HARBINGER RENEGADE

THE JUDGMENT OF SOLOMON

RAFER ROBERTS | DARICK ROBERTSON | JUAN JOSÉ RYP | RICHARD CLARK

CONTENTS

Collection Cover Art: Darick Robertson and
Richard Clark with Diego Rodriguez

Assistant Editor: Lauren Hitzhusen
Editor-in-Chief: Warren Simons

VALIANT.

Peter Cuneo
Chairman

Dinesh Shamdasani
CEO & Chief Creative Officer

Gavin Cuneo
Chief Operating Officer & CFO

Fred Pierce
Publisher

Warren Simons
Editor-in-Chief

Walter Black
VP Operations

Hunter Gorinson
VP Marketing & Communications

Atom! Freeman
Director of Sales

Andy Liegl
Alex Rae
Sales Managers

Annie Rosa
Sales Coordinator

Josh Johns
Director of Digital Media and
Development

Travis Escarfullery
Jeff Walker
Production & Design Managers

Kyle Andrukiewicz
Editor and Creative Executive

Robert Meyers
Managing Editor

Peter Stern
Publishing & Operations Manager

Andrew Steinbeiser
Marketing & Communications
Manager

Danny Khazem
Charlotte Greenbaum
Associate Editors

Lauren Hitzhusen
Assistant Editor

Benjamin Peterson
Editorial Assistant

Shanyce Lora
Digital Media Coordinator

Ivan Cohen
Collection Editor

Steve Blackwell
Collection Designer

Rian Hughes/Device
Original Trade Dress & Book Design

Russell Brown
President, Consumer Products,
Promotions and Ad Sales

Caritza Berlioz
Licensing Coodinator

Harbinger® Renegade: The Judgment of Solomon. Published by
Valiant Entertainment LLC. Office of Publication: 350 Seventh Avenue,
New York, NY 10001. Compilation copyright © 2017 Valiant Entertainment LLC.
All rights reserved. Contains materials originally published in single magazine
form as Harbinger Renegade #1-4. Copyright © 2017 Valiant Entertainment LLC.
All rights reserved. All characters, their distinctive likeness and related indicia
featured in this publication are trademarks of Valiant Entertainment LLC.
The stories, characters, and incidents featured in this publication are
entirely fictional. Valiant Entertainment does not read or accept
unsolicited submissions of ideas, stories, or artwork.
Printed in the U.S.A. First Printing. ISBN: 9781682151693.

Library of Congress Cataloging-in-Publication Data

Names: Roberts, Rafer, 1976- author. | Robertson, Darick, artist. | Ryp, Juan
    Jose, 1971- artist. | Rodriguez, Diego (Comic book artist), artist.
Title: Harbinger Renegade. Volume one, The judgment of Solomon / Rafer
    Roberts, Darick Robertson, Juan Jose Ryp, Diego Rodriguez.
Other titles: Judgment of Solomon
Description: New York, NY : Valiant Entertainment, 2017. | "Contains
    materials originally published in single magazine form as Harbinger
    Renegade #1/4."
Identifiers: LCCN 2017005547 (print) | LCCN 2017005652 (ebook) | ISBN
    9781682151693 (trade pbk. : alk. paper) | ISBN 9781682151709 (e-book)
Subjects: LCSH: Comic books, strips, etc.
Classification: LCC PN6728.H363 R63 2017 (print) | LCC PN6728.H363 (ebook) |
    DDC 741.5/973--dc23
LC record available at https://lccn.loc.gov/2017005547

VALIANT

RAFER ROBERTS | DARICK ROBERTSON
JUAN JOSÉ RYP | RAÚL ALLÉN

#1

Harbinger
RENEGADE

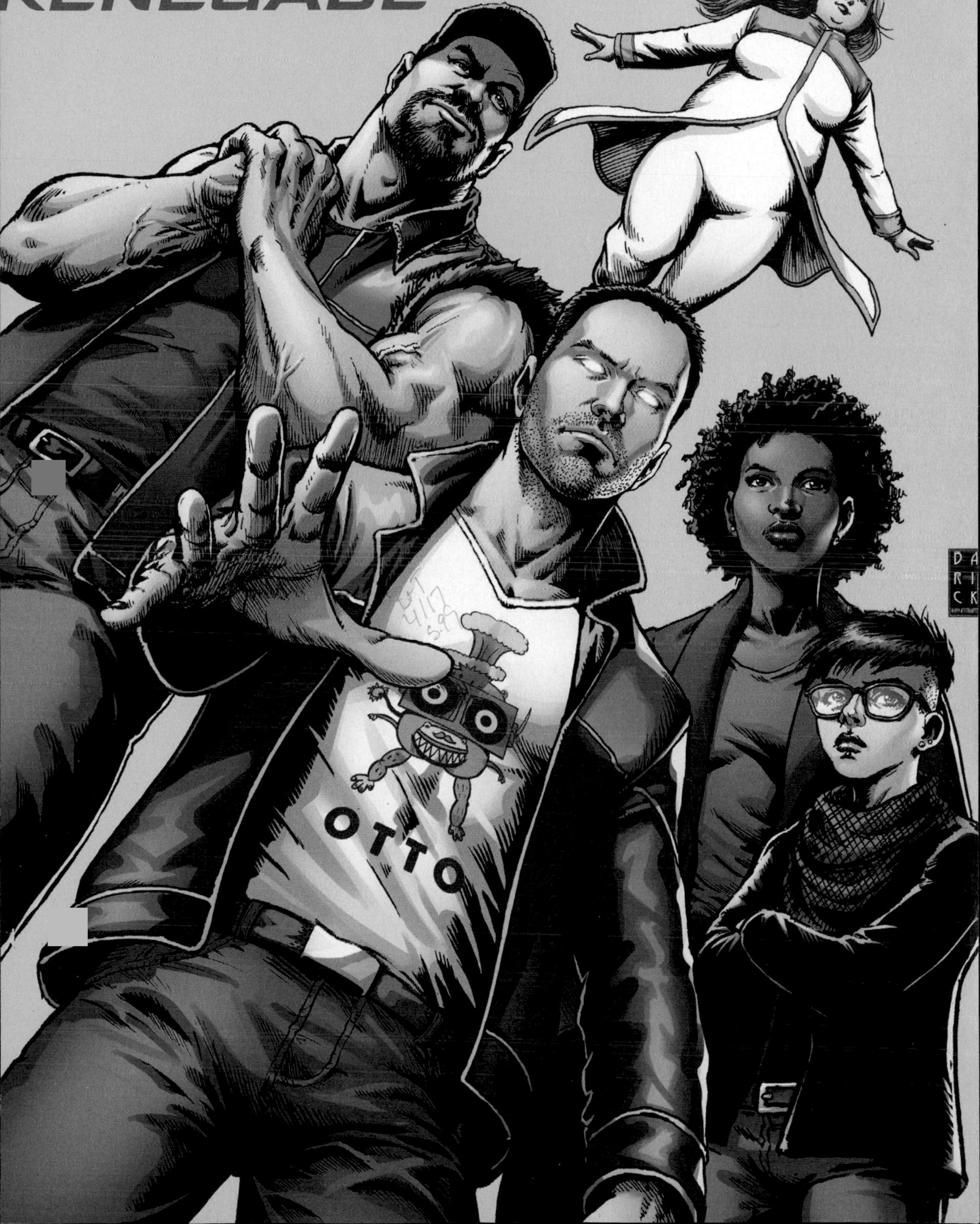
OTTO
DARICK

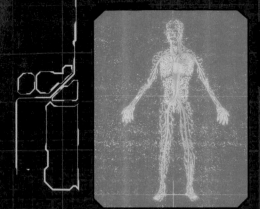

A psiot is an individual who possesses extraordinary powers, such as telepathy, telekinesis, or flight.

However, psiots are extremely rare. Only about four in every million people have the potential to gain powers.

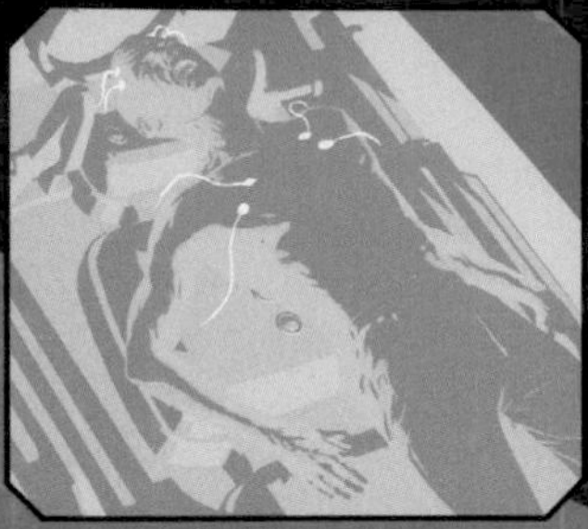

Activating a psiot's abilities requires a dangerous and invasive surgery that is frequently lethal. Many potential psiots choose not to undergo the procedure. Many others never learn of their potential in the first place.

LOCATION SCANER HUD
DANGER LEVEL

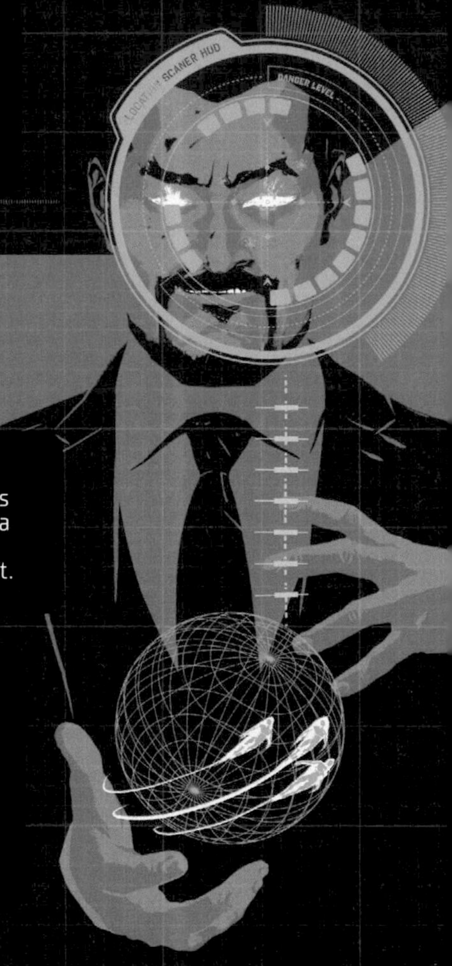

Until recently, the existence of psiots was a secret known only to a powerful few.

One such man was Toyo Harada, an Omega-level psiot who used his extraordinary gifts to build Harada Global Conglomerates, one of the largest corporations on the planet.

HGC

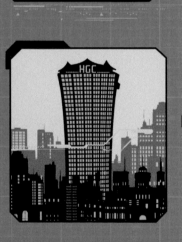

Within the sprawling HGC, Harada hid his most prized possession: The Harbinger Foundation. The Foundation recruited, activated, and trained psiots, all in an effort to realize Harada's vision for a more peaceful, egalitarian tomorrow.

But Harada and his psiot army often achieved peace through the violent manipulation of world events.

INTRODUCTION:
WRITER: Rafer Roberts
ART and LETTERING: Raúl Allén and Patricia Martín

PROLOGUE:
WRITER: Rafer Roberts
ART: Juan José Ryp
COLOR ART: Frankie D'Armata
LETTERER: Dave Lanphear

STORY:
WRITER: Rafer Roberts
PENCILER: Darick Robertson
INKER: Richard Clark
COLOR ART: Diego Rodriguez
LETTERER: Dave Lanphear

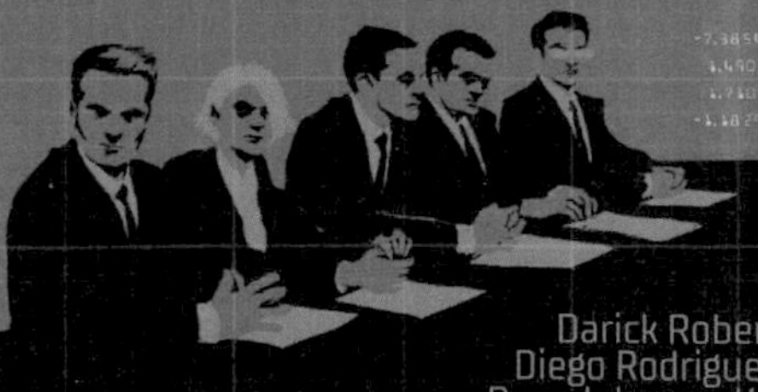

COVERS:
Darick Robertson, Richard Clark and Diego Rodriguez, Jelena Kevic-Djurdjevic, Dave Johnson, Kano, Pere Pérez and Andrew Dalhouse, Clayton Henry and Ulises Arreola, Bob Layton and David Baron, Jim Mahfood

ASSISTANT EDITOR – Lauren Hitzhusen
EDITOR – Warren Simons

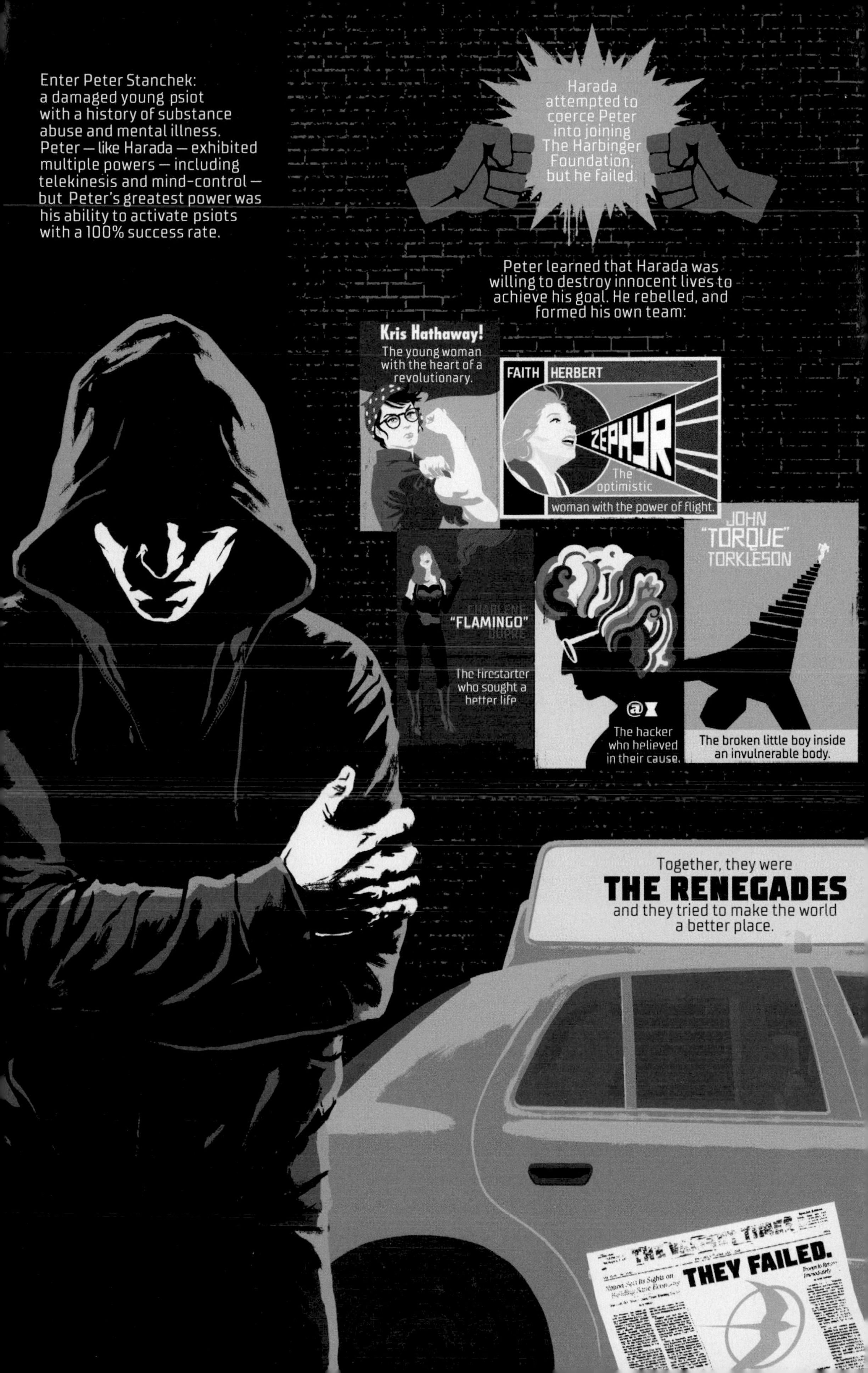
Enter Peter Stanchek: a damaged young psiot with a history of substance abuse and mental illness. Peter — like Harada — exhibited multiple powers — including telekinesis and mind-control — but Peter's greatest power was his ability to activate psiots with a 100% success rate.
Harada attempted to coerce Peter into joining The Harbinger Foundation, but he failed.
Peter learned that Harada was willing to destroy innocent lives to achieve his goal. He rebelled, and formed his own team:
Kris Hathaway!
The young woman with the heart of a revolutionary.
FAITH HERBERT
ZEPHYR
The optimistic woman with the power of flight.
"FLAMINGO"
The firestarter who sought a better life.
The hacker who believed in their cause.
JOHN "TORQUE" TORKLESON
The broken little boy inside an invulnerable body.
Together, they were
THE RENEGADES
and they tried to make the world a better place.
THEY FAILED.

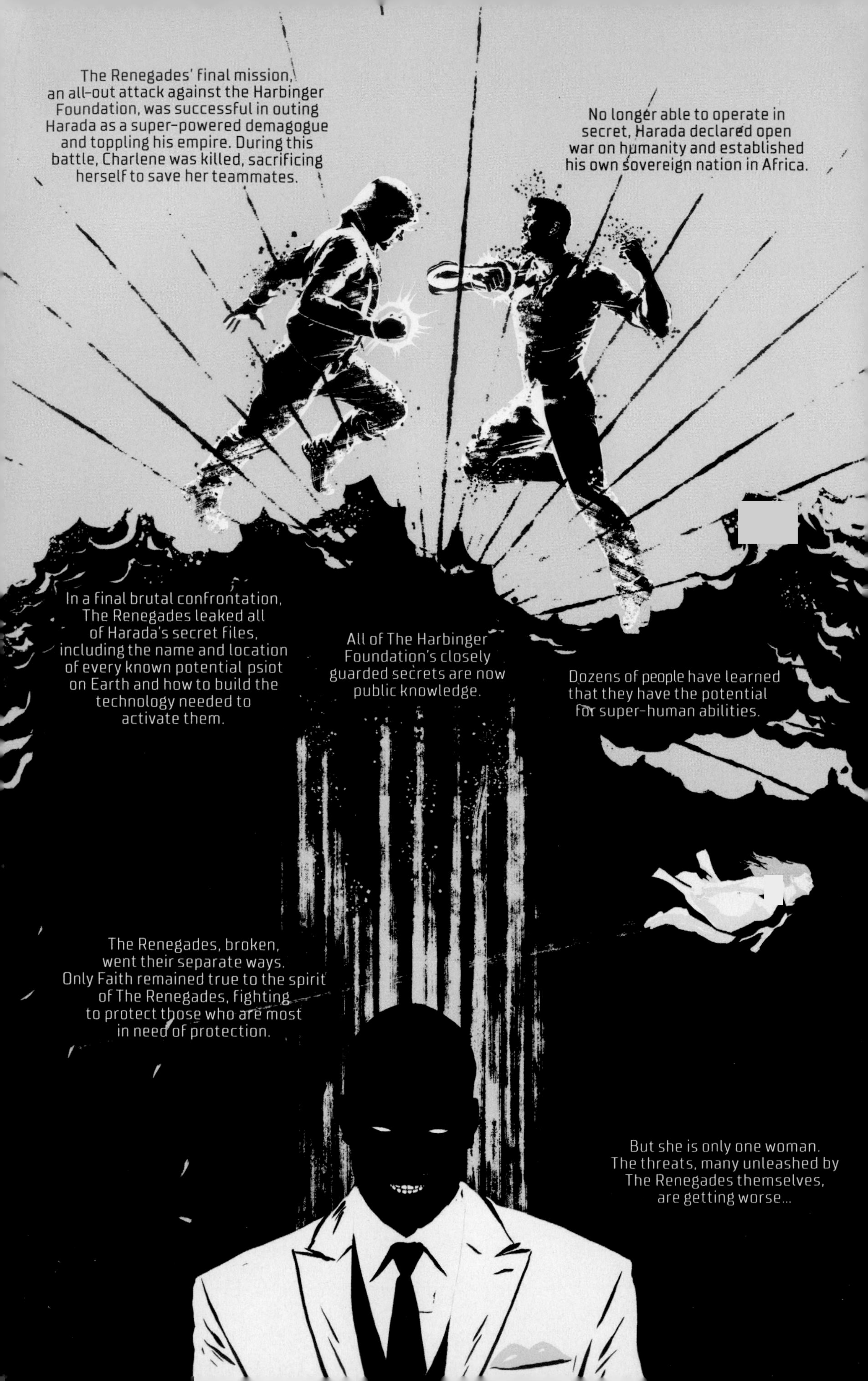
The Renegades' final mission, an all-out attack against the Harbinger Foundation, was successful in outing Harada as a super-powered demagogue and toppling his empire. During this battle, Charlene was killed, sacrificing herself to save her teammates.
No longer able to operate in secret, Harada declared open war on humanity and established his own sovereign nation in Africa.
In a final brutal confrontation, The Renegades leaked all of Harada's secret files, including the name and location of every known potential psiot on Earth and how to build the technology needed to activate them.
All of The Harbinger Foundation's closely guarded secrets are now public knowledge.
Dozens of people have learned that they have the potential for super-human abilities.
The Renegades, broken, went their separate ways. Only Faith remained true to the spirit of The Renegades, fighting to protect those who are most in need of protection.
But she is only one woman. The threats, many unleashed by The Renegades themselves, are getting worse...

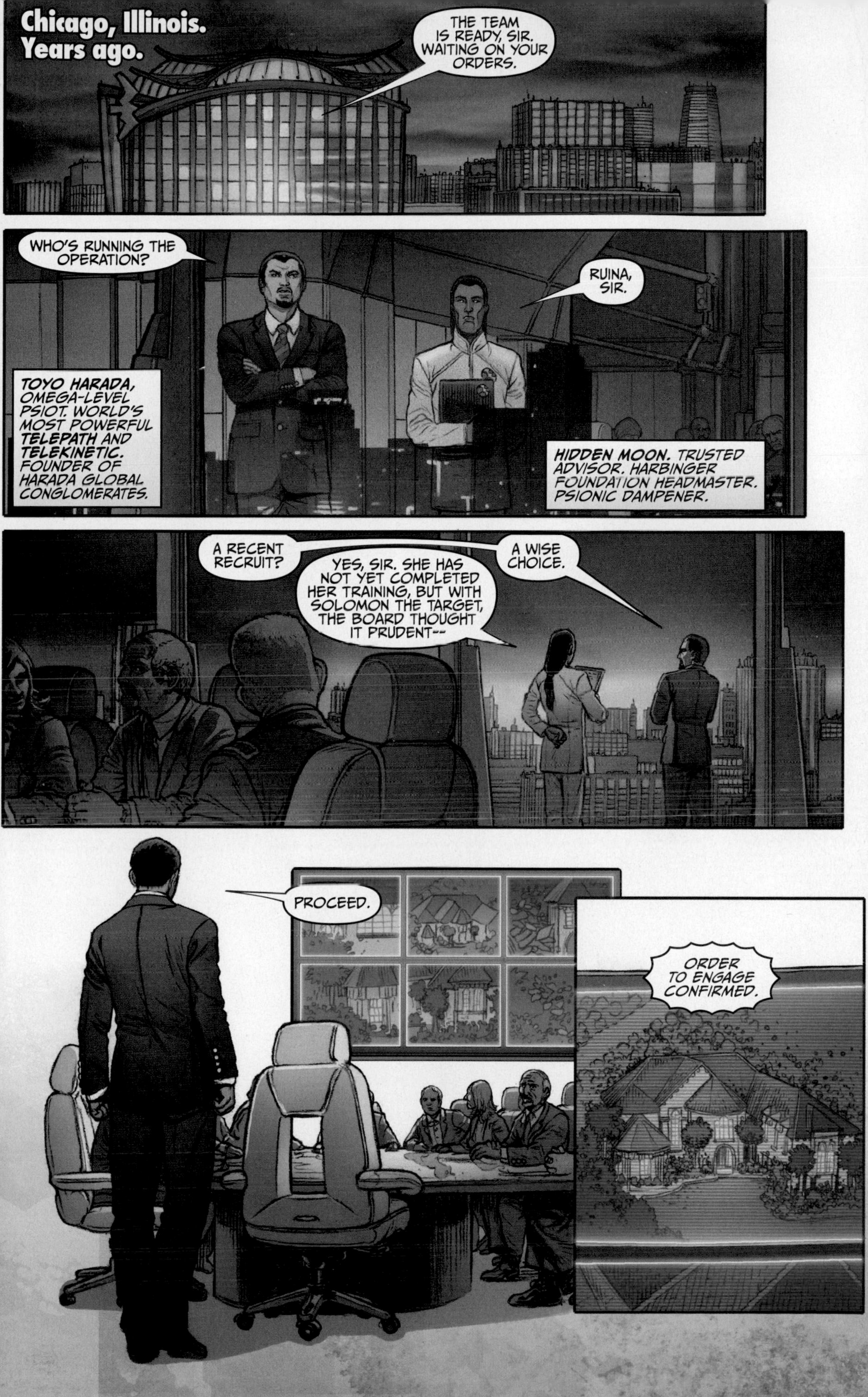
Chicago, Illinois.
Years ago.
THE TEAM IS READY, SIR. WAITING ON YOUR ORDERS.
WHO'S RUNNING THE OPERATION?
RUINA, SIR.
TOYO HARADA, OMEGA-LEVEL PSIOT. WORLD'S MOST POWERFUL TELEPATH AND TELEKINETIC. FOUNDER OF HARADA GLOBAL CONGLOMERATES.
HIDDEN MOON. TRUSTED ADVISOR. HARBINGER FOUNDATION HEADMASTER. PSIONIC DAMPENER.
A RECENT RECRUIT?
YES, SIR. SHE HAS NOT YET COMPLETED HER TRAINING, BUT WITH SOLOMON THE TARGET, THE BOARD THOUGHT IT PRUDENT--
A WISE CHOICE.
PROCEED.
ORDER TO ENGAGE CONFIRMED.

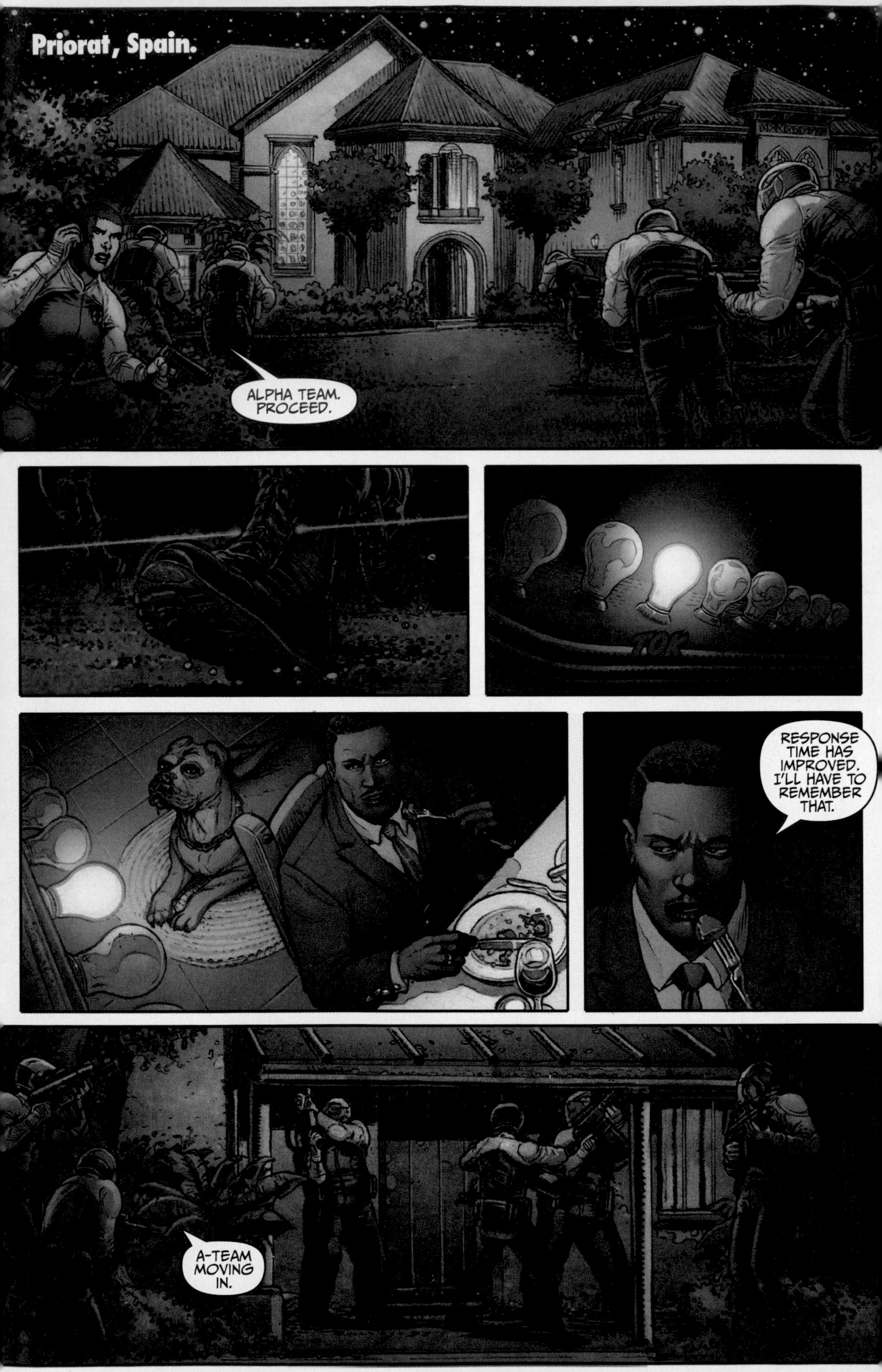

Priorat, Spain.
ALPHA TEAM. PROCEED.
RESPONSE TIME HAS IMPROVED. I'LL HAVE TO REMEMBER THAT.
A-TEAM MOVING IN.

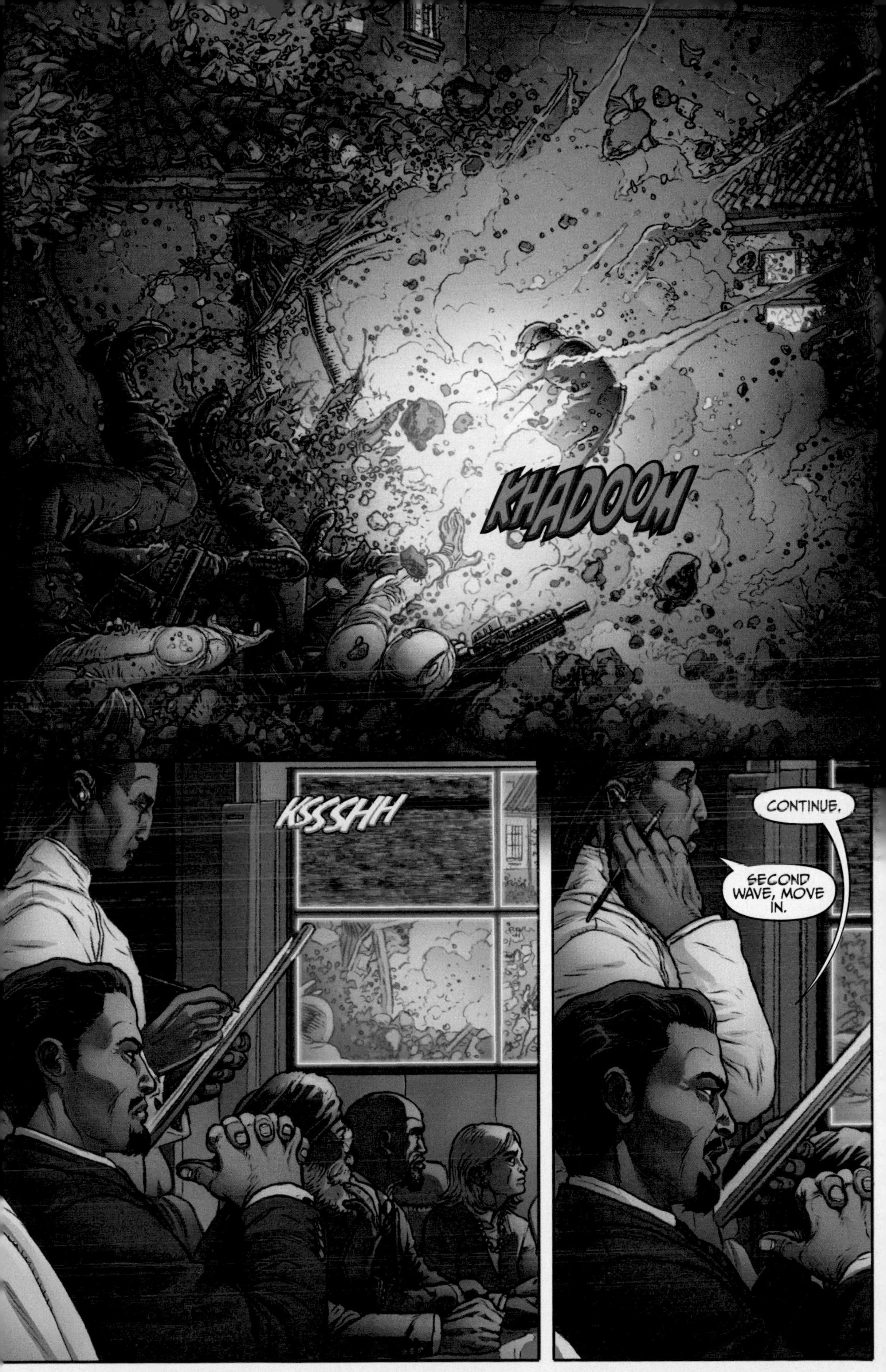
KHADOOM
KSSSHH
CONTINUE.
SECOND WAVE, MOVE IN.

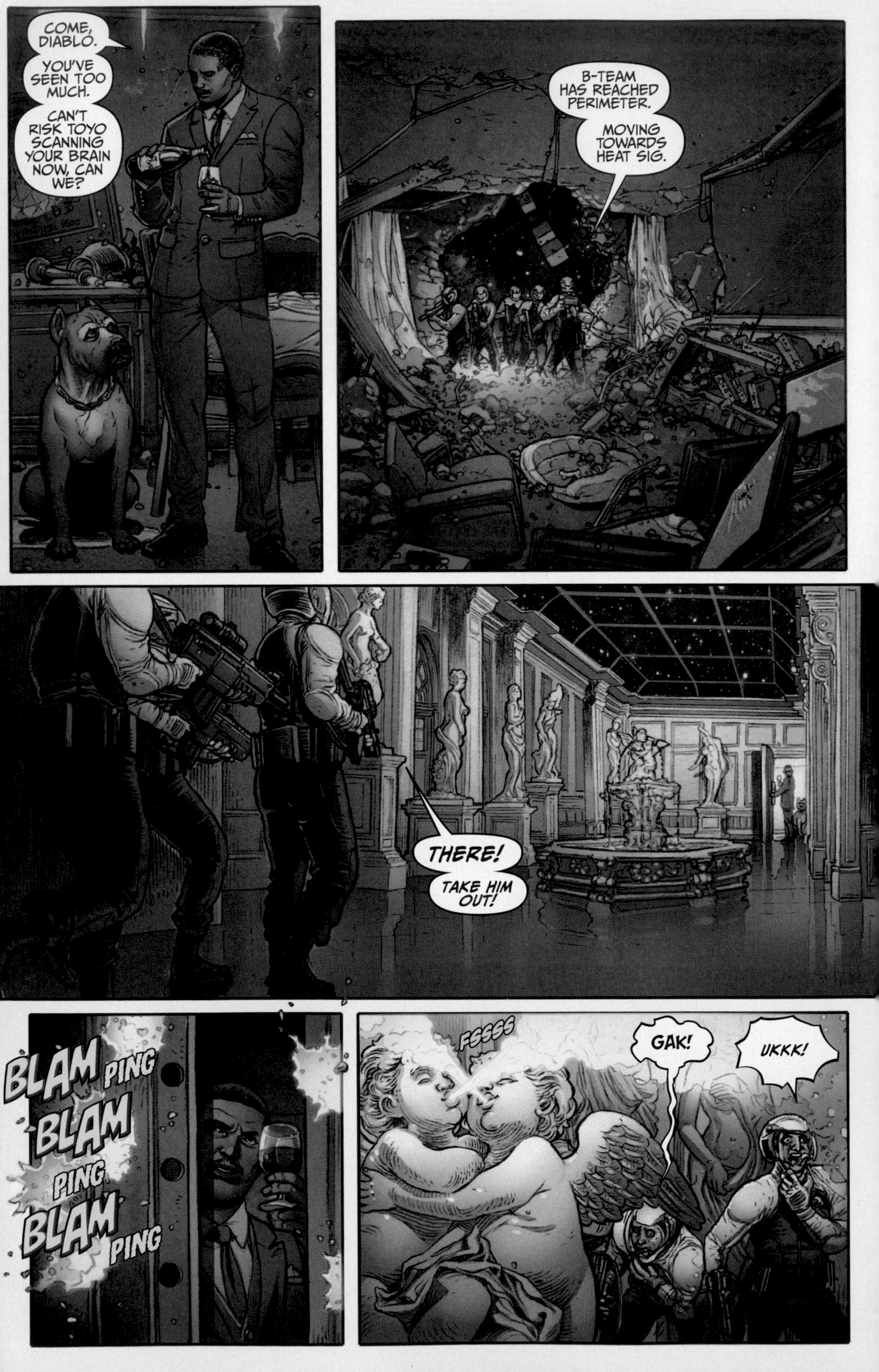
COME, DIABLO.
YOU'VE SEEN TOO MUCH.
CAN'T RISK TOYO SCANNING YOUR BRAIN NOW, CAN WE?
B-TEAM HAS REACHED PERIMETER.
MOVING TOWARDS HEAT SIG.
THERE!
TAKE HIM OUT!
BLAM PING
BLAM
PING
BLAM PING
FSSSS
GAK!
UKKK!

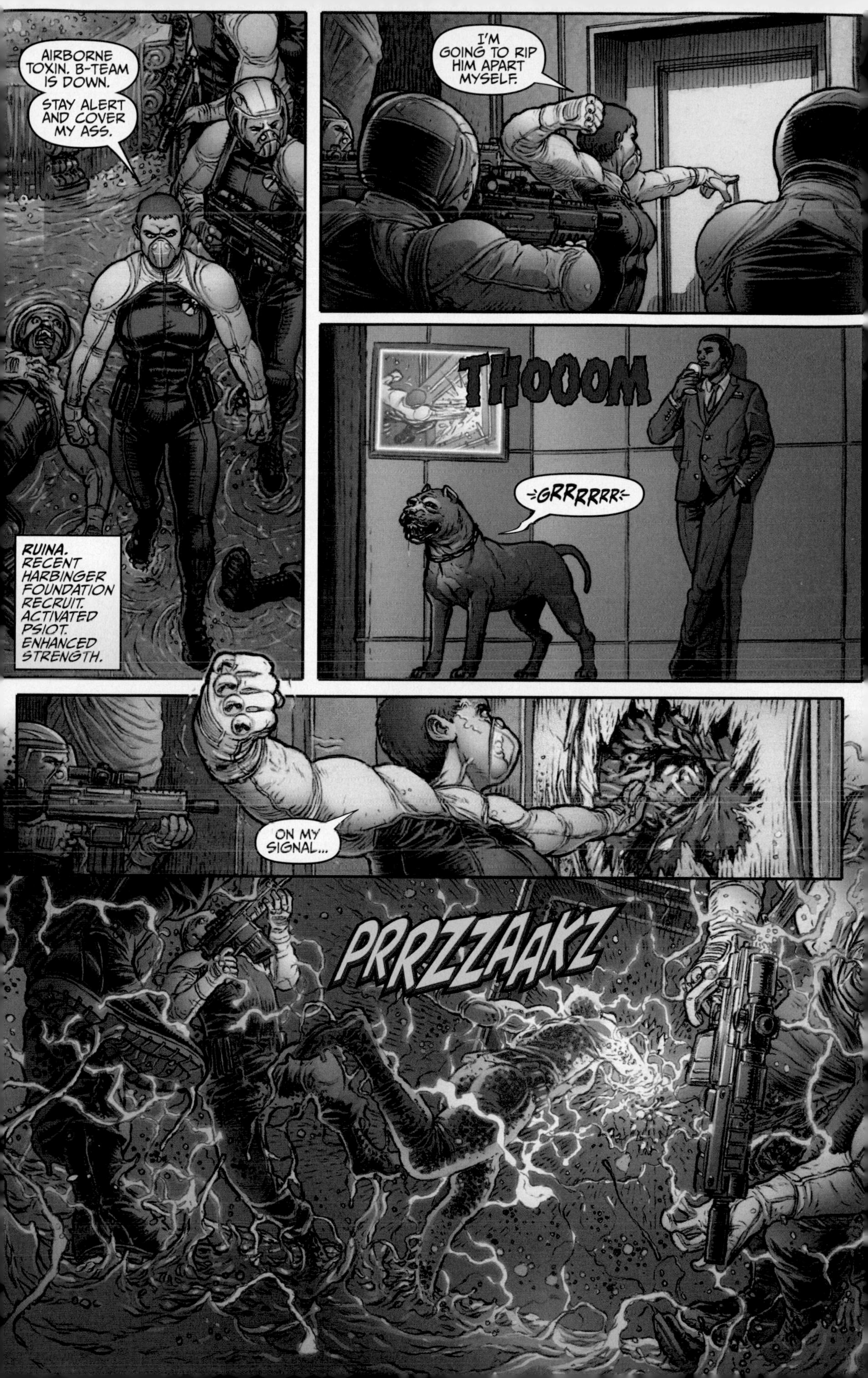
AIRBORNE TOXIN. B-TEAM IS DOWN.
STAY ALERT AND COVER MY ASS.
RUINA. RECENT HARBINGER FOUNDATION RECRUIT. ACTIVATED PSIOT. ENHANCED STRENGTH.
I'M GOING TO RIP HIM APART MYSELF.
THOOOM
GRRRRRR
ON MY SIGNAL...
PRRZZAAKZ

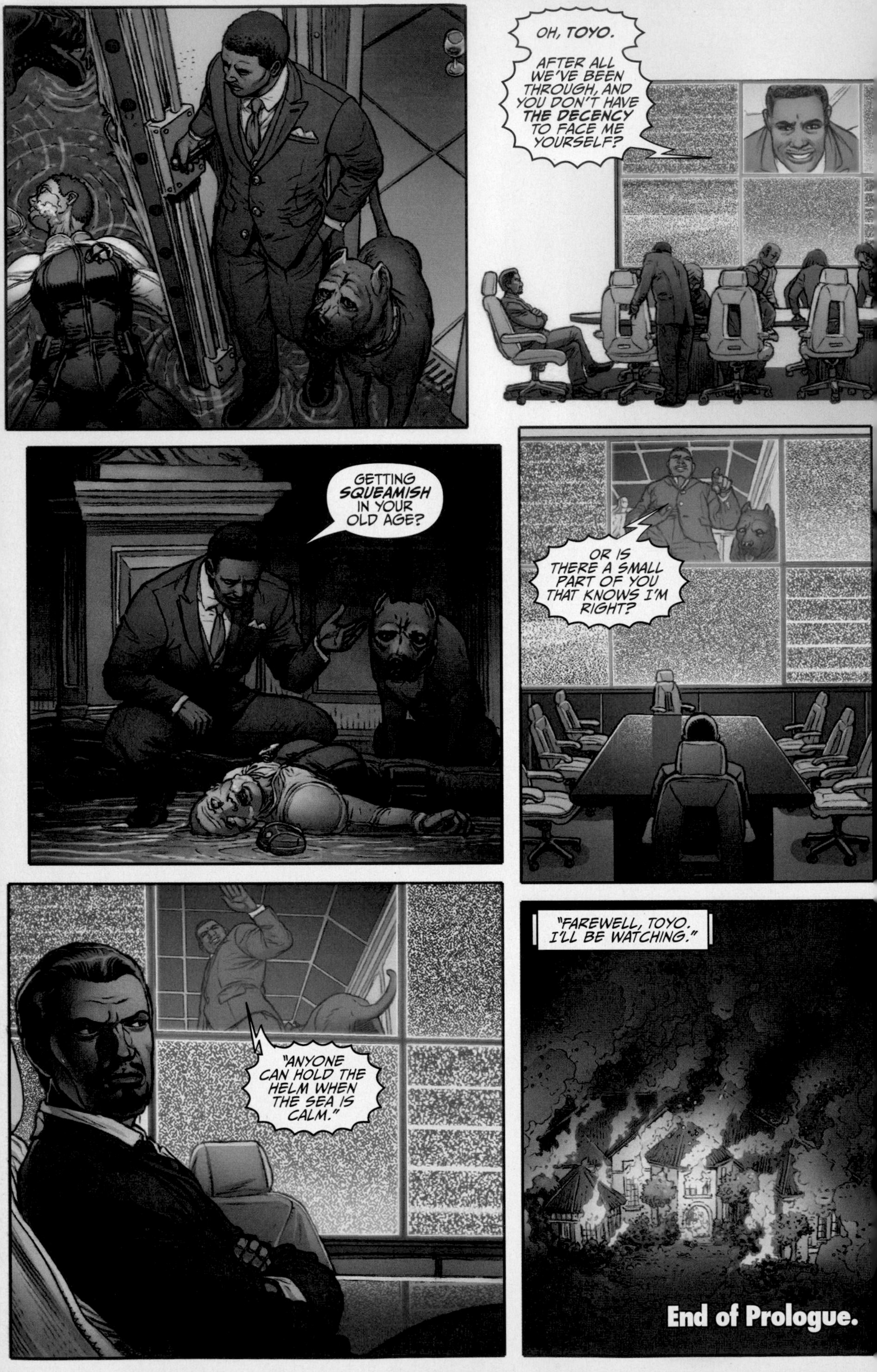
OH, TOYO.
AFTER ALL WE'VE BEEN THROUGH, AND YOU DON'T HAVE THE DECENCY TO FACE ME YOURSELF?
GETTING SQUEAMISH IN YOUR OLD AGE?
OR IS THERE A SMALL PART OF YOU THAT KNOWS I'M RIGHT?
"ANYONE CAN HOLD THE HELM WHEN THE SEA IS CALM."
"FAREWELL, TOYO. I'LL BE WATCHING."
End of Prologue.

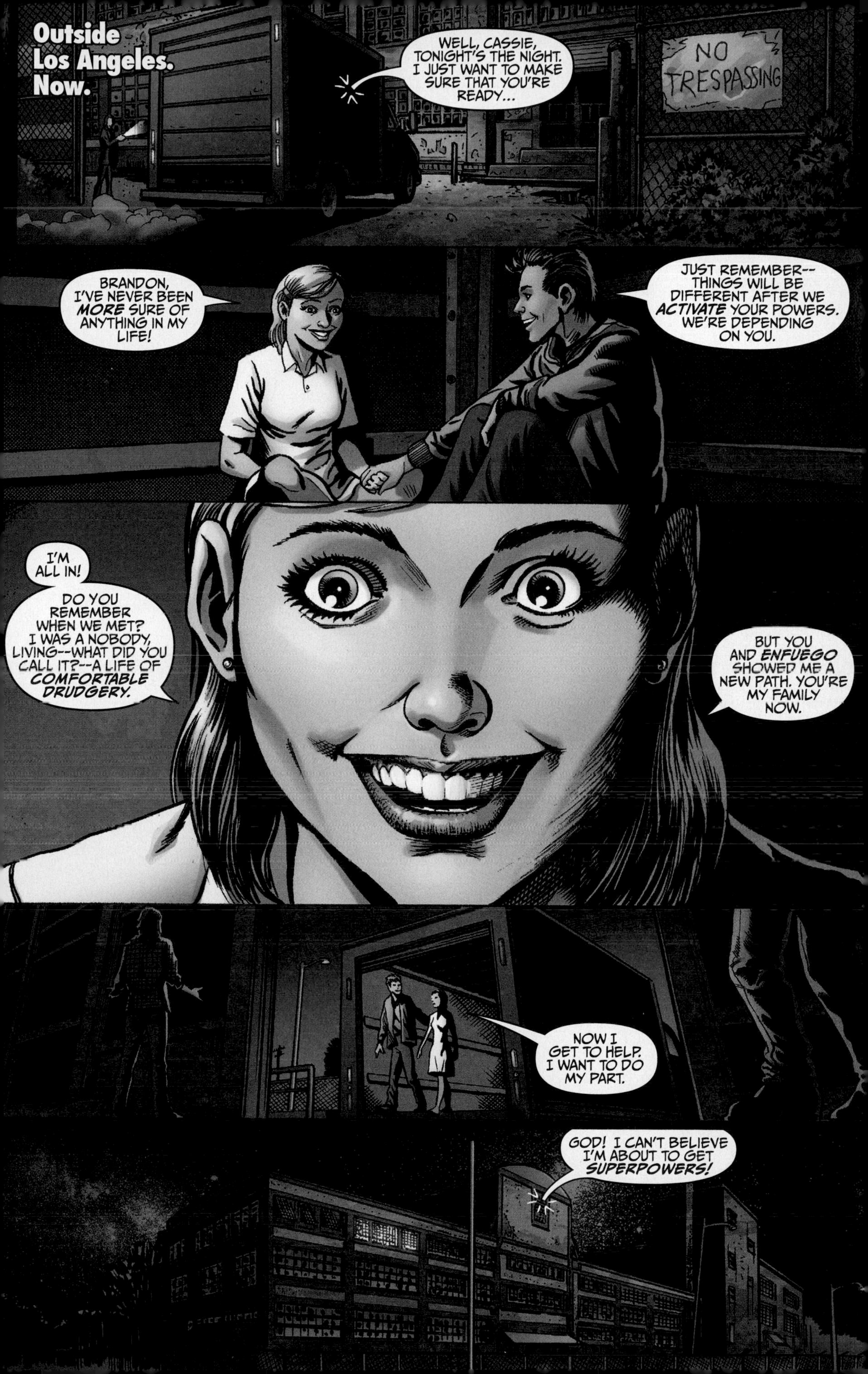
Outside Los Angeles. Now.
WELL, CASSIE, TONIGHT'S THE NIGHT. I JUST WANT TO MAKE SURE THAT YOU'RE READY...
NO TRESPASSING
BRANDON, I'VE NEVER BEEN MORE SURE OF ANYTHING IN MY LIFE!
JUST REMEMBER-- THINGS WILL BE DIFFERENT AFTER WE ACTIVATE YOUR POWERS. WE'RE DEPENDING ON YOU.
I'M ALL IN!
DO YOU REMEMBER WHEN WE MET? I WAS A NOBODY, LIVING--WHAT DID YOU CALL IT?--A LIFE OF COMFORTABLE DRUDGERY.
BUT YOU AND ENFUEGO SHOWED ME A NEW PATH. YOU'RE MY FAMILY NOW.
NOW I GET TO HELP. I WANT TO DO MY PART.
GOD! I CAN'T BELIEVE I'M ABOUT TO GET SUPERPOWERS!

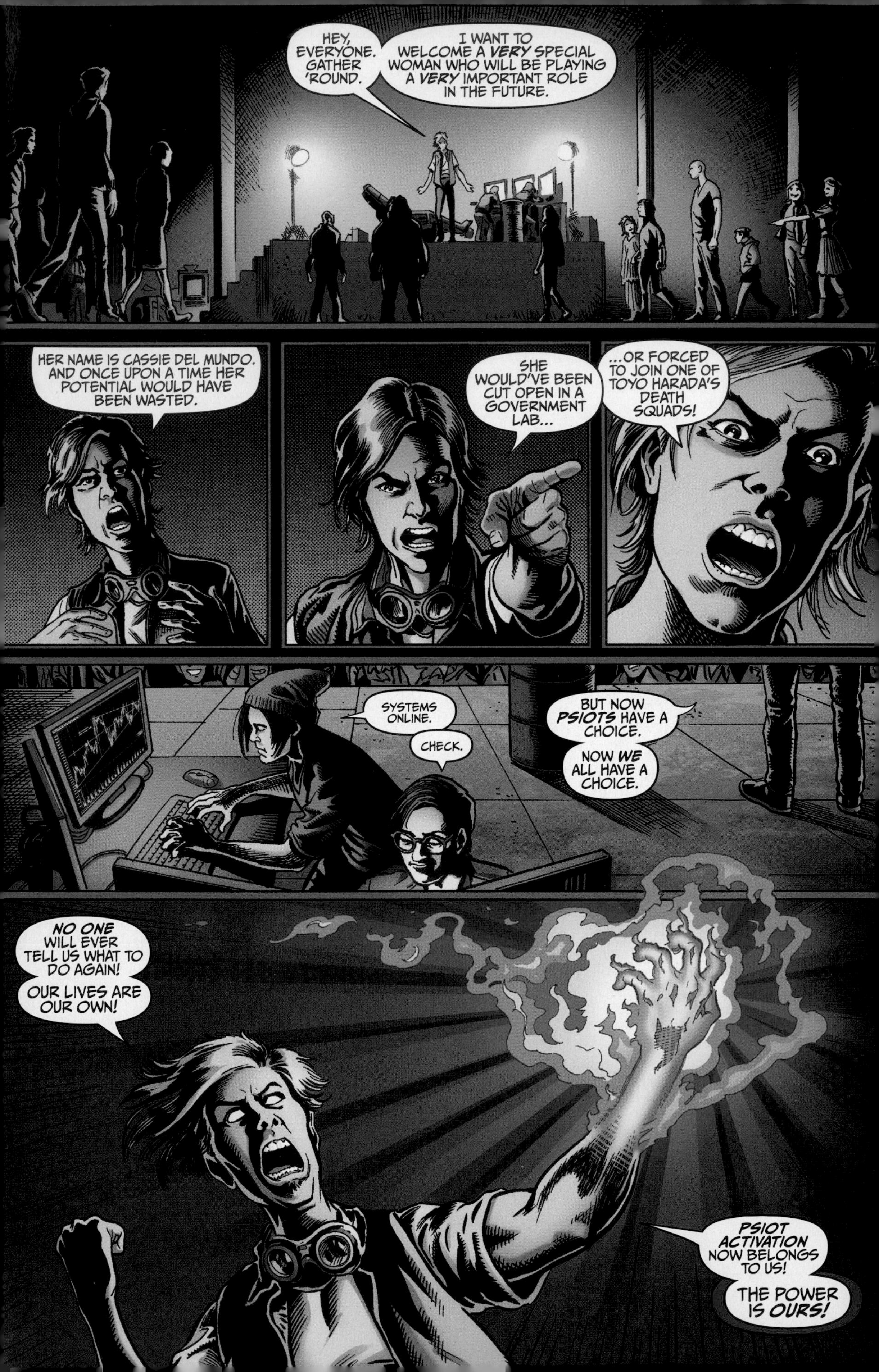
HEY, EVERYONE. GATHER 'ROUND.
I WANT TO WELCOME A VERY SPECIAL WOMAN WHO WILL BE PLAYING A VERY IMPORTANT ROLE IN THE FUTURE.
HER NAME IS CASSIE DEL MUNDO. AND ONCE UPON A TIME HER POTENTIAL WOULD HAVE BEEN WASTED.
SHE WOULD'VE BEEN CUT OPEN IN A GOVERNMENT LAB...
...OR FORCED TO JOIN ONE OF TOYO HARADA'S DEATH SQUADS!
SYSTEMS ONLINE.
CHECK.
BUT NOW PSIOTS HAVE A CHOICE.
NOW WE ALL HAVE A CHOICE.
NO ONE WILL EVER TELL US WHAT TO DO AGAIN!
OUR LIVES ARE OUR OWN!
PSIOT ACTIVATION NOW BELONGS TO US!
THE POWER IS OURS!

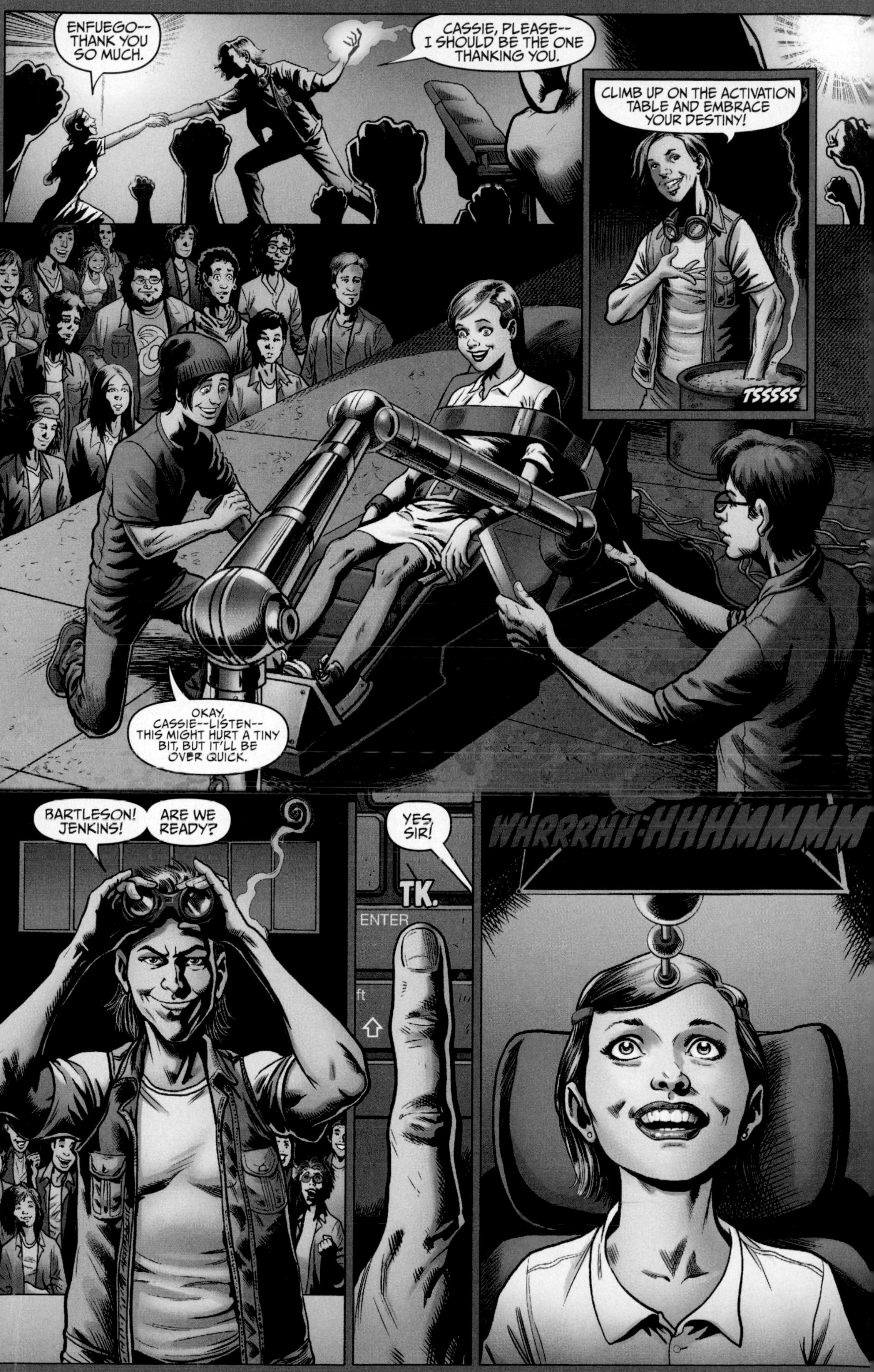
ENFUEGO-- THANK YOU SO MUCH.
CASSIE, PLEASE-- I SHOULD BE THE ONE THANKING YOU.
CLIMB UP ON THE ACTIVATION TABLE AND EMBRACE YOUR DESTINY!
TSSSSS
OKAY, CASSIE--LISTEN-- THIS MIGHT HURT A TINY BIT, BUT IT'LL BE OVER QUICK.
BARTLESON! JENKINS!
ARE WE READY?
YES, SIR!
TK.
ENTER
WHRRRHH-HHHMMMM

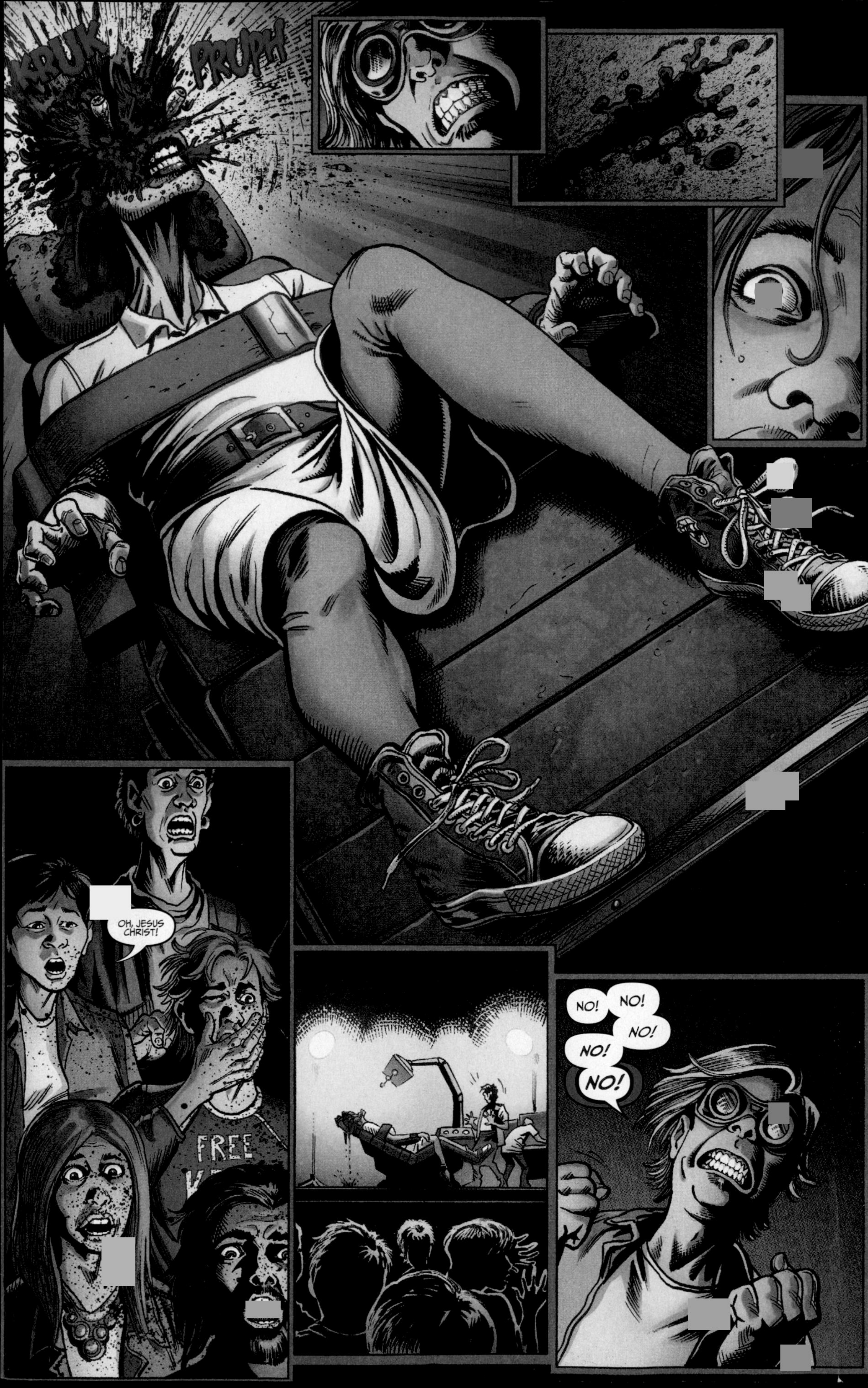
KRUK
PRUPH
OH, JESUS CHRIST!
NO!
NO!
NO!
NO!
NO!
FREE

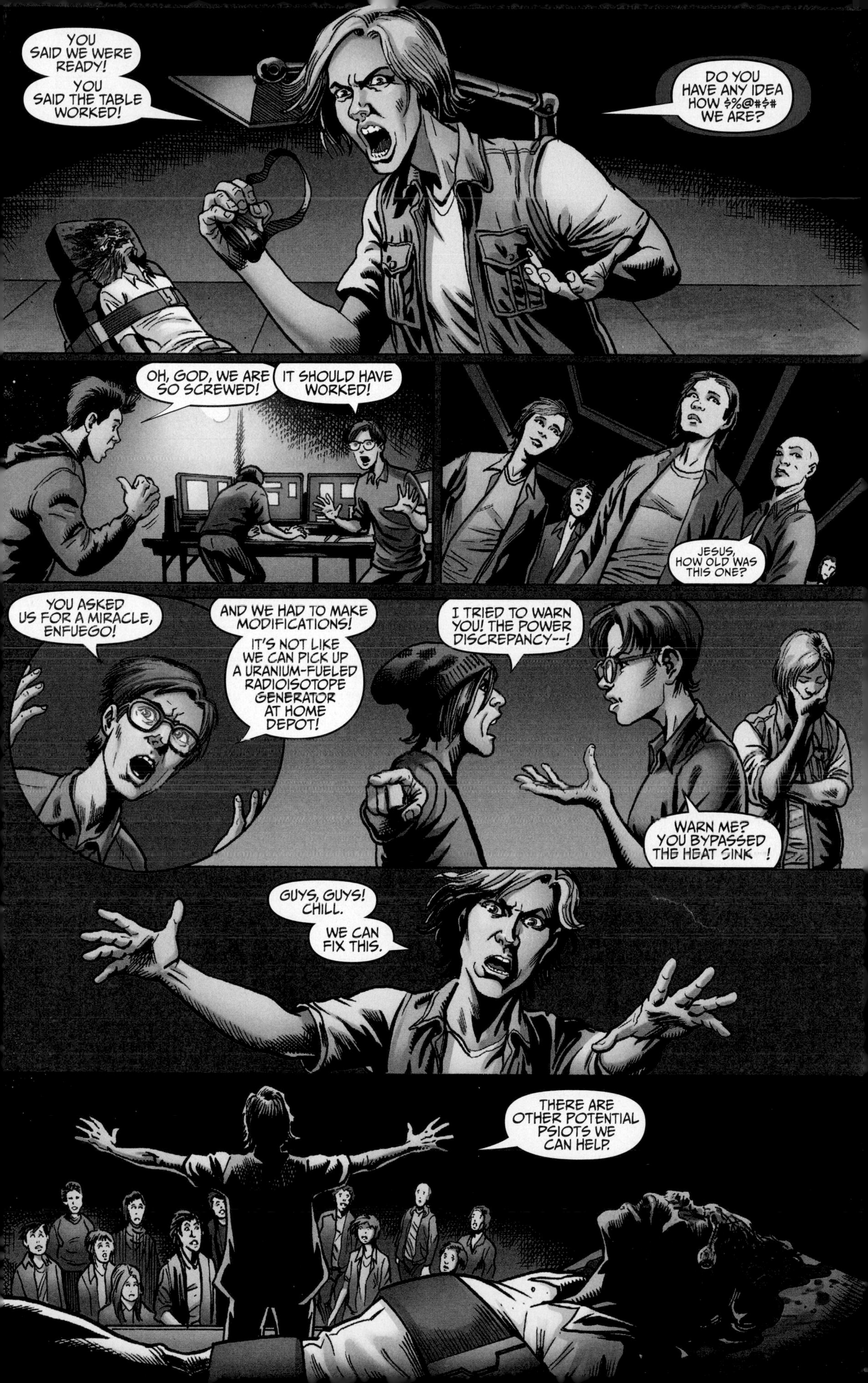
YOU SAID WE WERE READY!
YOU SAID THE TABLE WORKED!
DO YOU HAVE ANY IDEA HOW $%@#$# WE ARE?
OH, GOD, WE ARE SO SCREWED!
IT SHOULD HAVE WORKED!
JESUS, HOW OLD WAS THIS ONE?
YOU ASKED US FOR A MIRACLE, ENFUEGO!
AND WE HAD TO MAKE MODIFICATIONS!
IT'S NOT LIKE WE CAN PICK UP A URANIUM-FUELED RADIOISOTOPE GENERATOR AT HOME DEPOT!
I TRIED TO WARN YOU! THE POWER DISCREPANCY--!
WARN ME? YOU BYPASSED THE HEAT SINK!
GUYS, GUYS! CHILL.
WE CAN FIX THIS.
THERE ARE OTHER POTENTIAL PSIOTS WE CAN HELP.

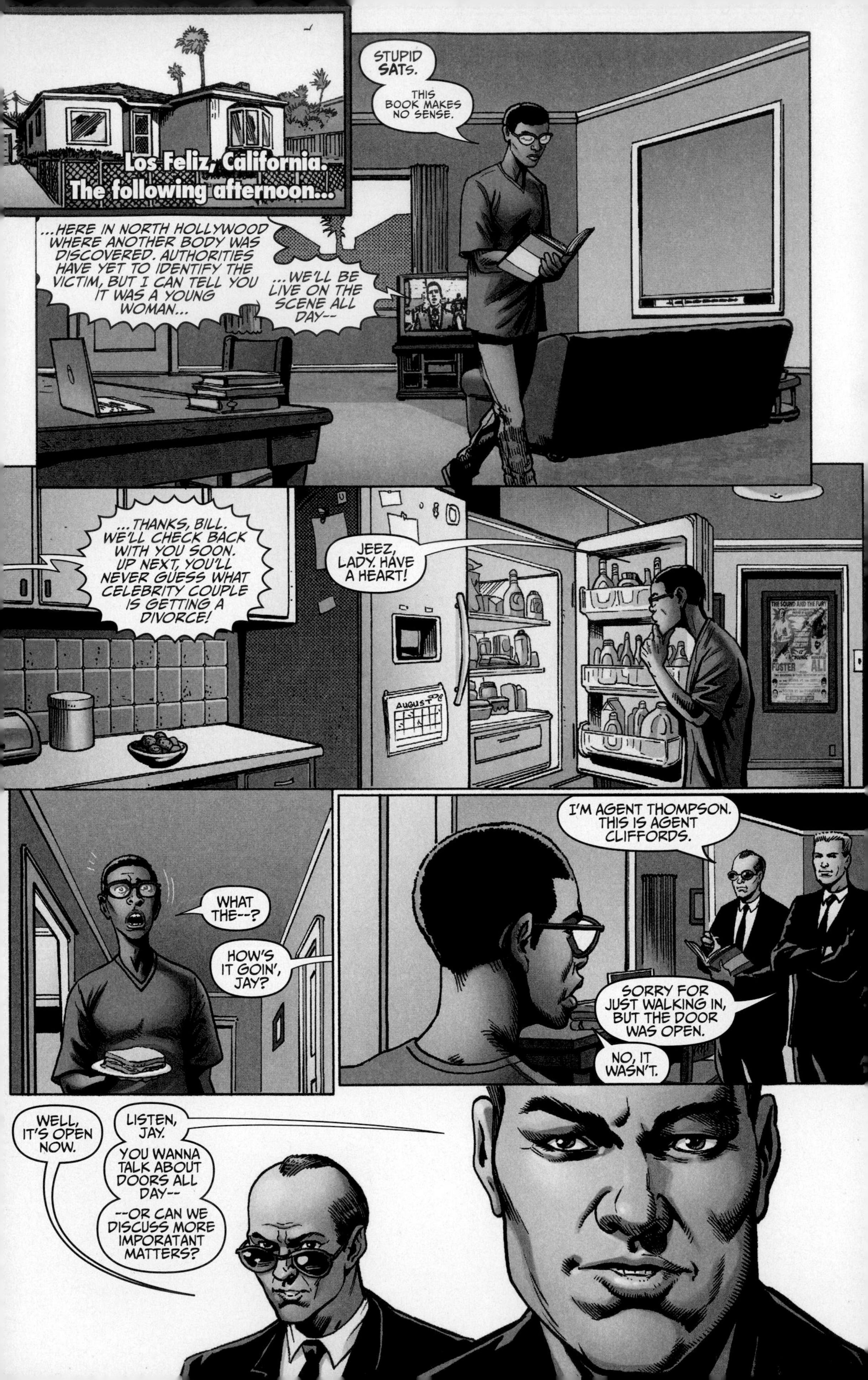
Los Feliz, California. The following afternoon...
STUPID SATS.
THIS BOOK MAKES NO SENSE.
...HERE IN NORTH HOLLYWOOD WHERE ANOTHER BODY WAS DISCOVERED. AUTHORITIES HAVE YET TO IDENTIFY THE VICTIM, BUT I CAN TELL YOU IT WAS A YOUNG WOMAN...
...WE'LL BE LIVE ON THE SCENE ALL DAY--
...THANKS, BILL. WE'LL CHECK BACK WITH YOU SOON. UP NEXT, YOU'LL NEVER GUESS WHAT CELEBRITY COUPLE IS GETTING A DIVORCE!
JEEZ, LADY. HAVE A HEART!
AUGUST
THE SOUND AND THE FURY
FOSTER
ALI
WHAT THE--?
HOW'S IT GOIN', JAY?
I'M AGENT THOMPSON. THIS IS AGENT CLIFFORDS.
SORRY FOR JUST WALKING IN, BUT THE DOOR WAS OPEN.
NO, IT WASN'T.
WELL, IT'S OPEN NOW.
LISTEN, JAY.
YOU WANNA TALK ABOUT DOORS ALL DAY--
--OR CAN WE DISCUSS MORE IMPORATANT MATTERS?

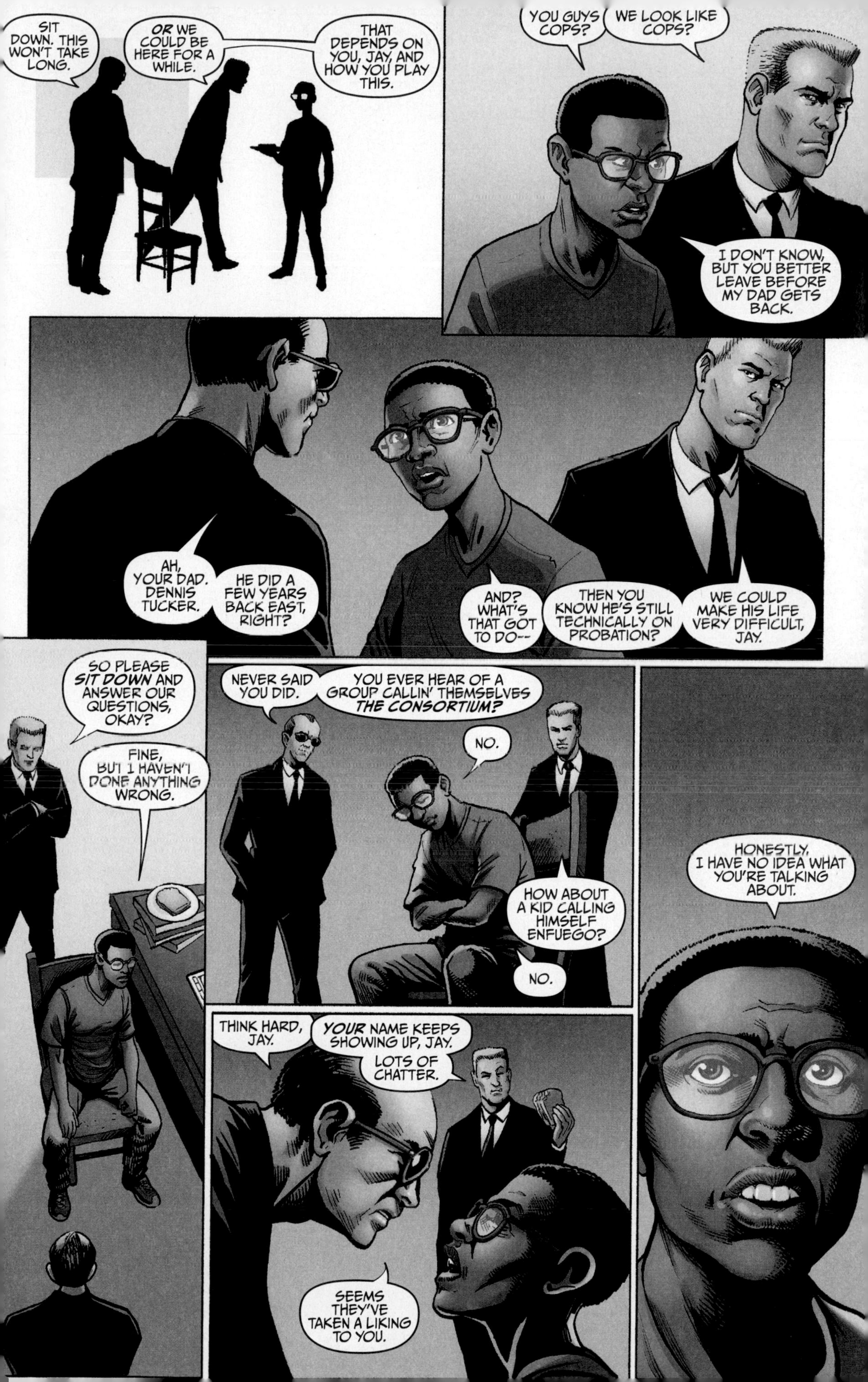
SIT DOWN. THIS WON'T TAKE LONG.
OR WE COULD BE HERE FOR A WHILE.
THAT DEPENDS ON YOU, JAY, AND HOW YOU PLAY THIS.
YOU GUYS COPS?
WE LOOK LIKE COPS?
I DON'T KNOW, BUT YOU BETTER LEAVE BEFORE MY DAD GETS BACK.
AH, YOUR DAD. DENNIS TUCKER.
HE DID A FEW YEARS BACK EAST, RIGHT?
AND? WHAT'S THAT GOT TO DO--
THEN YOU KNOW HE'S STILL TECHNICALLY ON PROBATION?
WE COULD MAKE HIS LIFE VERY DIFFICULT, JAY.
SO PLEASE SIT DOWN AND ANSWER OUR QUESTIONS, OKAY?
FINE, BUT I HAVEN'T DONE ANYTHING WRONG.
NEVER SAID YOU DID.
YOU EVER HEAR OF A GROUP CALLIN' THEMSELVES THE CONSORTIUM?
NO.
HOW ABOUT A KID CALLING HIMSELF ENFUEGO?
NO.
THINK HARD, JAY.
YOUR NAME KEEPS SHOWING UP, JAY.
LOTS OF CHATTER.
SEEMS THEY'VE TAKEN A LIKING TO YOU.
HONESTLY, I HAVE NO IDEA WHAT YOU'RE TALKING ABOUT.

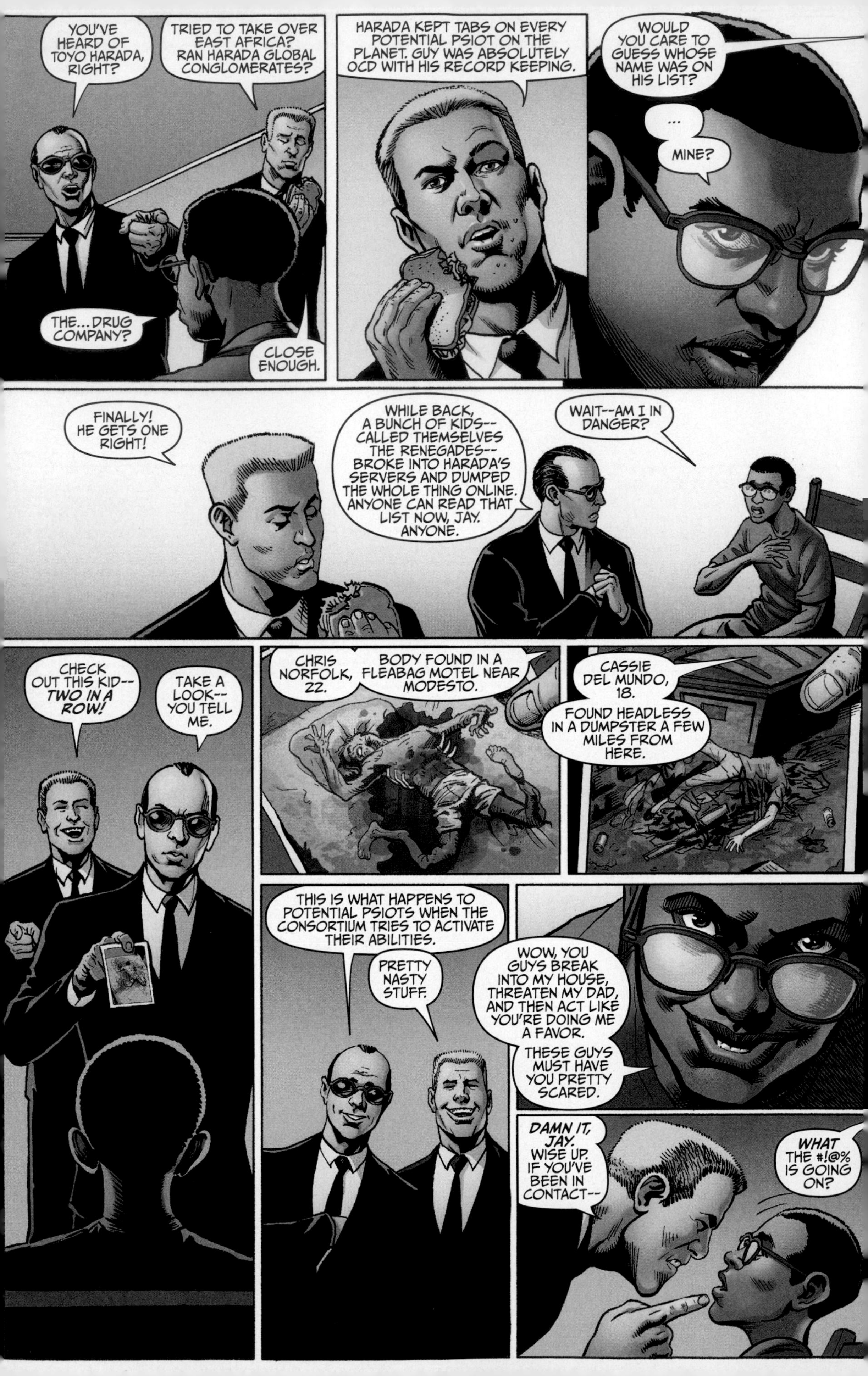
YOU'VE HEARD OF TOYO HARADA, RIGHT?
TRIED TO TAKE OVER EAST AFRICA? RAN HARADA GLOBAL CONGLOMERATES?
THE...DRUG COMPANY?
CLOSE ENOUGH.
HARADA KEPT TABS ON EVERY POTENTIAL PSIOT ON THE PLANET. GUY WAS ABSOLUTELY OCD WITH HIS RECORD KEEPING.
WOULD YOU CARE TO GUESS WHOSE NAME WAS ON HIS LIST?
...
MINE?
FINALLY! HE GETS ONE RIGHT!
WHILE BACK, A BUNCH OF KIDS-- CALLED THEMSELVES THE RENEGADES-- BROKE INTO HARADA'S SERVERS AND DUMPED THE WHOLE THING ONLINE. ANYONE CAN READ THAT LIST NOW, JAY. ANYONE.
WAIT--AM I IN DANGER?
CHECK OUT THIS KID-- TWO IN A ROW!
TAKE A LOOK-- YOU TELL ME.
CHRIS NORFOLK, 22.
BODY FOUND IN A FLEABAG MOTEL NEAR MODESTO.
CASSIE DEL MUNDO, 18.
FOUND HEADLESS IN A DUMPSTER A FEW MILES FROM HERE.
THIS IS WHAT HAPPENS TO POTENTIAL PSIOTS WHEN THE CONSORTIUM TRIES TO ACTIVATE THEIR ABILITIES.
PRETTY NASTY STUFF.
WOW, YOU GUYS BREAK INTO MY HOUSE, THREATEN MY DAD, AND THEN ACT LIKE YOU'RE DOING ME A FAVOR.
THESE GUYS MUST HAVE YOU PRETTY SCARED.
DAMN IT, JAY. WISE UP. IF YOU'VE BEEN IN CONTACT--
WHAT THE #!@% IS GOING ON?

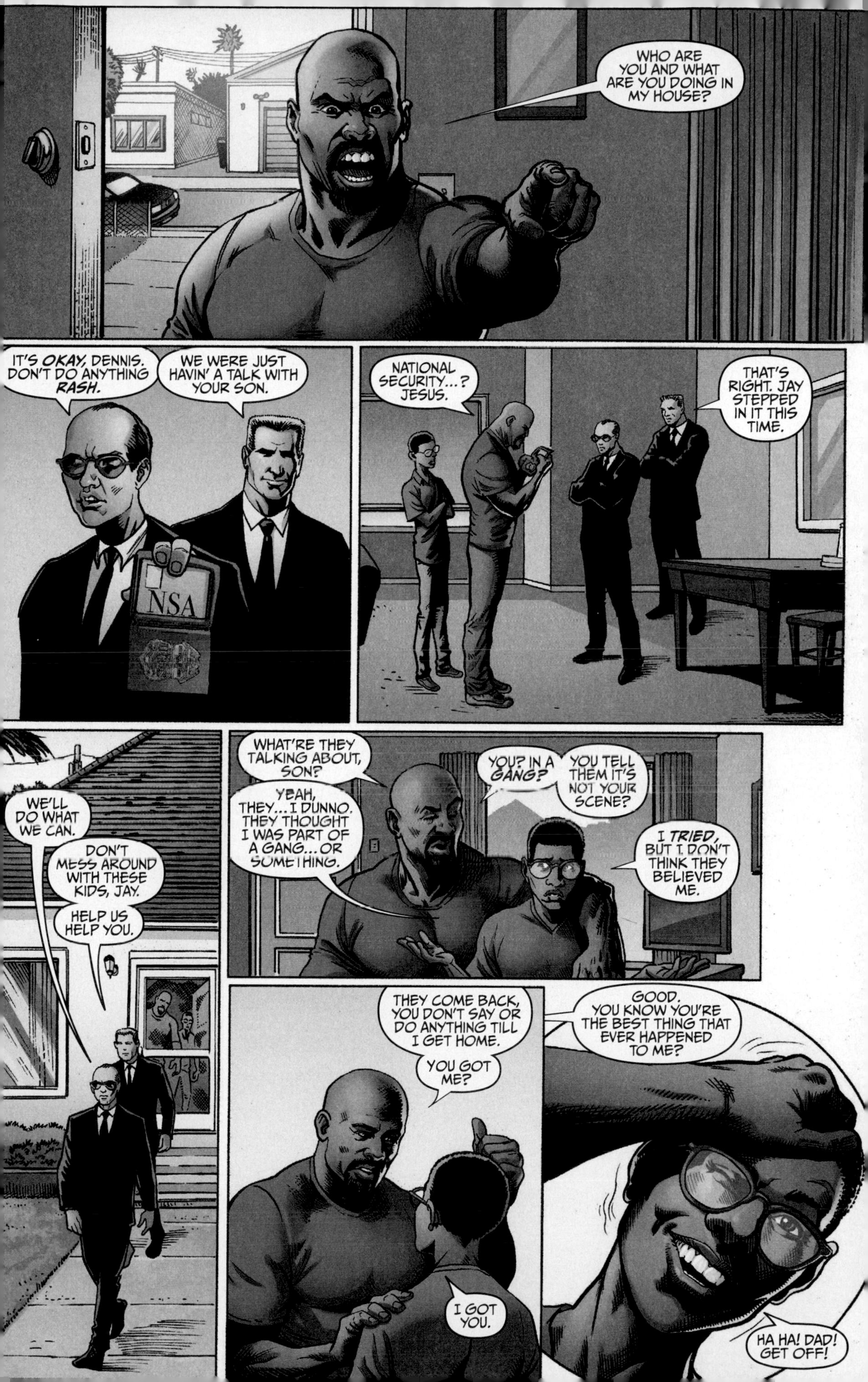
WHO ARE YOU AND WHAT ARE YOU DOING IN MY HOUSE?
IT'S OKAY, DENNIS. DON'T DO ANYTHING RASH.
WE WERE JUST HAVIN' A TALK WITH YOUR SON.
NSA
NATIONAL SECURITY...? JESUS.
THAT'S RIGHT. JAY STEPPED IN IT THIS TIME.
WE'LL DO WHAT WE CAN.
DON'T MESS AROUND WITH THESE KIDS, JAY.
HELP US HELP YOU.
WHAT'RE THEY TALKING ABOUT, SON?
YEAH, THEY... I DUNNO. THEY THOUGHT I WAS PART OF A GANG... OR SOMETHING.
YOU? IN A GANG?
YOU TELL THEM IT'S NOT YOUR SCENE?
I TRIED, BUT I DON'T THINK THEY BELIEVED ME.
THEY COME BACK, YOU DON'T SAY OR DO ANYTHING TILL I GET HOME.
YOU GOT ME?
I GOT YOU.
GOOD. YOU KNOW YOU'RE THE BEST THING THAT EVER HAPPENED TO ME?
HA HA! DAD! GET OFF!

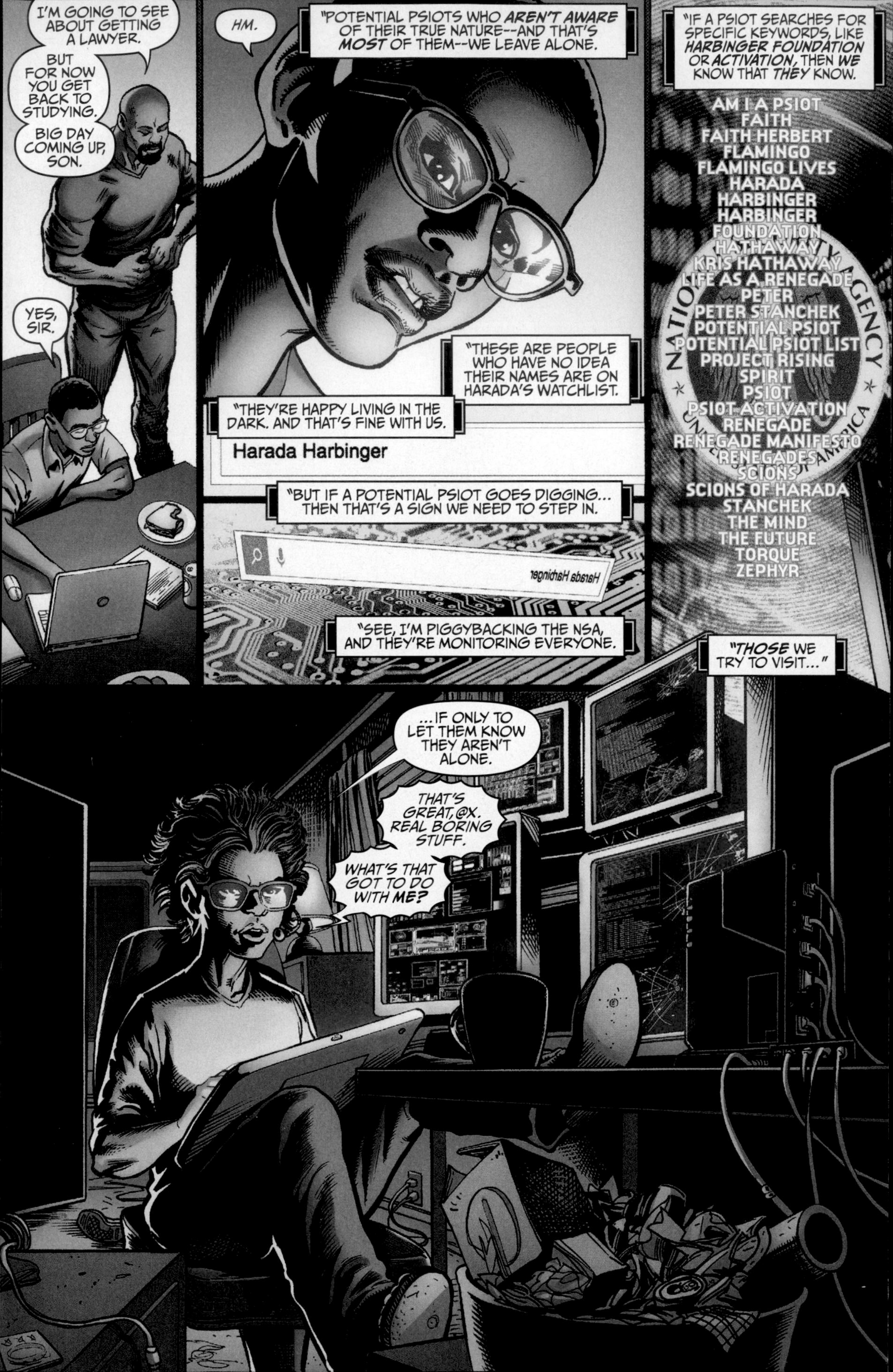

I'M GOING TO SEE ABOUT GETTING A LAWYER.
BUT FOR NOW YOU GET BACK TO STUDYING.
BIG DAY COMING UP, SON.
YES, SIR.
HM.
"POTENTIAL PSIOTS WHO AREN'T AWARE OF THEIR TRUE NATURE--AND THAT'S MOST OF THEM--WE LEAVE ALONE.
"THESE ARE PEOPLE WHO HAVE NO IDEA THEIR NAMES ARE ON HARADA'S WATCHLIST.
"THEY'RE HAPPY LIVING IN THE DARK. AND THAT'S FINE WITH US.
Harada Harbinger
"BUT IF A POTENTIAL PSIOT GOES DIGGING... THEN THAT'S A SIGN WE NEED TO STEP IN.
Harada Harbinger
"SEE, I'M PIGGYBACKING THE NSA, AND THEY'RE MONITORING EVERYONE.
"IF A PSIOT SEARCHES FOR SPECIFIC KEYWORDS, LIKE HARBINGER FOUNDATION OR ACTIVATION, THEN WE KNOW THAT THEY KNOW.
AM I A PSIOT
FAITH
FAITH HERBERT
FLAMINGO
FLAMINGO LIVES
HARADA
HARBINGER
HARBINGER FOUNDATION
HATHAWAY
KRIS HATHAWAY
LIFE AS A RENEGADE
PETER
PETER STANCHEK
POTENTIAL PSIOT
POTENTIAL PSIOT LIST
PROJECT RISING
SPIRIT
PSIOT
PSIOT ACTIVATION
RENEGADE
RENEGADE MANIFESTO
RENEGADES
SCIONS
SCIONS OF HARADA
STANCHEK
THE MIND
THE FUTURE
TORQUE
ZEPHYR
"THOSE WE TRY TO VISIT..."
...IF ONLY TO LET THEM KNOW THEY AREN'T ALONE.
THAT'S GREAT, @X. REAL BORING STUFF.
WHAT'S THAT GOT TO DO WITH ME?

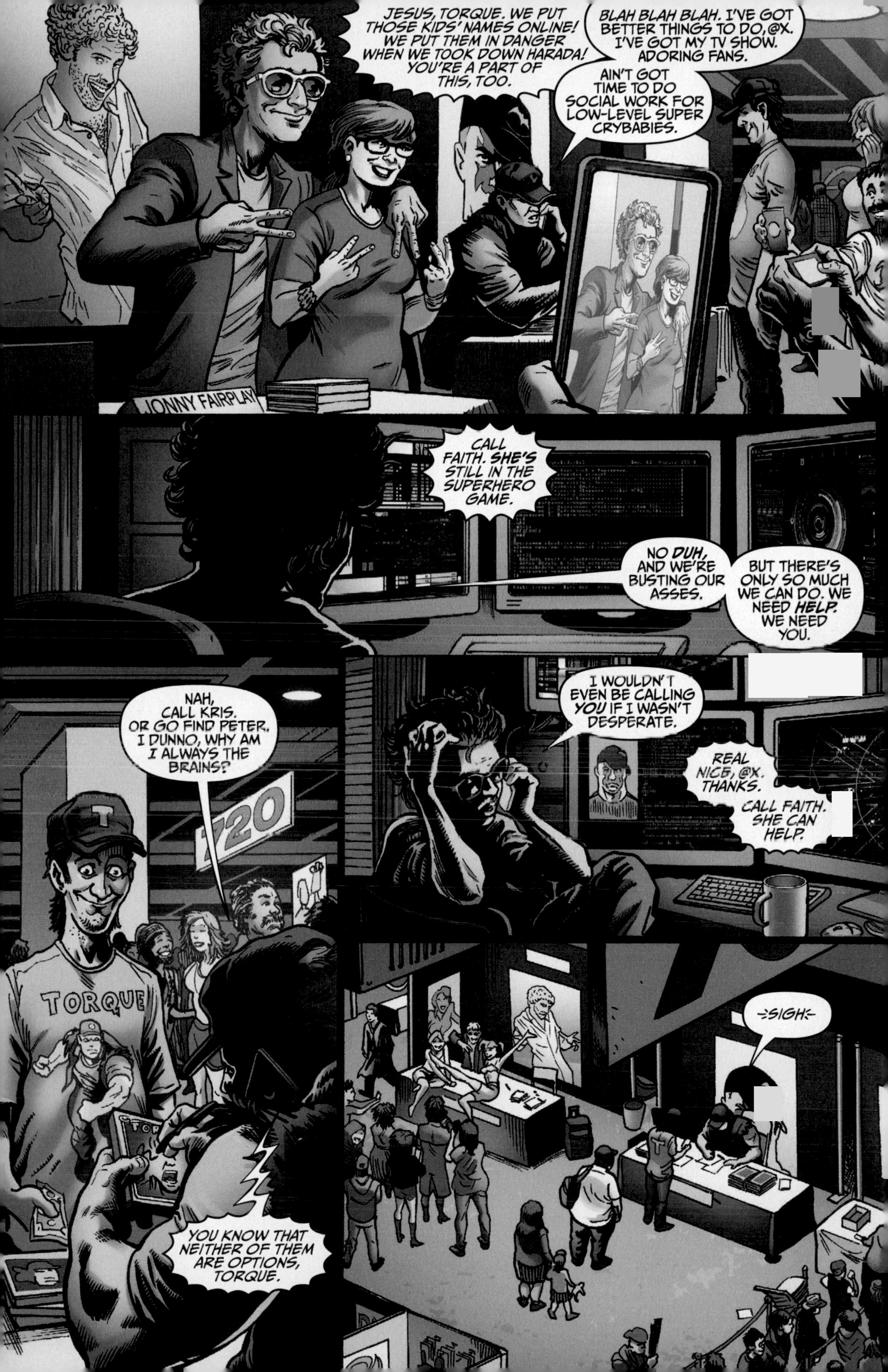
JESUS, TORQUE. WE PUT THOSE KIDS' NAMES ONLINE! WE PUT THEM IN DANGER WHEN WE TOOK DOWN HARADA! YOU'RE A PART OF THIS, TOO.
BLAH BLAH BLAH. I'VE GOT BETTER THINGS TO DO, @X. I'VE GOT MY TV SHOW. ADORING FANS.
AIN'T GOT TIME TO DO SOCIAL WORK FOR LOW-LEVEL SUPER CRYBABIES.
JONNY FAIRPLAY
CALL FAITH. SHE'S STILL IN THE SUPERHERO GAME.
NO DUH, AND WE'RE BUSTING OUR ASSES.
BUT THERE'S ONLY SO MUCH WE CAN DO. WE NEED HELP. WE NEED YOU.
NAH, CALL KRIS. OR GO FIND PETER. I DUNNO, WHY AM I ALWAYS THE BRAINS?
I WOULDN'T EVEN BE CALLING YOU IF I WASN'T DESPERATE.
REAL NICE, @X. THANKS.
CALL FAITH. SHE CAN HELP.
720
TORQUE
YOU KNOW THAT NEITHER OF THEM ARE OPTIONS, TORQUE.
-SIGH-

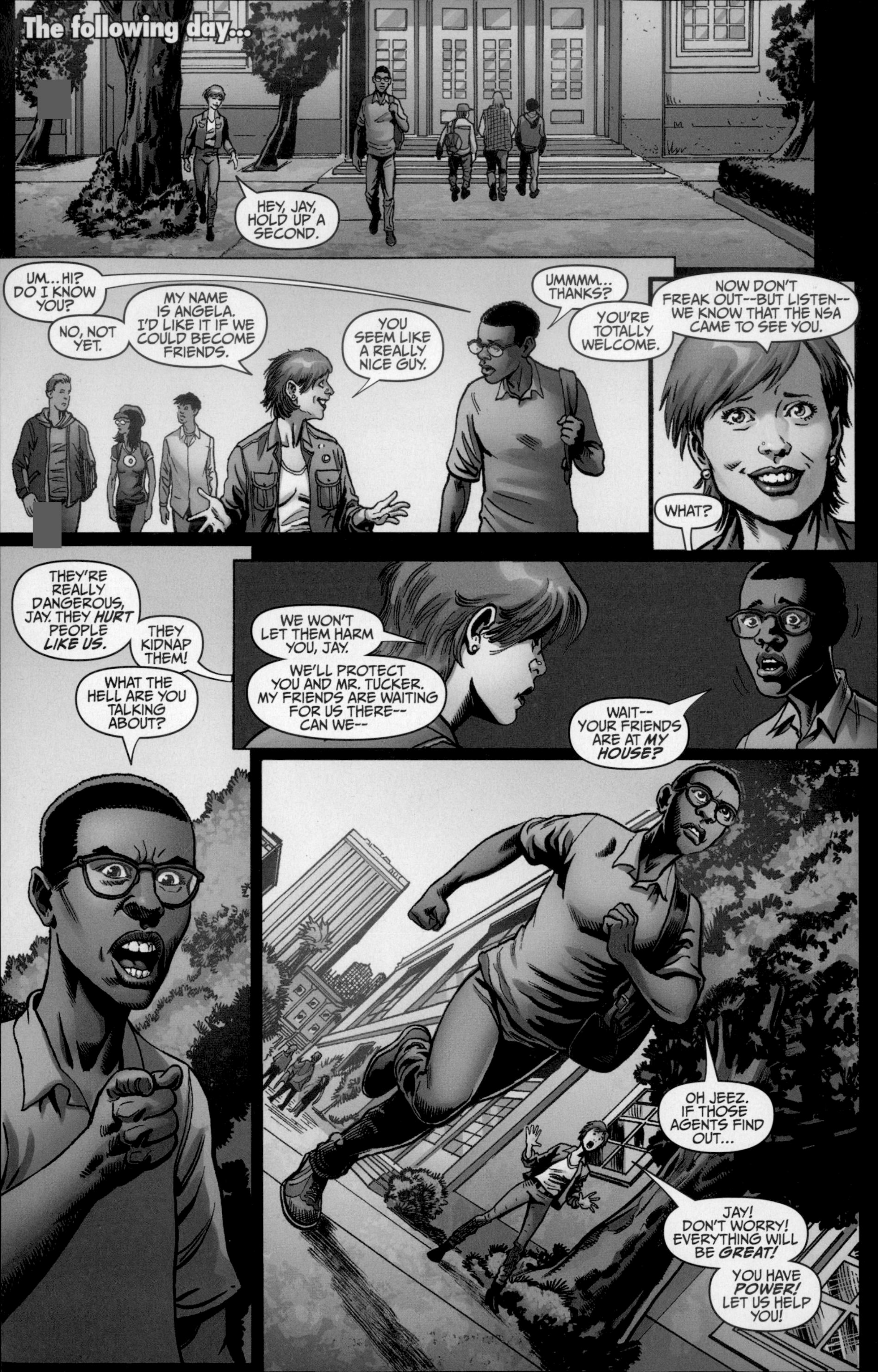
The following day...
HEY, JAY, HOLD UP A SECOND.
UM...HI? DO I KNOW YOU?
NO, NOT YET.
MY NAME IS ANGELA. I'D LIKE IT IF WE COULD BECOME FRIENDS.
YOU SEEM LIKE A REALLY NICE GUY.
UMMMM... THANKS?
YOU'RE TOTALLY WELCOME.
NOW DON'T FREAK OUT--BUT LISTEN--WE KNOW THAT THE NSA CAME TO SEE YOU.
WHAT?
THEY'RE REALLY DANGEROUS, JAY. THEY *HURT* PEOPLE *LIKE US*.
THEY KIDNAP THEM!
WHAT THE HELL ARE YOU TALKING ABOUT?
WE WON'T LET THEM HARM YOU, JAY.
WE'LL PROTECT YOU AND MR. TUCKER. MY FRIENDS ARE WAITING FOR US THERE--CAN WE--
WAIT--YOUR FRIENDS ARE AT *MY HOUSE?*
OH JEEZ. IF THOSE AGENTS FIND OUT...
JAY! DON'T WORRY! EVERYTHING WILL BE *GREAT!*
YOU HAVE *POWER!* LET US HELP YOU!

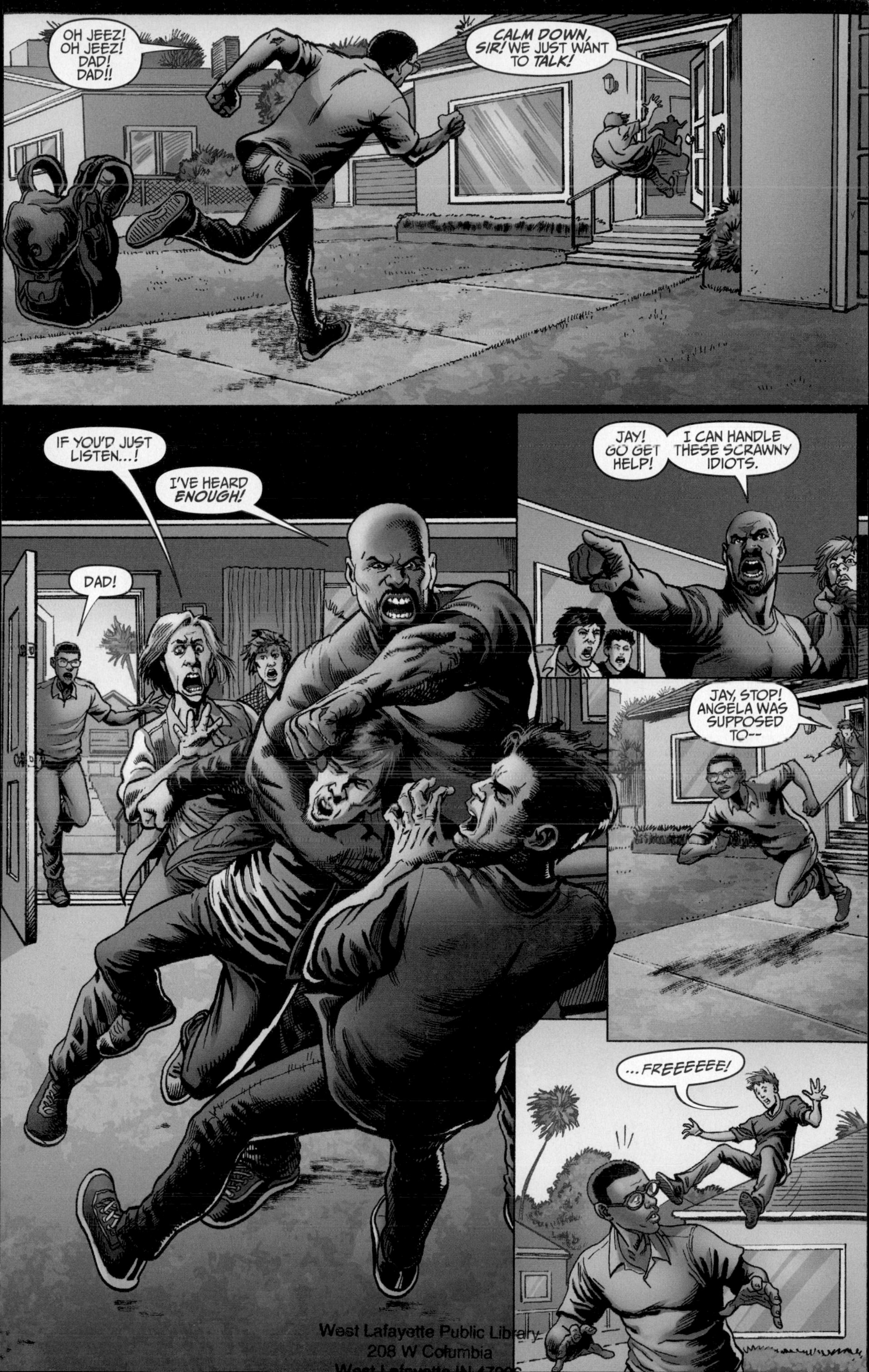
OH JEEZ! OH JEEZ! DAD! DAD!!
CALM DOWN, SIR! WE JUST WANT TO TALK!
IF YOU'D JUST LISTEN...!
I'VE HEARD ENOUGH!
DAD!
JAY! GO GET HELP!
I CAN HANDLE THESE SCRAWNY IDIOTS.
JAY, STOP! ANGELA WAS SUPPOSED TO--
...FREEEEEEE!

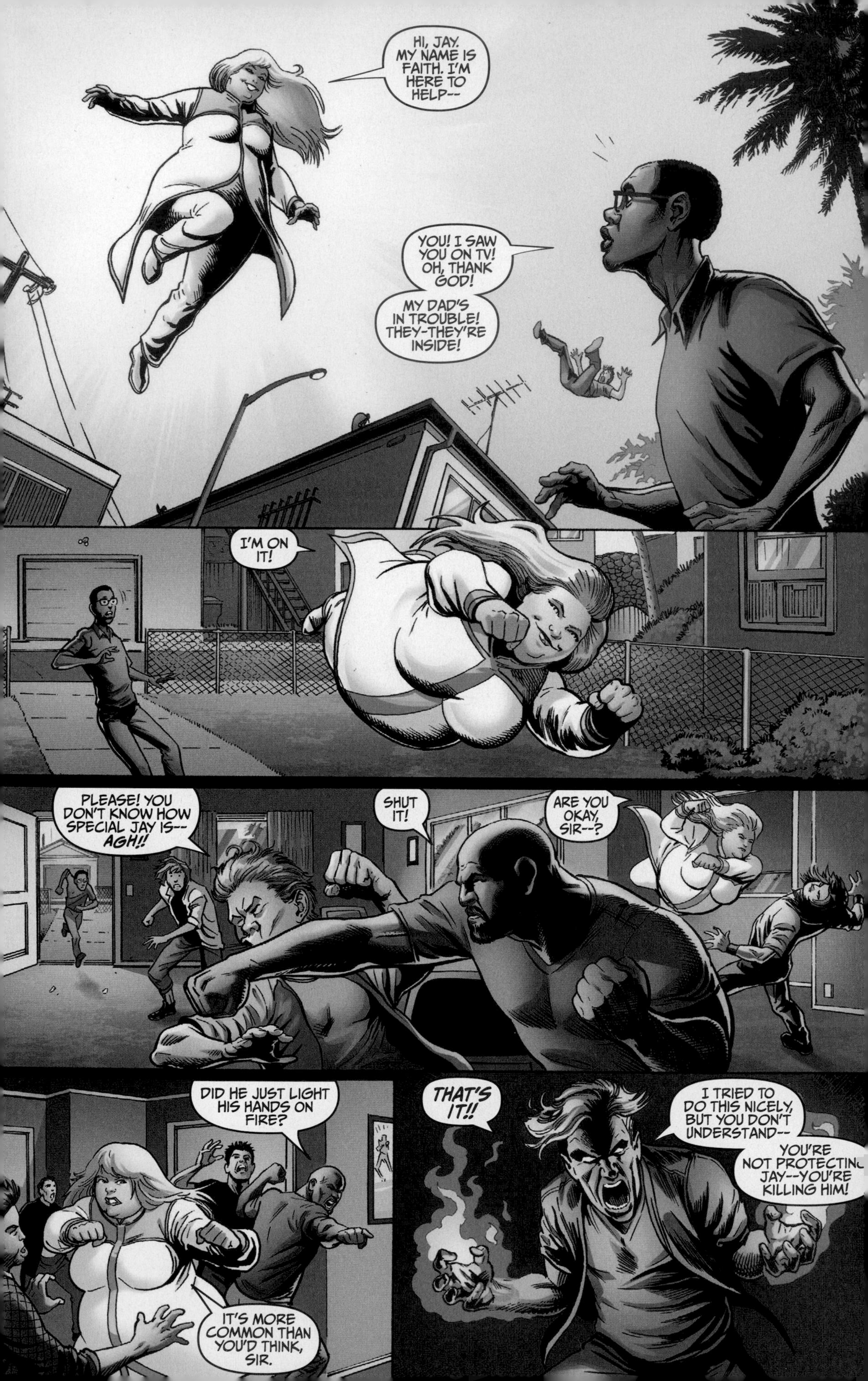
HI, JAY. MY NAME IS FAITH. I'M HERE TO HELP--
YOU! I SAW YOU ON TV! OH, THANK GOD!
MY DAD'S IN TROUBLE! THEY-THEY'RE INSIDE!
I'M ON IT!
PLEASE! YOU DON'T KNOW HOW SPECIAL JAY IS-- AGH!!
SHUT IT!
ARE YOU OKAY, SIR--?
DID HE JUST LIGHT HIS HANDS ON FIRE?
IT'S MORE COMMON THAN YOU'D THINK, SIR.
THAT'S IT!!
I TRIED TO DO THIS NICELY, BUT YOU DON'T UNDERSTAND--
YOU'RE NOT PROTECTING JAY--YOU'RE KILLING HIM!

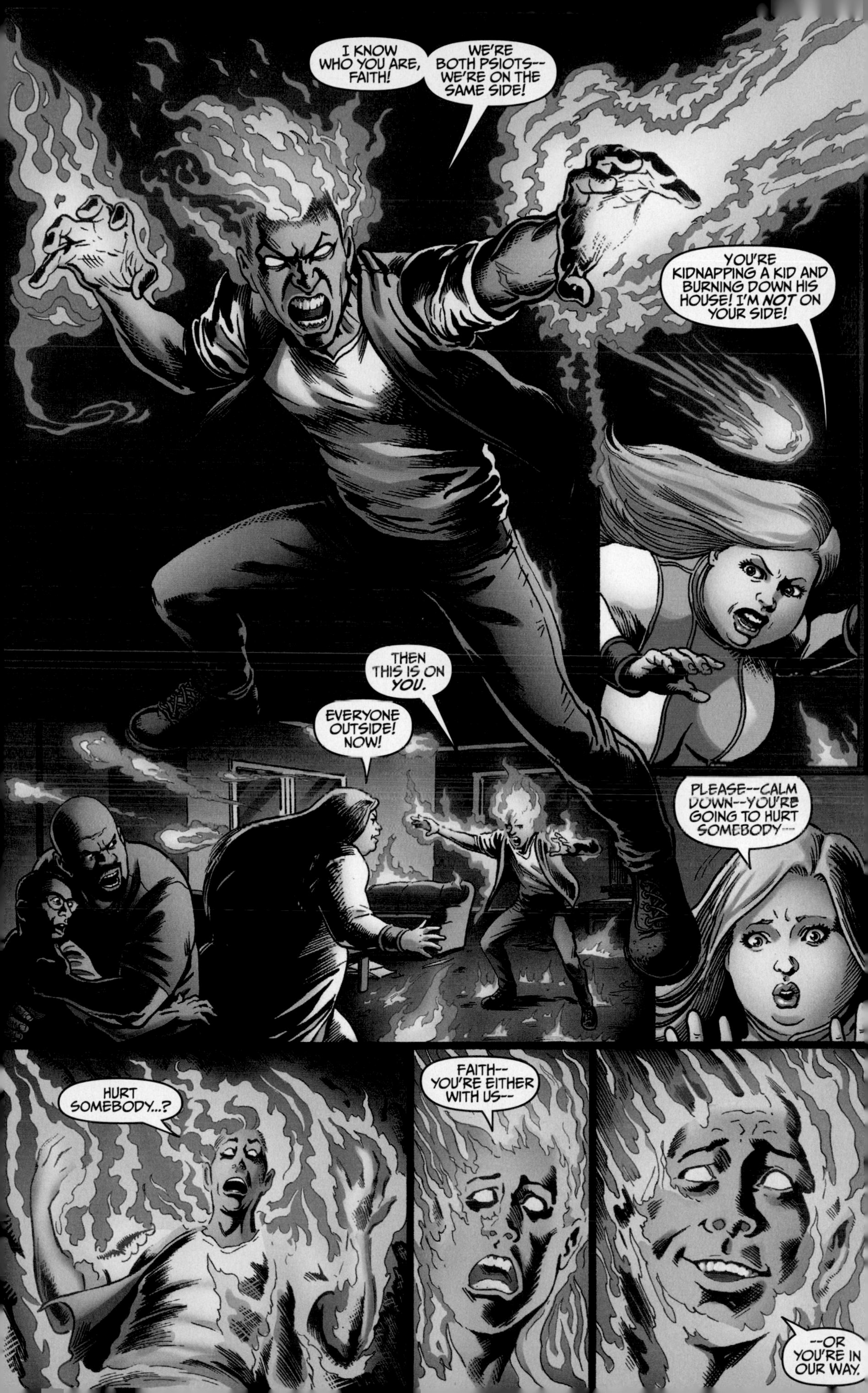
I KNOW WHO YOU ARE, FAITH!
WE'RE BOTH PSIOTS-- WE'RE ON THE SAME SIDE!
YOU'RE KIDNAPPING A KID AND BURNING DOWN HIS HOUSE! I'M NOT ON YOUR SIDE!
THEN THIS IS ON YOU.
EVERYONE OUTSIDE! NOW!
PLEASE--CALM DOWN--YOU'RE GOING TO HURT SOMEBODY---
HURT SOMEBODY...?
FAITH-- YOU'RE EITHER WITH US--
--OR YOU'RE IN OUR WAY.

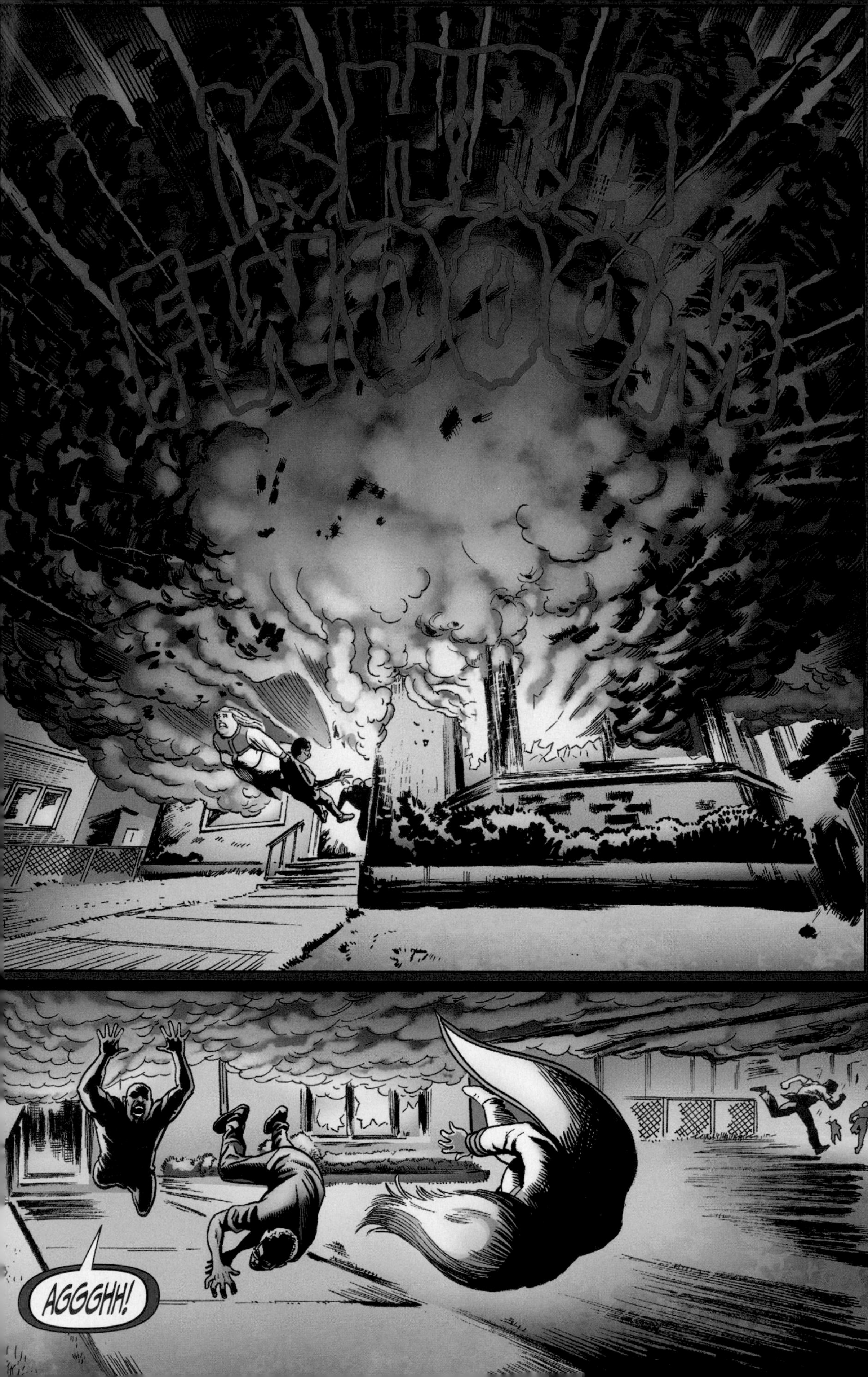
AGGGHH!

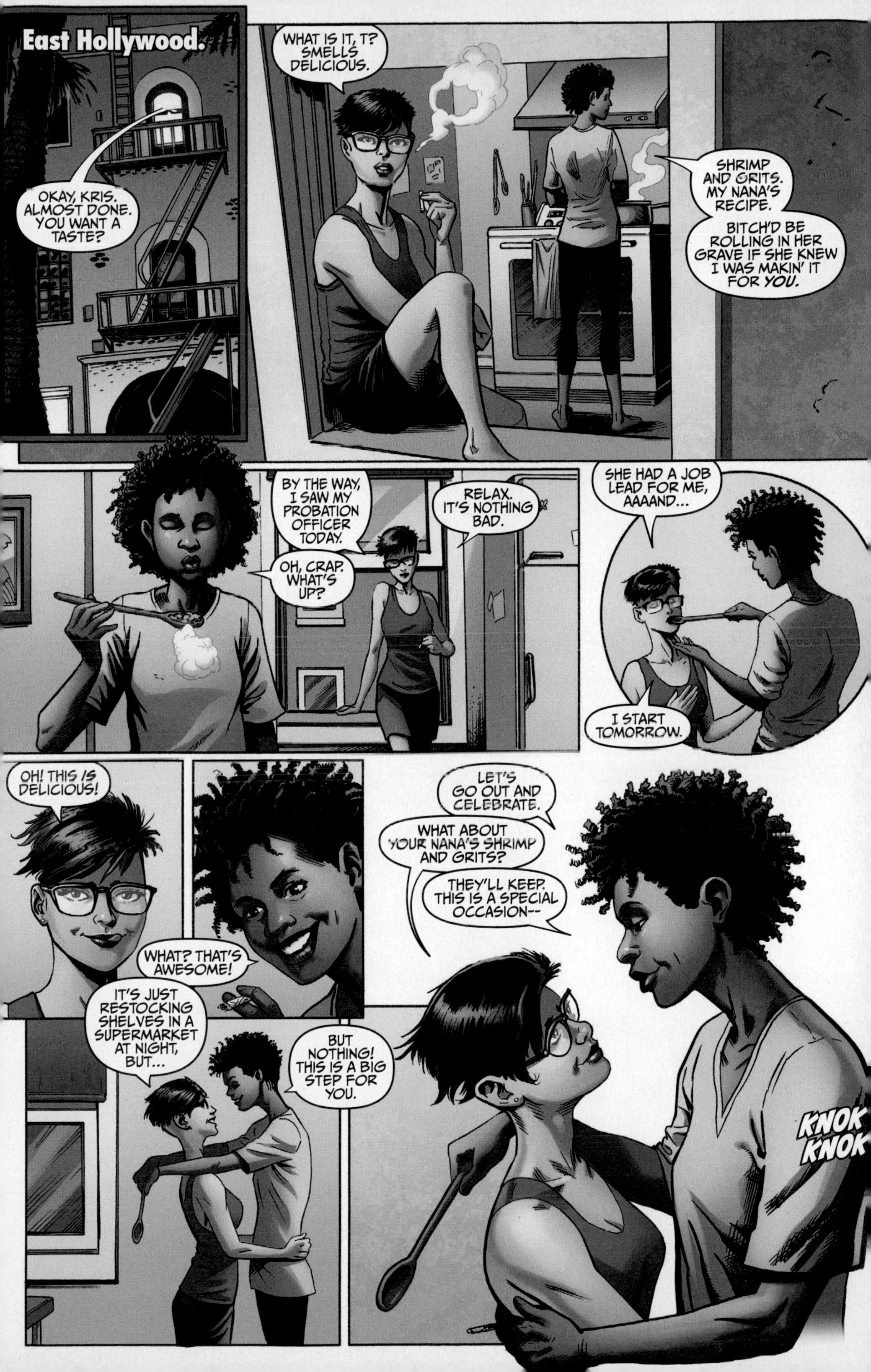
East Hollywood.
OKAY, KRIS. ALMOST DONE. YOU WANT A TASTE?
WHAT IS IT, T? SMELLS DELICIOUS.
SHRIMP AND GRITS. MY NANA'S RECIPE.
BITCH'D BE ROLLING IN HER GRAVE IF SHE KNEW I WAS MAKIN' IT FOR YOU.
BY THE WAY, I SAW MY PROBATION OFFICER TODAY.
OH, CRAP. WHAT'S UP?
RELAX. IT'S NOTHING BAD.
SHE HAD A JOB LEAD FOR ME, AAAAND...
I START TOMORROW.
OH! THIS IS DELICIOUS!
WHAT? THAT'S AWESOME!
IT'S JUST RESTOCKING SHELVES IN A SUPERMARKET AT NIGHT, BUT...
BUT NOTHING! THIS IS A BIG STEP FOR YOU.
LET'S GO OUT AND CELEBRATE.
WHAT ABOUT YOUR NANA'S SHRIMP AND GRITS?
THEY'LL KEEP. THIS IS A SPECIAL OCCASION--
KNOK KNOK

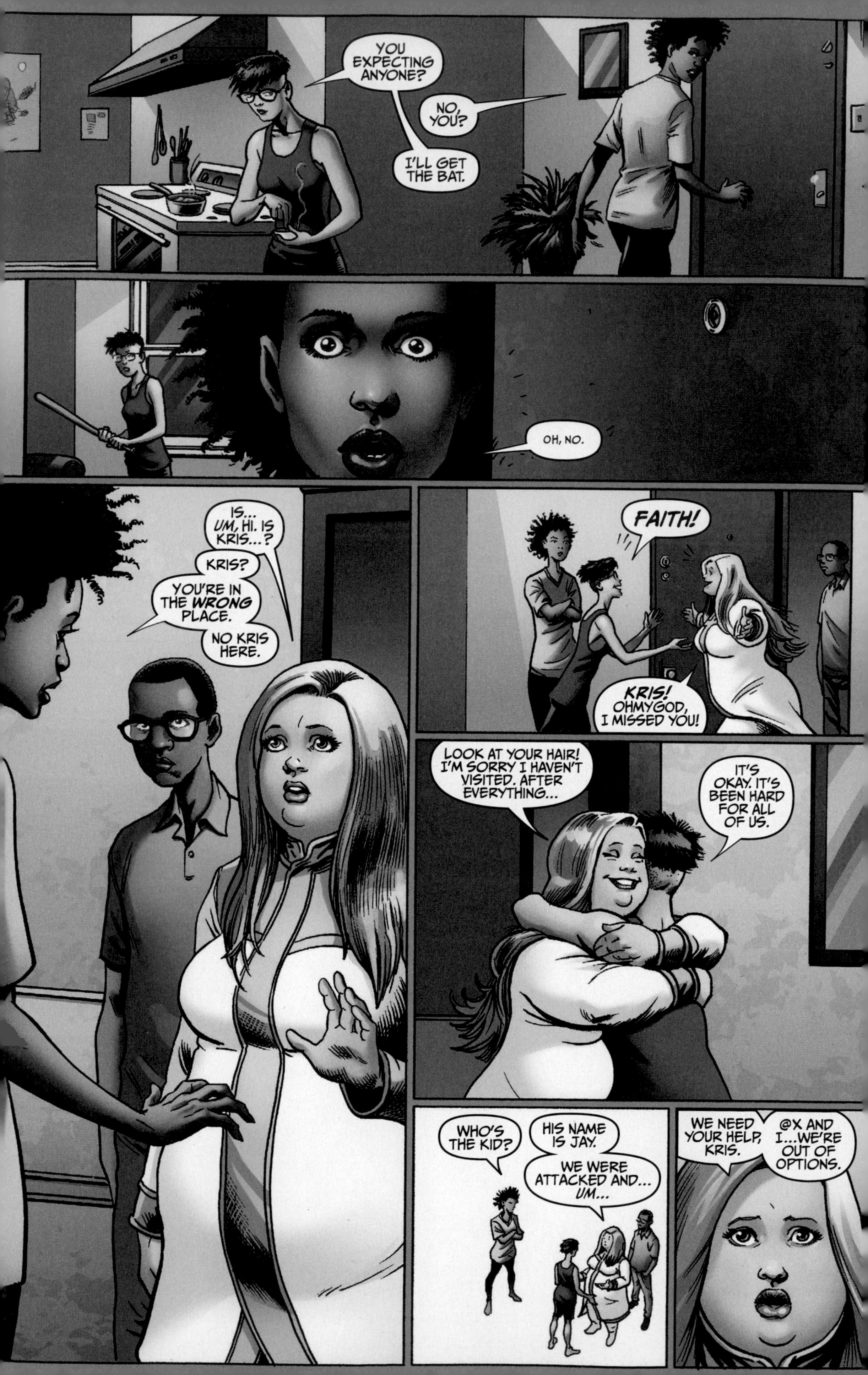
YOU EXPECTING ANYONE?
NO, YOU?
I'LL GET THE BAT.
OH, NO.
IS... UM, HI. IS KRIS...?
KRIS?
YOU'RE IN THE WRONG PLACE.
NO KRIS HERE.
FAITH!
KRIS! OHMYGOD, I MISSED YOU!
LOOK AT YOUR HAIR! I'M SORRY I HAVEN'T VISITED. AFTER EVERYTHING...
IT'S OKAY. IT'S BEEN HARD FOR ALL OF US.
WHO'S THE KID?
HIS NAME IS JAY.
WE WERE ATTACKED AND... UM...
WE NEED YOUR HELP, KRIS.
@X AND I...WE'RE OUT OF OPTIONS.

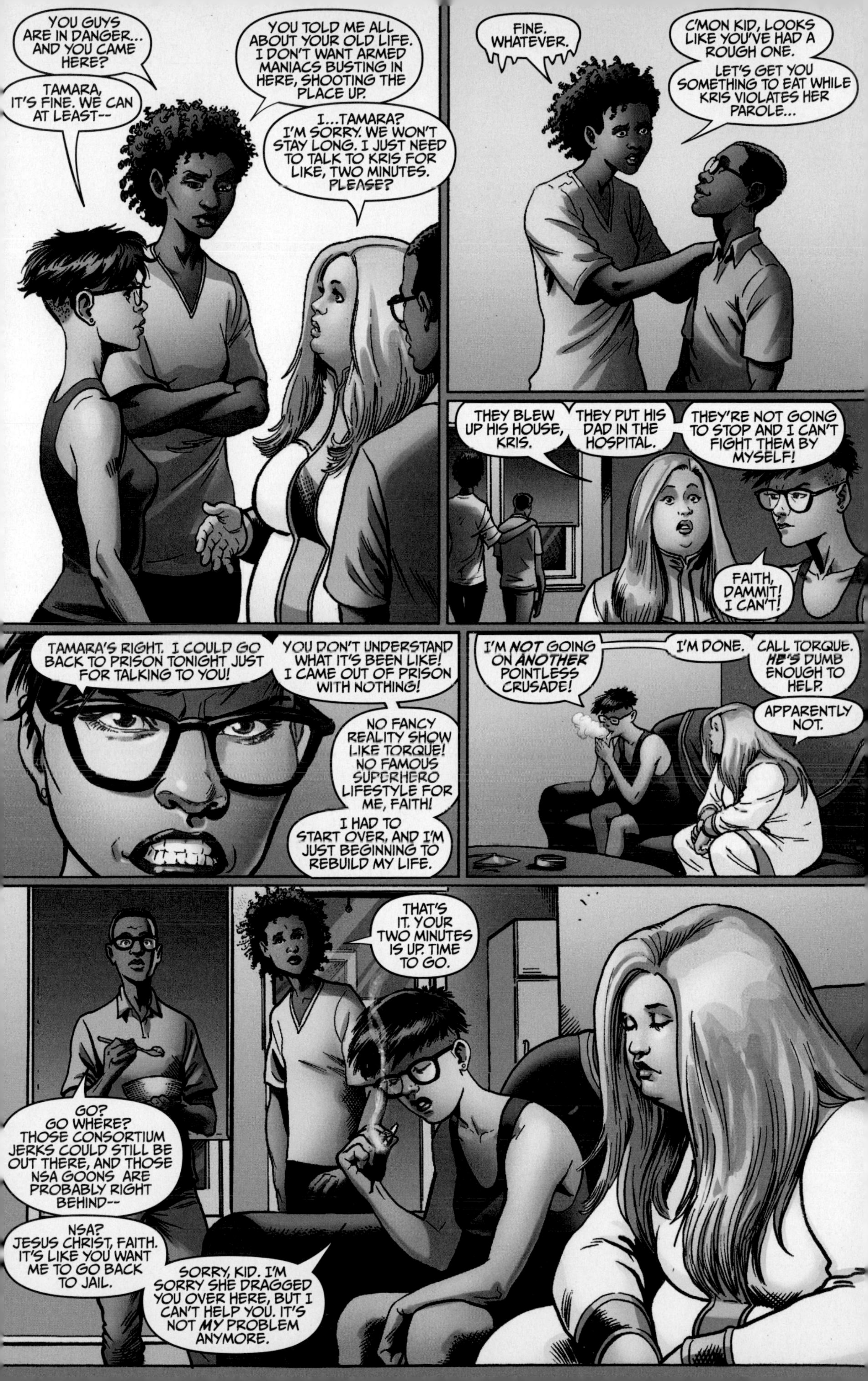
YOU GUYS ARE IN DANGER... AND YOU CAME HERE?
YOU TOLD ME ALL ABOUT YOUR OLD LIFE. I DON'T WANT ARMED MANIACS BUSTING IN HERE, SHOOTING THE PLACE UP.
TAMARA, IT'S FINE. WE CAN AT LEAST--
I...TAMARA? I'M SORRY. WE WON'T STAY LONG. I JUST NEED TO TALK TO KRIS FOR LIKE, TWO MINUTES. PLEASE?
FINE. WHATEVER.
C'MON KID, LOOKS LIKE YOU'VE HAD A ROUGH ONE.
LET'S GET YOU SOMETHING TO EAT WHILE KRIS VIOLATES HER PAROLE...
THEY BLEW UP HIS HOUSE, KRIS.
THEY PUT HIS DAD IN THE HOSPITAL.
THEY'RE NOT GOING TO STOP AND I CAN'T FIGHT THEM BY MYSELF!
FAITH, DAMMIT! I CAN'T!
TAMARA'S RIGHT. I COULD GO BACK TO PRISON TONIGHT JUST FOR TALKING TO YOU!
YOU DON'T UNDERSTAND WHAT IT'S BEEN LIKE! I CAME OUT OF PRISON WITH NOTHING!
NO FANCY REALITY SHOW LIKE TORQUE! NO FAMOUS SUPERHERO LIFESTYLE FOR ME, FAITH!
I HAD TO START OVER, AND I'M JUST BEGINNING TO REBUILD MY LIFE.
I'M NOT GOING ON ANOTHER POINTLESS CRUSADE!
I'M DONE.
CALL TORQUE. HE'S DUMB ENOUGH TO HELP.
APPARENTLY NOT.
THAT'S IT. YOUR TWO MINUTES IS UP. TIME TO GO.
GO? GO WHERE? THOSE CONSORTIUM JERKS COULD STILL BE OUT THERE, AND THOSE NSA GOONS ARE PROBABLY RIGHT BEHIND--
NSA? JESUS CHRIST, FAITH. IT'S LIKE YOU WANT ME TO GO BACK TO JAIL.
SORRY, KID. I'M SORRY SHE DRAGGED YOU OVER HERE, BUT I CAN'T HELP YOU. IT'S NOT MY PROBLEM ANYMORE.

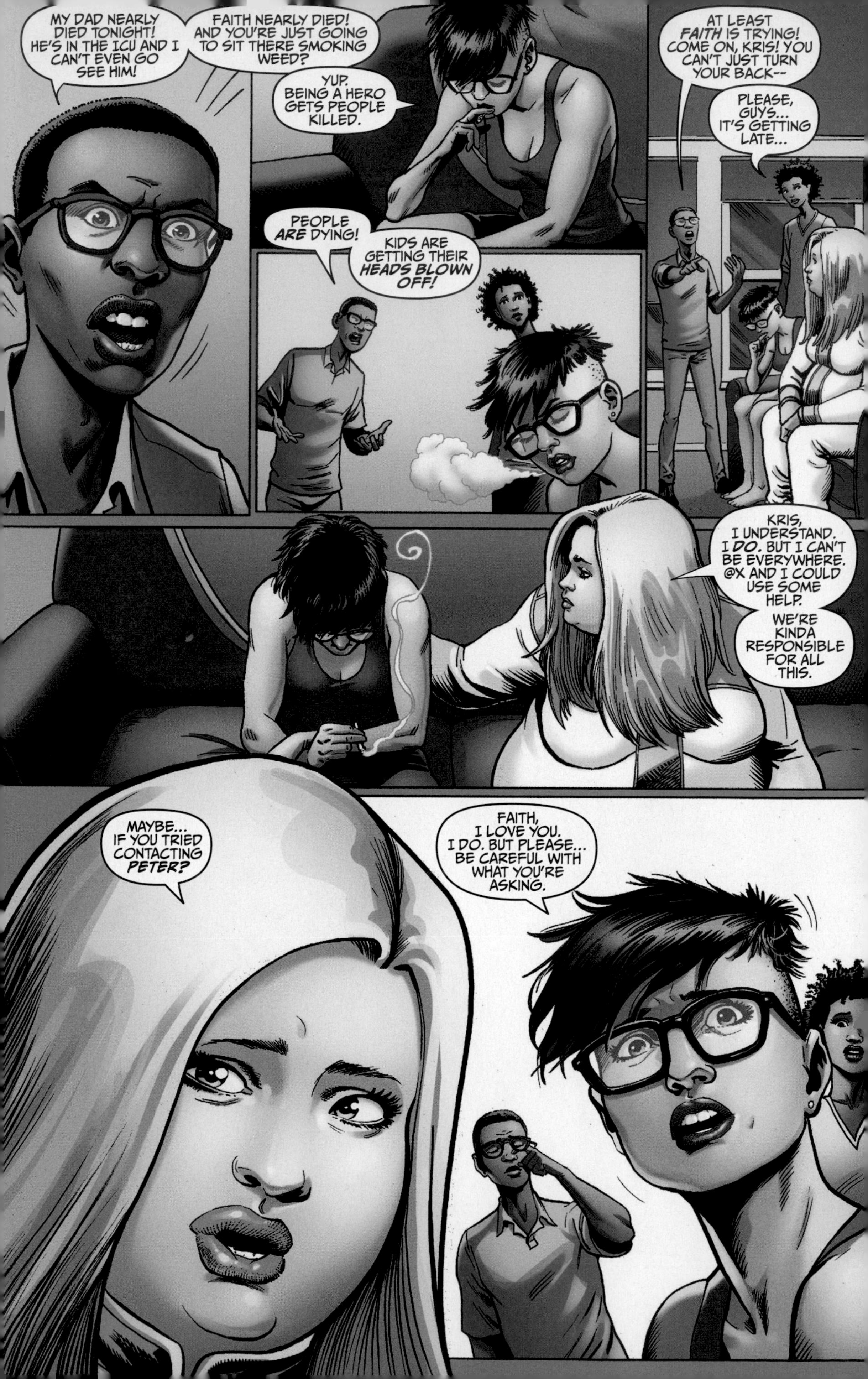
MY DAD NEARLY DIED TONIGHT! HE'S IN THE ICU AND I CAN'T EVEN GO SEE HIM!
FAITH NEARLY DIED! AND YOU'RE JUST GOING TO SIT THERE SMOKING WEED?
YUP. BEING A HERO GETS PEOPLE KILLED.
PEOPLE *ARE* DYING!
KIDS ARE GETTING THEIR *HEADS BLOWN OFF!*
AT LEAST *FAITH* IS TRYING! COME ON, KRIS! YOU CAN'T JUST TURN YOUR BACK--
PLEASE, GUYS... IT'S GETTING LATE...
KRIS, I UNDERSTAND. I *DO*. BUT I CAN'T BE EVERYWHERE. @X AND I COULD USE SOME HELP.
WE'RE KINDA RESPONSIBLE FOR ALL THIS.
MAYBE... IF YOU TRIED CONTACTING *PETER?*
FAITH, I LOVE YOU. I DO. BUT PLEASE... BE CAREFUL WITH WHAT YOU'RE ASKING.

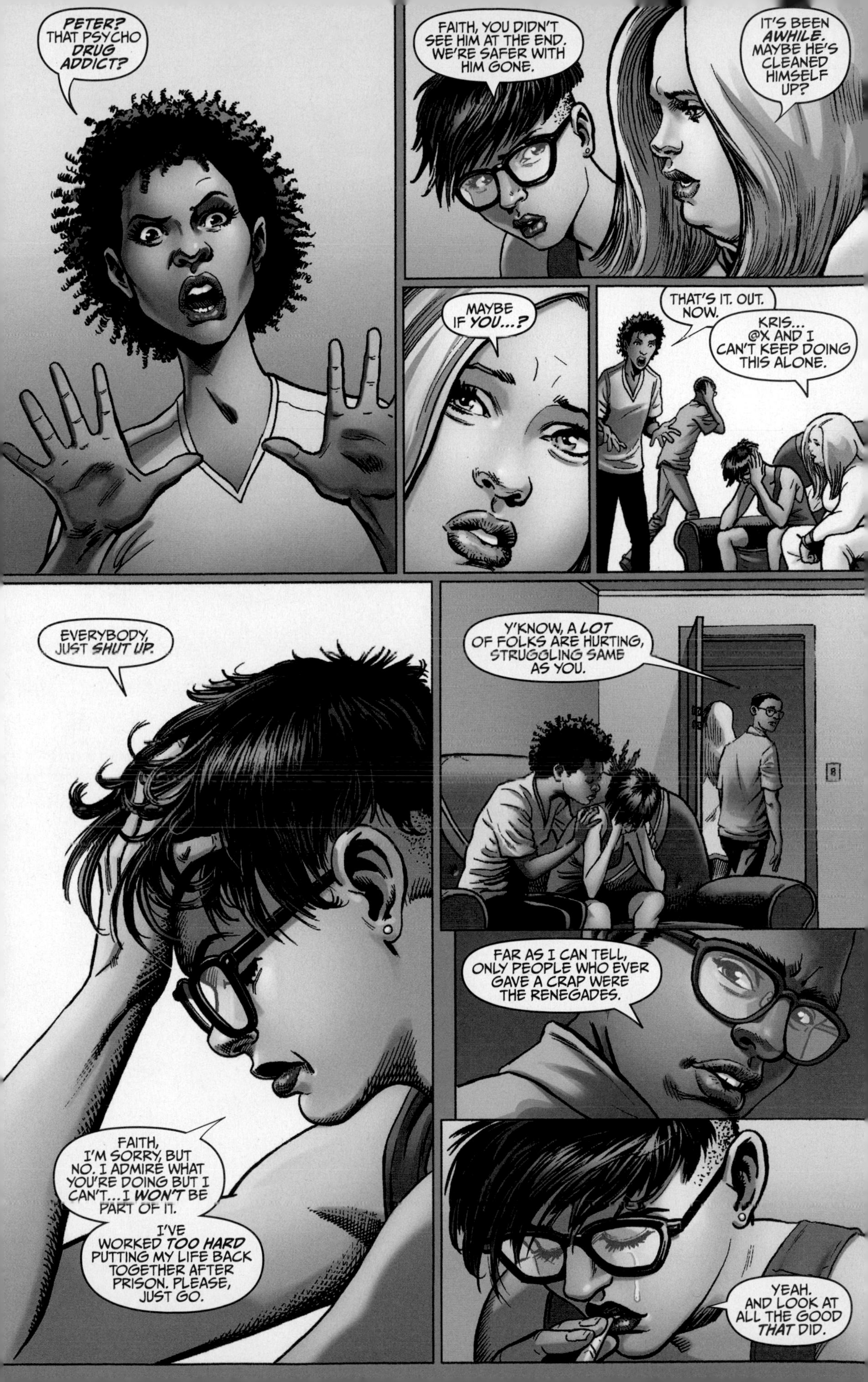
PETER? THAT PSYCHO DRUG ADDICT?
FAITH, YOU DIDN'T SEE HIM AT THE END. WE'RE SAFER WITH HIM GONE.
IT'S BEEN AWHILE. MAYBE HE'S CLEANED HIMSELF UP?
MAYBE IF YOU...?
THAT'S IT. OUT. NOW.
KRIS... @X AND I CAN'T KEEP DOING THIS ALONE.
EVERYBODY, JUST SHUT UP.
FAITH, I'M SORRY, BUT NO. I ADMIRE WHAT YOU'RE DOING BUT I CAN'T... I WON'T BE PART OF IT.
I'VE WORKED TOO HARD PUTTING MY LIFE BACK TOGETHER AFTER PRISON. PLEASE, JUST GO.
Y'KNOW, A LOT OF FOLKS ARE HURTING, STRUGGLING SAME AS YOU.
FAR AS I CAN TELL, ONLY PEOPLE WHO EVER GAVE A CRAP WERE THE RENEGADES.
YEAH. AND LOOK AT ALL THE GOOD THAT DID.

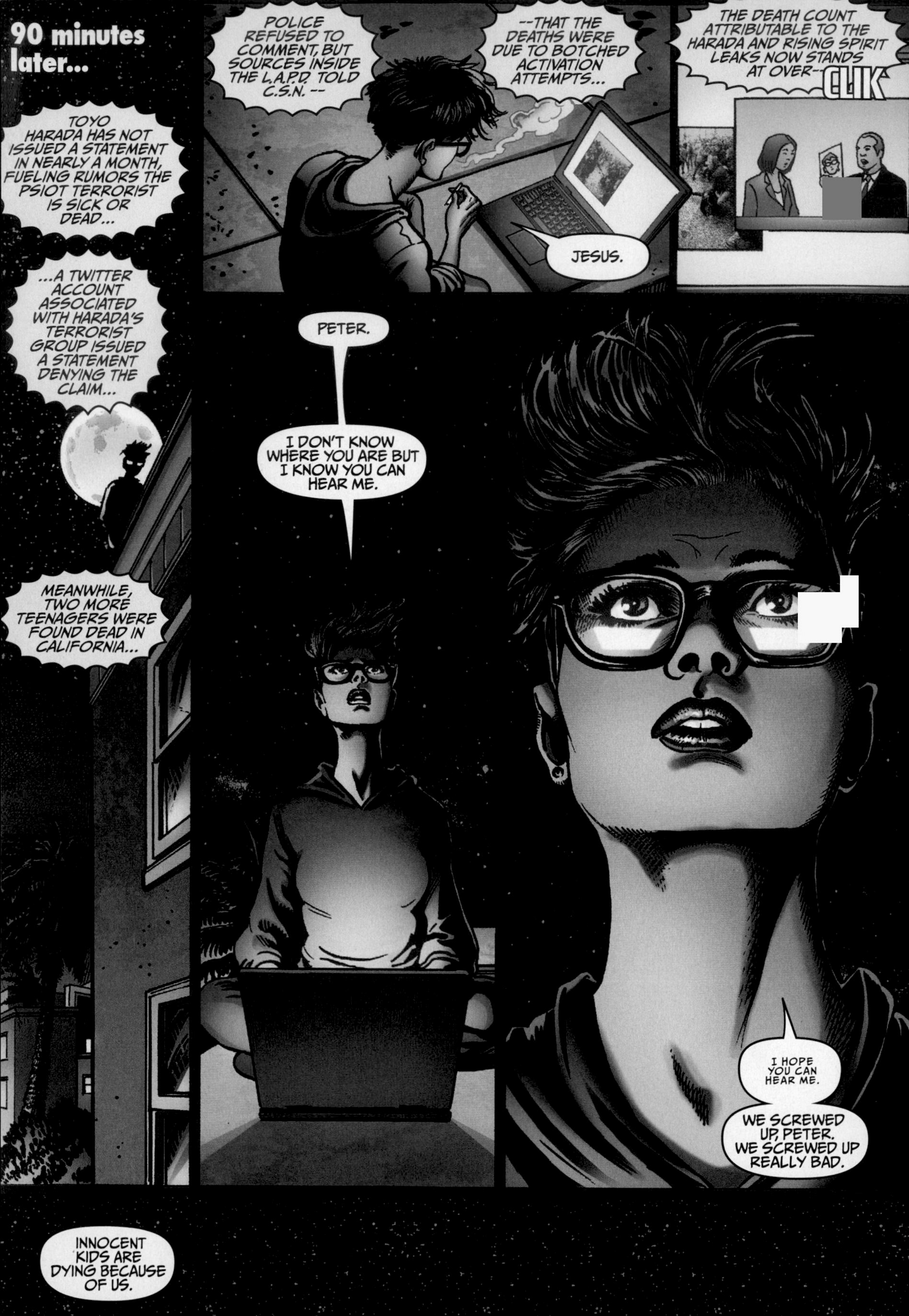
90 minutes later...
TOYO HARADA HAS NOT ISSUED A STATEMENT IN NEARLY A MONTH, FUELING RUMORS THE PSIOT TERRORIST IS SICK OR DEAD...
POLICE REFUSED TO COMMENT, BUT SOURCES INSIDE THE L.A.P.D. TOLD C.S.N. --
--THAT THE DEATHS WERE DUE TO BOTCHED ACTIVATION ATTEMPTS...
JESUS.
THE DEATH COUNT ATTRIBUTABLE TO THE HARADA AND RISING SPIRIT LEAKS NOW STANDS AT OVER--
CLIK
...A TWITTER ACCOUNT ASSOCIATED WITH HARADA'S TERRORIST GROUP ISSUED A STATEMENT DENYING THE CLAIM...
PETER.
I DON'T KNOW WHERE YOU ARE BUT I KNOW YOU CAN HEAR ME.
MEANWHILE, TWO MORE TEENAGERS WERE FOUND DEAD IN CALIFORNIA...
I HOPE YOU CAN HEAR ME.
WE SCREWED UP, PETER. WE SCREWED UP REALLY BAD.
INNOCENT KIDS ARE DYING BECAUSE OF US.

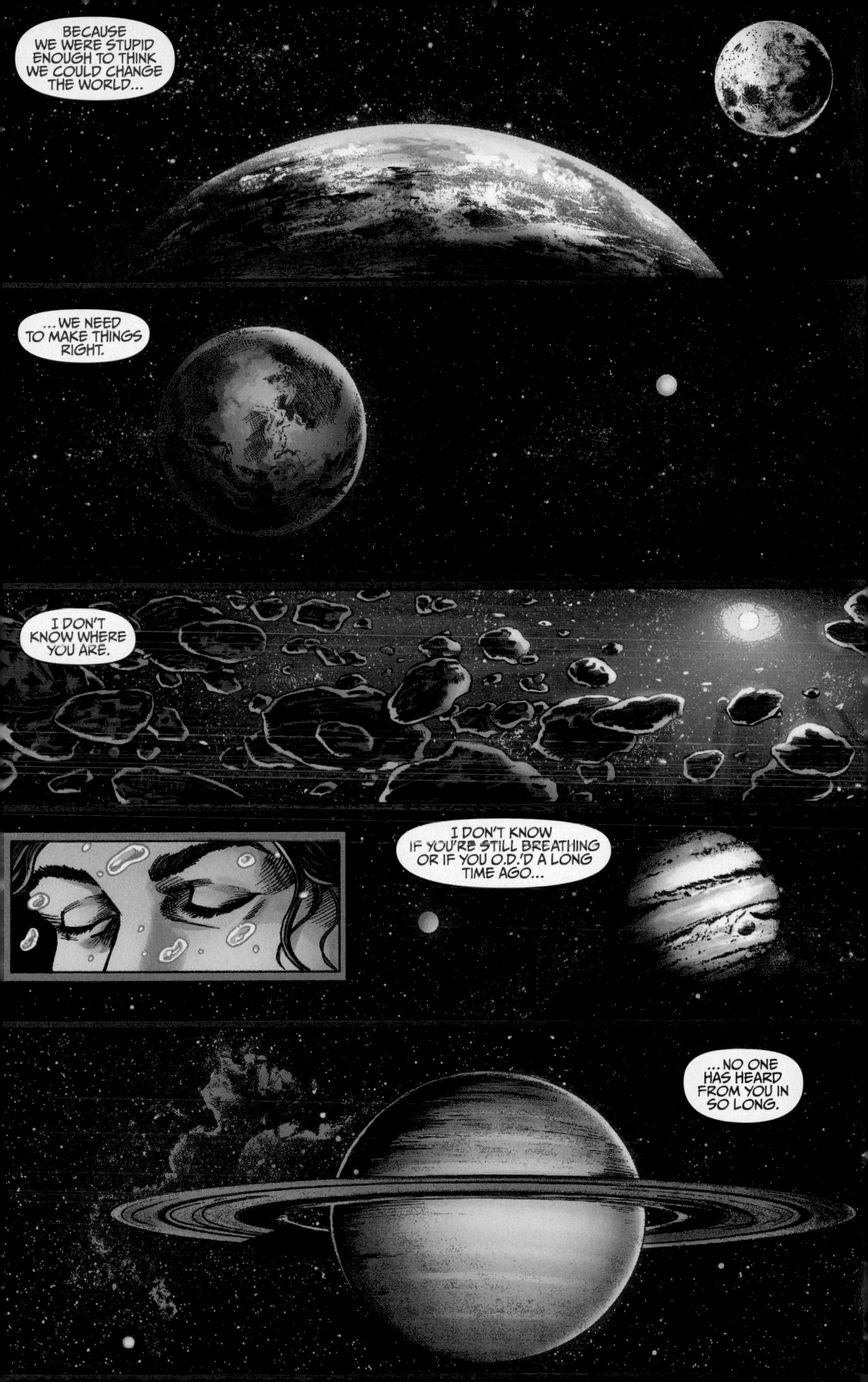
BECAUSE WE WERE STUPID ENOUGH TO THINK WE COULD CHANGE THE WORLD...
...WE NEED TO MAKE THINGS RIGHT.
I DON'T KNOW WHERE YOU ARE.
I DON'T KNOW IF YOU'RE STILL BREATHING OR IF YOU O.D.'D A LONG TIME AGO...
...NO ONE HAS HEARD FROM YOU IN SO LONG.

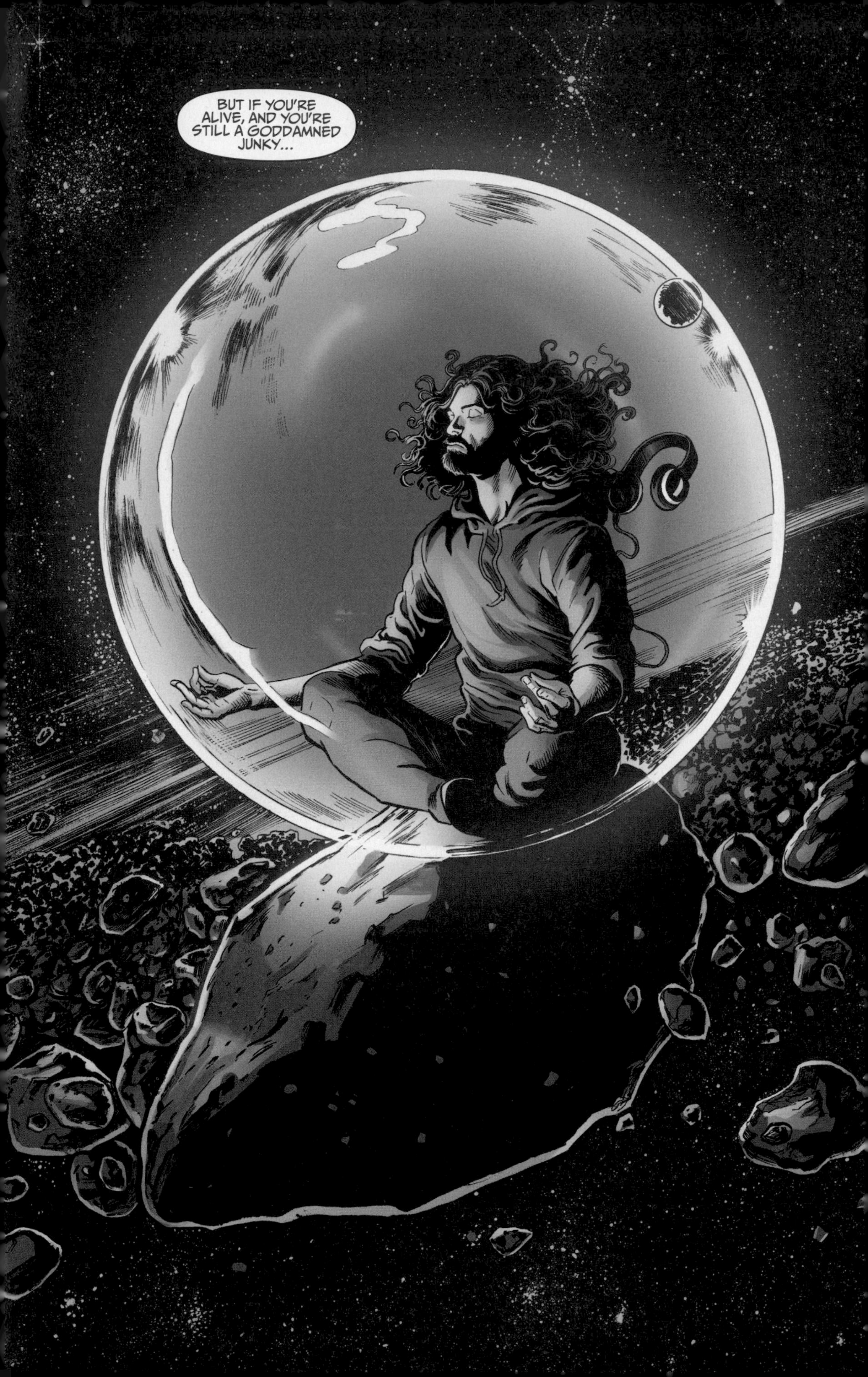
BUT IF YOU'RE ALIVE, AND YOU'RE STILL A GODDAMNED JUNKY...

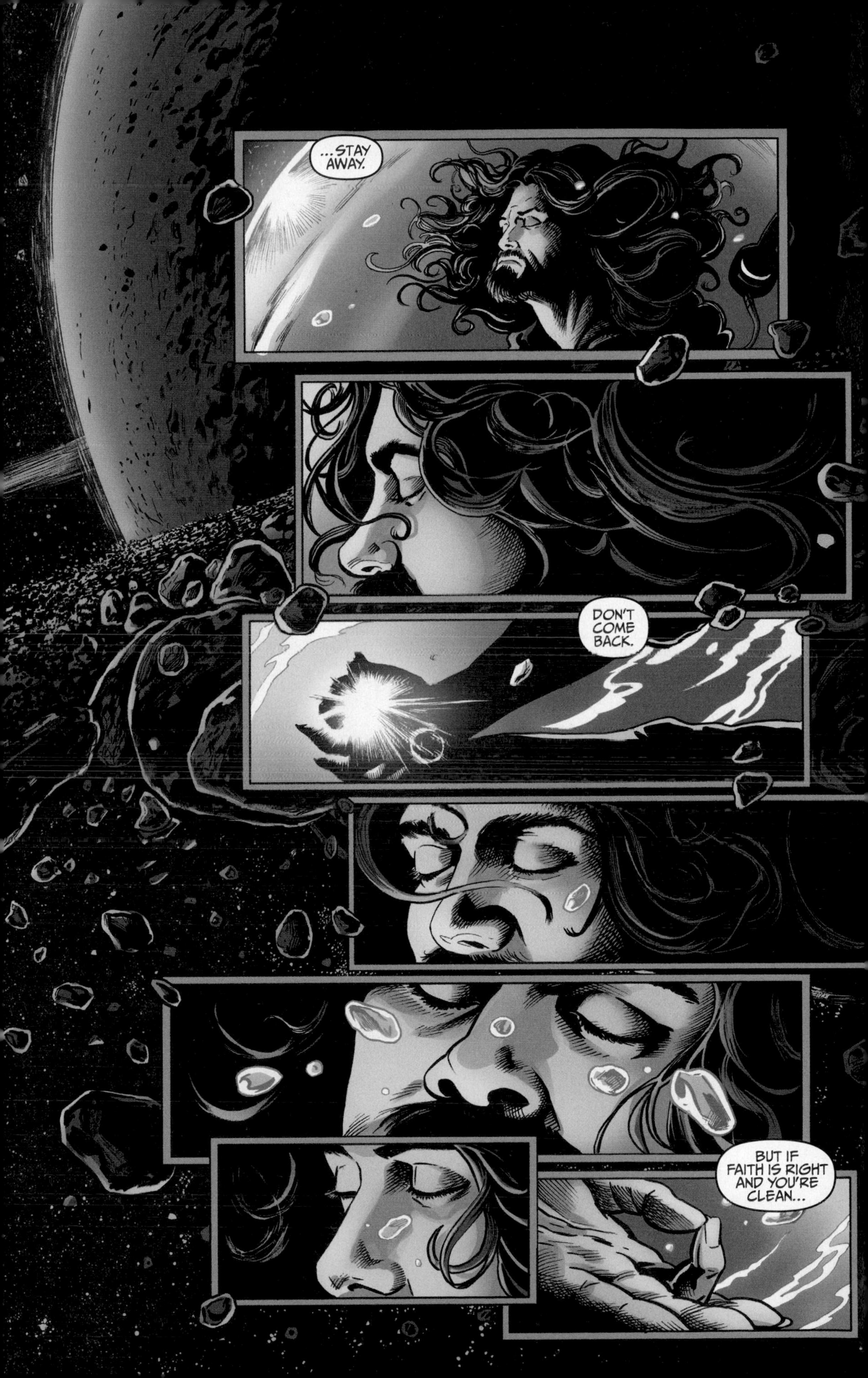
...STAY AWAY.
DON'T COME BACK.
BUT IF FAITH IS RIGHT AND YOU'RE CLEAN...

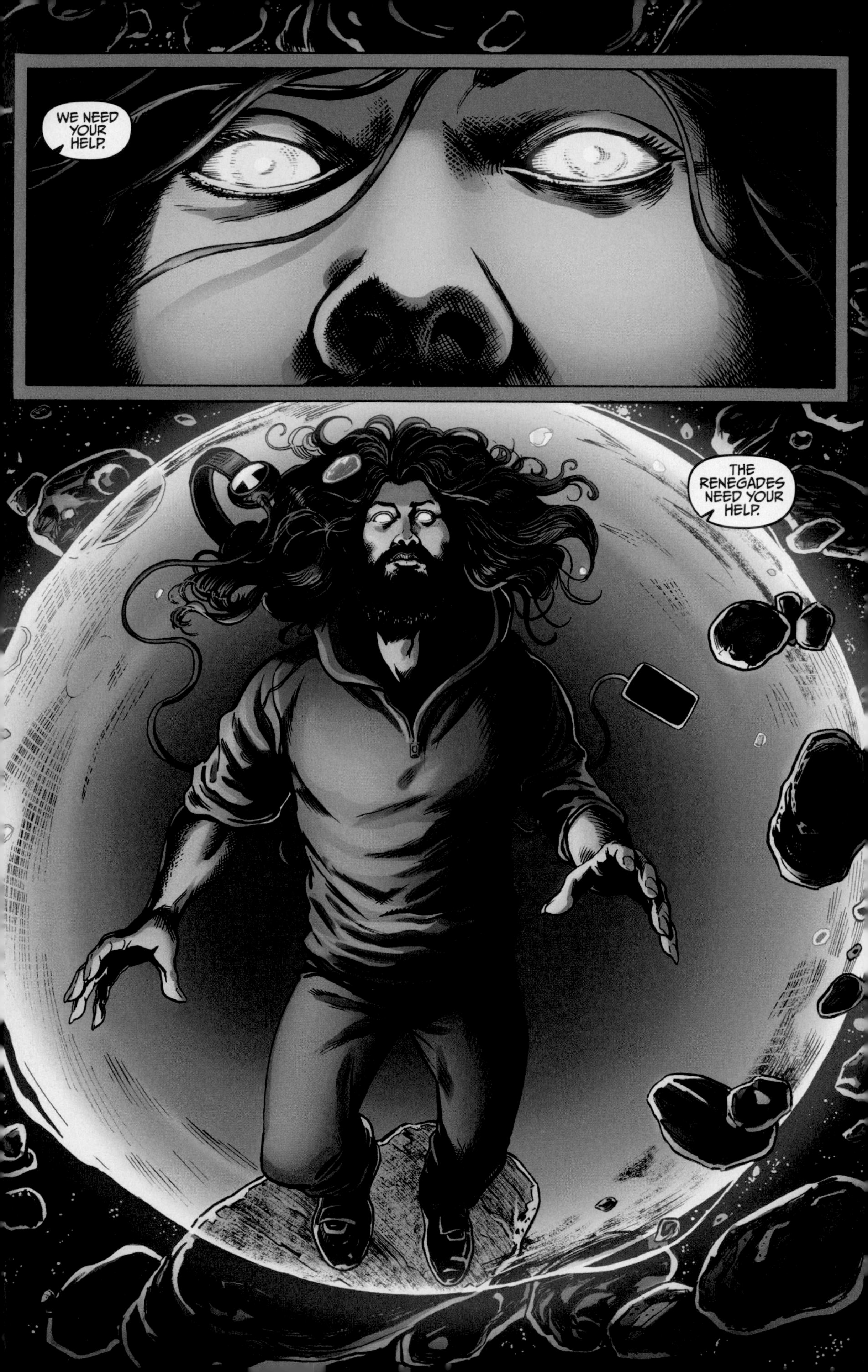
WE NEED YOUR HELP.
THE RENEGADES NEED YOUR HELP.

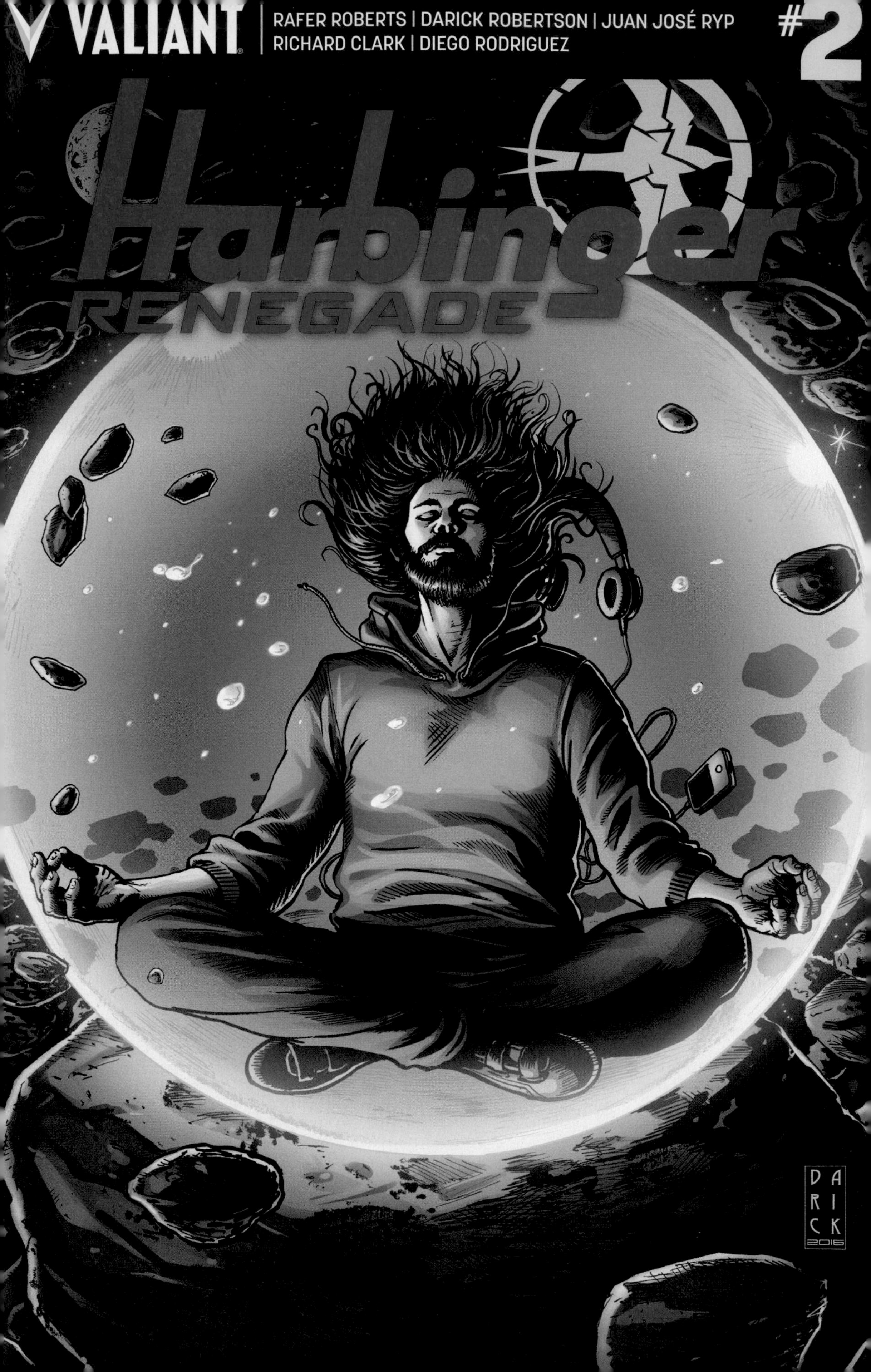
VALIANT
RAFER ROBERTS | DARICK ROBERTSON | JUAN JOSÉ RYP
RICHARD CLARK | DIEGO RODRIGUEZ
#2
Harbinger
RENEGADE
DARICK 2016

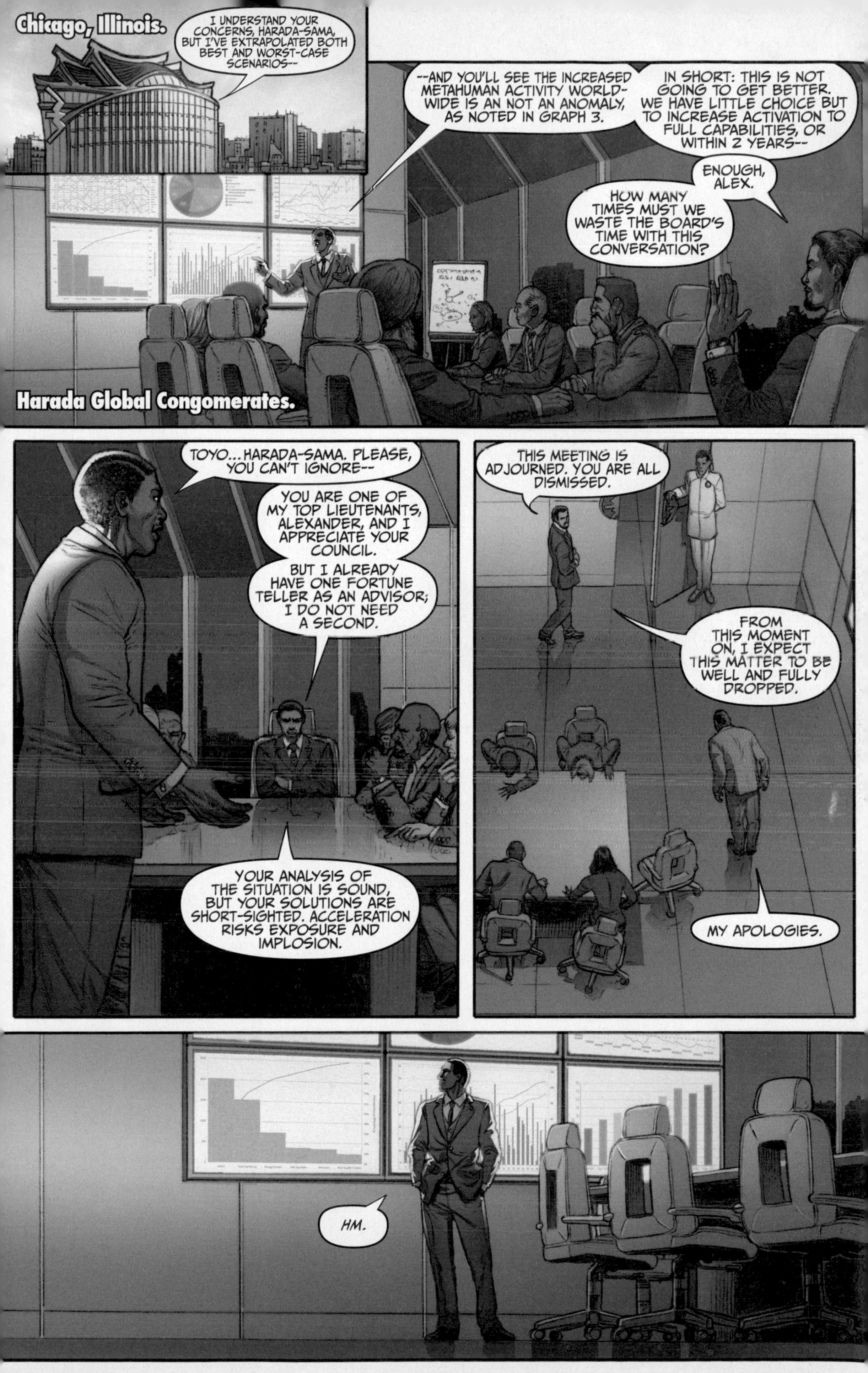
Chicago, Illinois.
I UNDERSTAND YOUR CONCERNS, HARADA-SAMA, BUT I'VE EXTRAPOLATED BOTH BEST AND WORST-CASE SCENARIOS--
--AND YOU'LL SEE THE INCREASED METAHUMAN ACTIVITY WORLD-WIDE IS AN NOT AN ANOMALY, AS NOTED IN GRAPH 3.
IN SHORT: THIS IS NOT GOING TO GET BETTER. WE HAVE LITTLE CHOICE BUT TO INCREASE ACTIVATION TO FULL CAPABILITIES, OR WITHIN 2 YEARS--
ENOUGH, ALEX.
HOW MANY TIMES MUST WE WASTE THE BOARD'S TIME WITH THIS CONVERSATION?
Harada Global Congomerates.
TOYO... HARADA-SAMA. PLEASE, YOU CAN'T IGNORE--
YOU ARE ONE OF MY TOP LIEUTENANTS, ALEXANDER, AND I APPRECIATE YOUR COUNCIL.
BUT I ALREADY HAVE ONE FORTUNE TELLER AS AN ADVISOR; I DO NOT NEED A SECOND.
YOUR ANALYSIS OF THE SITUATION IS SOUND, BUT YOUR SOLUTIONS ARE SHORT-SIGHTED. ACCELERATION RISKS EXPOSURE AND IMPLOSION.
THIS MEETING IS ADJOURNED. YOU ARE ALL DISMISSED.
FROM THIS MOMENT ON, I EXPECT THIS MATTER TO BE WELL AND FULLY DROPPED.
MY APOLOGIES.
HM.

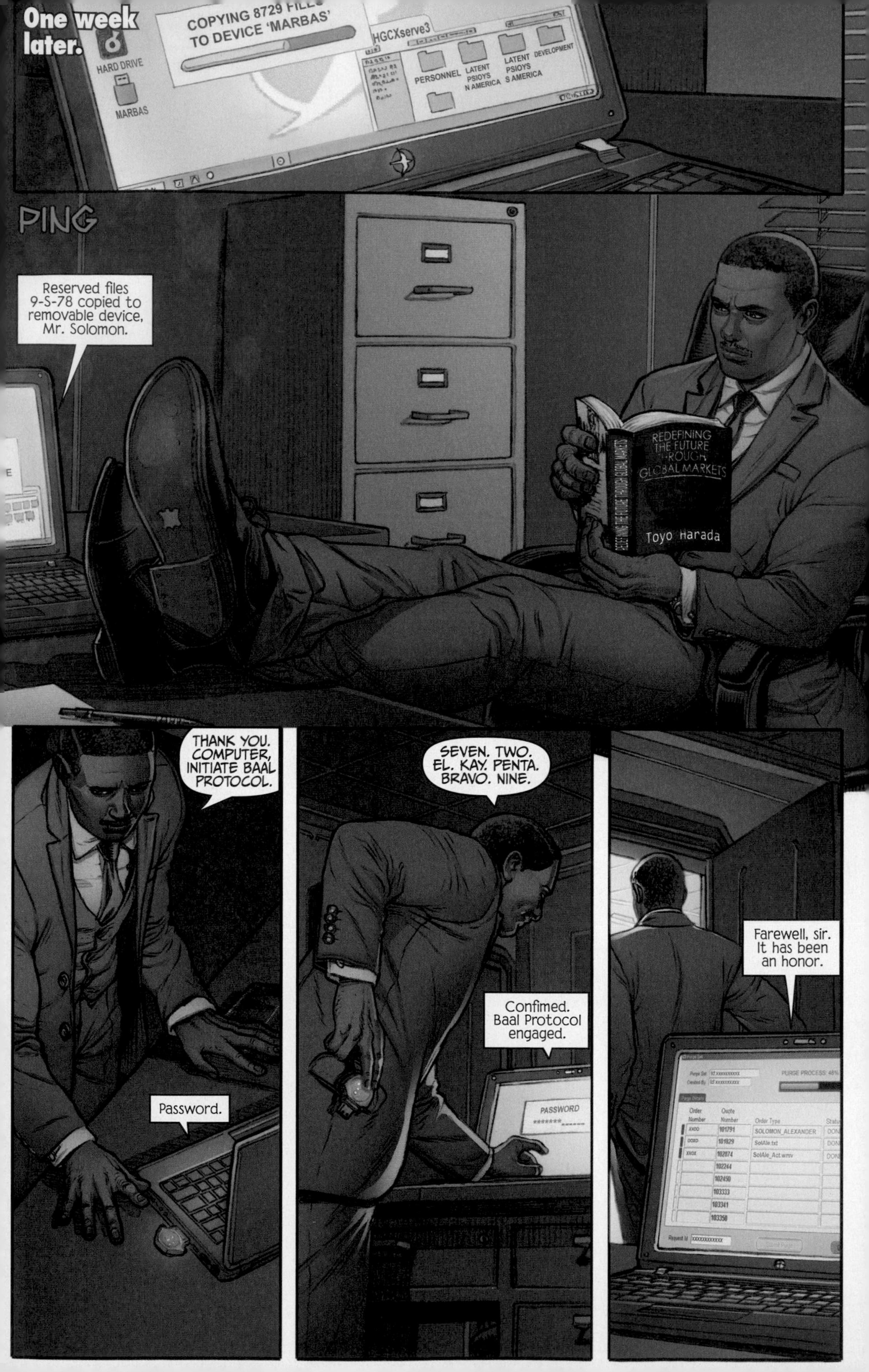
One week later.
COPYING 8729 FILES TO DEVICE 'MARBAS'
HARD DRIVE
MARBAS
HGCXserve3
PERSONNEL
LATENT PSIOYS N AMERICA
LATENT PSIOYS S AMERICA
DEVELOPMENT
PING
Reserved files 9-S-78 copied to removable device, Mr. Solomon.
REDEFINING THE FUTURE THROUGH GLOBAL MARKETS
Toyo Harada
THANK YOU. COMPUTER, INITIATE BAAL PROTOCOL.
Password.
SEVEN. TWO. EL. KAY. PENTA. BRAVO. NINE.
Confimed. Baal Protocol engaged.
PASSWORD
Farewell, sir. It has been an honor.
PURGE PROCESS: 48%
SOLOMON_ALEXANDER
SolAle.txt
SolAle_Act.wmv

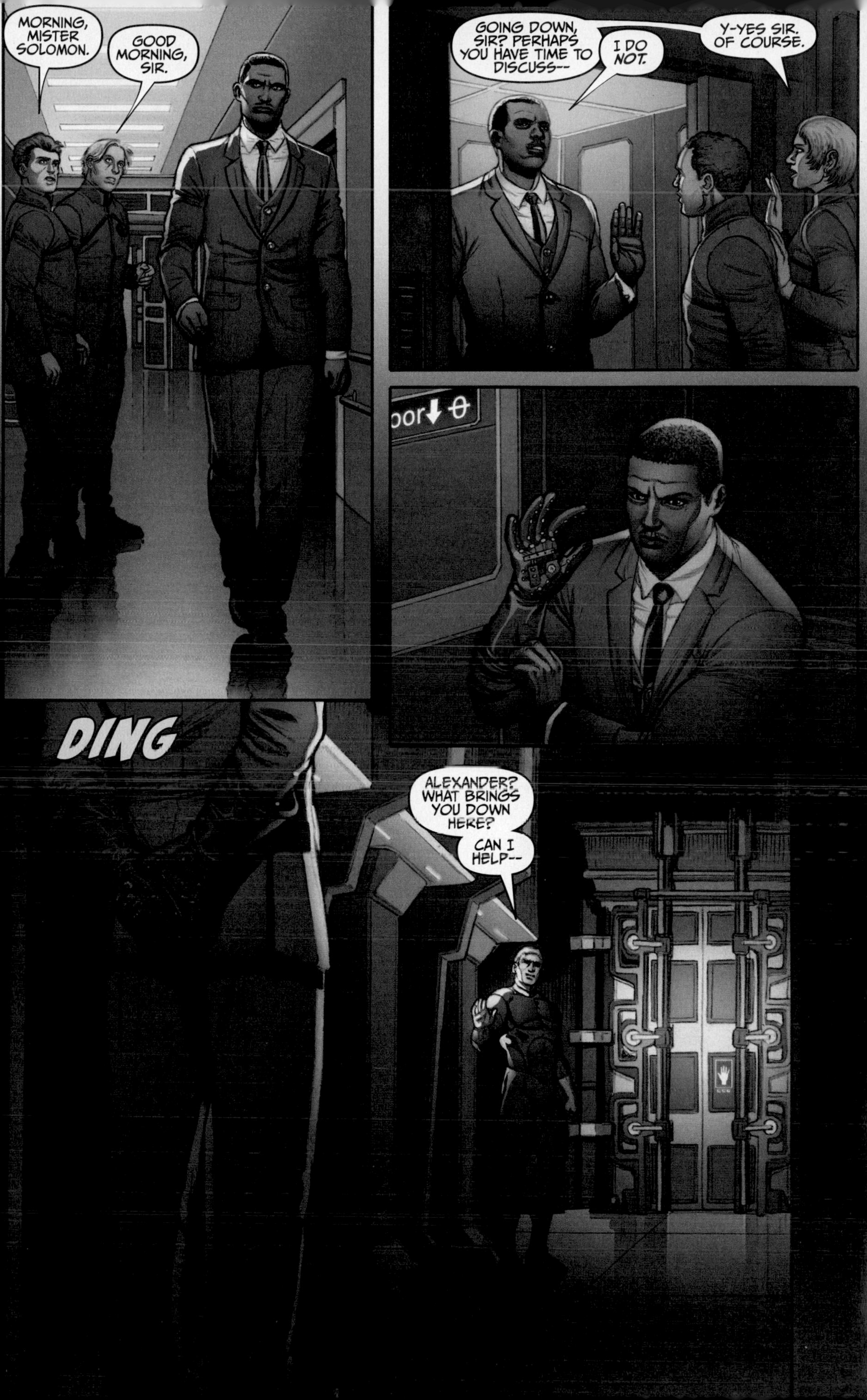
MORNING, MISTER SOLOMON.
GOOD MORNING, SIR.
GOING DOWN, SIR? PERHAPS YOU HAVE TIME TO DISCUSS--
I DO NOT.
Y-YES SIR. OF COURSE.
oor
DING
ALEXANDER? WHAT BRINGS YOU DOWN HERE?
CAN I HELP--

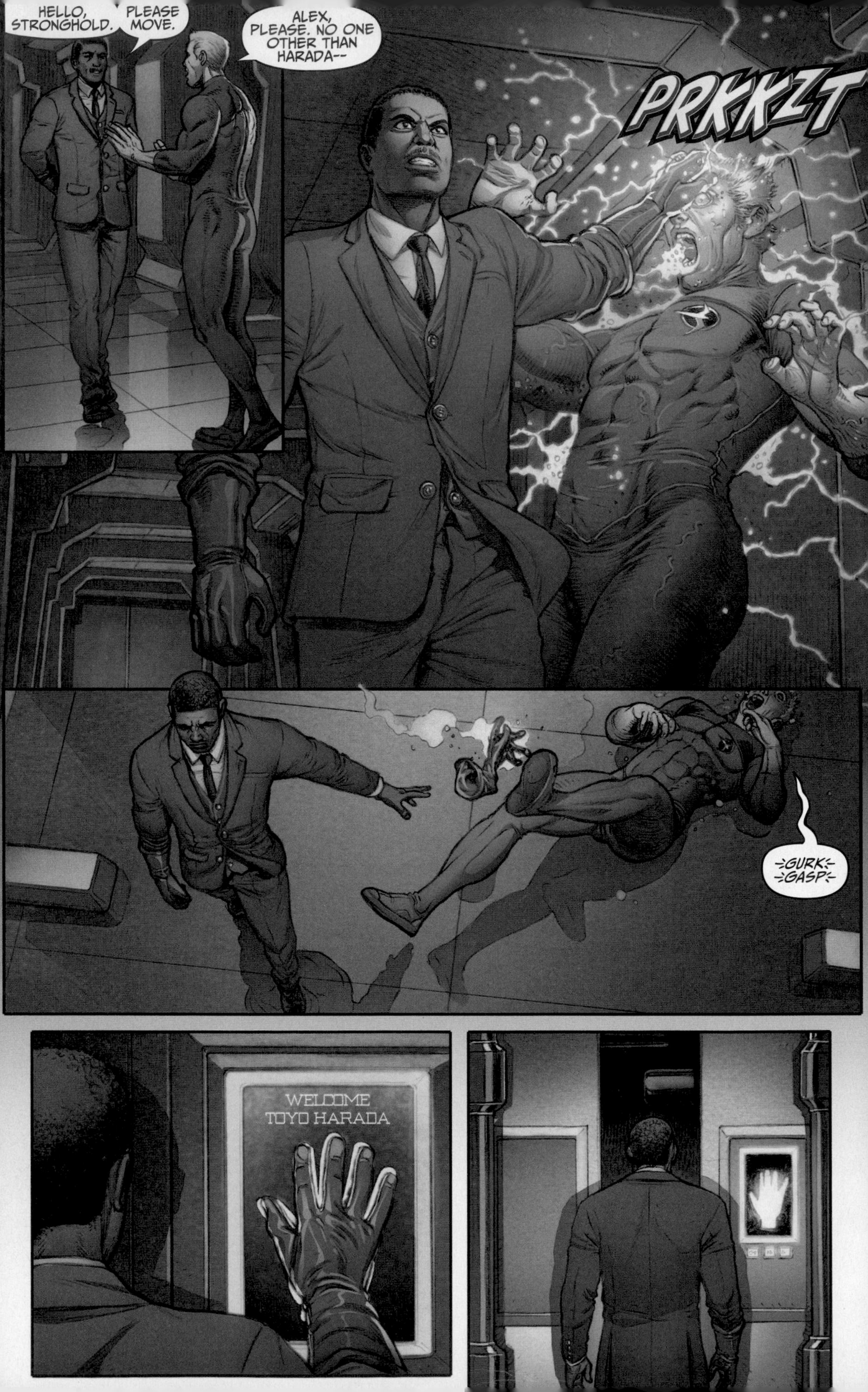
HELLO, STRONGHOLD.
PLEASE MOVE.
ALEX, PLEASE. NO ONE OTHER THAN HARADA--
PRKKZT
GURK GASP
WELCOME TOYO HARADA

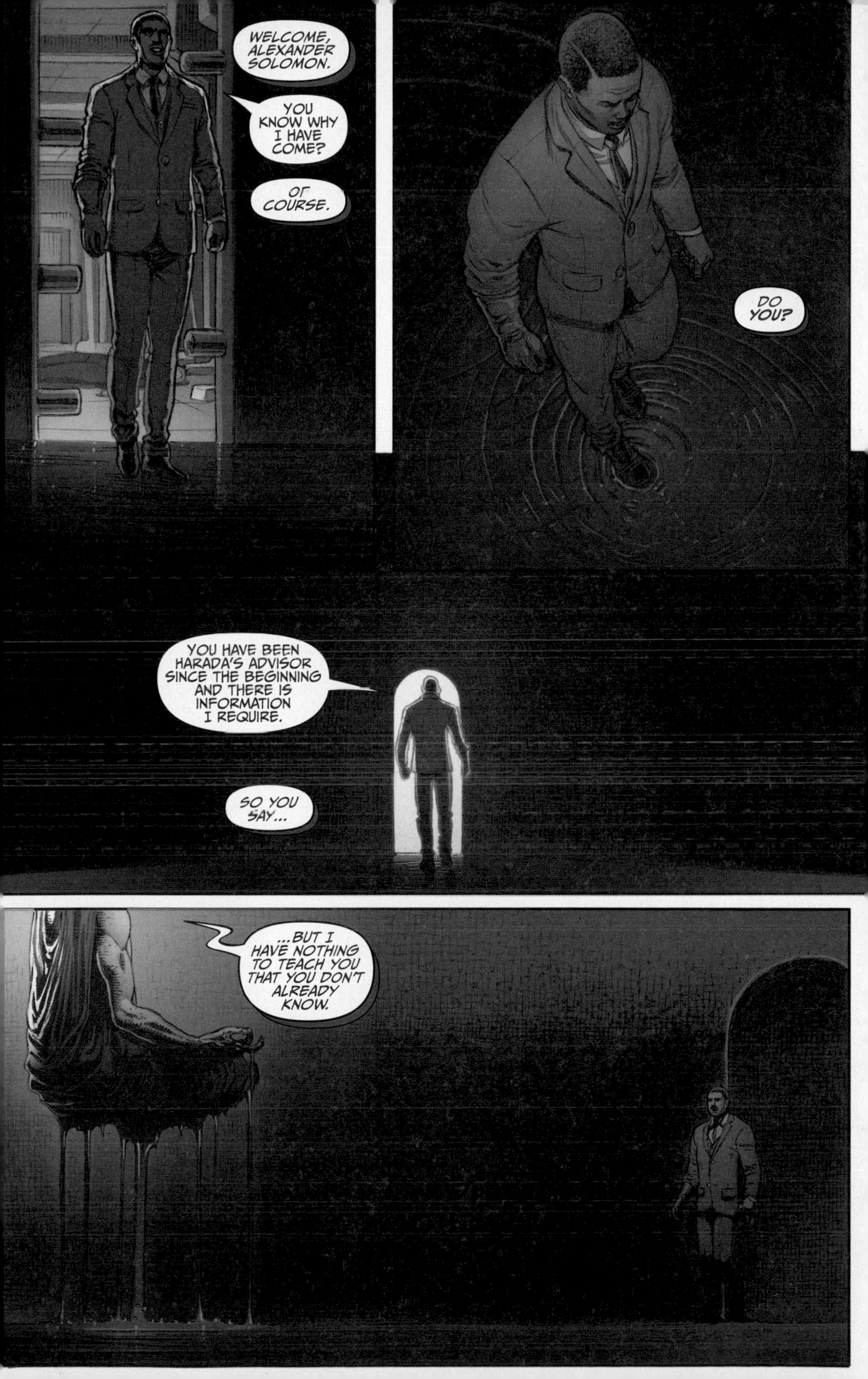
WELCOME, ALEXANDER SOLOMON.
YOU KNOW WHY I HAVE COME?
OF COURSE.
DO YOU?
YOU HAVE BEEN HARADA'S ADVISOR SINCE THE BEGINNING AND THERE IS INFORMATION I REQUIRE.
SO YOU SAY...
...BUT I HAVE NOTHING TO TEACH YOU THAT YOU DON'T ALREADY KNOW.

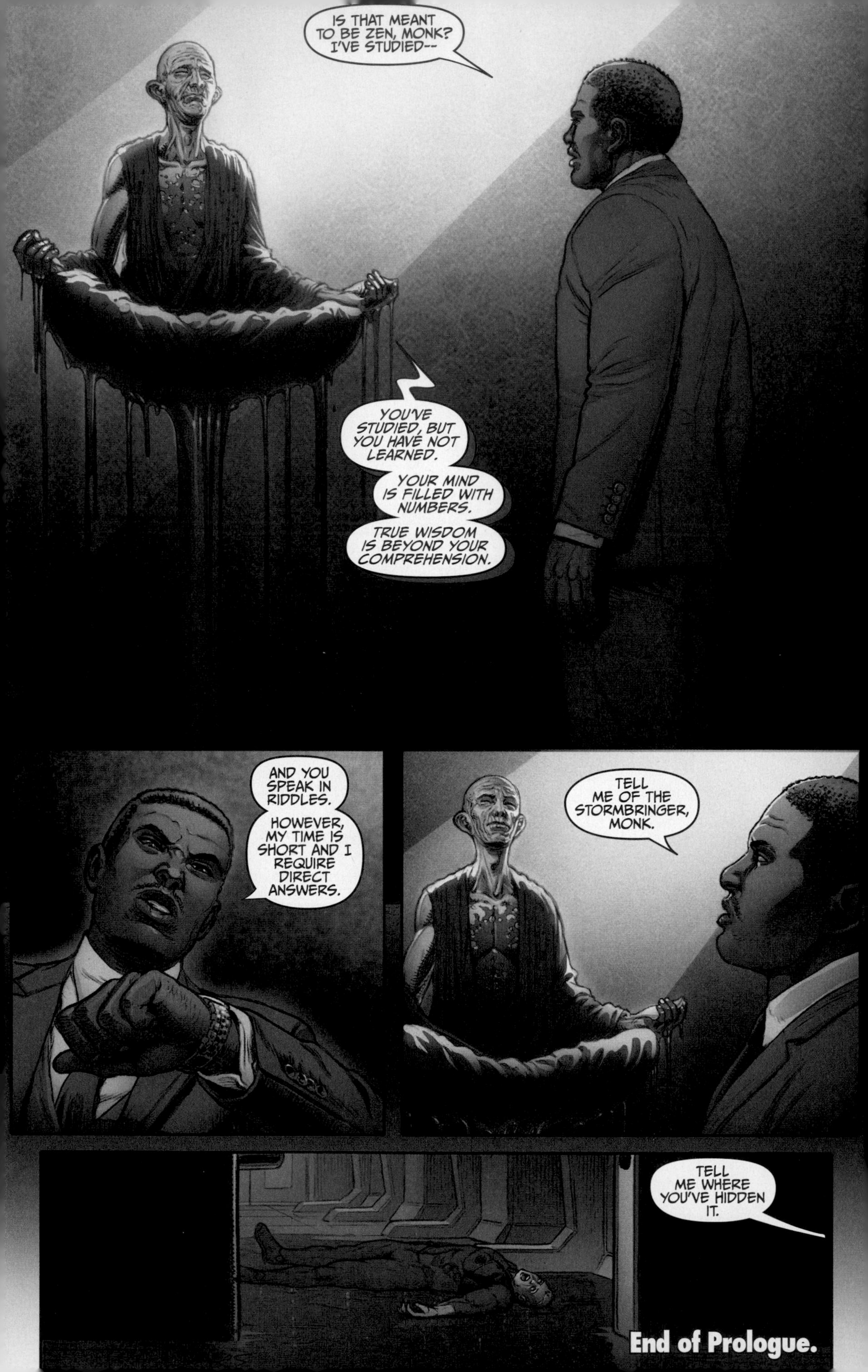
IS THAT MEANT TO BE ZEN, MONK? I'VE STUDIED--
YOU'VE STUDIED, BUT YOU HAVE NOT LEARNED.
YOUR MIND IS FILLED WITH NUMBERS.
TRUE WISDOM IS BEYOND YOUR COMPREHENSION.
AND YOU SPEAK IN RIDDLES.
HOWEVER, MY TIME IS SHORT AND I REQUIRE DIRECT ANSWERS.
TELL ME OF THE STORMBRINGER, MONK.
TELL ME WHERE YOU'VE HIDDEN IT.
End of Prologue.

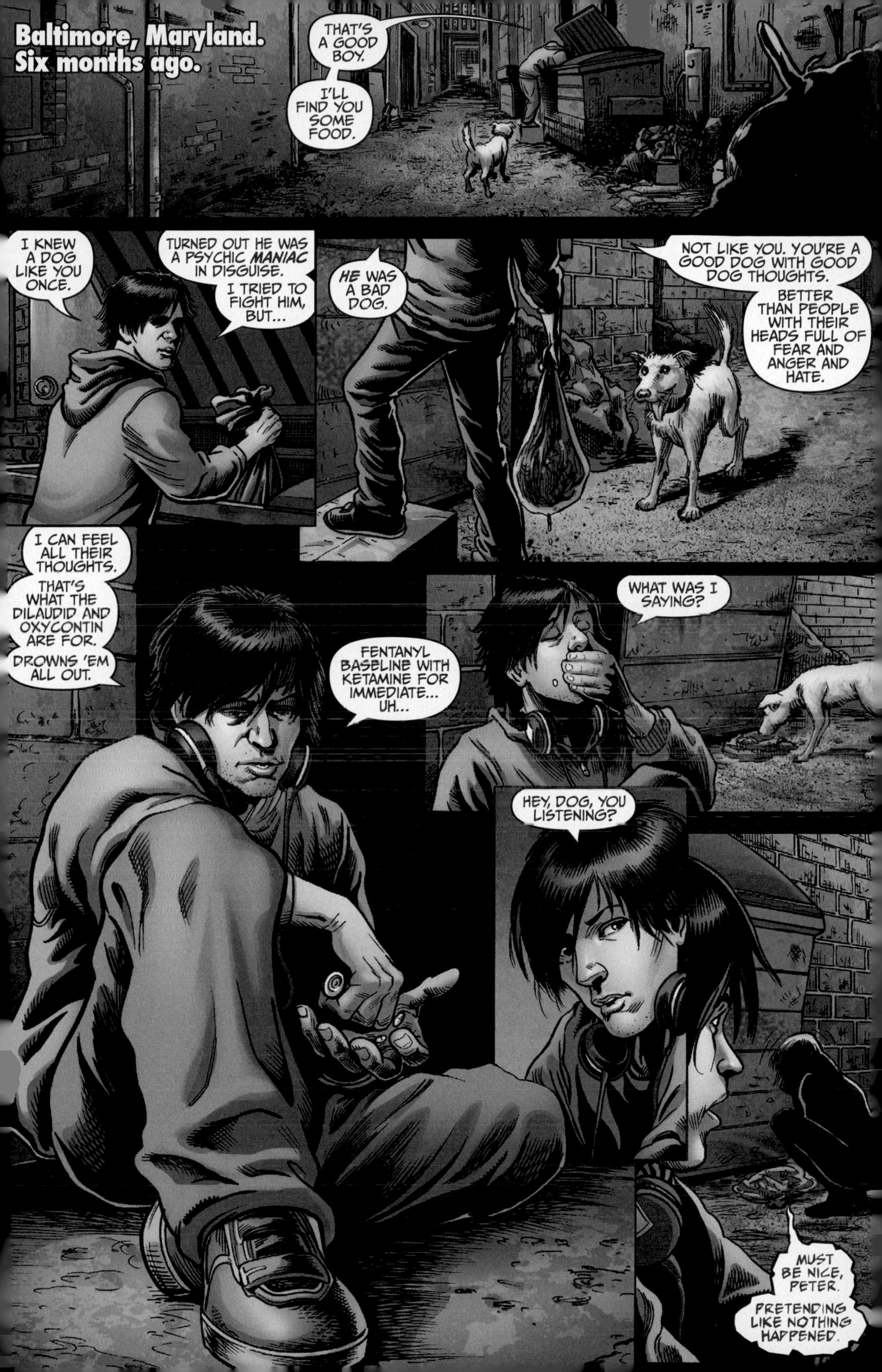
Baltimore, Maryland.
Six months ago.
THAT'S A GOOD BOY.
I'LL FIND YOU SOME FOOD.
I KNEW A DOG LIKE YOU ONCE.
TURNED OUT HE WAS A PSYCHIC MANIAC IN DISGUISE.
I TRIED TO FIGHT HIM, BUT...
HE WAS A BAD DOG.
NOT LIKE YOU. YOU'RE A GOOD DOG WITH GOOD DOG THOUGHTS.
BETTER THAN PEOPLE WITH THEIR HEADS FULL OF FEAR AND ANGER AND HATE.
I CAN FEEL ALL THEIR THOUGHTS.
THAT'S WHAT THE DILAUDID AND OXYCONTIN ARE FOR.
DROWNS 'EM ALL OUT.
FENTANYL BASELINE WITH KETAMINE FOR IMMEDIATE... UH...
WHAT WAS I SAYING?
HEY, DOG, YOU LISTENING?
MUST BE NICE, PETER.
PRETENDING LIKE NOTHING HAPPENED.

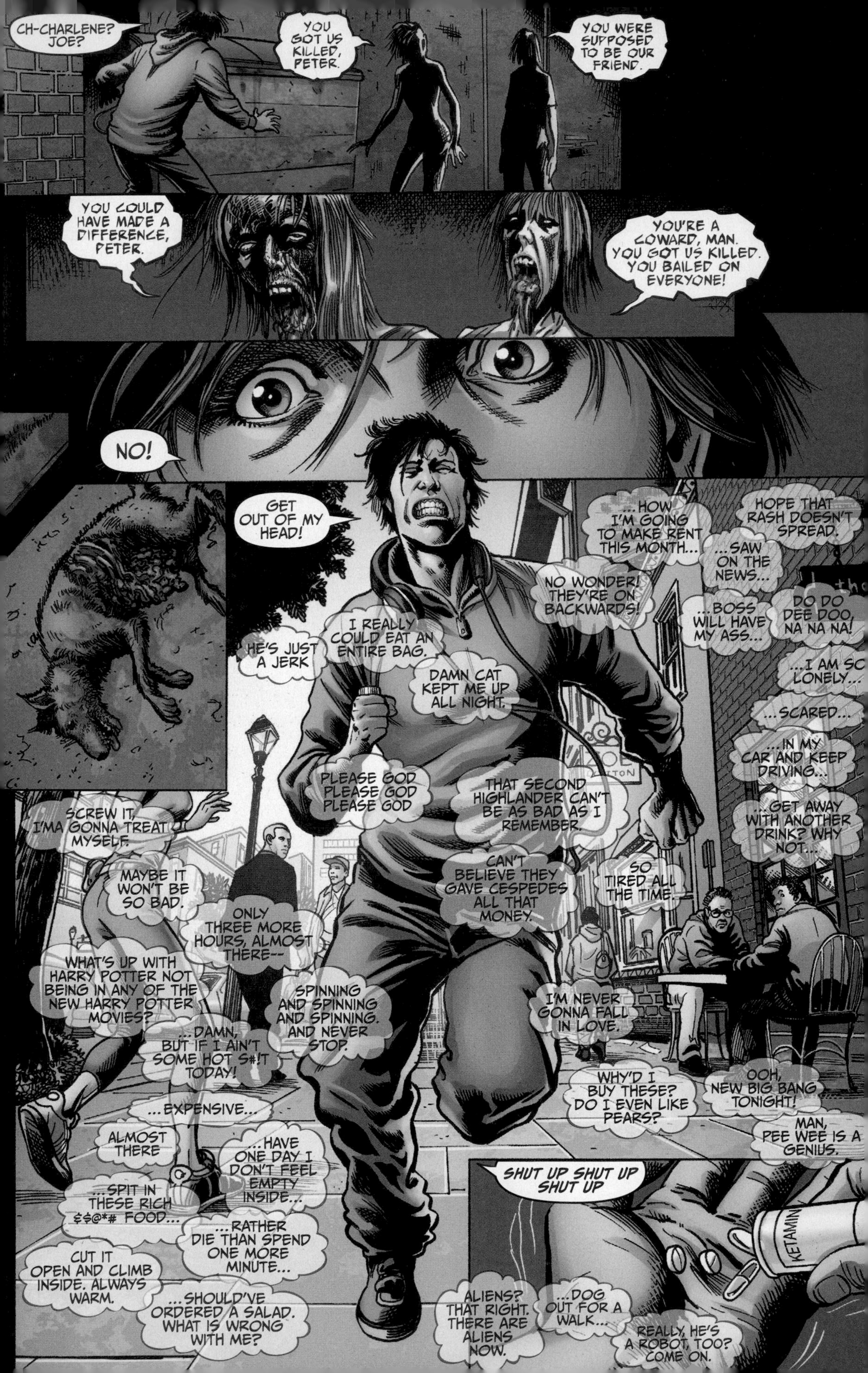
CH-CHARLENE? JOE?
YOU GOT US KILLED, PETER.
YOU WERE SUPPOSED TO BE OUR FRIEND.
YOU COULD HAVE MADE A DIFFERENCE, PETER.
YOU'RE A COWARD, MAN. YOU GOT US KILLED. YOU BAILED ON EVERYONE!
NO!
GET OUT OF MY HEAD!
...HOW I'M GOING TO MAKE RENT THIS MONTH...
HOPE THAT RASH DOESN'T SPREAD.
...SAW ON THE NEWS...
NO WONDER! THEY'RE ON BACKWARDS!
...BOSS WILL HAVE MY ASS...
DO DO DEE DOO, NA NA NA!
I REALLY COULD EAT AN ENTIRE BAG.
HE'S JUST A JERK
DAMN CAT KEPT ME UP ALL NIGHT.
...I AM SO LONELY...
...SCARED...
...IN MY CAR AND KEEP DRIVING...
PLEASE GOD PLEASE GOD PLEASE GOD
THAT SECOND HIGHLANDER CAN'T BE AS BAD AS I REMEMBER.
...GET AWAY WITH ANOTHER DRINK? WHY NOT...
SCREW IT, I'MA GONNA TREAT MYSELF.
MAYBE IT WON'T BE SO BAD.
CAN'T BELIEVE THEY GAVE CESPEDES ALL THAT MONEY.
SO TIRED ALL THE TIME.
ONLY THREE MORE HOURS, ALMOST THERE--
WHAT'S UP WITH HARRY POTTER NOT BEING IN ANY OF THE NEW HARRY POTTER MOVIES?
SPINNING AND SPINNING AND SPINNING. AND NEVER STOP.
I'M NEVER GONNA FALL IN LOVE.
...DAMN, BUT IF I AIN'T SOME HOT S#!T TODAY!
WHY'D I BUY THESE? DO I EVEN LIKE PEARS?
OOH, NEW BIG BANG TONIGHT!
...EXPENSIVE...
ALMOST THERE
...HAVE ONE DAY I DON'T FEEL EMPTY INSIDE...
MAN, PEE WEE IS A GENIUS.
SHUT UP SHUT UP SHUT UP
...SPIT IN THESE RICH $$@*# FOOD...
...RATHER DIE THAN SPEND ONE MORE MINUTE...
CUT IT OPEN AND CLIMB INSIDE. ALWAYS WARM.
...SHOULD'VE ORDERED A SALAD. WHAT IS WRONG WITH ME?
ALIENS? THAT RIGHT. THERE ARE ALIENS NOW.
...DOG OUT FOR A WALK...
REALLY, HE'S A ROBOT, TOO? COME ON.
KETAMIN

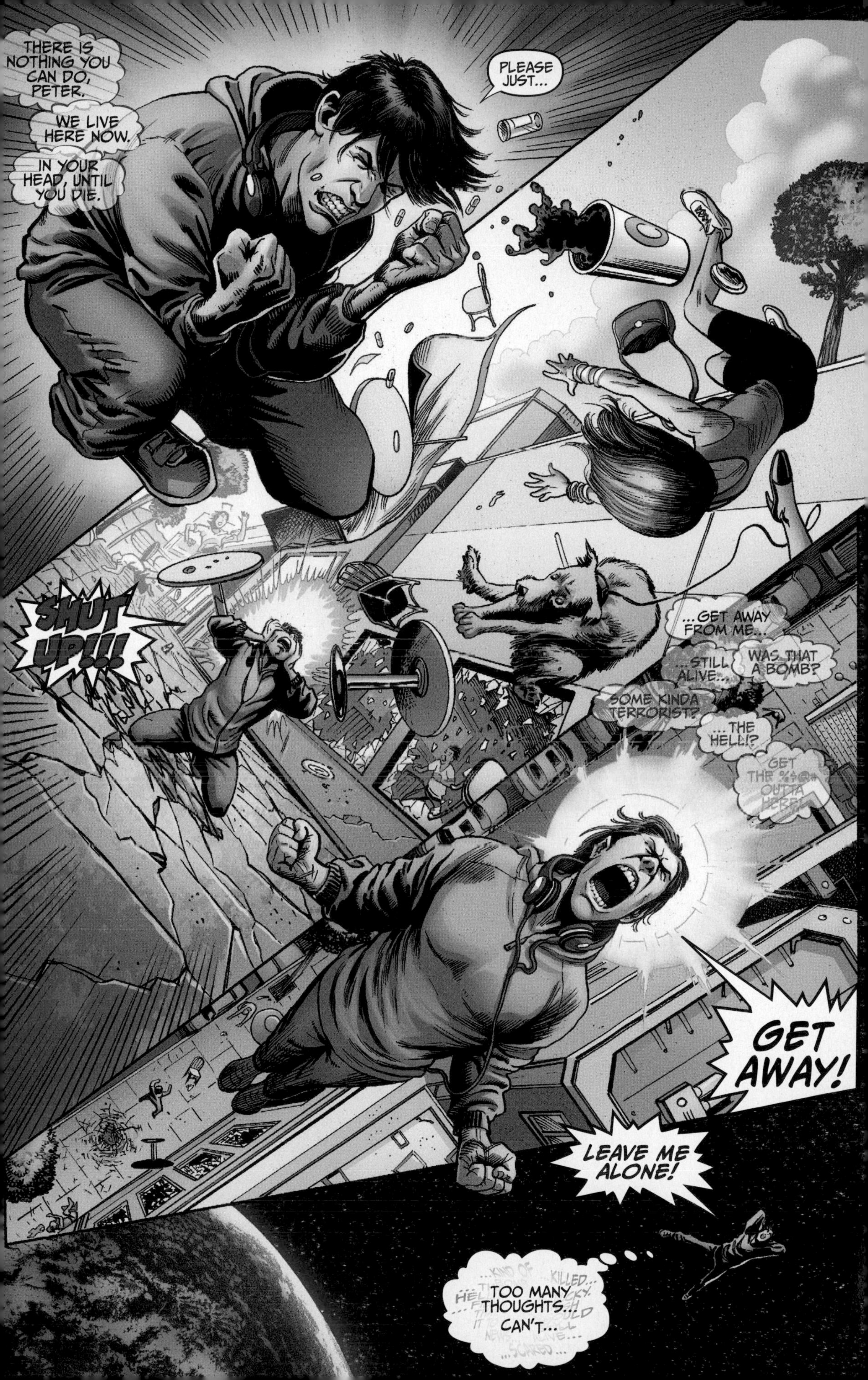
THERE IS NOTHING YOU CAN DO, PETER.
WE LIVE HERE NOW.
IN YOUR HEAD, UNTIL YOU DIE.
PLEASE JUST...
SHUT UP!!!
...GET AWAY FROM ME...
...STILL ALIVE...
WAS THAT A BOMB?
SOME KINDA TERRORIST?
...THE HELL!?
GET THE %$@# OUTTA
GET AWAY!
LEAVE ME ALONE!
TOO MANY THOUGHTS... CAN'T...

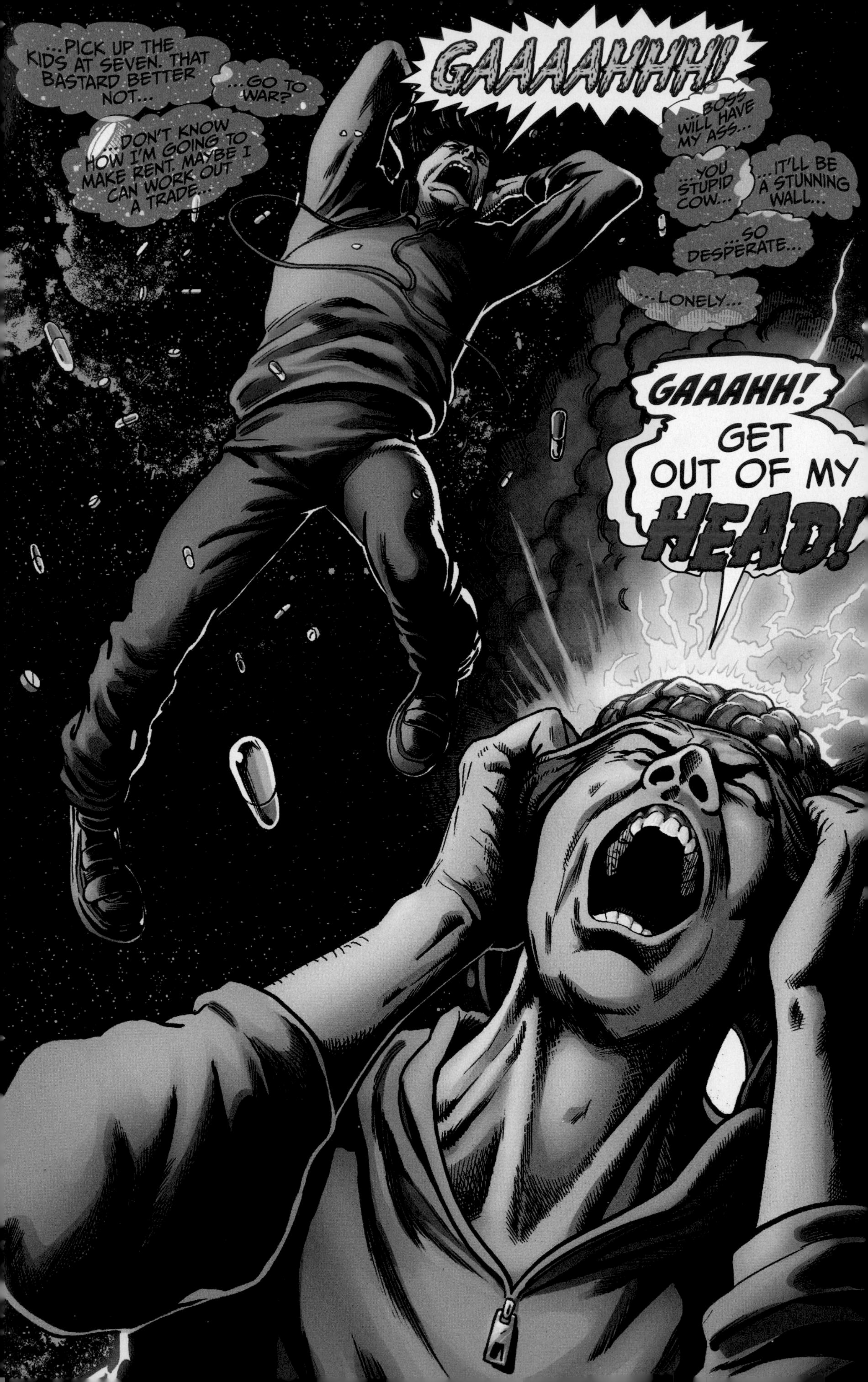
...PICK UP THE KIDS AT SEVEN. THAT BASTARD BETTER NOT...
...GO TO WAR?
...DON'T KNOW HOW I'M GOING TO MAKE RENT. MAYBE I CAN WORK OUT A TRADE...
GAAAAHHH!
...BOSS WILL HAVE MY ASS...
...YOU STUPID COW...
...IT'LL BE A STUNNING WALL...
...SO DESPERATE...
...LONELY...
GAAAHH! GET OUT OF MY HEAD!

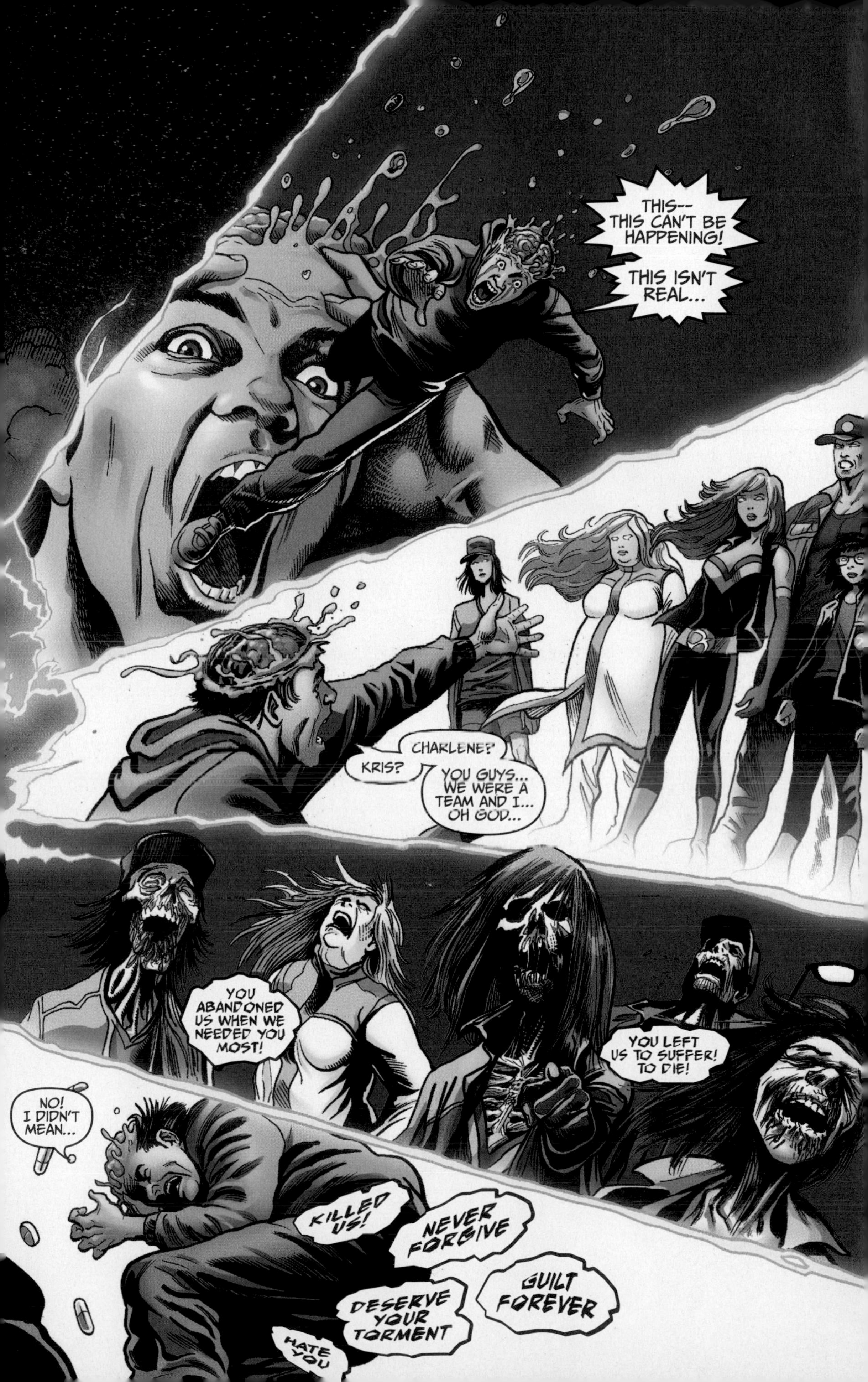
THIS-- THIS CAN'T BE HAPPENING!
THIS ISN'T REAL...
CHARLENE?
KRIS?
YOU GUYS... WE WERE A TEAM AND I... OH GOD...
YOU ABANDONED US WHEN WE NEEDED YOU MOST!
YOU LEFT US TO SUFFER! TO DIE!
NO! I DIDN'T MEAN...
KILLED US!
NEVER FORGIVE
GUILT FOREVER
DESERVE YOUR TORMENT
HATE YOU

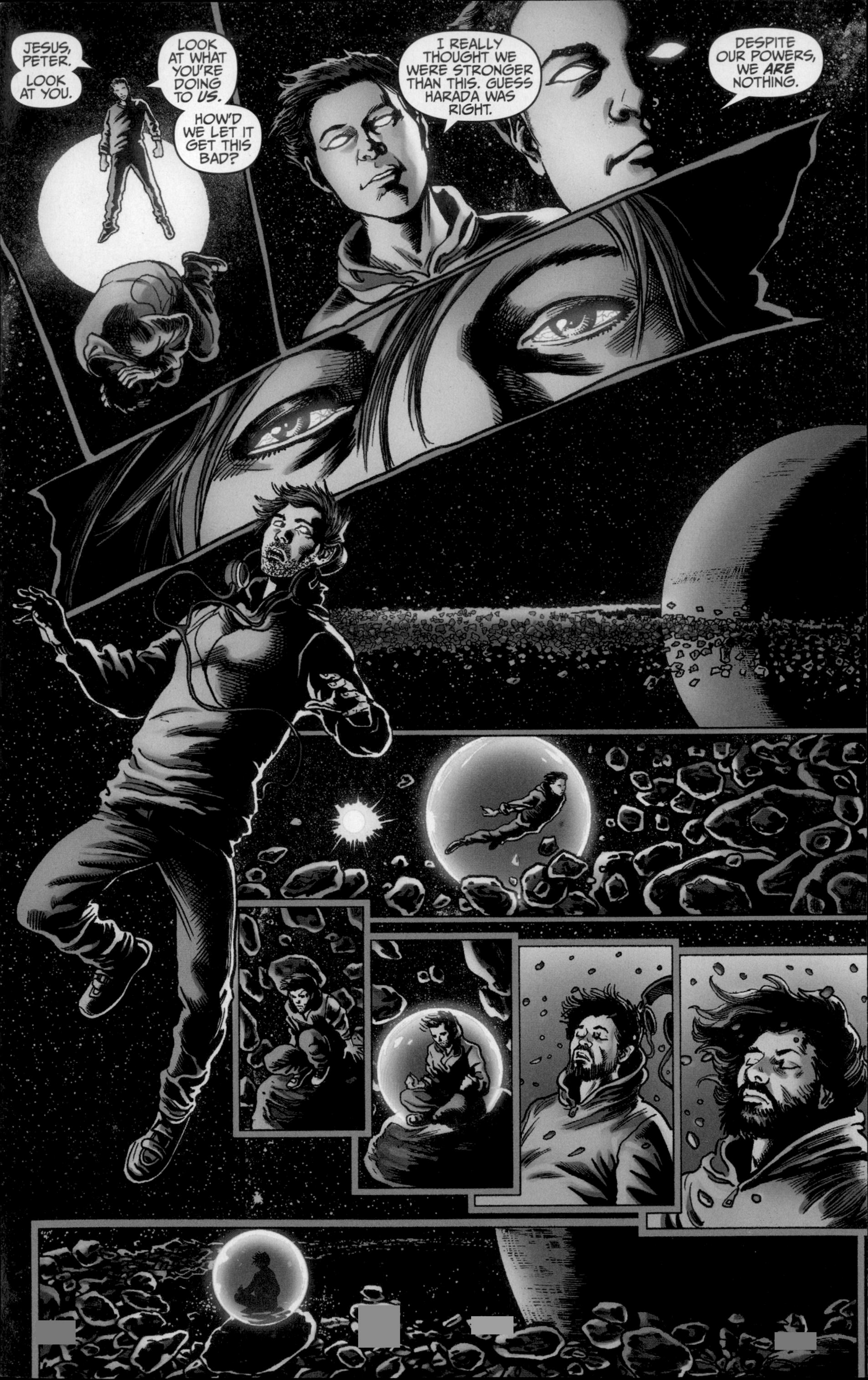
JESUS, PETER.
LOOK AT YOU.
LOOK AT WHAT YOU'RE DOING TO *US*.
HOW'D WE LET IT GET THIS BAD?
I REALLY THOUGHT WE WERE STRONGER THAN THIS. GUESS HARADA WAS RIGHT.
DESPITE OUR POWERS, WE *ARE* NOTHING.

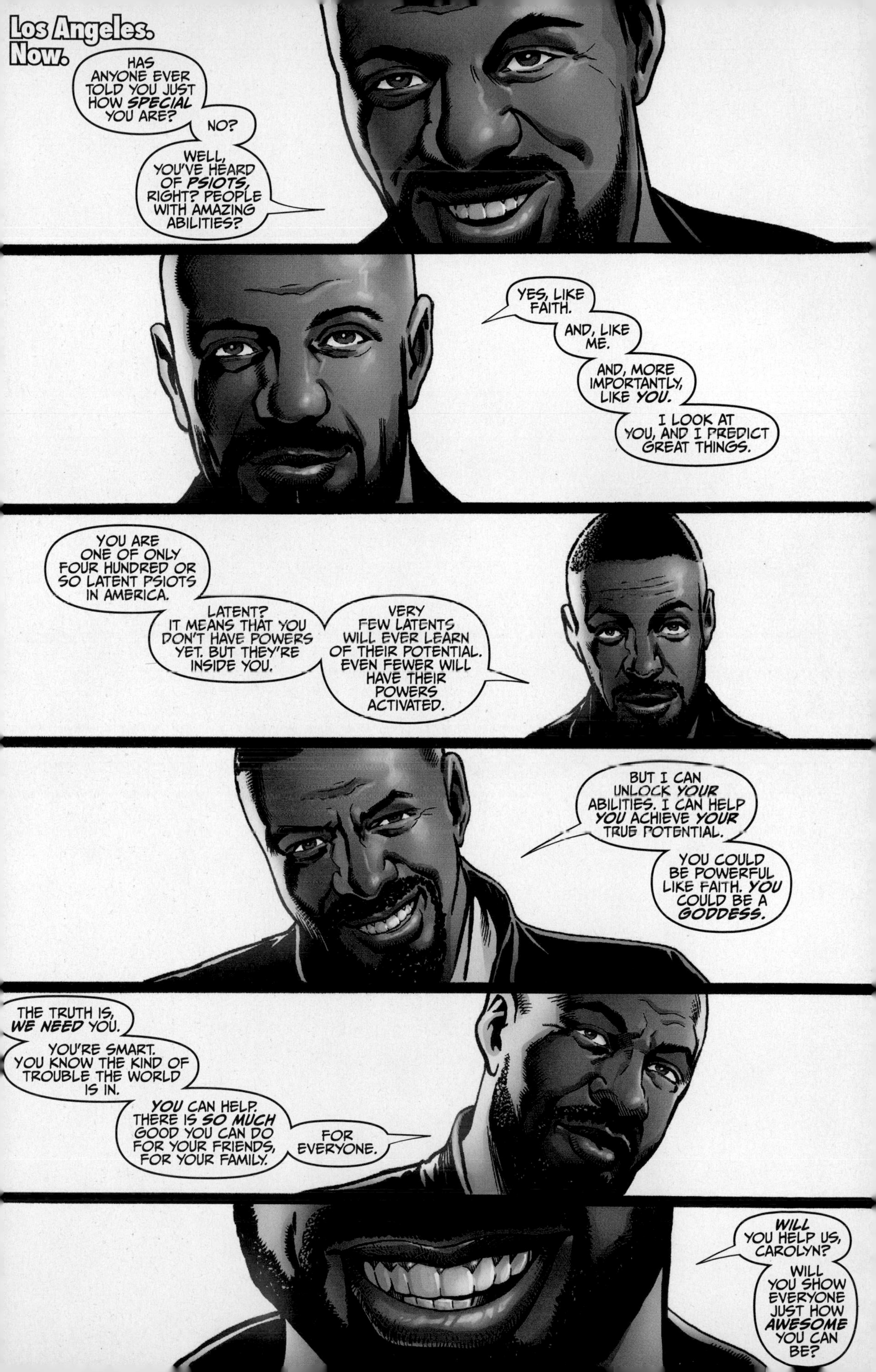
Los Angeles. Now.
HAS ANYONE EVER TOLD YOU JUST HOW SPECIAL YOU ARE?
NO?
WELL, YOU'VE HEARD OF PSIOTS, RIGHT? PEOPLE WITH AMAZING ABILITIES?
YES, LIKE FAITH.
AND, LIKE ME.
AND, MORE IMPORTANTLY, LIKE YOU.
I LOOK AT YOU, AND I PREDICT GREAT THINGS.
YOU ARE ONE OF ONLY FOUR HUNDRED OR SO LATENT PSIOTS IN AMERICA.
LATENT? IT MEANS THAT YOU DON'T HAVE POWERS YET. BUT THEY'RE INSIDE YOU.
VERY FEW LATENTS WILL EVER LEARN OF THEIR POTENTIAL. EVEN FEWER WILL HAVE THEIR POWERS ACTIVATED.
BUT I CAN UNLOCK YOUR ABILITIES. I CAN HELP YOU ACHIEVE YOUR TRUE POTENTIAL.
YOU COULD BE POWERFUL LIKE FAITH. YOU COULD BE A GODDESS.
THE TRUTH IS, WE NEED YOU.
YOU'RE SMART. YOU KNOW THE KIND OF TROUBLE THE WORLD IS IN.
YOU CAN HELP. THERE IS SO MUCH GOOD YOU CAN DO FOR YOUR FRIENDS, FOR YOUR FAMILY.
FOR EVERYONE.
WILL YOU HELP US, CAROLYN?
WILL YOU SHOW EVERYONE JUST HOW AWESOME YOU CAN BE?

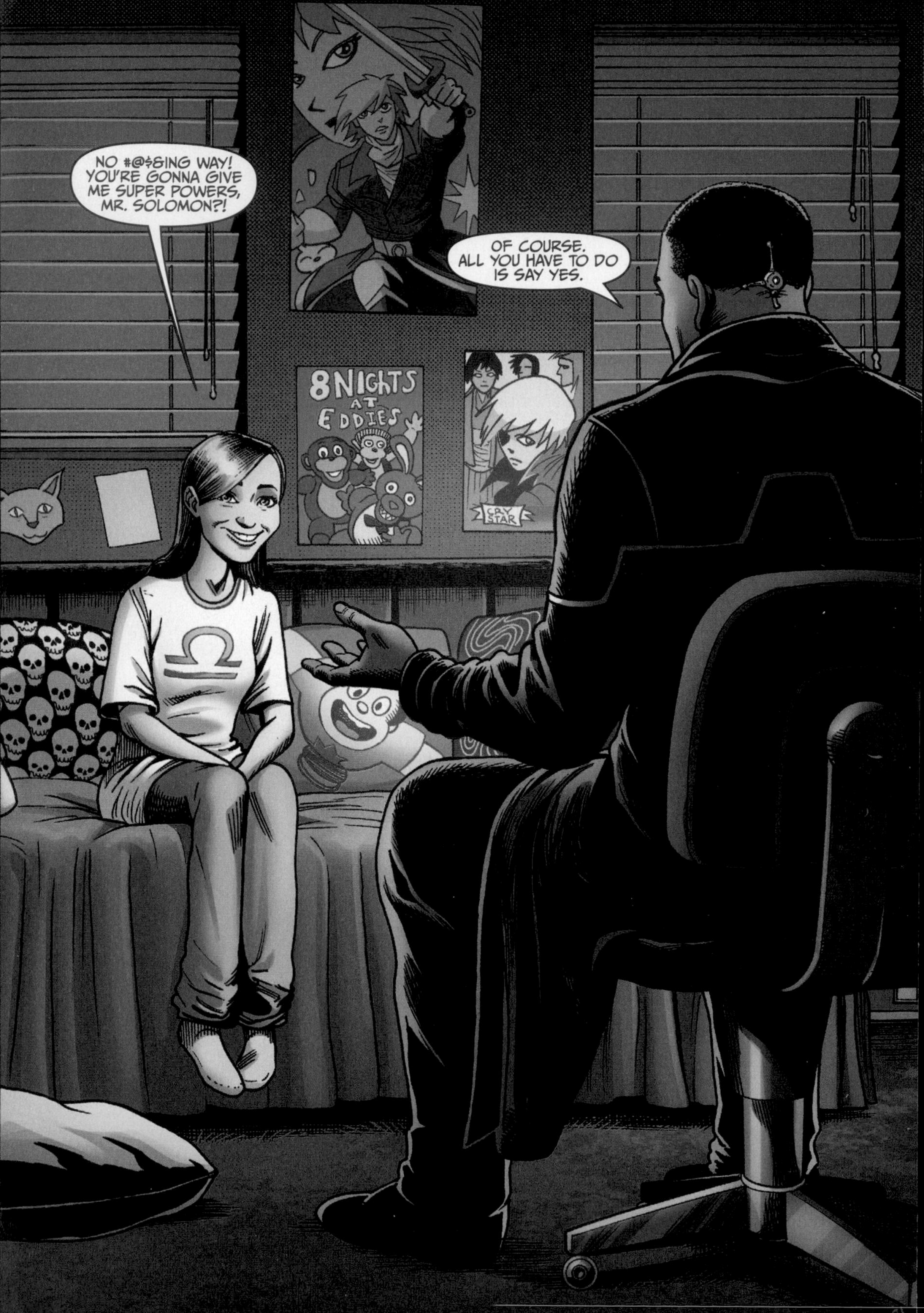
NO #@$&ING WAY! YOU'RE GONNA GIVE ME SUPER POWERS, MR. SOLOMON?!
OF COURSE. ALL YOU HAVE TO DO IS SAY YES.
8 NIGHTS AT EDDIES
CRY STAR

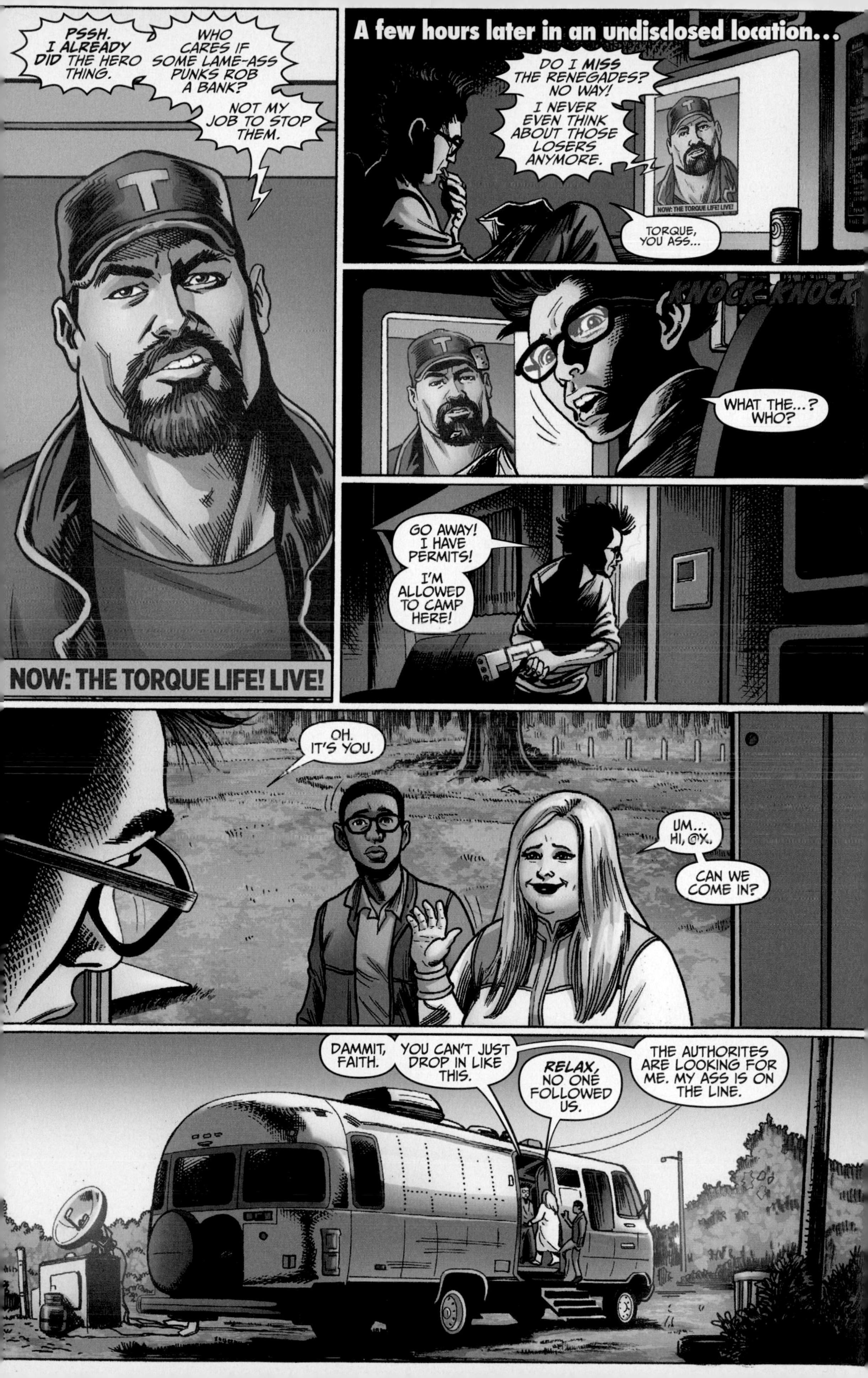
PSSH. I ALREADY DID THE HERO THING.
WHO CARES IF SOME LAME-ASS PUNKS ROB A BANK?
NOT MY JOB TO STOP THEM.
NOW: THE TORQUE LIFE! LIVE!
A few hours later in an undisclosed location...
DO I MISS THE RENEGADES? NO WAY!
I NEVER EVEN THINK ABOUT THOSE LOSERS ANYMORE.
NOW: THE TORQUE LIFE! LIVE!
TORQUE, YOU ASS...
KNOCK KNOCK
WHAT THE...? WHO?
GO AWAY! I HAVE PERMITS!
I'M ALLOWED TO CAMP HERE!
OH. IT'S YOU.
UM... HI, @X.
CAN WE COME IN?
DAMMIT, FAITH.
YOU CAN'T JUST DROP IN LIKE THIS.
RELAX, NO ONE FOLLOWED US.
THE AUTHORITES ARE LOOKING FOR ME. MY ASS IS ON THE LINE.

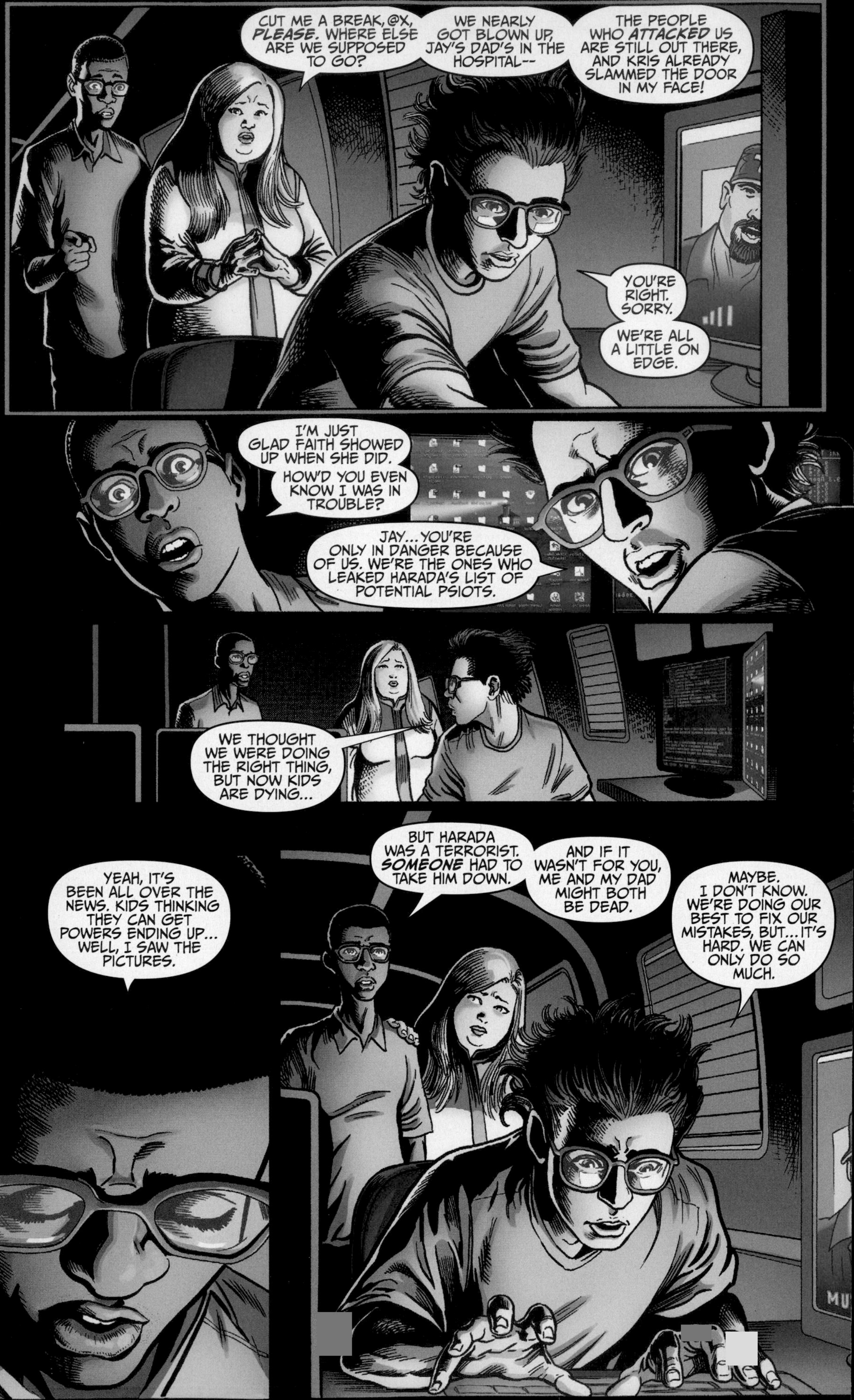
CUT ME A BREAK, @X, PLEASE. WHERE ELSE ARE WE SUPPOSED TO GO?
WE NEARLY GOT BLOWN UP, JAY'S DAD'S IN THE HOSPITAL--
THE PEOPLE WHO ATTACKED US ARE STILL OUT THERE, AND KRIS ALREADY SLAMMED THE DOOR IN MY FACE!
YOU'RE RIGHT. SORRY.
WE'RE ALL A LITTLE ON EDGE.
I'M JUST GLAD FAITH SHOWED UP WHEN SHE DID.
HOW'D YOU EVEN KNOW I WAS IN TROUBLE?
JAY...YOU'RE ONLY IN DANGER BECAUSE OF US. WE'RE THE ONES WHO LEAKED HARADA'S LIST OF POTENTIAL PSIOTS.
WE THOUGHT WE WERE DOING THE RIGHT THING, BUT NOW KIDS ARE DYING...
YEAH, IT'S BEEN ALL OVER THE NEWS. KIDS THINKING THEY CAN GET POWERS ENDING UP... WELL, I SAW THE PICTURES.
BUT HARADA WAS A TERRORIST. SOMEONE HAD TO TAKE HIM DOWN.
AND IF IT WASN'T FOR YOU, ME AND MY DAD MIGHT BOTH BE DEAD.
MAYBE. I DON'T KNOW. WE'RE DOING OUR BEST TO FIX OUR MISTAKES, BUT...IT'S HARD. WE CAN ONLY DO SO MUCH.

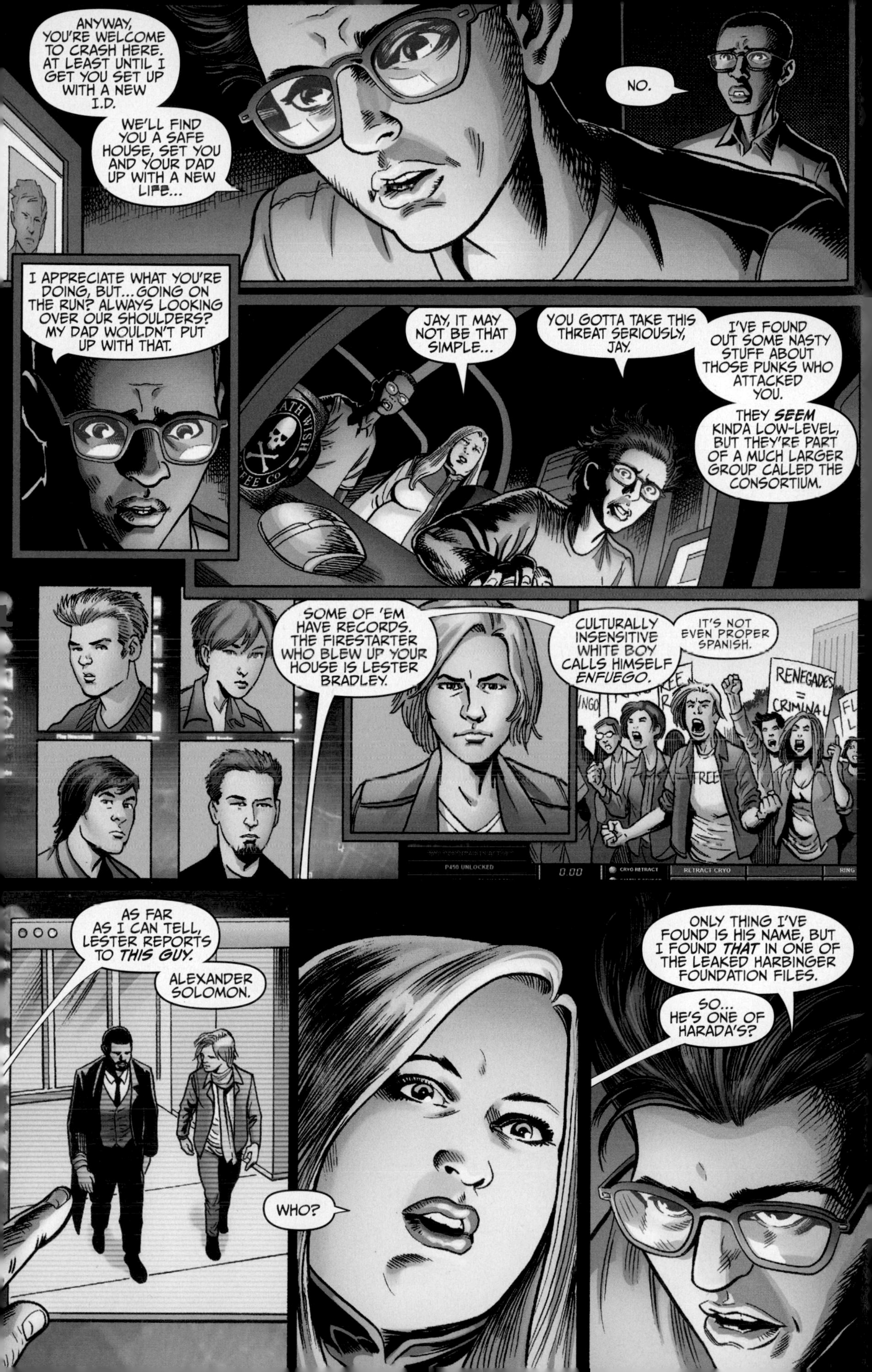
ANYWAY, YOU'RE WELCOME TO CRASH HERE. AT LEAST UNTIL I GET YOU SET UP WITH A NEW I.D.
WE'LL FIND YOU A SAFE HOUSE, SET YOU AND YOUR DAD UP WITH A NEW LIFE...
NO.
I APPRECIATE WHAT YOU'RE DOING, BUT...GOING ON THE RUN? ALWAYS LOOKING OVER OUR SHOULDERS? MY DAD WOULDN'T PUT UP WITH THAT.
JAY, IT MAY NOT BE THAT SIMPLE...
YOU GOTTA TAKE THIS THREAT SERIOUSLY, JAY.
I'VE FOUND OUT SOME NASTY STUFF ABOUT THOSE PUNKS WHO ATTACKED YOU.
THEY *SEEM* KINDA LOW-LEVEL, BUT THEY'RE PART OF A MUCH LARGER GROUP CALLED THE CONSORTIUM.
SOME OF 'EM HAVE RECORDS. THE FIRESTARTER WHO BLEW UP YOUR HOUSE IS LESTER BRADLEY.
CULTURALLY INSENSITIVE WHITE BOY CALLS HIMSELF *ENFUEGO.*
IT'S NOT EVEN PROPER SPANISH.
AS FAR AS I CAN TELL, LESTER REPORTS TO *THIS GUY.*
ALEXANDER SOLOMON.
WHO?
ONLY THING I'VE FOUND IS HIS NAME, BUT I FOUND *THAT* IN ONE OF THE LEAKED HARBINGER FOUNDATION FILES.
SO... HE'S ONE OF HARADA'S?

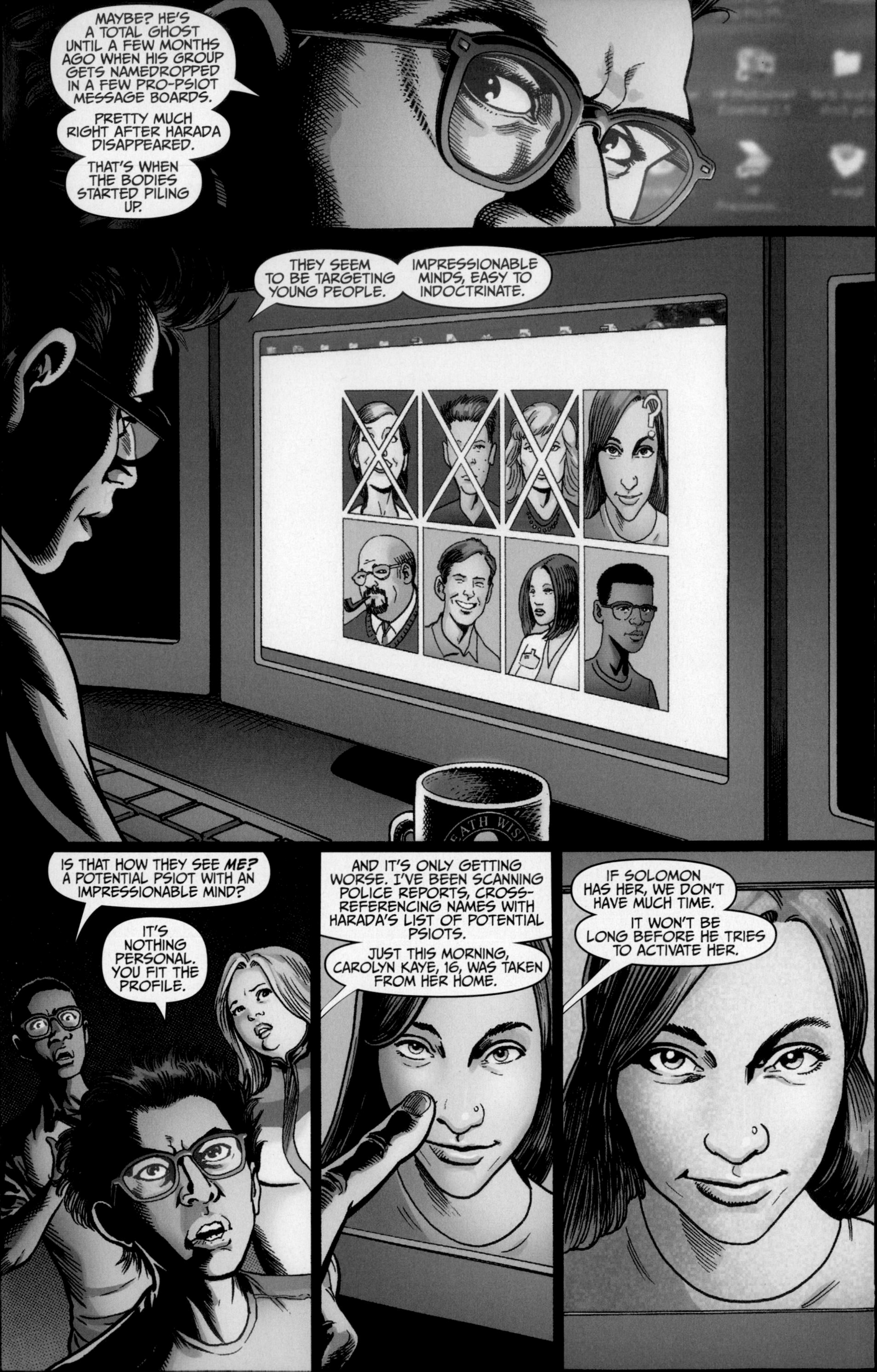
MAYBE? HE'S A TOTAL GHOST UNTIL A FEW MONTHS AGO WHEN HIS GROUP GETS NAMEDROPPED IN A FEW PRO-PSIOT MESSAGE BOARDS.
PRETTY MUCH RIGHT AFTER HARADA DISAPPEARED.
THAT'S WHEN THE BODIES STARTED PILING UP.
THEY SEEM TO BE TARGETING YOUNG PEOPLE.
IMPRESSIONABLE MINDS, EASY TO INDOCTRINATE.
IS THAT HOW THEY SEE ME? A POTENTIAL PSIOT WITH AN IMPRESSIONABLE MIND?
IT'S NOTHING PERSONAL. YOU FIT THE PROFILE.
AND IT'S ONLY GETTING WORSE. I'VE BEEN SCANNING POLICE REPORTS, CROSS-REFERENCING NAMES WITH HARADA'S LIST OF POTENTIAL PSIOTS.
JUST THIS MORNING, CAROLYN KAYE, 16, WAS TAKEN FROM HER HOME.
IF SOLOMON HAS HER, WE DON'T HAVE MUCH TIME.
IT WON'T BE LONG BEFORE HE TRIES TO ACTIVATE HER.

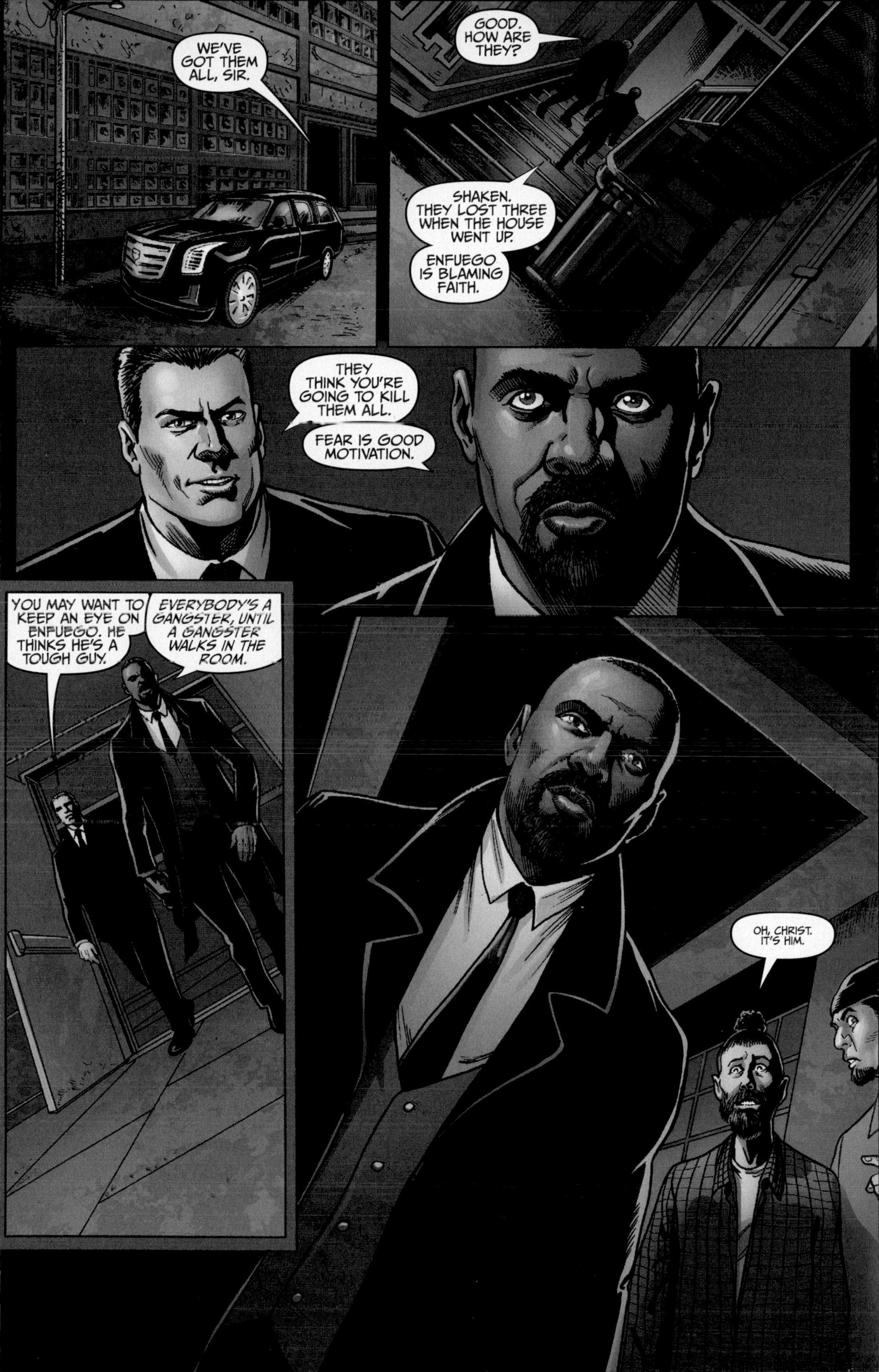
WE'VE GOT THEM ALL, SIR.
GOOD. HOW ARE THEY?
SHAKEN. THEY LOST THREE WHEN THE HOUSE WENT UP.
ENFUEGO IS BLAMING FAITH.
THEY THINK YOU'RE GOING TO KILL THEM ALL.
FEAR IS GOOD MOTIVATION.
YOU MAY WANT TO KEEP AN EYE ON ENFUEGO. HE THINKS HE'S A TOUGH GUY.
EVERYBODY'S A GANGSTER, UNTIL A GANGSTER WALKS IN THE ROOM.
OH, CHRIST. IT'S HIM.

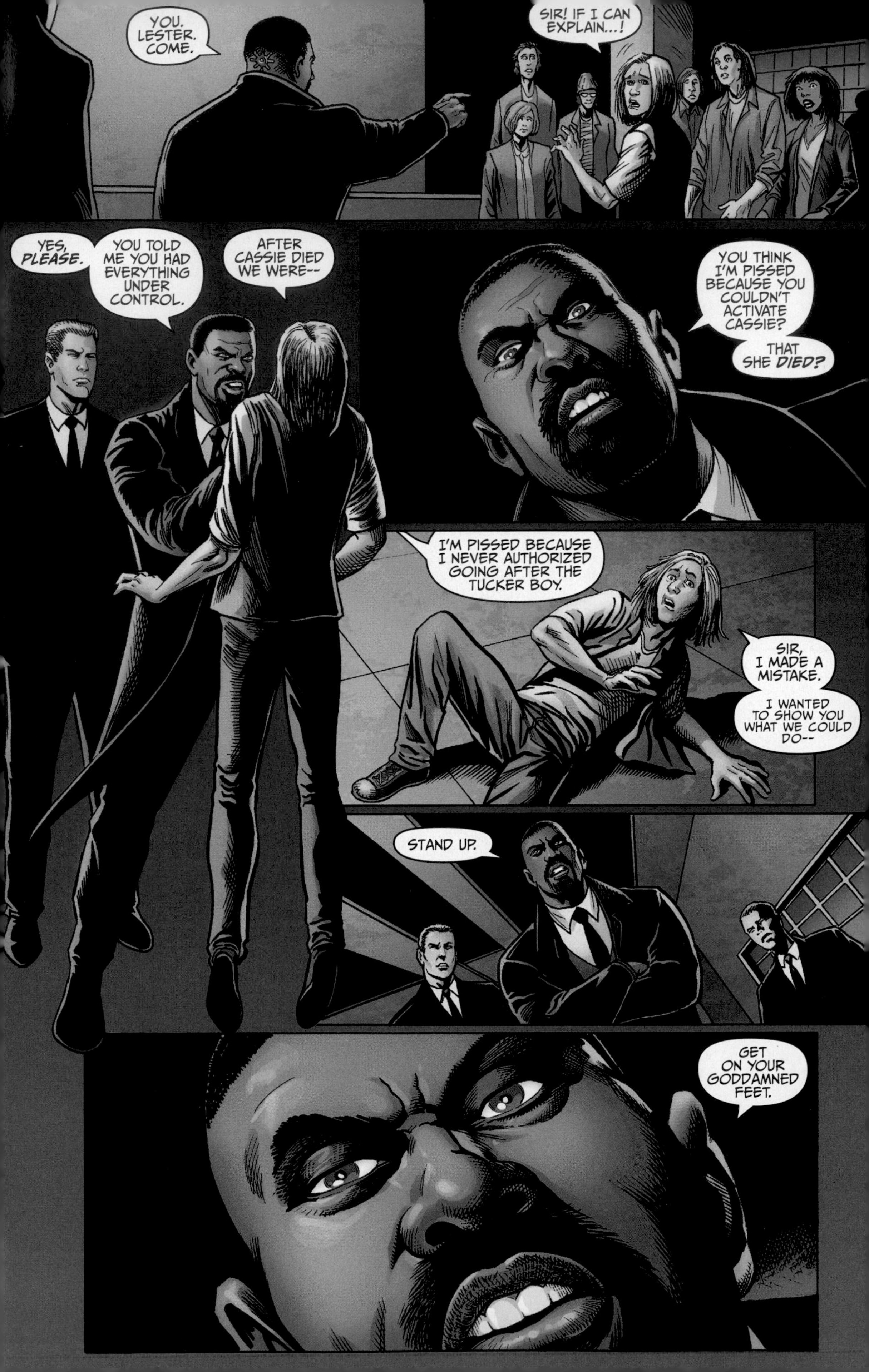
YOU. LESTER. COME.
SIR! IF I CAN EXPLAIN...!
YES, PLEASE.
YOU TOLD ME YOU HAD EVERYTHING UNDER CONTROL.
AFTER CASSIE DIED WE WERE--
YOU THINK I'M PISSED BECAUSE YOU COULDN'T ACTIVATE CASSIE?
THAT SHE DIED?
I'M PISSED BECAUSE I NEVER AUTHORIZED GOING AFTER THE TUCKER BOY.
SIR, I MADE A MISTAKE.
I WANTED TO SHOW YOU WHAT WE COULD DO--
STAND UP.
GET ON YOUR GODDAMNED FEET.

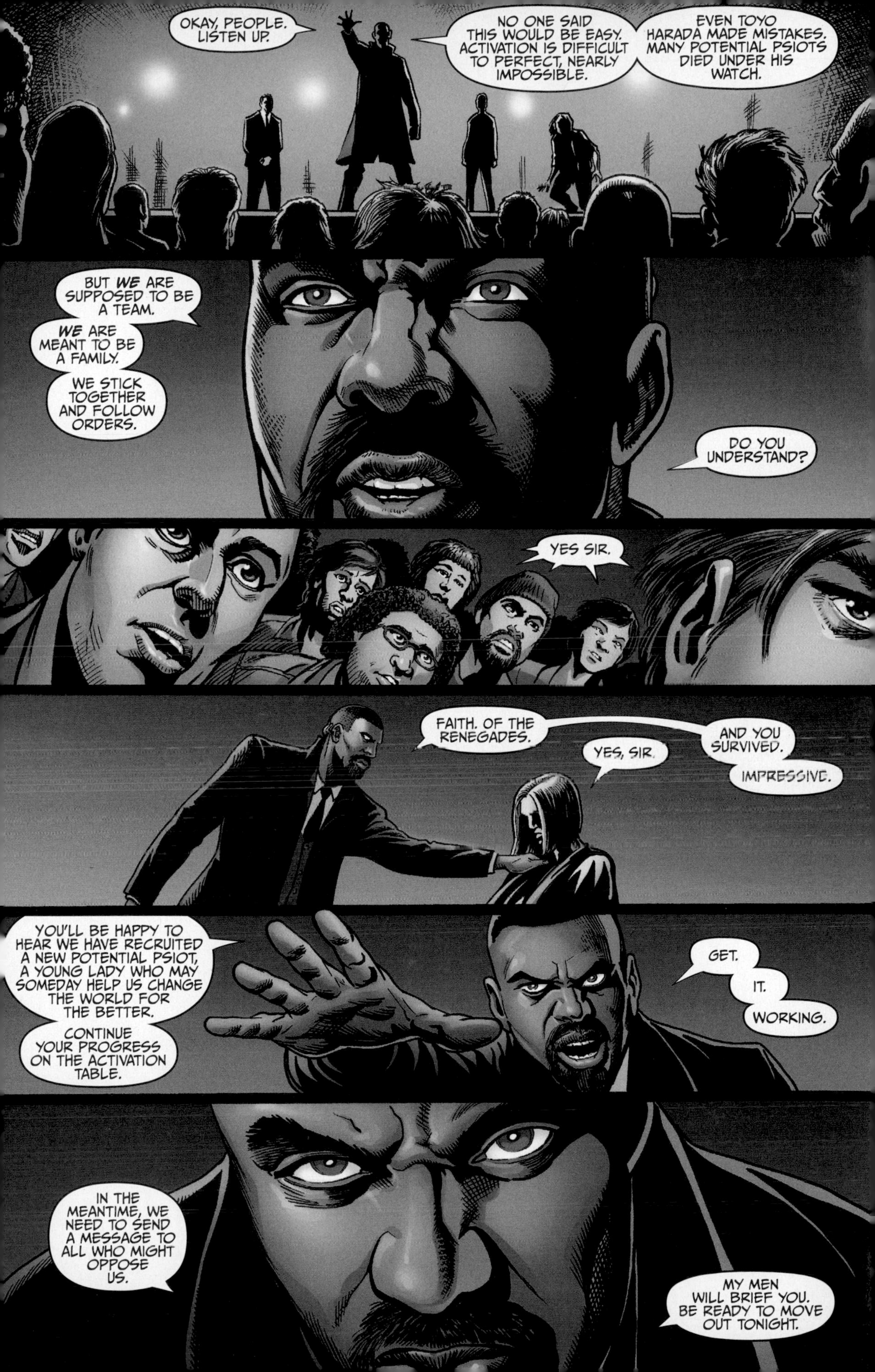
OKAY, PEOPLE. LISTEN UP.
NO ONE SAID THIS WOULD BE EASY. ACTIVATION IS DIFFICULT TO PERFECT, NEARLY IMPOSSIBLE.
EVEN TOYO HARADA MADE MISTAKES. MANY POTENTIAL PSIOTS DIED UNDER HIS WATCH.
BUT *WE* ARE SUPPOSED TO BE A TEAM.
WE ARE MEANT TO BE A FAMILY.
WE STICK TOGETHER AND FOLLOW ORDERS.
DO YOU UNDERSTAND?
YES SIR.
FAITH. OF THE RENEGADES.
AND YOU SURVIVED.
IMPRESSIVE.
YES, SIR.
YOU'LL BE HAPPY TO HEAR WE HAVE RECRUITED A NEW POTENTIAL PSIOT, A YOUNG LADY WHO MAY SOMEDAY HELP US CHANGE THE WORLD FOR THE BETTER.
CONTINUE YOUR PROGRESS ON THE ACTIVATION TABLE.
GET.
IT.
WORKING.
IN THE MEANTIME, WE NEED TO SEND A MESSAGE TO ALL WHO MIGHT OPPOSE US.
MY MEN WILL BRIEF YOU. BE READY TO MOVE OUT TONIGHT.

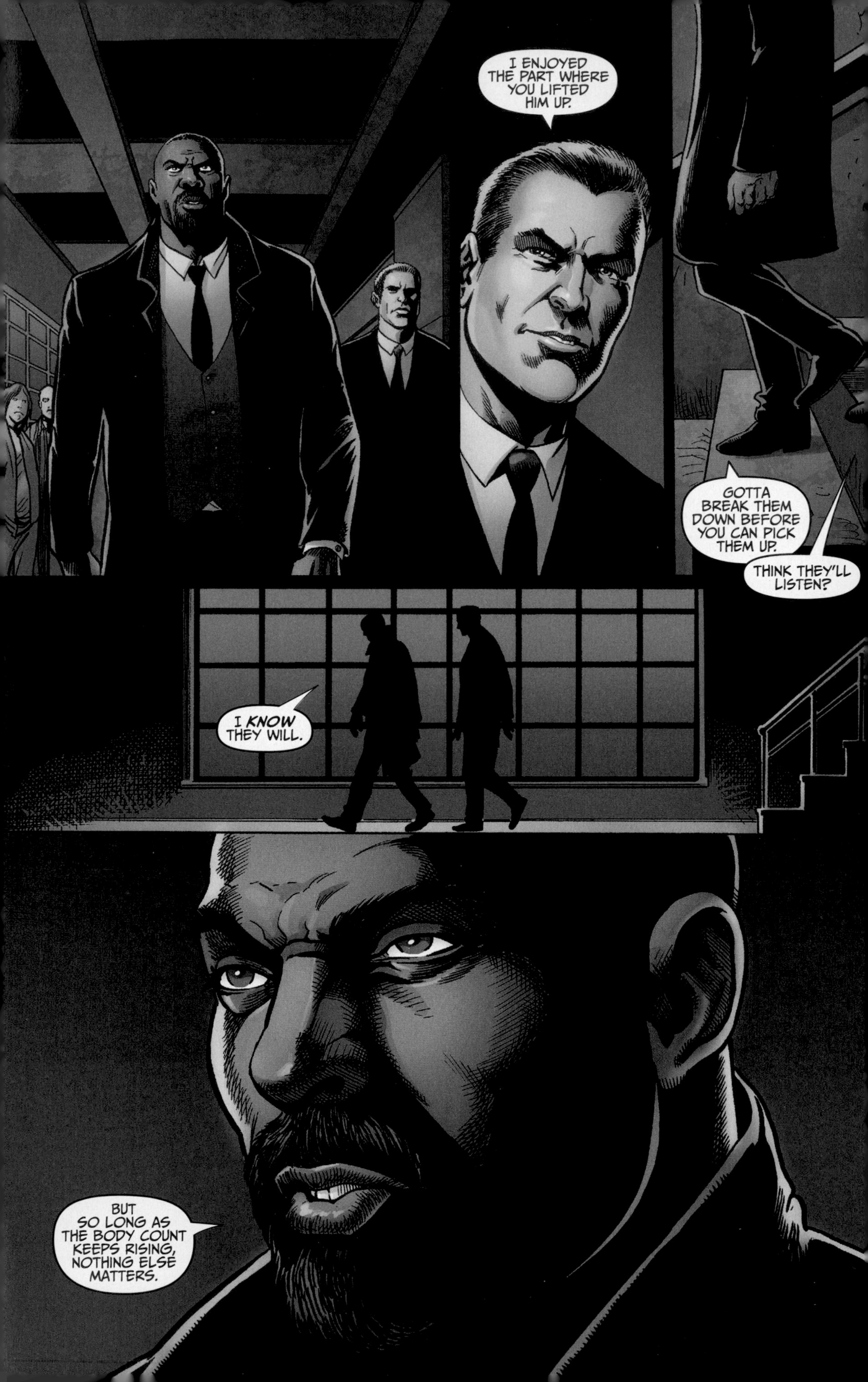
I ENJOYED THE PART WHERE YOU LIFTED HIM UP.
GOTTA BREAK THEM DOWN BEFORE YOU CAN PICK THEM UP.
THINK THEY'LL LISTEN?
I KNOW THEY WILL.
BUT SO LONG AS THE BODY COUNT KEEPS RISING, NOTHING ELSE MATTERS.

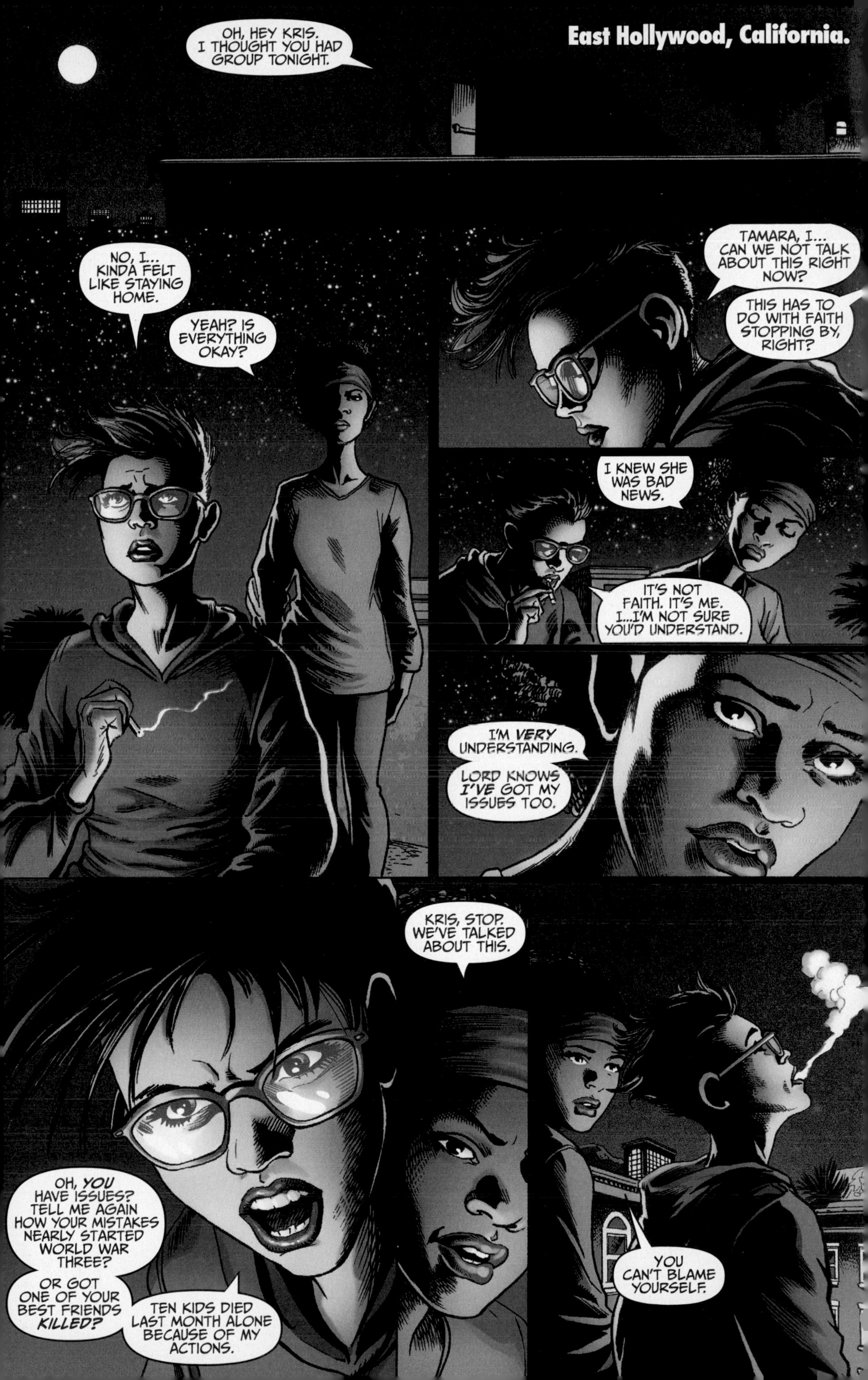
East Hollywood, California.
OH, HEY KRIS. I THOUGHT YOU HAD GROUP TONIGHT.
NO, I... KINDA FELT LIKE STAYING HOME.
YEAH? IS EVERYTHING OKAY?
TAMARA, I... CAN WE NOT TALK ABOUT THIS RIGHT NOW?
THIS HAS TO DO WITH FAITH STOPPING BY, RIGHT?
I KNEW SHE WAS BAD NEWS.
IT'S NOT FAITH. IT'S ME. I...I'M NOT SURE YOU'D UNDERSTAND.
I'M *VERY* UNDERSTANDING.
LORD KNOWS *I'VE* GOT MY ISSUES TOO.
OH, *YOU* HAVE ISSUES? TELL ME AGAIN HOW YOUR MISTAKES NEARLY STARTED WORLD WAR THREE?
OR GOT ONE OF YOUR BEST FRIENDS *KILLED?*
TEN KIDS DIED LAST MONTH ALONE BECAUSE OF MY ACTIONS.
KRIS, STOP. WE'VE TALKED ABOUT THIS.
YOU CAN'T BLAME YOURSELF.

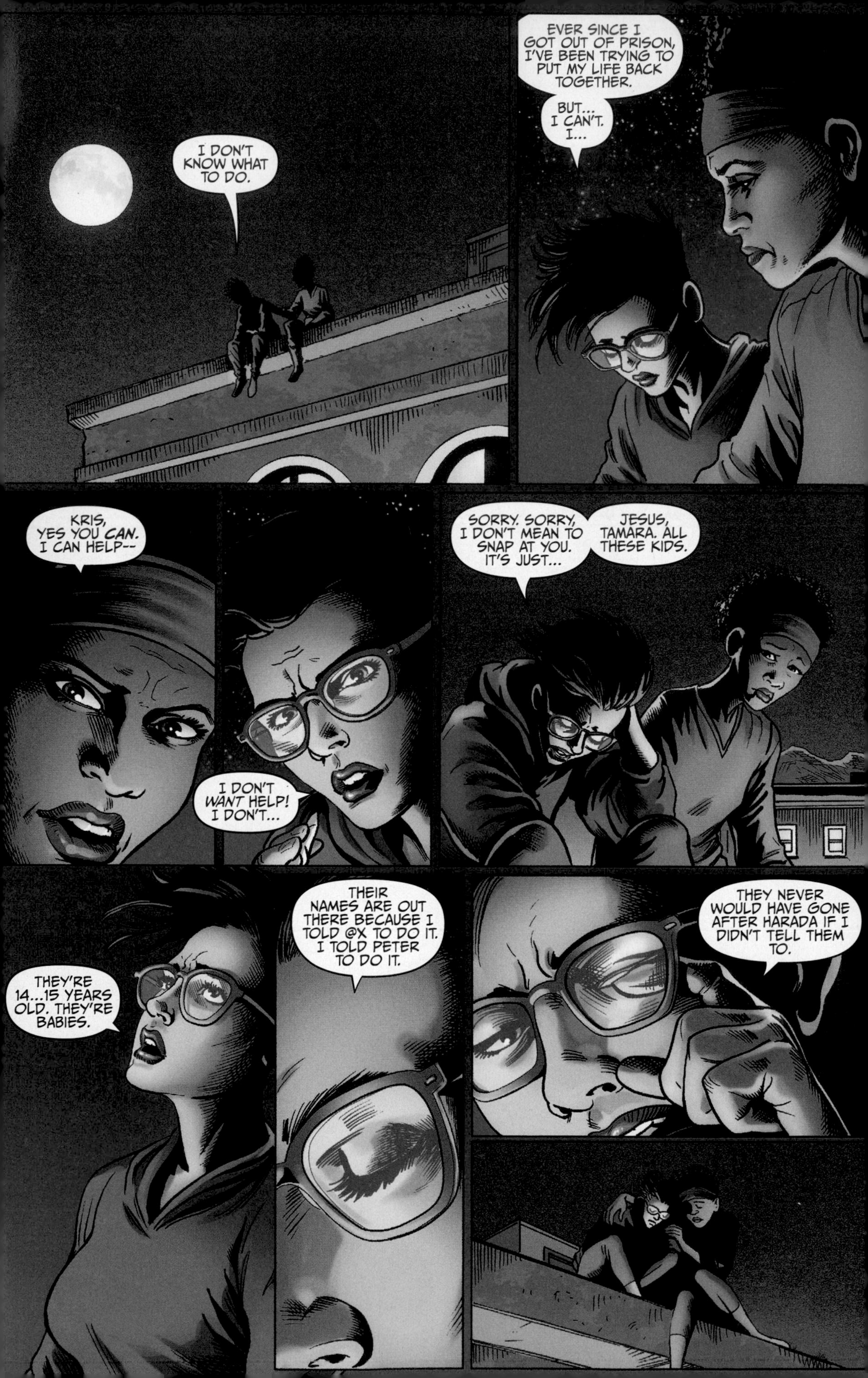
I DON'T KNOW WHAT TO DO.
EVER SINCE I GOT OUT OF PRISON, I'VE BEEN TRYING TO PUT MY LIFE BACK TOGETHER.
BUT... I CAN'T. I...
KRIS, YES YOU CAN. I CAN HELP--
I DON'T WANT HELP! I DON'T...
SORRY. SORRY, I DON'T MEAN TO SNAP AT YOU. IT'S JUST...
JESUS, TAMARA. ALL THESE KIDS.
THEY'RE 14...15 YEARS OLD. THEY'RE BABIES.
THEIR NAMES ARE OUT THERE BECAUSE I TOLD @X TO DO IT. I TOLD PETER TO DO IT.
THEY NEVER WOULD HAVE GONE AFTER HARADA IF I DIDN'T TELL THEM TO.

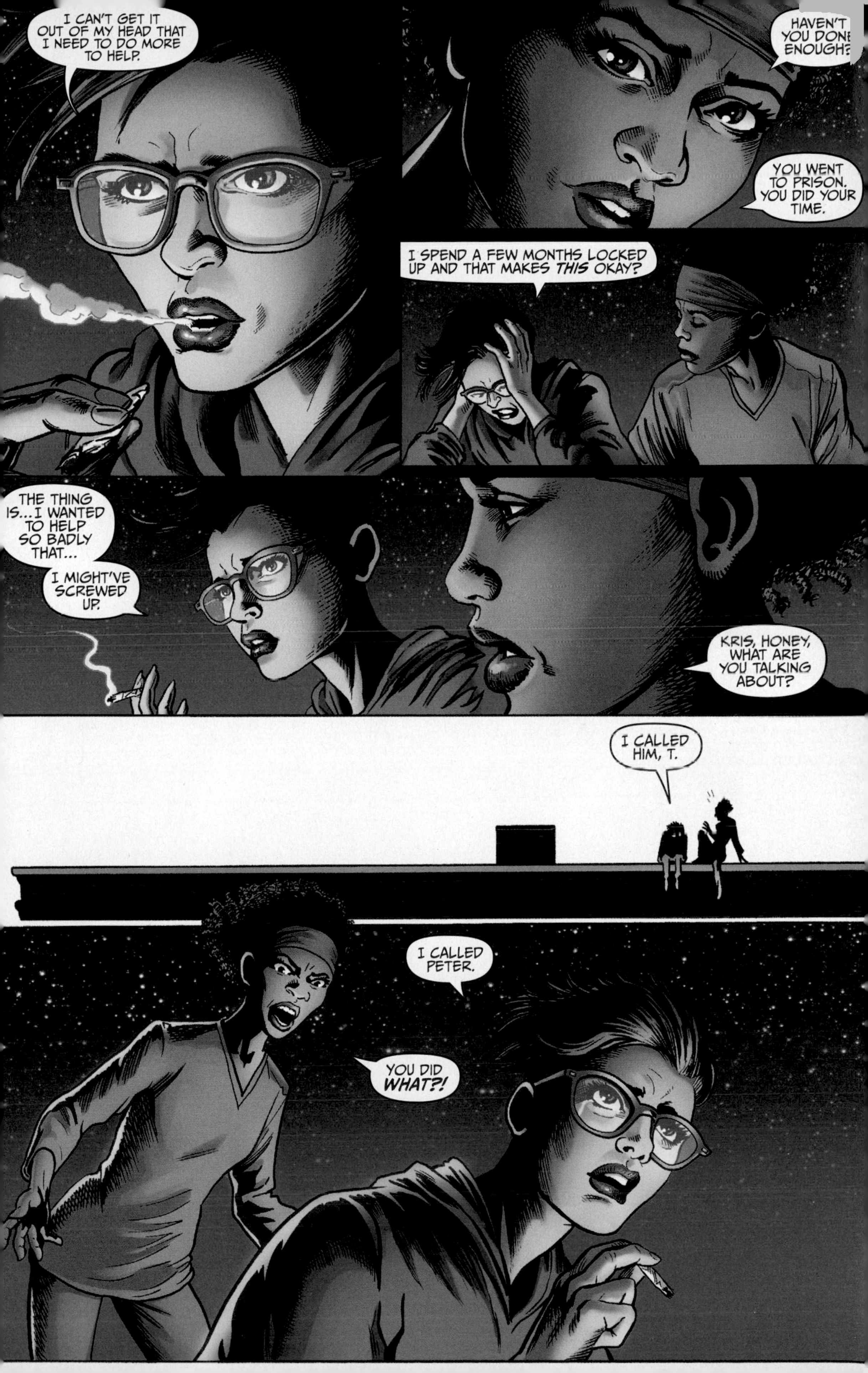
I CAN'T GET IT OUT OF MY HEAD THAT I NEED TO DO MORE TO HELP.
HAVEN'T YOU DONE ENOUGH?
YOU WENT TO PRISON. YOU DID YOUR TIME.
I SPEND A FEW MONTHS LOCKED UP AND THAT MAKES *THIS* OKAY?
THE THING IS...I WANTED TO HELP SO BADLY THAT...
I MIGHT'VE SCREWED UP.
KRIS, HONEY, WHAT ARE YOU TALKING ABOUT?
I CALLED HIM, T.
I CALLED PETER.
YOU DID *WHAT?!*

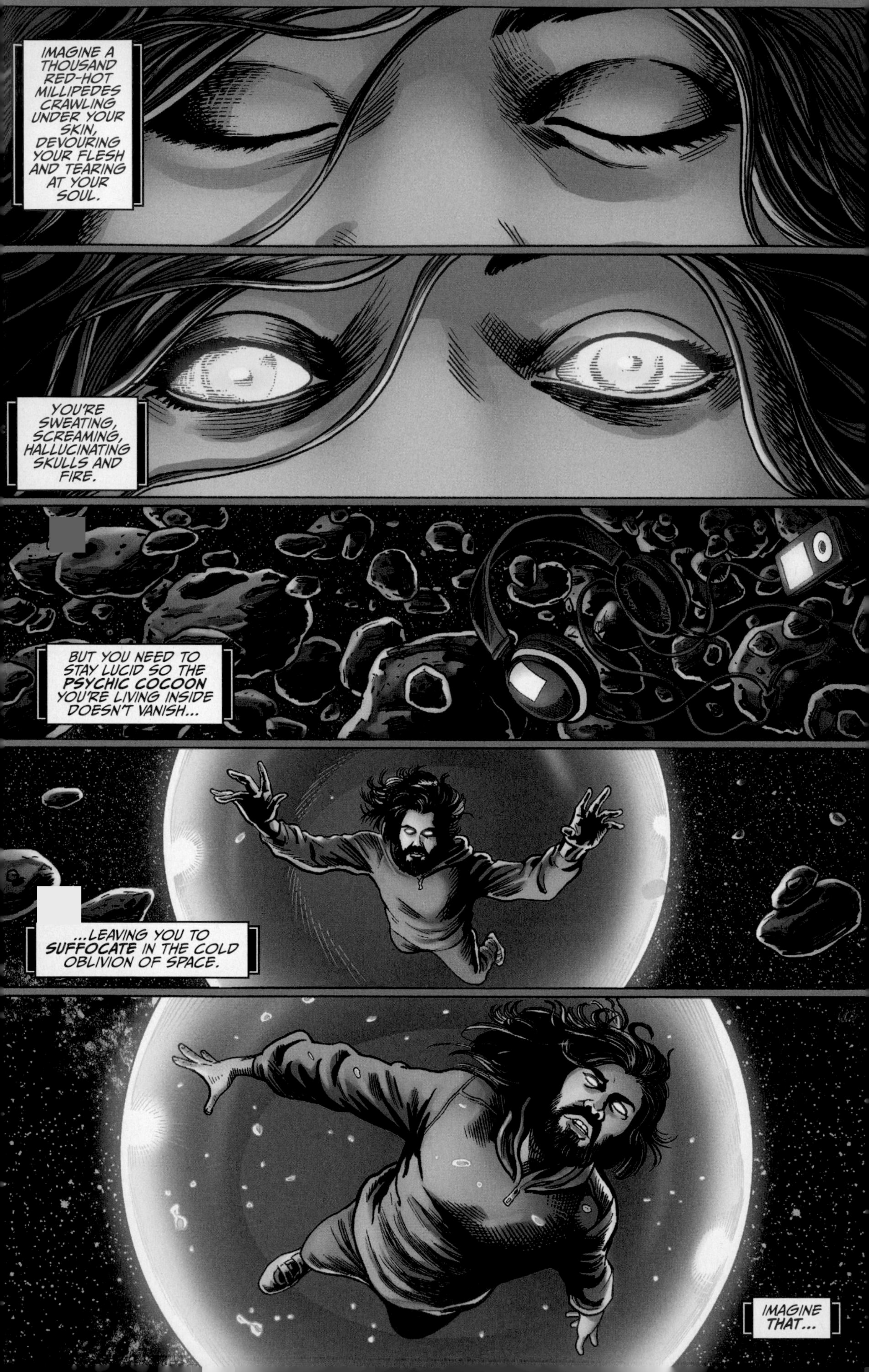
IMAGINE A THOUSAND RED-HOT MILLIPEDES CRAWLING UNDER YOUR SKIN, DEVOURING YOUR FLESH AND TEARING AT YOUR SOUL.
YOU'RE SWEATING, SCREAMING, HALLUCINATING SKULLS AND FIRE.
BUT YOU NEED TO STAY LUCID SO THE PSYCHIC COCOON YOU'RE LIVING INSIDE DOESN'T VANISH...
...LEAVING YOU TO SUFFOCATE IN THE COLD OBLIVION OF SPACE.
IMAGINE THAT...

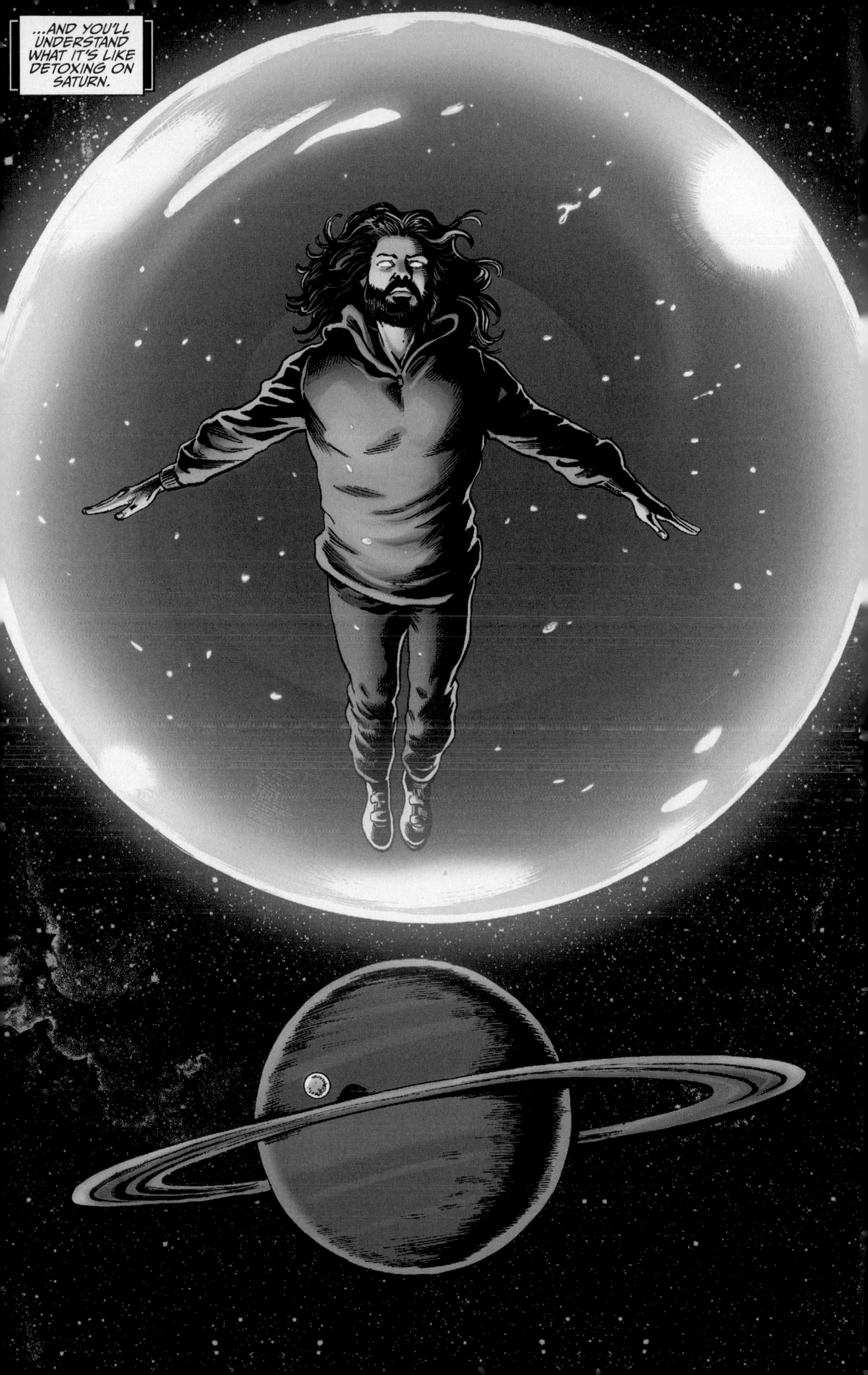
...AND YOU'LL UNDERSTAND WHAT IT'S LIKE DETOXING ON SATURN.

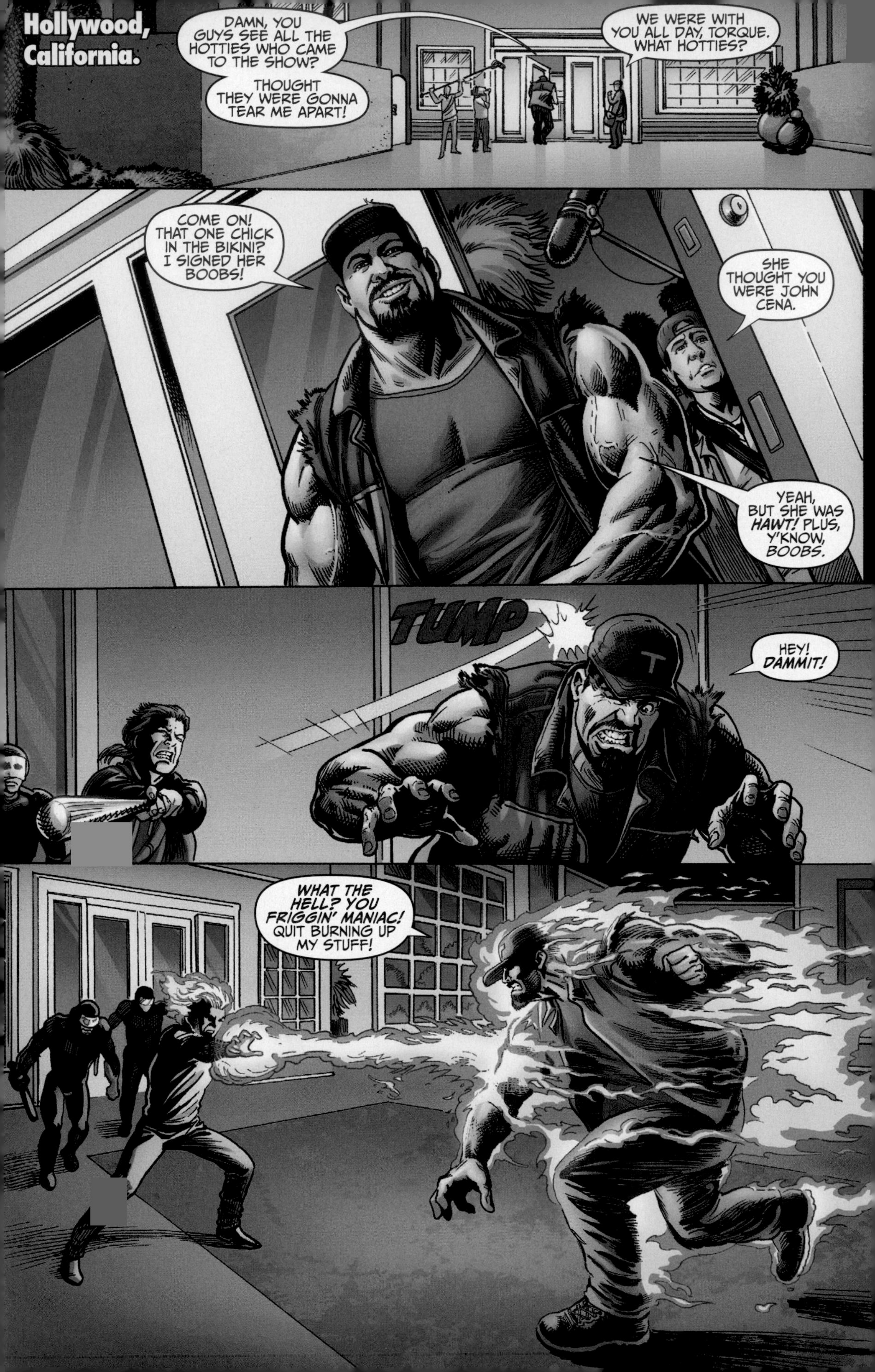
Hollywood, California.
DAMN, YOU GUYS SEE ALL THE HOTTIES WHO CAME TO THE SHOW?
THOUGHT THEY WERE GONNA TEAR ME APART!
WE WERE WITH YOU ALL DAY, TORQUE. WHAT HOTTIES?
COME ON! THAT ONE CHICK IN THE BIKINI? I SIGNED HER BOOBS!
SHE THOUGHT YOU WERE JOHN CENA.
YEAH, BUT SHE WAS HAWT! PLUS, Y'KNOW, BOOBS.
TUMP
HEY! DAMMIT!
WHAT THE HELL? YOU FRIGGIN' MANIAC! QUIT BURNING UP MY STUFF!

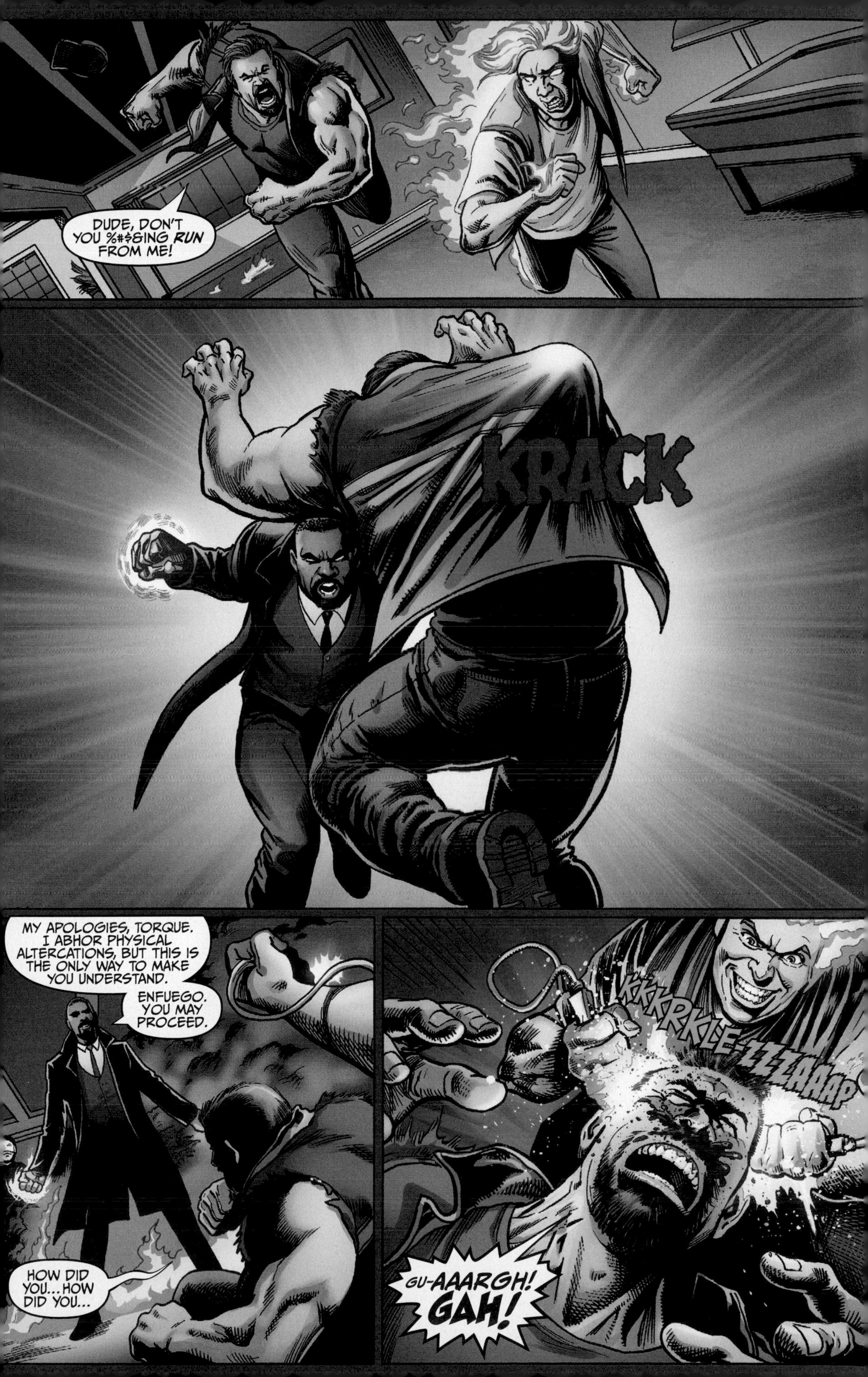
DUDE, DON'T YOU %#$&ING RUN FROM ME!
KRACK
MY APOLOGIES, TORQUE. I ABHOR PHYSICAL ALTERCATIONS, BUT THIS IS THE ONLY WAY TO MAKE YOU UNDERSTAND.
ENFUEGO. YOU MAY PROCEED.
HOW DID YOU... HOW DID YOU...
KKKRKLE-ZZZAAAP
GU-AAARGH! GAH!

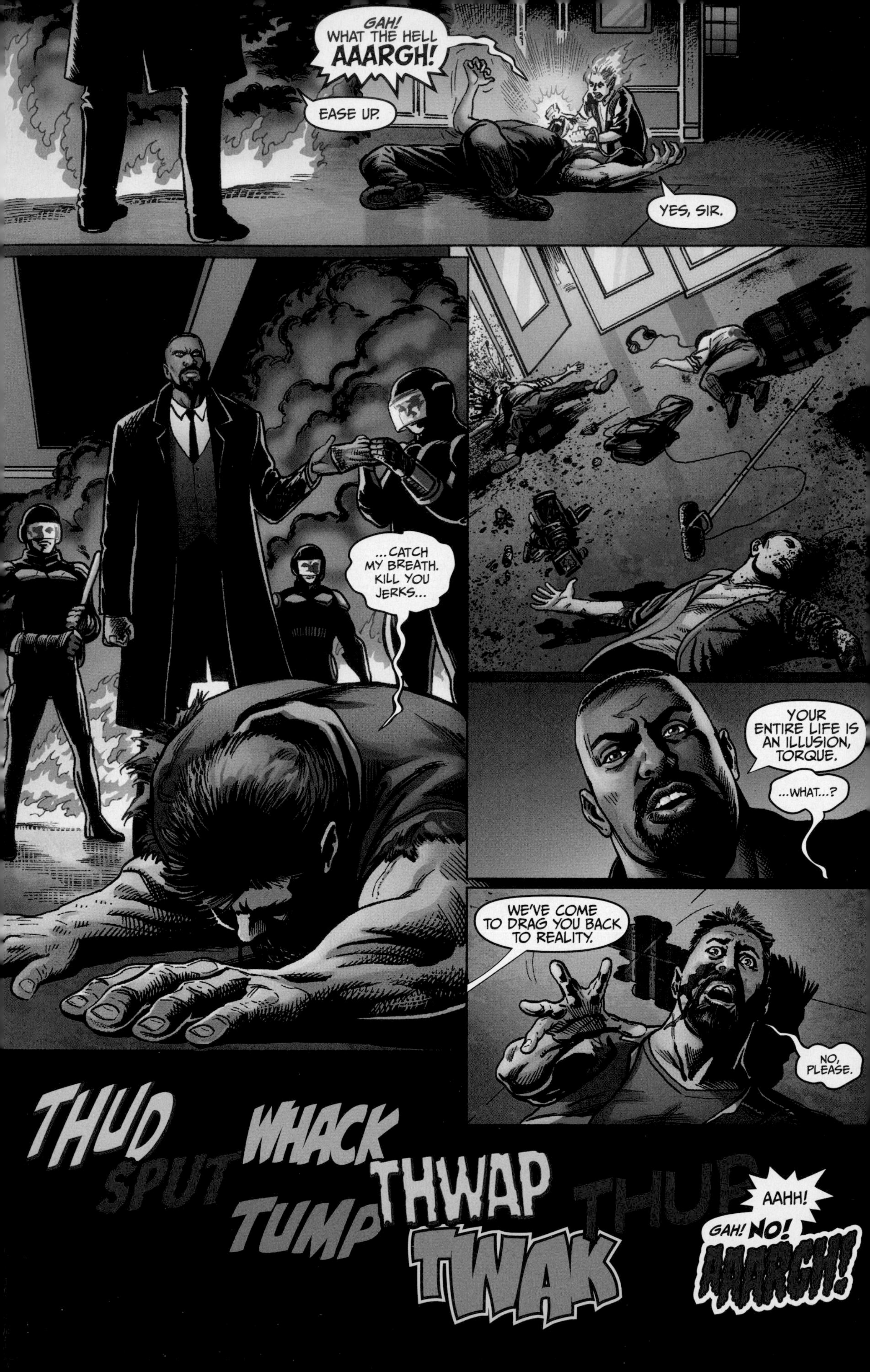
GAH! WHAT THE HELL AAARGH!
EASE UP.
YES, SIR.
...CATCH MY BREATH. KILL YOU JERKS...
YOUR ENTIRE LIFE IS AN ILLUSION, TORQUE.
...WHAT...?
WE'VE COME TO DRAG YOU BACK TO REALITY.
NO, PLEASE.
THUD
SPUT
WHACK
TUMP
THWAP
TWAK
AAHH!
GAH! NO!
AAARGH!

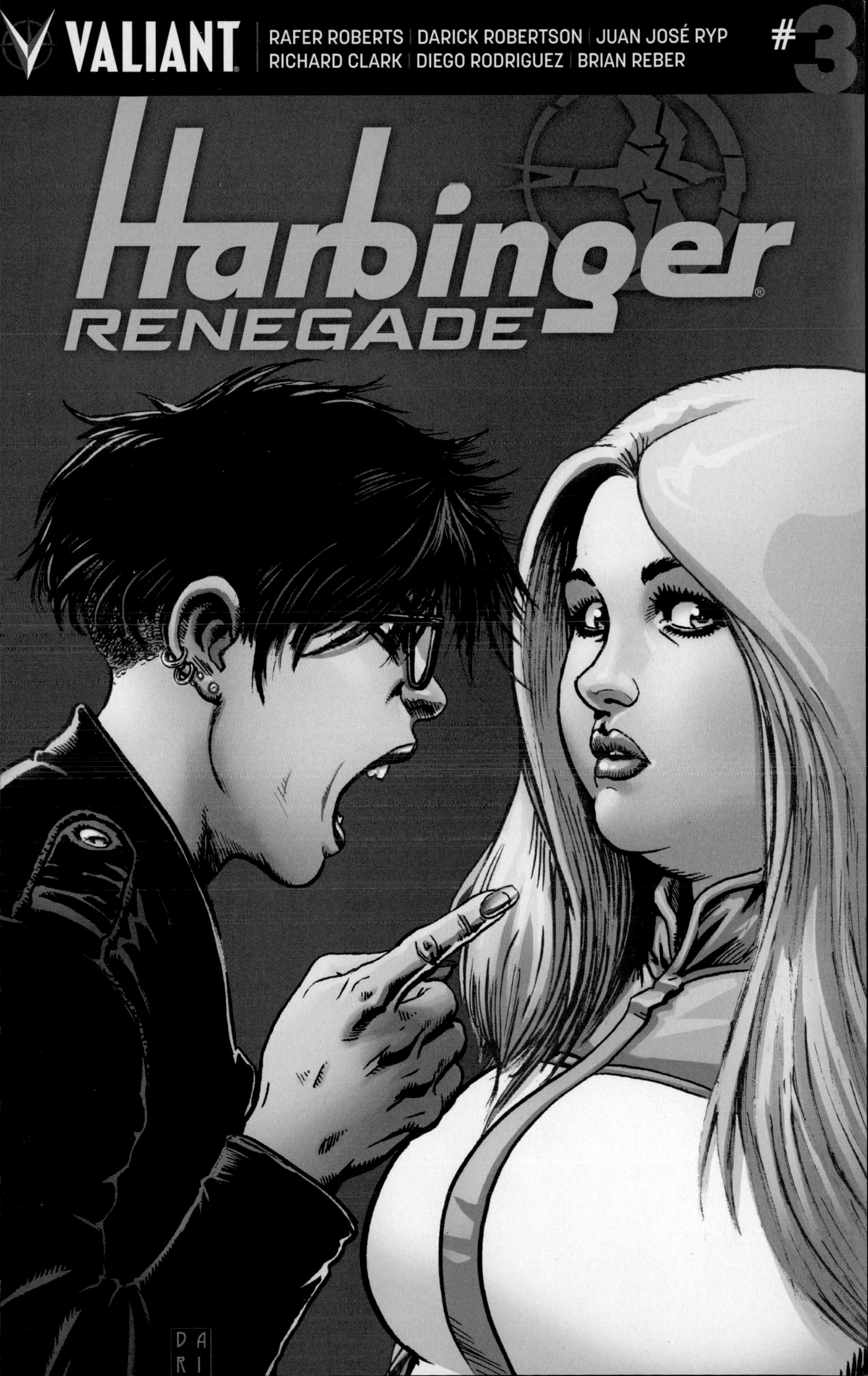
VALIANT
RAFER ROBERTS | DARICK ROBERTSON | JUAN JOSÉ RYP
RICHARD CLARK | DIEGO RODRIGUEZ | BRIAN REBER
#3
Harbinger
RENEGADE
DARI

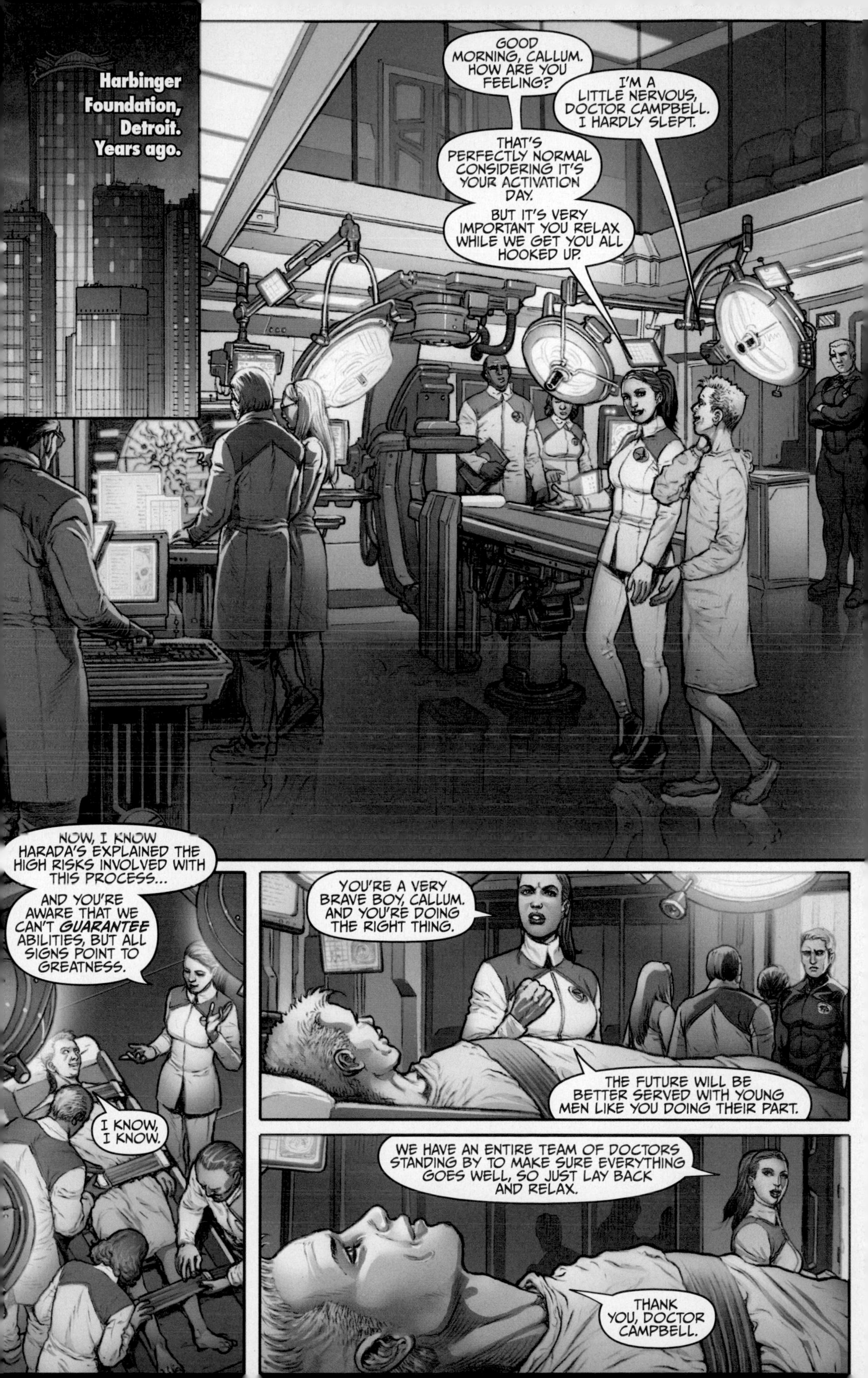
Harbinger Foundation, Detroit. Years ago.
GOOD MORNING, CALLUM. HOW ARE YOU FEELING?
I'M A LITTLE NERVOUS, DOCTOR CAMPBELL. I HARDLY SLEPT.
THAT'S PERFECTLY NORMAL CONSIDERING IT'S YOUR ACTIVATION DAY.
BUT IT'S VERY IMPORTANT YOU RELAX WHILE WE GET YOU ALL HOOKED UP.
NOW, I KNOW HARADA'S EXPLAINED THE HIGH RISKS INVOLVED WITH THIS PROCESS...
AND YOU'RE AWARE THAT WE CAN'T GUARANTEE ABILITIES, BUT ALL SIGNS POINT TO GREATNESS.
I KNOW, I KNOW.
YOU'RE A VERY BRAVE BOY, CALLUM. AND YOU'RE DOING THE RIGHT THING.
THE FUTURE WILL BE BETTER SERVED WITH YOUNG MEN LIKE YOU DOING THEIR PART.
WE HAVE AN ENTIRE TEAM OF DOCTORS STANDING BY TO MAKE SURE EVERYTHING GOES WELL, SO JUST LAY BACK AND RELAX.
THANK YOU, DOCTOR CAMPBELL.

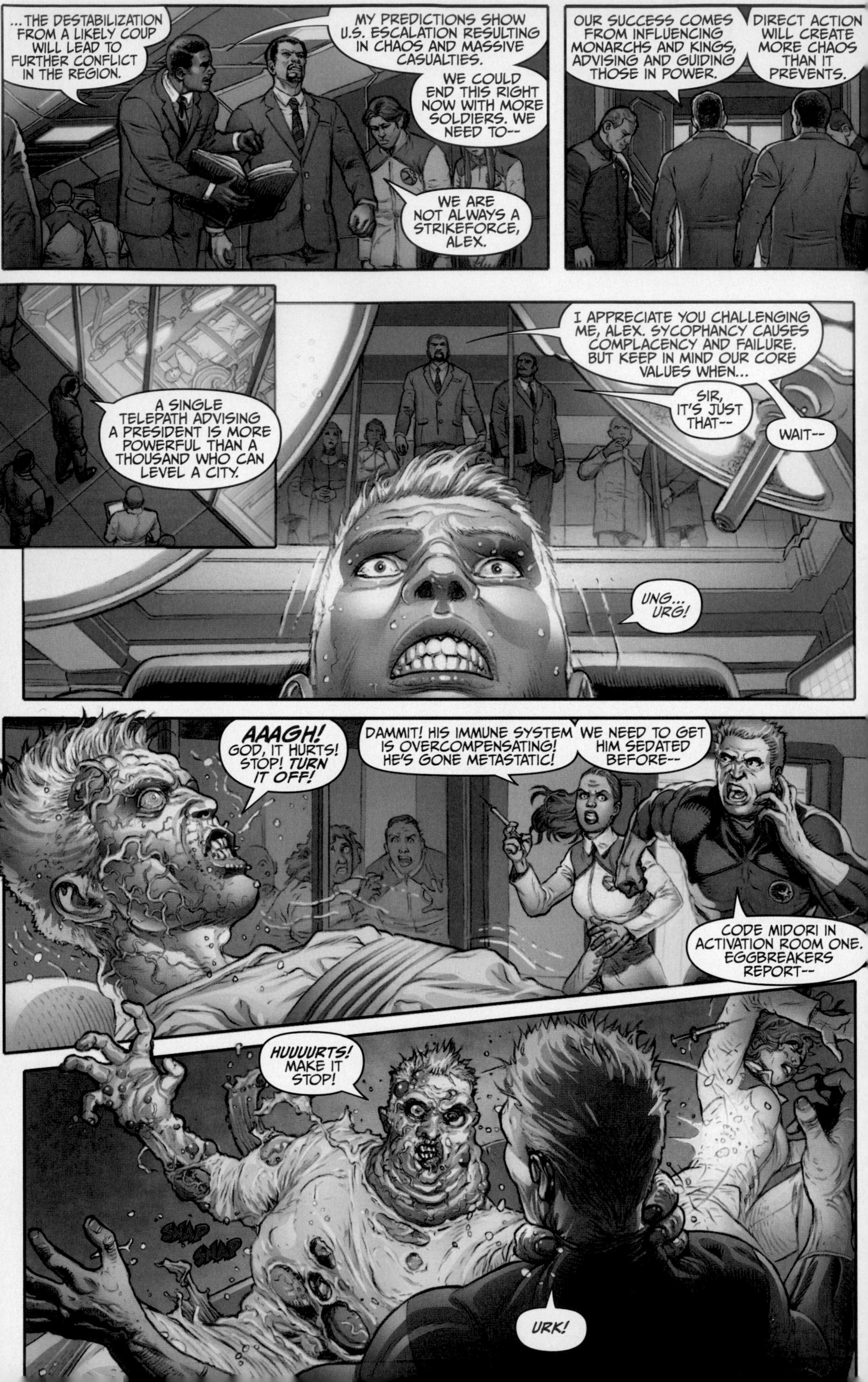
...THE DESTABILIZATION FROM A LIKELY COUP WILL LEAD TO FURTHER CONFLICT IN THE REGION.
MY PREDICTIONS SHOW U.S. ESCALATION RESULTING IN CHAOS AND MASSIVE CASUALTIES.
WE COULD END THIS RIGHT NOW WITH MORE SOLDIERS. WE NEED TO--
WE ARE NOT ALWAYS A STRIKEFORCE, ALEX.
OUR SUCCESS COMES FROM INFLUENCING MONARCHS AND KINGS, ADVISING AND GUIDING THOSE IN POWER.
DIRECT ACTION WILL CREATE MORE CHAOS THAN IT PREVENTS.
A SINGLE TELEPATH ADVISING A PRESIDENT IS MORE POWERFUL THAN A THOUSAND WHO CAN LEVEL A CITY.
I APPRECIATE YOU CHALLENGING ME, ALEX. SYCOPHANCY CAUSES COMPLACENCY AND FAILURE. BUT KEEP IN MIND OUR CORE VALUES WHEN...
SIR, IT'S JUST THAT--
WAIT--
UNG... URG!
AAAGH! GOD, IT HURTS! STOP! TURN IT OFF!
DAMMIT! HIS IMMUNE SYSTEM IS OVERCOMPENSATING! HE'S GONE METASTATIC!
WE NEED TO GET HIM SEDATED BEFORE--
CODE MIDORI IN ACTIVATION ROOM ONE. EGGBREAKERS REPORT--
HUUUURTS! MAKE IT STOP!
SNAP
SNAP
URK!

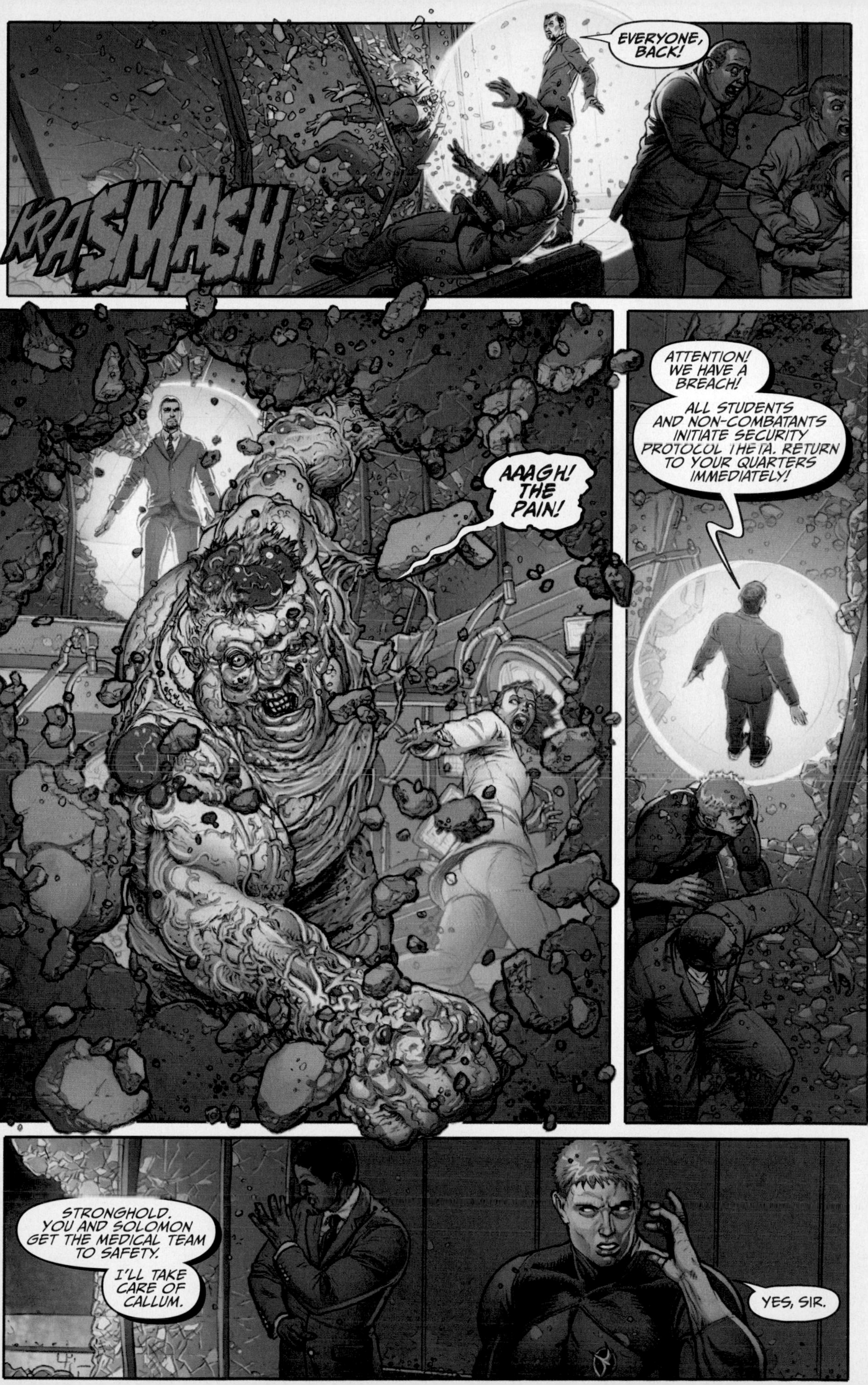
EVERYONE, BACK!
KRASMASH
AAAGH! THE PAIN!
ATTENTION! WE HAVE A BREACH!
ALL STUDENTS AND NON-COMBATANTS INITIATE SECURITY PROTOCOL THETA. RETURN TO YOUR QUARTERS IMMEDIATELY!
STRONGHOLD. YOU AND SOLOMON GET THE MEDICAL TEAM TO SAFETY.
I'LL TAKE CARE OF CALLUM.
YES, SIR.

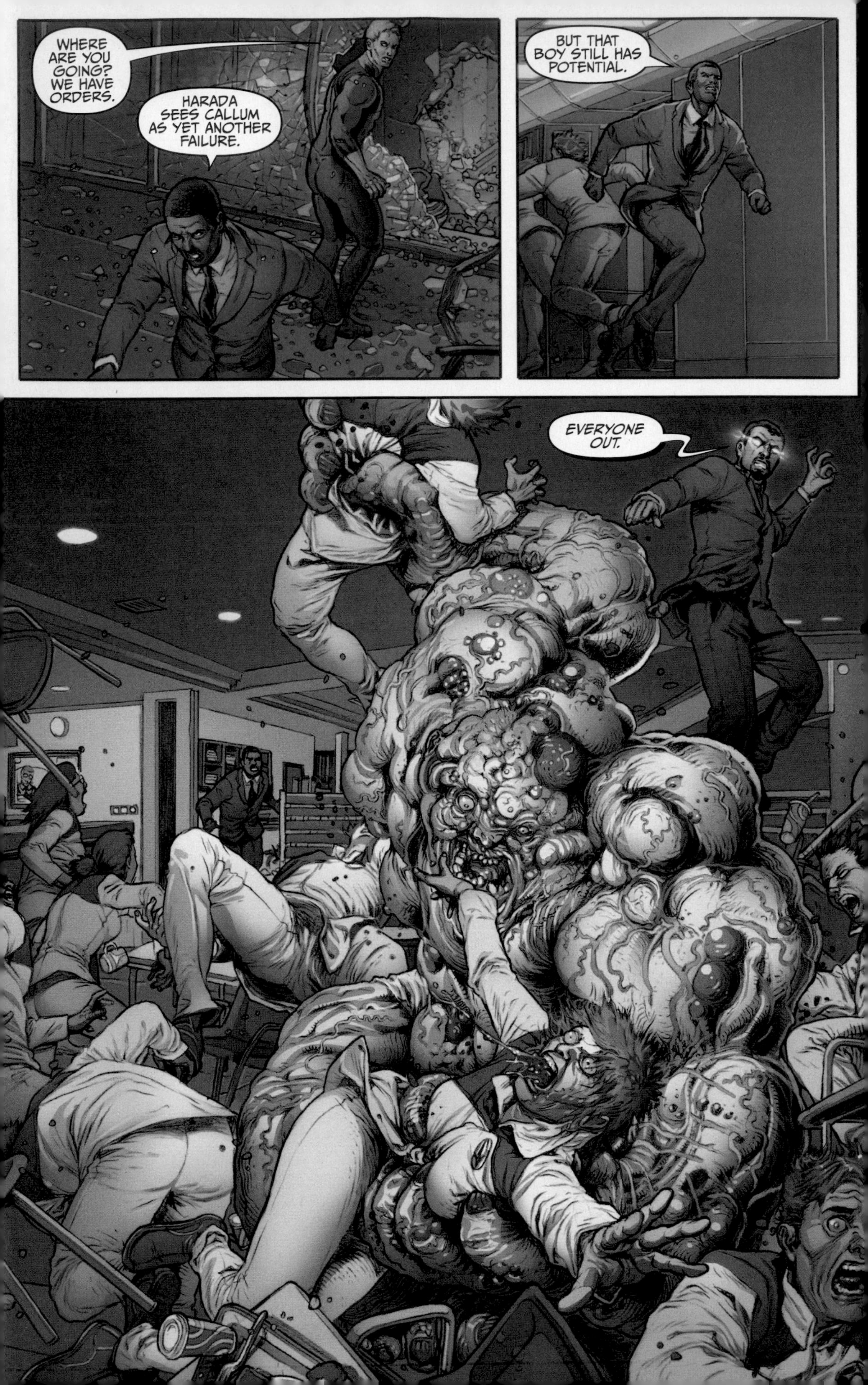
WHERE ARE YOU GOING? WE HAVE ORDERS.
HARADA SEES CALLUM AS YET ANOTHER FAILURE.
BUT THAT BOY STILL HAS POTENTIAL.
EVERYONE OUT.

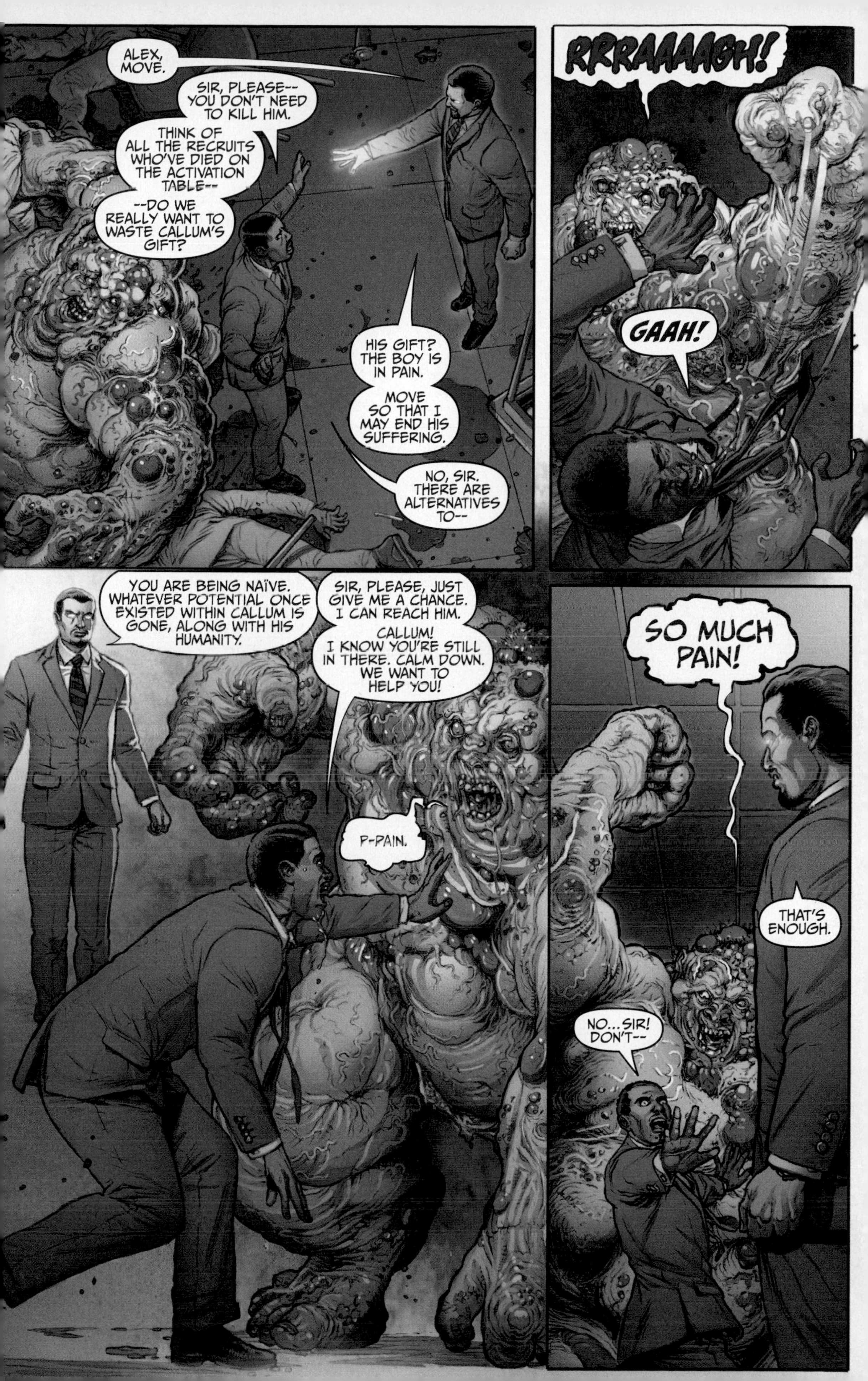
ALEX, MOVE.
SIR, PLEASE-- YOU DON'T NEED TO KILL HIM.
THINK OF ALL THE RECRUITS WHO'VE DIED ON THE ACTIVATION TABLE--
--DO WE REALLY WANT TO WASTE CALLUM'S GIFT?
HIS GIFT? THE BOY IS IN PAIN.
MOVE SO THAT I MAY END HIS SUFFERING.
NO, SIR. THERE ARE ALTERNATIVES TO--
RRRAAAAAGH!
GAAH!
YOU ARE BEING NAÏVE. WHATEVER POTENTIAL ONCE EXISTED WITHIN CALLUM IS GONE, ALONG WITH HIS HUMANITY.
SIR, PLEASE, JUST GIVE ME A CHANCE. I CAN REACH HIM.
CALLUM! I KNOW YOU'RE STILL IN THERE. CALM DOWN. WE WANT TO HELP YOU!
P-PAIN.
SO MUCH PAIN!
THAT'S ENOUGH.
NO...SIR! DON'T--

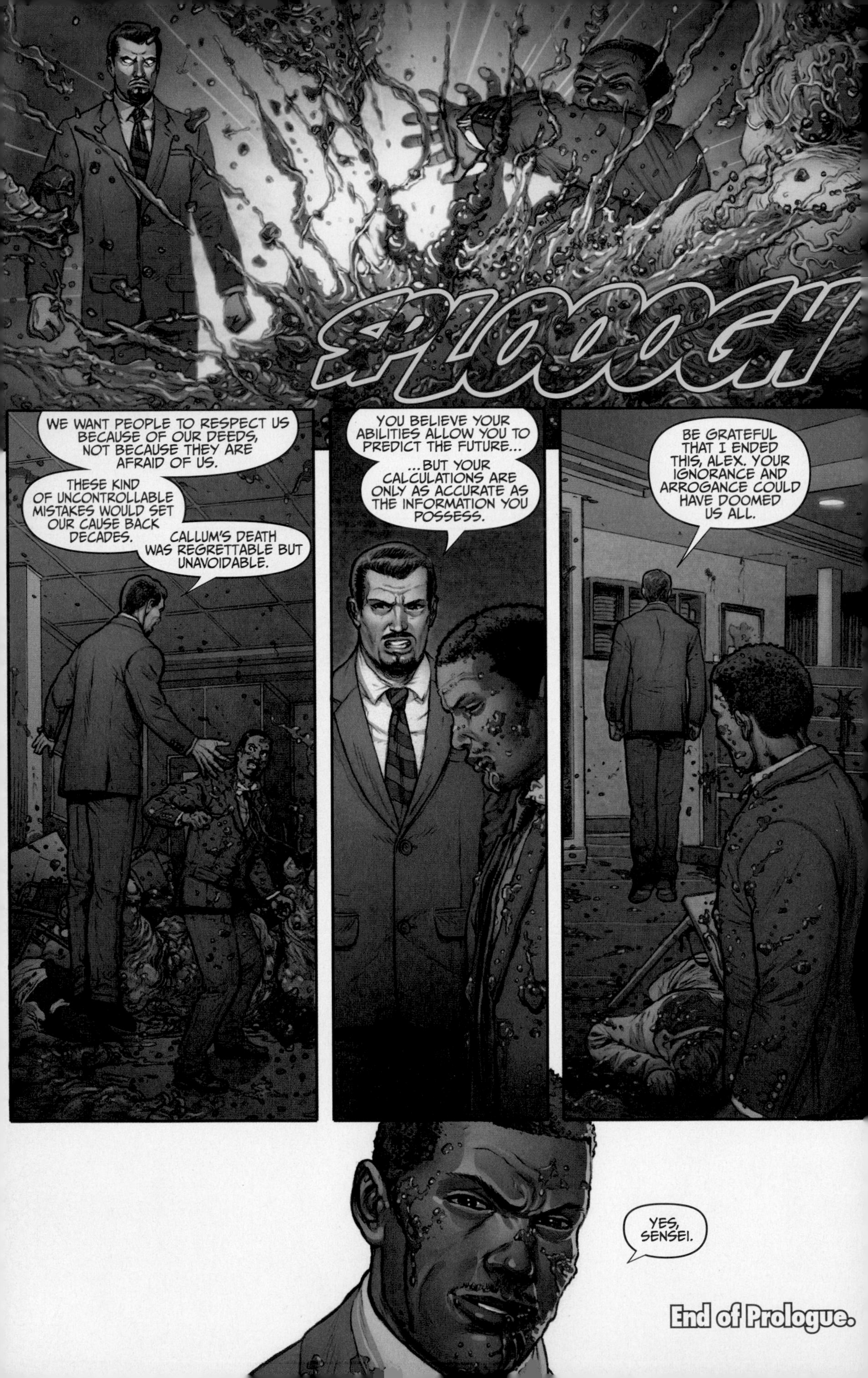
SPLOOOCH
WE WANT PEOPLE TO RESPECT US BECAUSE OF OUR DEEDS, NOT BECAUSE THEY ARE AFRAID OF US.
THESE KIND OF UNCONTROLLABLE MISTAKES WOULD SET OUR CAUSE BACK DECADES.
CALLUM'S DEATH WAS REGRETTABLE BUT UNAVOIDABLE.
YOU BELIEVE YOUR ABILITIES ALLOW YOU TO PREDICT THE FUTURE...
...BUT YOUR CALCULATIONS ARE ONLY AS ACCURATE AS THE INFORMATION YOU POSSESS.
BE GRATEFUL THAT I ENDED THIS, ALEX. YOUR IGNORANCE AND ARROGANCE COULD HAVE DOOMED US ALL.
YES, SENSEI.
End of Prologue.

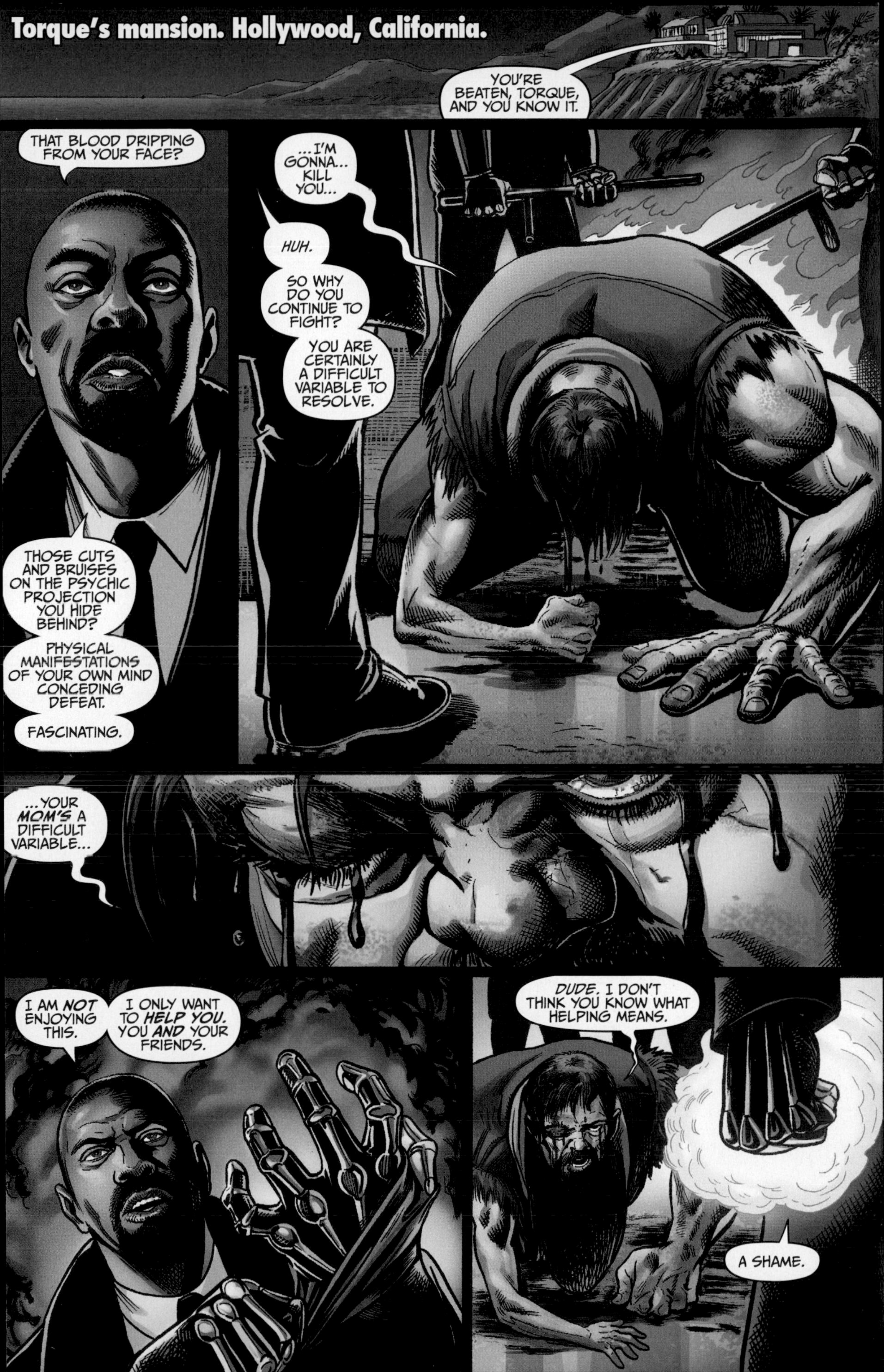
Torque's mansion. Hollywood, California.
YOU'RE BEATEN, TORQUE, AND YOU KNOW IT.
THAT BLOOD DRIPPING FROM YOUR FACE?
THOSE CUTS AND BRUISES ON THE PSYCHIC PROJECTION YOU HIDE BEHIND?
PHYSICAL MANIFESTATIONS OF YOUR OWN MIND CONCEDING DEFEAT.
FASCINATING.
...I'M GONNA... KILL YOU...
HUH.
SO WHY DO YOU CONTINUE TO FIGHT?
YOU ARE CERTAINLY A DIFFICULT VARIABLE TO RESOLVE.
...YOUR MOM'S A DIFFICULT VARIABLE...
I AM NOT ENJOYING THIS.
I ONLY WANT TO HELP YOU. YOU AND YOUR FRIENDS.
DUDE. I DON'T THINK YOU KNOW WHAT HELPING MEANS.
A SHAME.

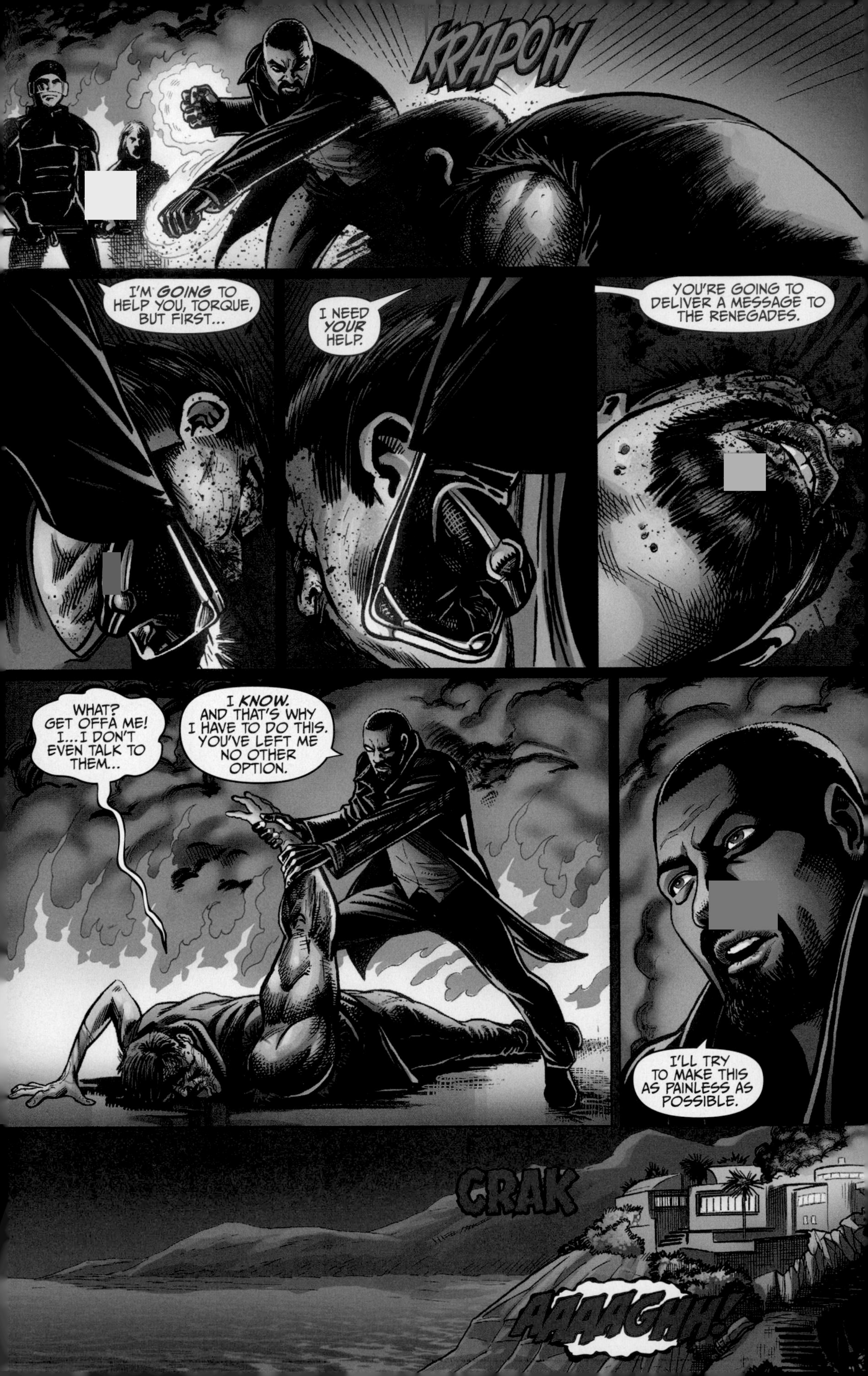
KRAPOW
I'M GOING TO HELP YOU, TORQUE, BUT FIRST...
I NEED YOUR HELP.
YOU'RE GOING TO DELIVER A MESSAGE TO THE RENEGADES.
WHAT? GET OFFA ME! I...I DON'T EVEN TALK TO THEM...
I KNOW. AND THAT'S WHY I HAVE TO DO THIS. YOU'VE LEFT ME NO OTHER OPTION.
I'LL TRY TO MAKE THIS AS PAINLESS AS POSSIBLE.
CRAK
AAAAGHH!

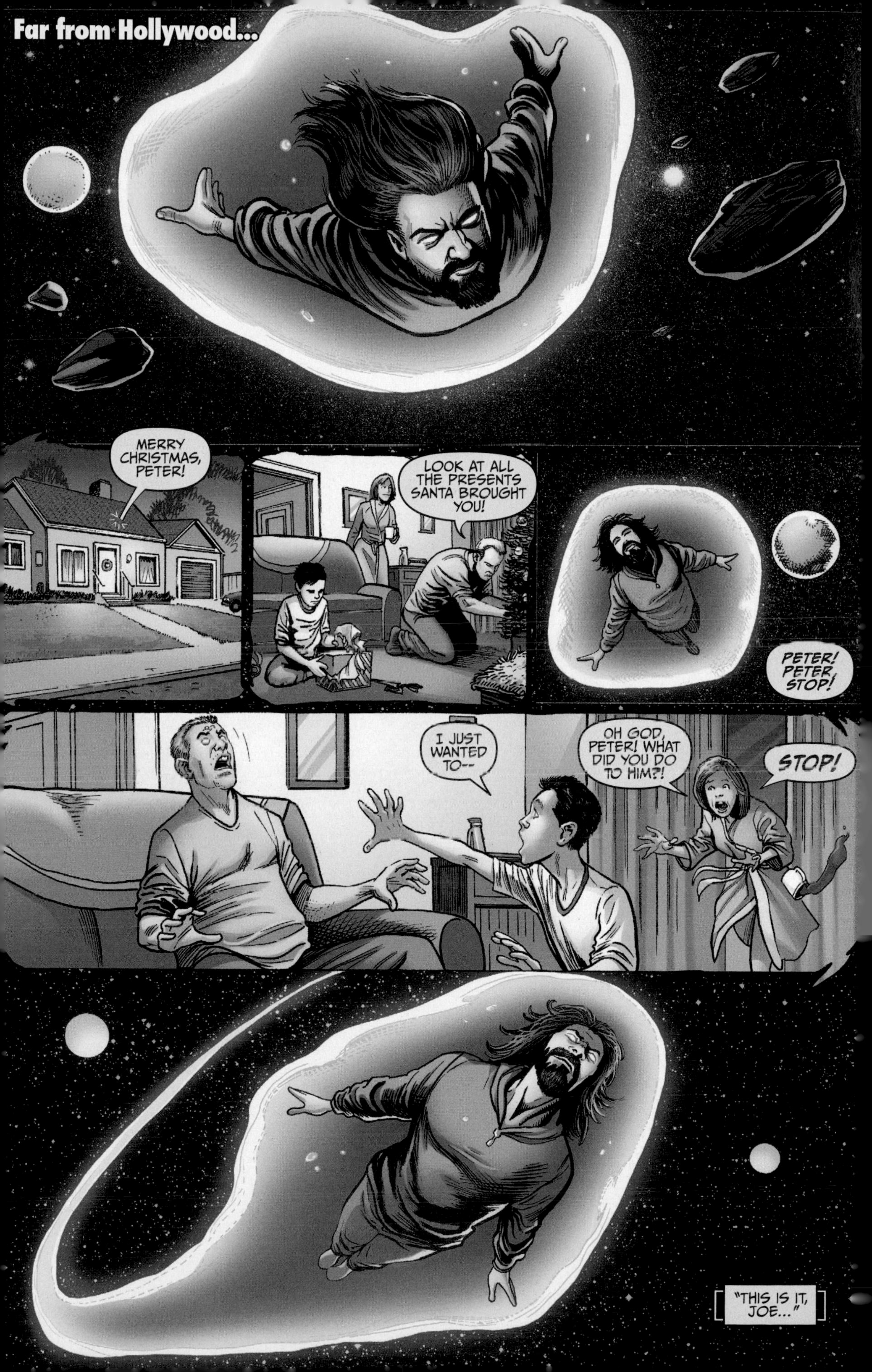
Far from Hollywood...
MERRY CHRISTMAS, PETER!
LOOK AT ALL THE PRESENTS SANTA BROUGHT YOU!
PETER! PETER, STOP!
I JUST WANTED TO--
OH GOD, PETER! WHAT DID YOU DO TO HIM?!
STOP!
"THIS IS IT, JOE..."

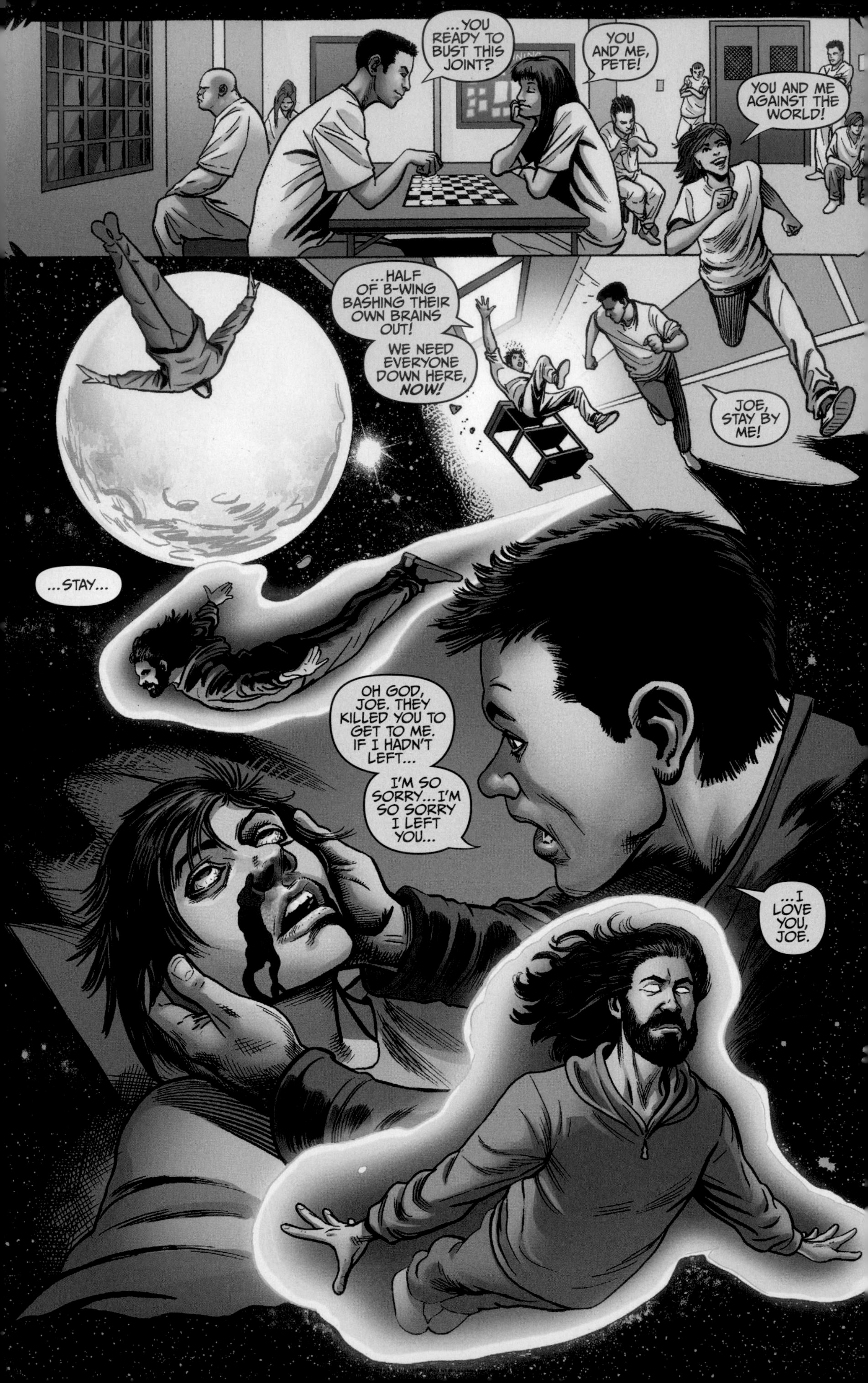
...YOU READY TO BUST THIS JOINT?
YOU AND ME, PETE!
YOU AND ME AGAINST THE WORLD!
...HALF OF B-WING BASHING THEIR OWN BRAINS OUT!
WE NEED EVERYONE DOWN HERE, NOW!
JOE, STAY BY ME!
...STAY...
OH GOD, JOE. THEY KILLED YOU TO GET TO ME. IF I HADN'T LEFT...
I'M SO SORRY...I'M SO SORRY I LEFT YOU...
...I LOVE YOU, JOE.

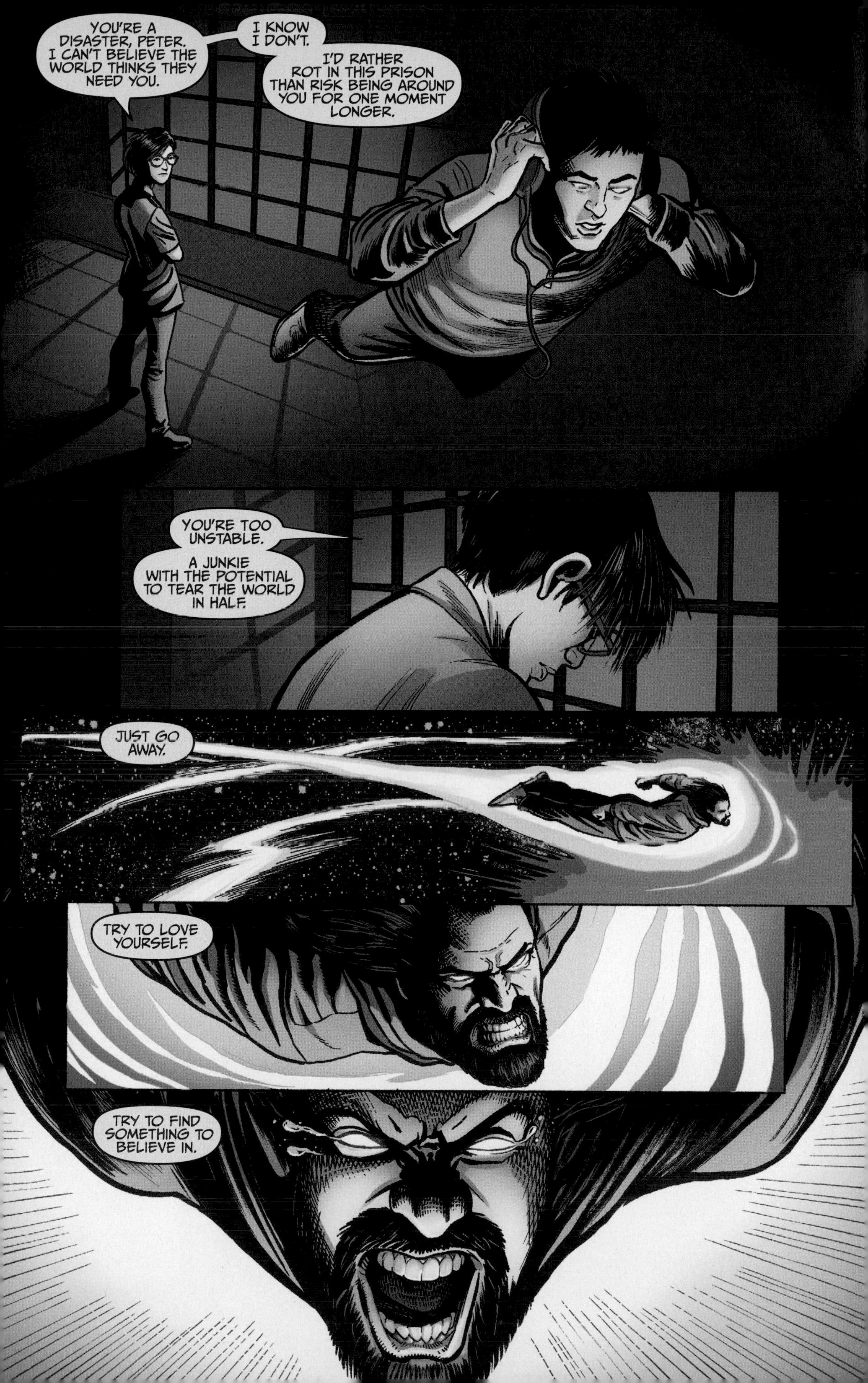
YOU'RE A DISASTER, PETER. I CAN'T BELIEVE THE WORLD THINKS THEY NEED YOU.
I KNOW I DON'T.
I'D RATHER ROT IN THIS PRISON THAN RISK BEING AROUND YOU FOR ONE MOMENT LONGER.
YOU'RE TOO UNSTABLE.
A JUNKIE WITH THE POTENTIAL TO TEAR THE WORLD IN HALF.
JUST GO AWAY.
TRY TO LOVE YOURSELF.
TRY TO FIND SOMETHING TO BELIEVE IN.

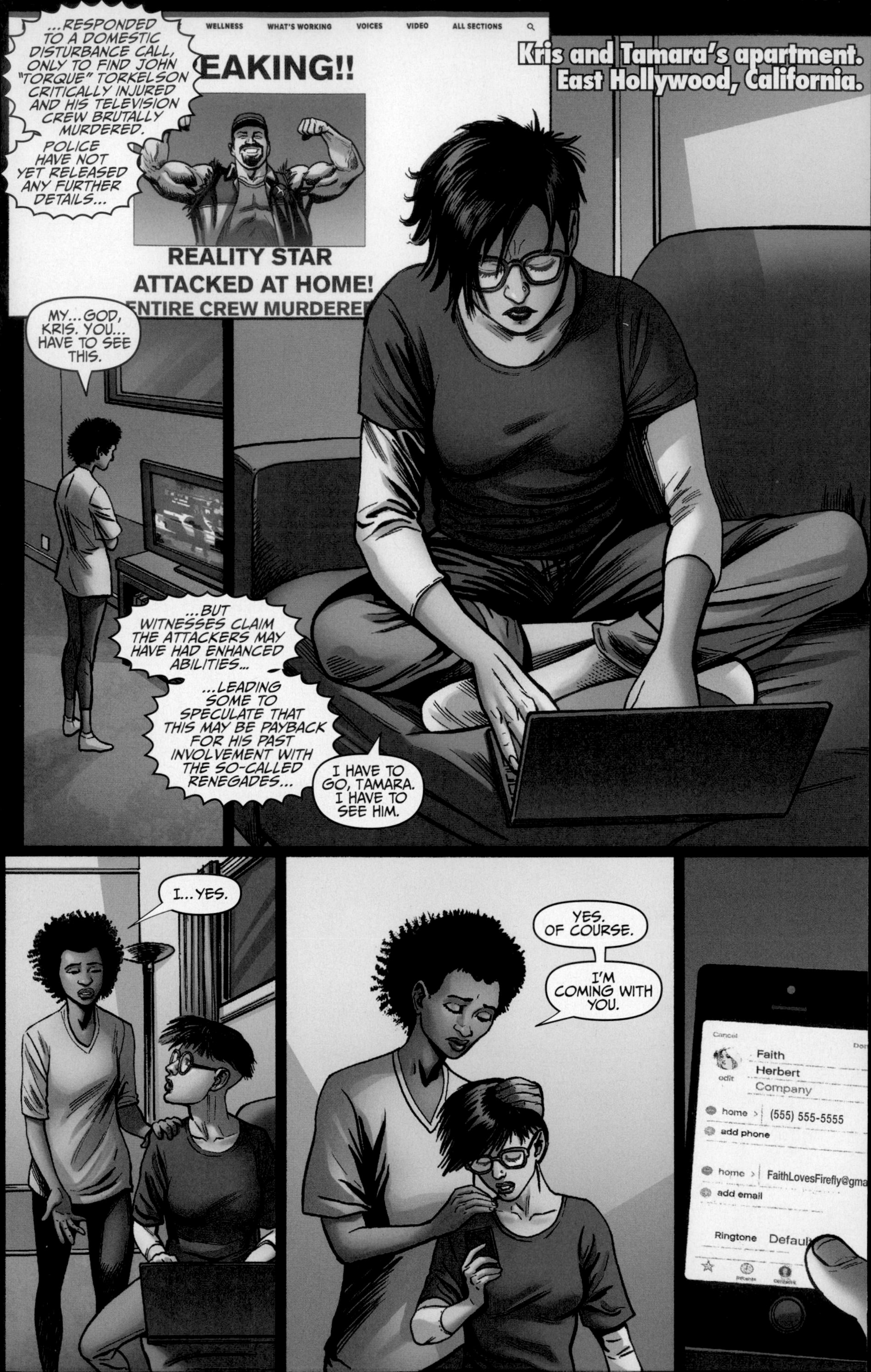
...RESPONDED TO A DOMESTIC DISTURBANCE CALL, ONLY TO FIND JOHN "TORQUE" TORKELSON CRITICALLY INJURED AND HIS TELEVISION CREW BRUTALLY MURDERED.
POLICE HAVE NOT YET RELEASED ANY FURTHER DETAILS...
WELLNESS
WHAT'S WORKING
VOICES
VIDEO
ALL SECTIONS
EAKING!!
REALITY STAR
ATTACKED AT HOME!
ENTIRE CREW MURDERE
Kris and Tamara's apartment. East Hollywood, California.
MY...GOD, KRIS. YOU... HAVE TO SEE THIS.
...BUT WITNESSES CLAIM THE ATTACKERS MAY HAVE HAD ENHANCED ABILITIES...
...LEADING SOME TO SPECULATE THAT THIS MAY BE PAYBACK FOR HIS PAST INVOLVEMENT WITH THE SO-CALLED RENEGADES...
I HAVE TO GO, TAMARA. I HAVE TO SEE HIM.
I...YES.
YES. OF COURSE.
I'M COMING WITH YOU.
Cancel
edit
Faith
Herbert
Company
home
(555) 555-5555
add phone
home
FaithLovesFirefly@gma
add email
Ringtone
Default

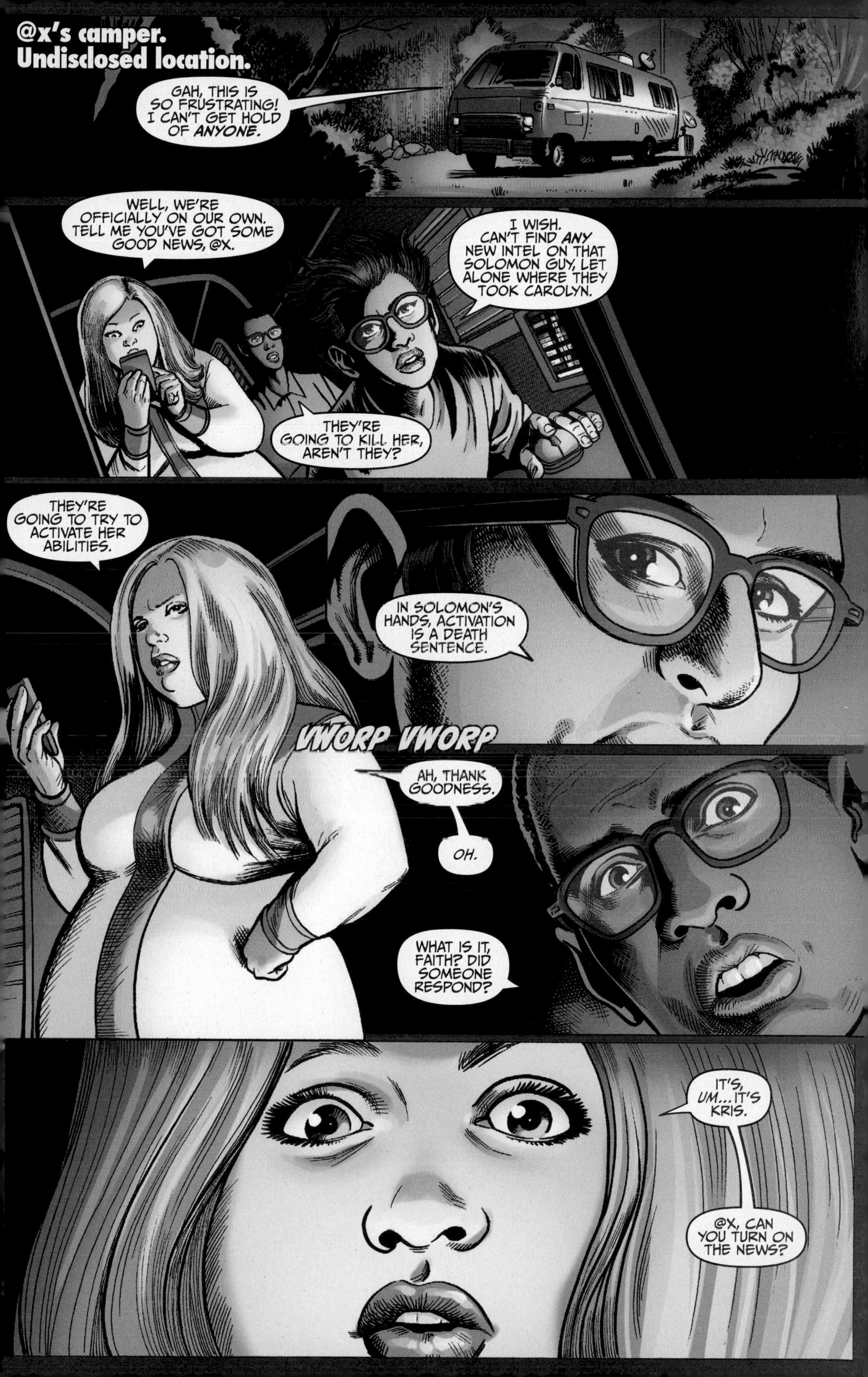
@x's camper.
Undisclosed location.
GAH, THIS IS SO FRUSTRATING! I CAN'T GET HOLD OF ANYONE.
WELL, WE'RE OFFICIALLY ON OUR OWN. TELL ME YOU'VE GOT SOME GOOD NEWS, @X.
I WISH. CAN'T FIND ANY NEW INTEL ON THAT SOLOMON GUY, LET ALONE WHERE THEY TOOK CAROLYN.
THEY'RE GOING TO KILL HER, AREN'T THEY?
THEY'RE GOING TO TRY TO ACTIVATE HER ABILITIES.
IN SOLOMON'S HANDS, ACTIVATION IS A DEATH SENTENCE.
VWORP VWORP
AH, THANK GOODNESS.
OH.
WHAT IS IT, FAITH? DID SOMEONE RESPOND?
IT'S, UM... IT'S KRIS.
@X, CAN YOU TURN ON THE NEWS?

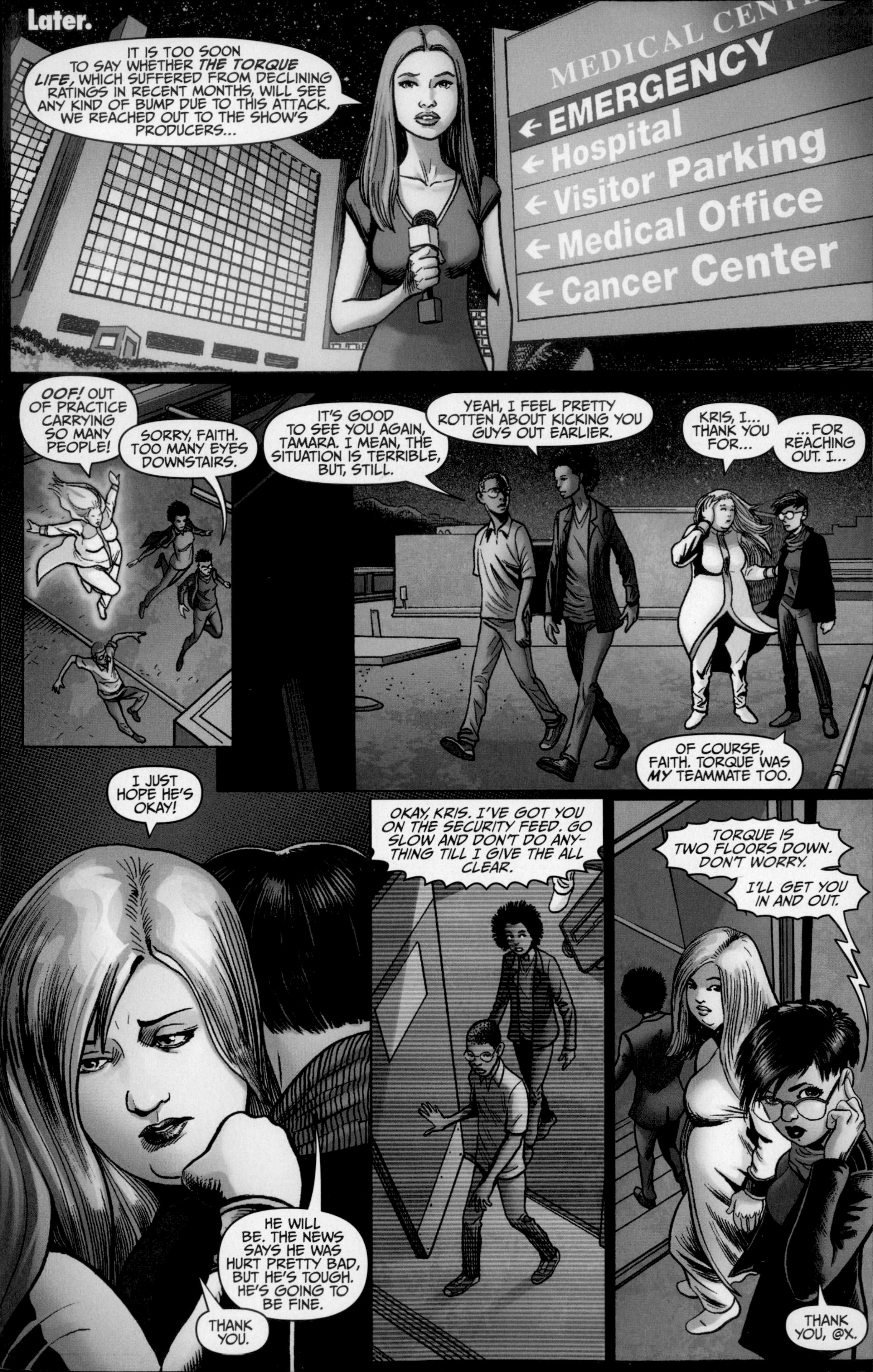
Later.
IT IS TOO SOON TO SAY WHETHER THE TORQUE LIFE, WHICH SUFFERED FROM DECLINING RATINGS IN RECENT MONTHS, WILL SEE ANY KIND OF BUMP DUE TO THIS ATTACK. WE REACHED OUT TO THE SHOW'S PRODUCERS...
MEDICAL CENT
EMERGENCY
Hospital
Visitor Parking
Medical Office
Cancer Center
OOF! OUT OF PRACTICE CARRYING SO MANY PEOPLE!
SORRY, FAITH. TOO MANY EYES DOWNSTAIRS.
IT'S GOOD TO SEE YOU AGAIN, TAMARA. I MEAN, THE SITUATION IS TERRIBLE, BUT, STILL.
YEAH, I FEEL PRETTY ROTTEN ABOUT KICKING YOU GUYS OUT EARLIER.
KRIS, I... THANK YOU FOR...
...FOR REACHING OUT. I...
OF COURSE, FAITH. TORQUE WAS MY TEAMMATE TOO.
I JUST HOPE HE'S OKAY!
HE WILL BE. THE NEWS SAYS HE WAS HURT PRETTY BAD, BUT HE'S TOUGH. HE'S GOING TO BE FINE.
THANK YOU.
OKAY, KRIS. I'VE GOT YOU ON THE SECURITY FEED. GO SLOW AND DON'T DO ANYTHING TILL I GIVE THE ALL CLEAR.
TORQUE IS TWO FLOORS DOWN. DON'T WORRY.
I'LL GET YOU IN AND OUT.
THANK YOU, @X.

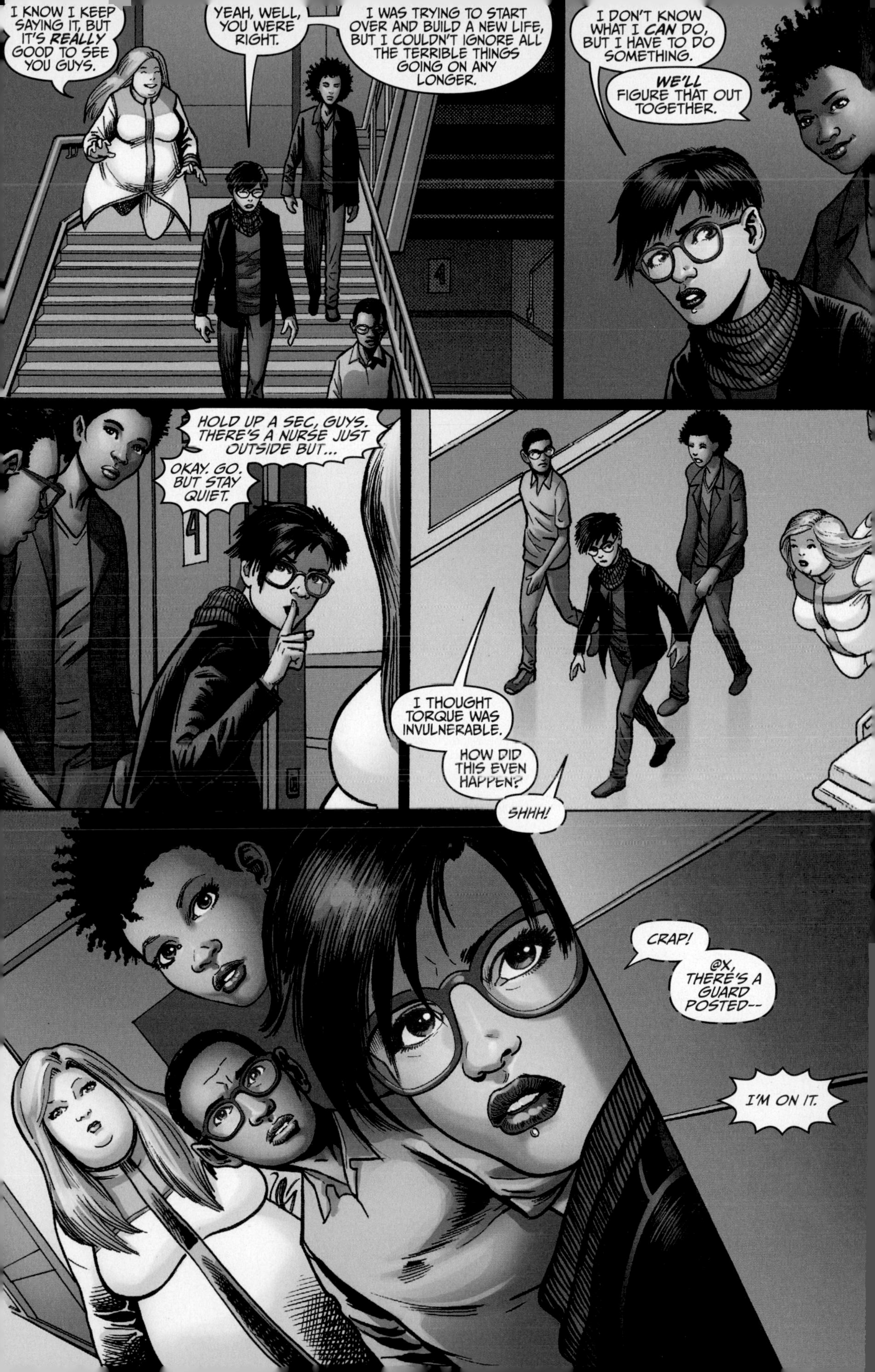
I KNOW I KEEP SAYING IT, BUT IT'S *REALLY* GOOD TO SEE YOU GUYS.
YEAH, WELL, YOU WERE RIGHT.
I WAS TRYING TO START OVER AND BUILD A NEW LIFE, BUT I COULDN'T IGNORE ALL THE TERRIBLE THINGS GOING ON ANY LONGER.
I DON'T KNOW WHAT I *CAN* DO, BUT I HAVE TO DO SOMETHING.
WE'LL FIGURE THAT OUT TOGETHER.
HOLD UP A SEC, GUYS. THERE'S A NURSE JUST OUTSIDE BUT...
OKAY. GO. BUT STAY QUIET.
4
I THOUGHT TORQUE WAS INVULNERABLE.
HOW DID THIS EVEN HAPPEN?
SHHH!
CRAP!
@X, THERE'S A GUARD POSTED--
I'M ON IT.

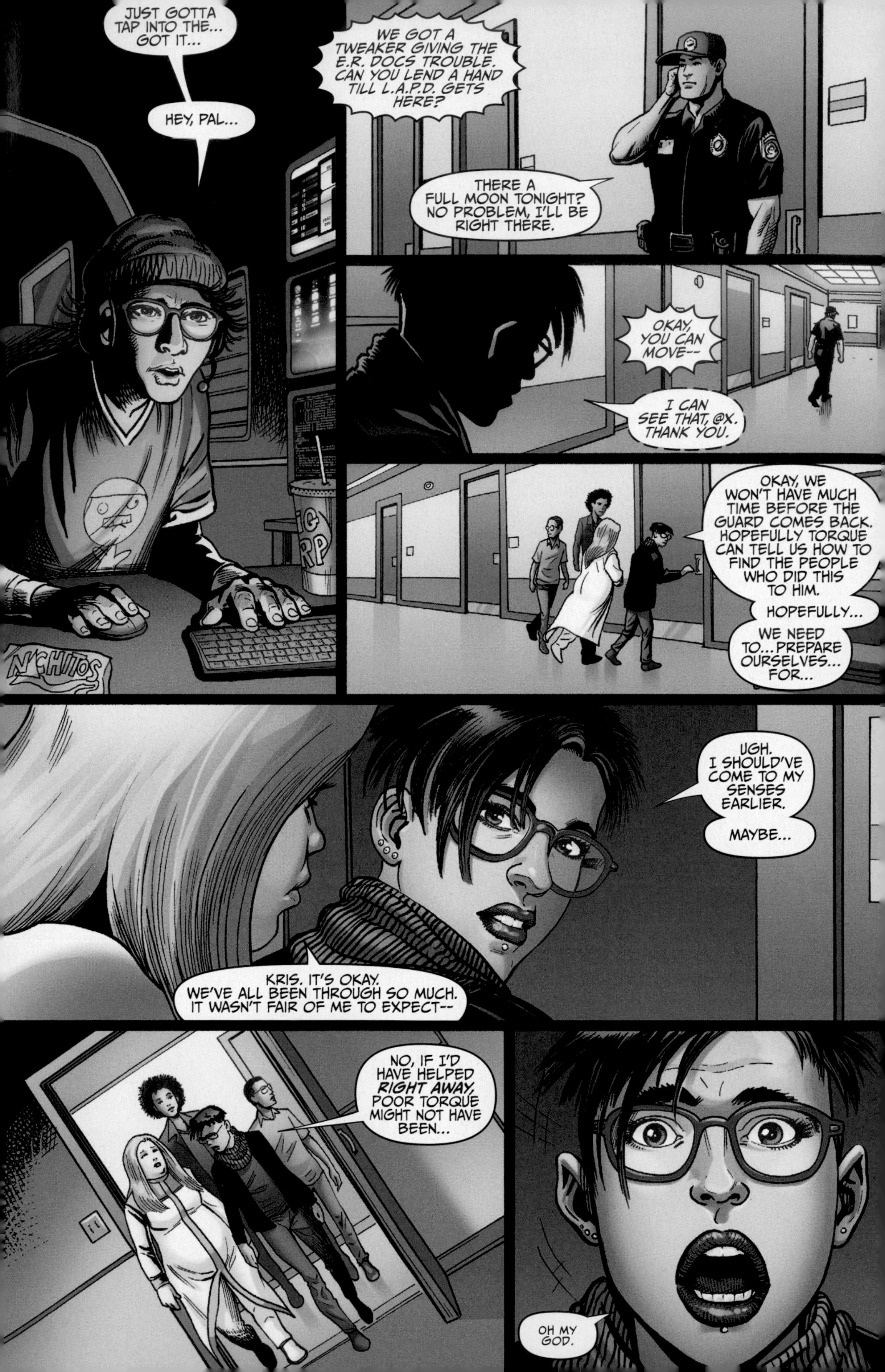
JUST GOTTA TAP INTO THE... GOT IT...
HEY, PAL...
WE GOT A TWEAKER GIVING THE E.R. DOCS TROUBLE. CAN YOU LEND A HAND TILL L.A.P.D. GETS HERE?
THERE A FULL MOON TONIGHT? NO PROBLEM, I'LL BE RIGHT THERE.
N'CHITOS
OKAY, YOU CAN MOVE--
I CAN SEE THAT, @X. THANK YOU.
OKAY, WE WON'T HAVE MUCH TIME BEFORE THE GUARD COMES BACK. HOPEFULLY TORQUE CAN TELL US HOW TO FIND THE PEOPLE WHO DID THIS TO HIM.
HOPEFULLY...
WE NEED TO...PREPARE OURSELVES... FOR...
UGH. I SHOULD'VE COME TO MY SENSES EARLIER.
MAYBE...
KRIS. IT'S OKAY. WE'VE ALL BEEN THROUGH SO MUCH. IT WASN'T FAIR OF ME TO EXPECT--
NO, IF I'D HAVE HELPED RIGHT AWAY, POOR TORQUE MIGHT NOT HAVE BEEN...
OH MY GOD.

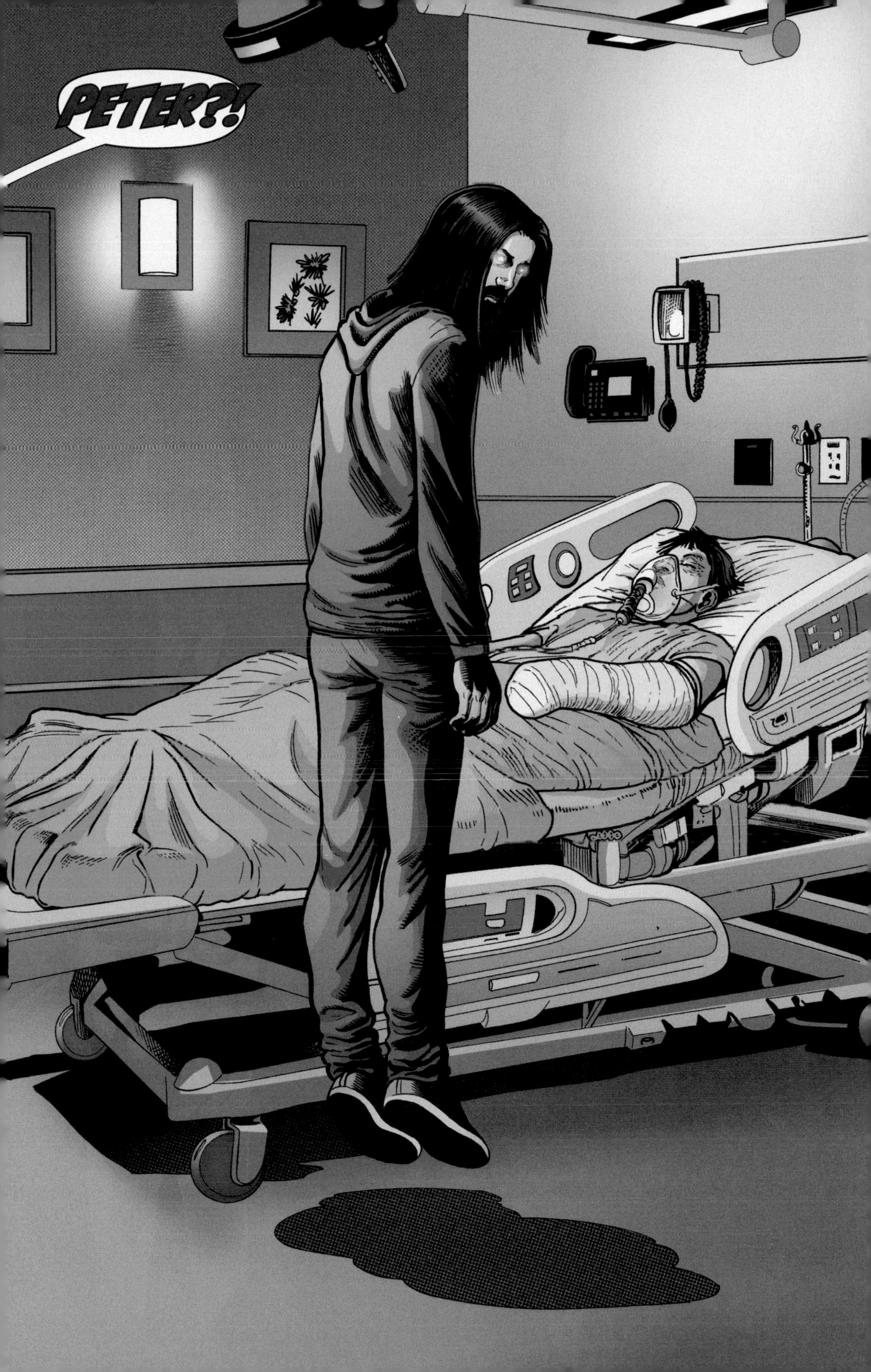
PETER?!

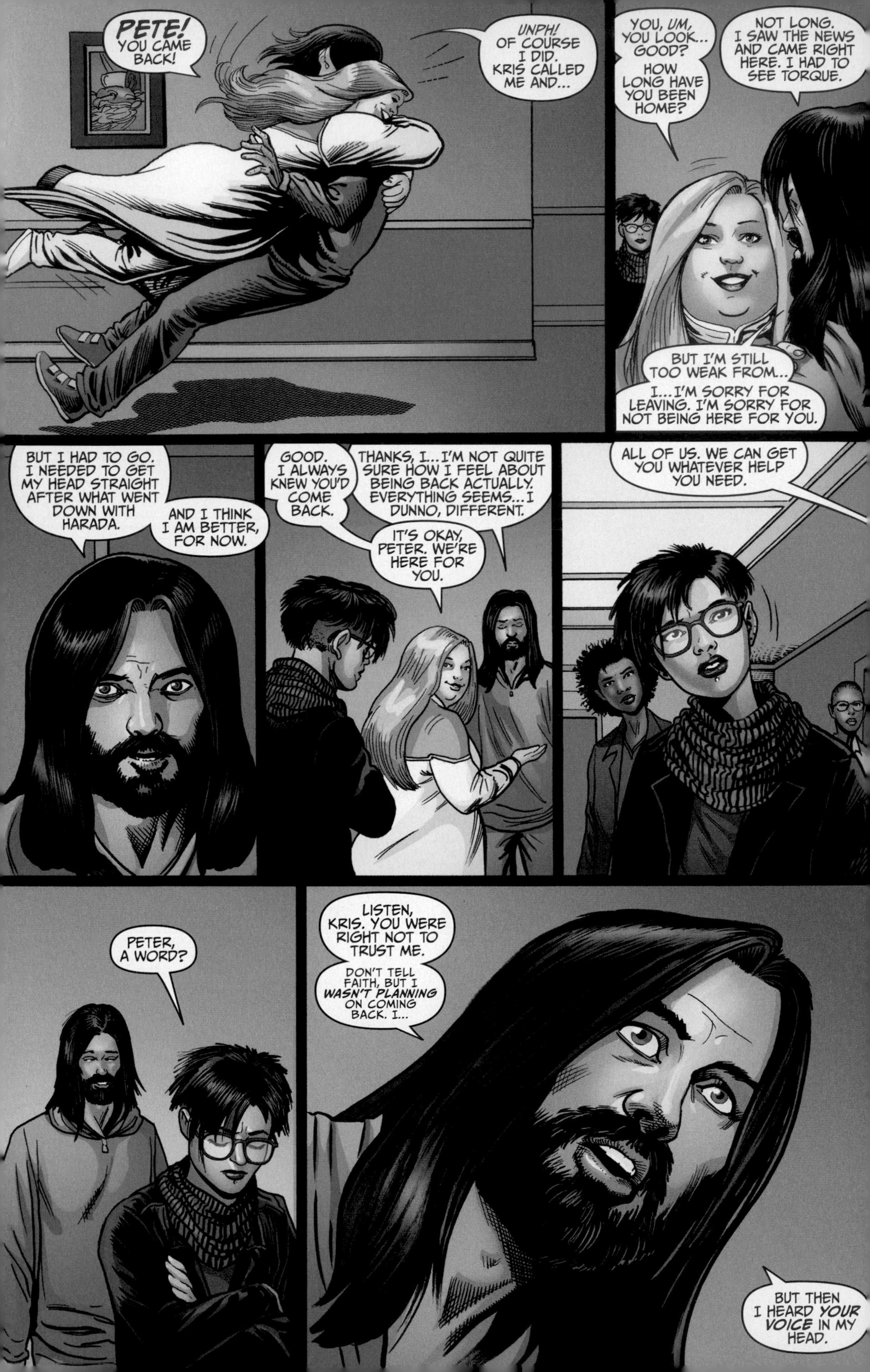
PETE! YOU CAME BACK!
UNPH! OF COURSE I DID. KRIS CALLED ME AND...
YOU, UM, YOU LOOK... GOOD?
HOW LONG HAVE YOU BEEN HOME?
NOT LONG. I SAW THE NEWS AND CAME RIGHT HERE. I HAD TO SEE TORQUE.
BUT I'M STILL TOO WEAK FROM...
I...I'M SORRY FOR LEAVING. I'M SORRY FOR NOT BEING HERE FOR YOU.
BUT I HAD TO GO. I NEEDED TO GET MY HEAD STRAIGHT AFTER WHAT WENT DOWN WITH HARADA.
AND I THINK I AM BETTER, FOR NOW.
GOOD. I ALWAYS KNEW YOU'D COME BACK.
THANKS, I...I'M NOT QUITE SURE HOW I FEEL ABOUT BEING BACK ACTUALLY. EVERYTHING SEEMS...I DUNNO, DIFFERENT.
IT'S OKAY, PETER. WE'RE HERE FOR YOU.
ALL OF US. WE CAN GET YOU WHATEVER HELP YOU NEED.
PETER, A WORD?
LISTEN, KRIS. YOU WERE RIGHT NOT TO TRUST ME.
DON'T TELL FAITH, BUT I WASN'T PLANNING ON COMING BACK. I...
BUT THEN I HEARD YOUR VOICE IN MY HEAD.

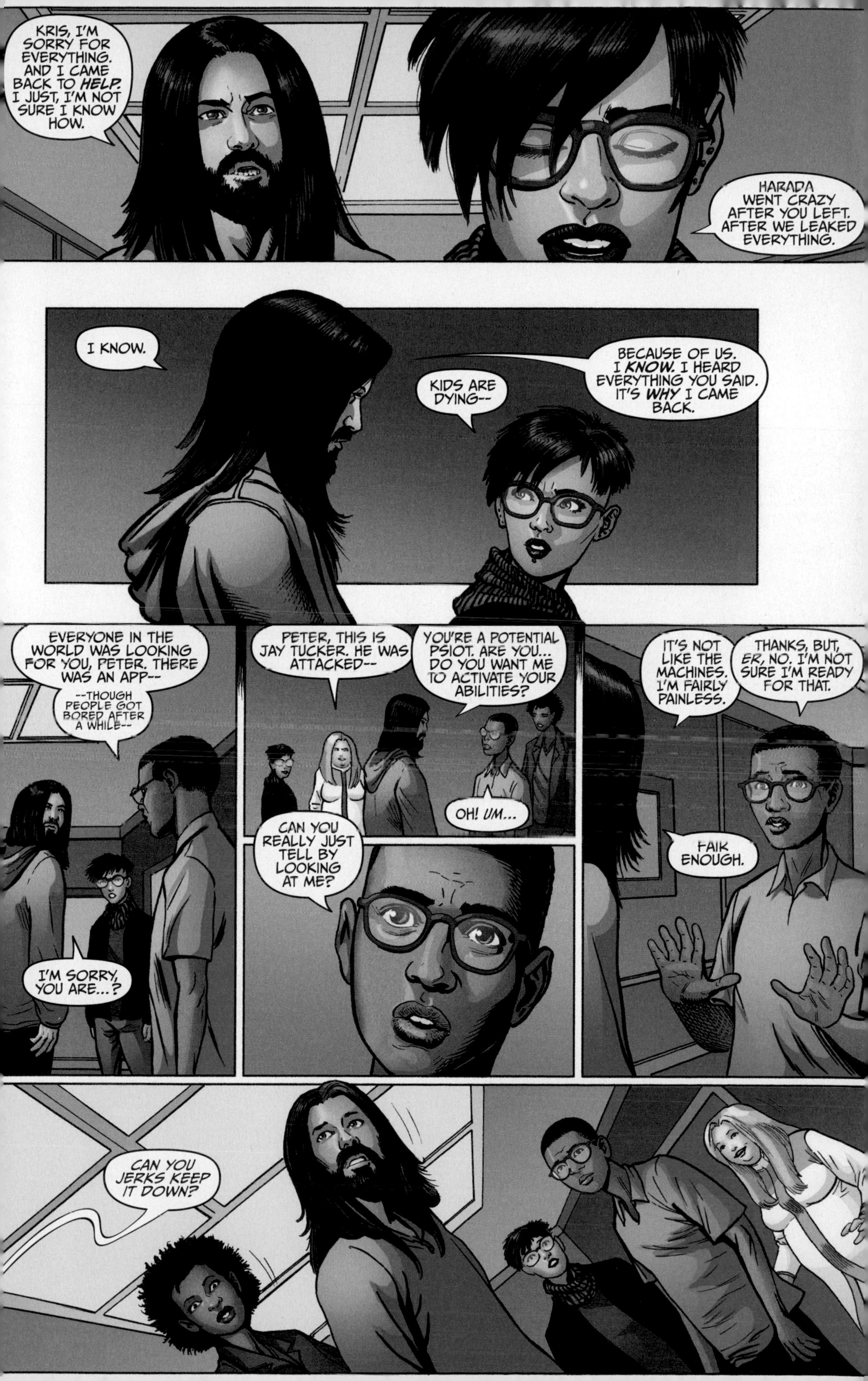
KRIS, I'M SORRY FOR EVERYTHING. AND I CAME BACK TO HELP. I JUST, I'M NOT SURE I KNOW HOW.
HARADA WENT CRAZY AFTER YOU LEFT. AFTER WE LEAKED EVERYTHING.
I KNOW.
KIDS ARE DYING--
BECAUSE OF US. I KNOW. I HEARD EVERYTHING YOU SAID. IT'S WHY I CAME BACK.
EVERYONE IN THE WORLD WAS LOOKING FOR YOU, PETER. THERE WAS AN APP--
--THOUGH PEOPLE GOT BORED AFTER A WHILE--
I'M SORRY, YOU ARE...?
PETER, THIS IS JAY TUCKER. HE WAS ATTACKED--
YOU'RE A POTENTIAL PSIOT. ARE YOU... DO YOU WANT ME TO ACTIVATE YOUR ABILITIES?
OH! UM...
CAN YOU REALLY JUST TELL BY LOOKING AT ME?
IT'S NOT LIKE THE MACHINES. I'M FAIRLY PAINLESS.
THANKS, BUT, ER, NO. I'M NOT SURE I'M READY FOR THAT.
FAIR ENOUGH.
CAN YOU JERKS KEEP IT DOWN?

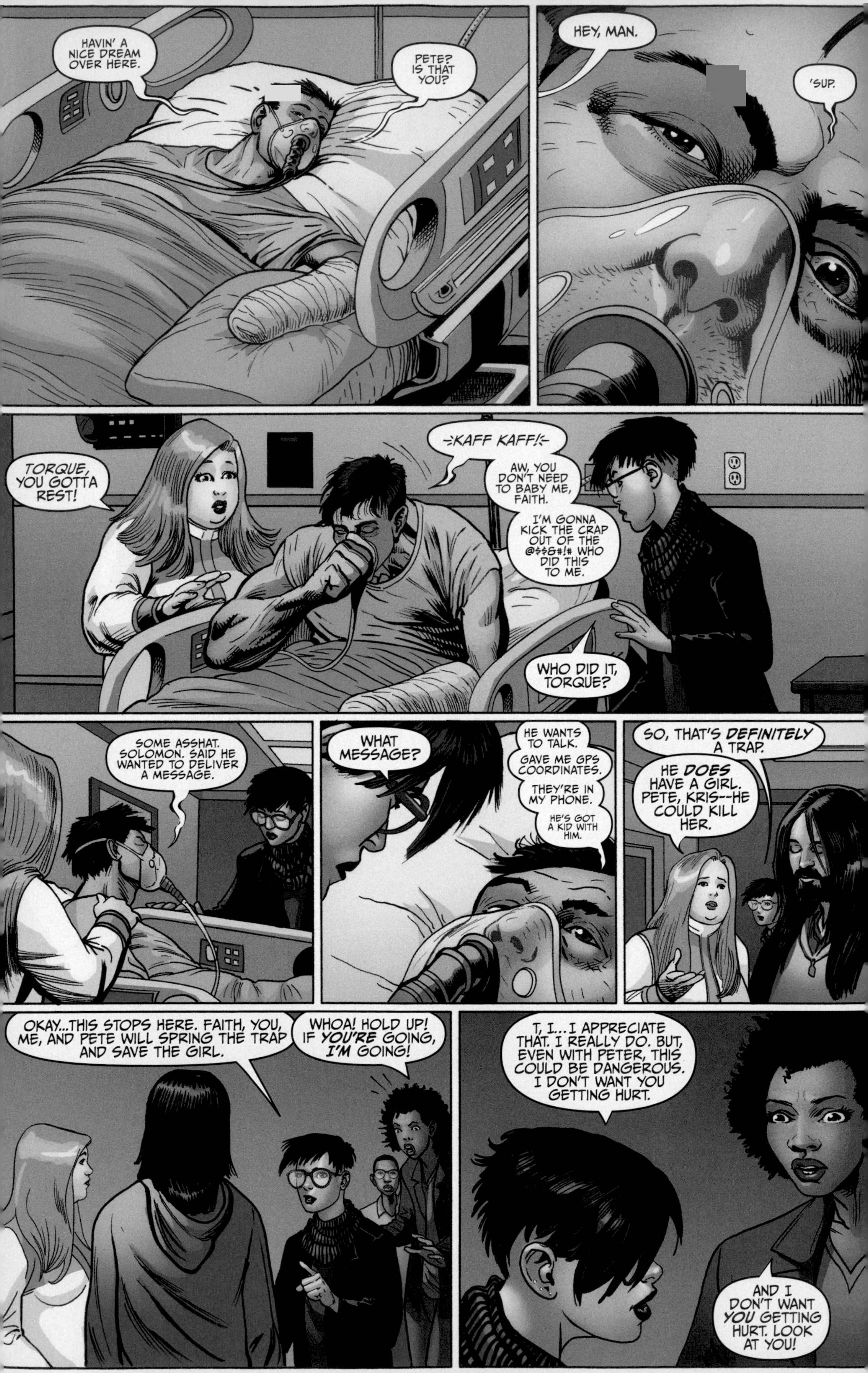
HAVIN' A NICE DREAM OVER HERE.
PETE? IS THAT YOU?
HEY, MAN.
'SUP.
TORQUE, YOU GOTTA REST!
-KAFF KAFF!-
AW, YOU DON'T NEED TO BABY ME, FAITH.
I'M GONNA KICK THE CRAP OUT OF THE @$$&#!# WHO DID THIS TO ME.
WHO DID IT, TORQUE?
SOME ASSHAT. SOLOMON. SAID HE WANTED TO DELIVER A MESSAGE.
WHAT MESSAGE?
HE WANTS TO TALK.
GAVE ME GPS COORDINATES.
THEY'RE IN MY PHONE.
HE'S GOT A KID WITH HIM.
SO, THAT'S DEFINITELY A TRAP.
HE DOES HAVE A GIRL. PETE, KRIS--HE COULD KILL HER.
OKAY...THIS STOPS HERE. FAITH, YOU, ME, AND PETE WILL SPRING THE TRAP AND SAVE THE GIRL.
WHOA! HOLD UP! IF YOU'RE GOING, I'M GOING!
T, I...I APPRECIATE THAT. I REALLY DO. BUT, EVEN WITH PETER, THIS COULD BE DANGEROUS. I DON'T WANT YOU GETTING HURT.
AND I DON'T WANT YOU GETTING HURT. LOOK AT YOU!

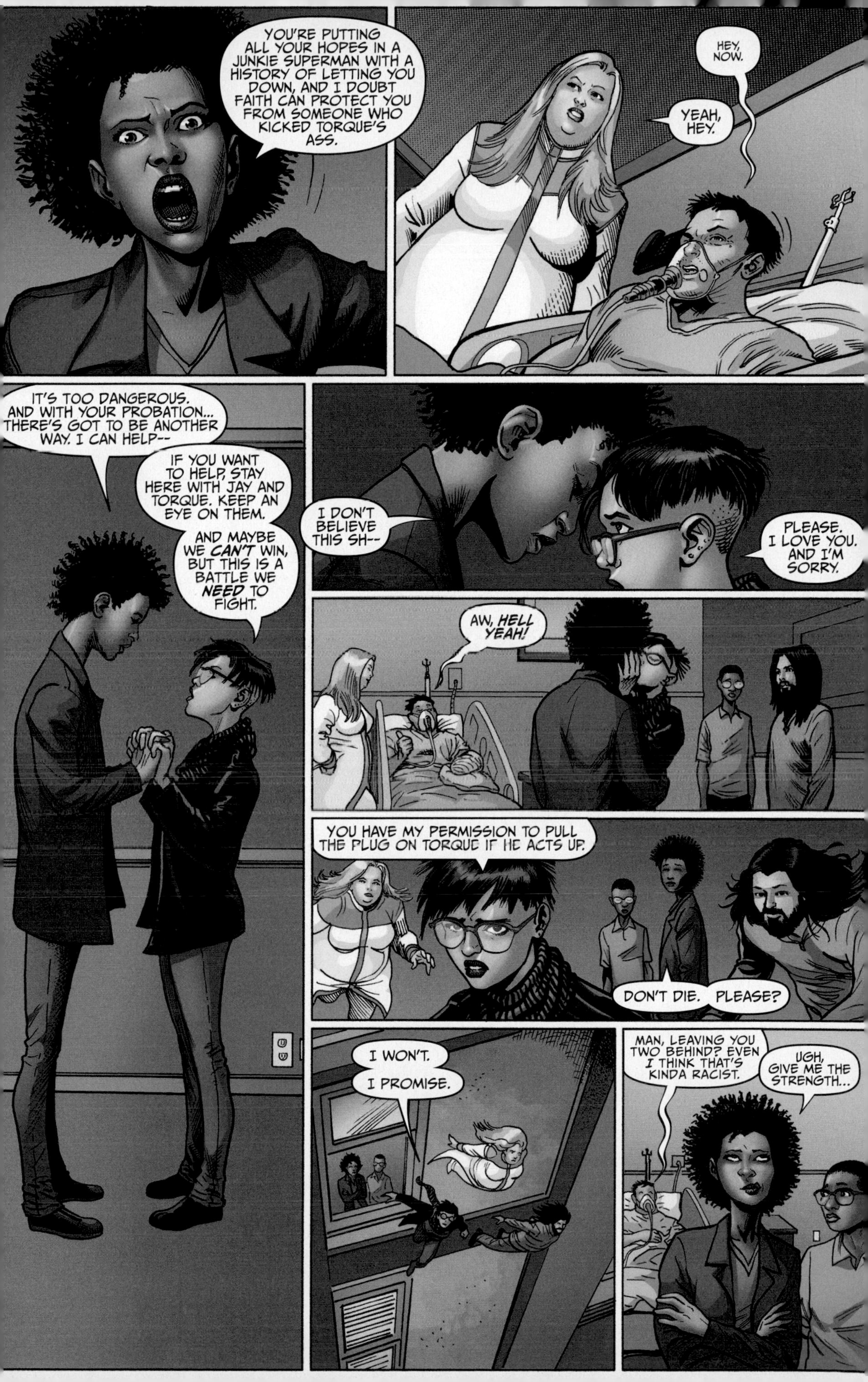
YOU'RE PUTTING ALL YOUR HOPES IN A JUNKIE SUPERMAN WITH A HISTORY OF LETTING YOU DOWN, AND I DOUBT FAITH CAN PROTECT YOU FROM SOMEONE WHO KICKED TORQUE'S ASS.
HEY, NOW.
YEAH, HEY.
IT'S TOO DANGEROUS. AND WITH YOUR PROBATION... THERE'S GOT TO BE ANOTHER WAY. I CAN HELP--
IF YOU WANT TO HELP, STAY HERE WITH JAY AND TORQUE. KEEP AN EYE ON THEM.
AND MAYBE WE CAN'T WIN, BUT THIS IS A BATTLE WE NEED TO FIGHT.
I DON'T BELIEVE THIS SH--
PLEASE. I LOVE YOU. AND I'M SORRY.
AW, HELL YEAH!
YOU HAVE MY PERMISSION TO PULL THE PLUG ON TORQUE IF HE ACTS UP.
DON'T DIE.
PLEASE?
I WON'T.
I PROMISE.
MAN, LEAVING YOU TWO BEHIND? EVEN I THINK THAT'S KINDA RACIST.
UGH, GIVE ME THE STRENGTH...

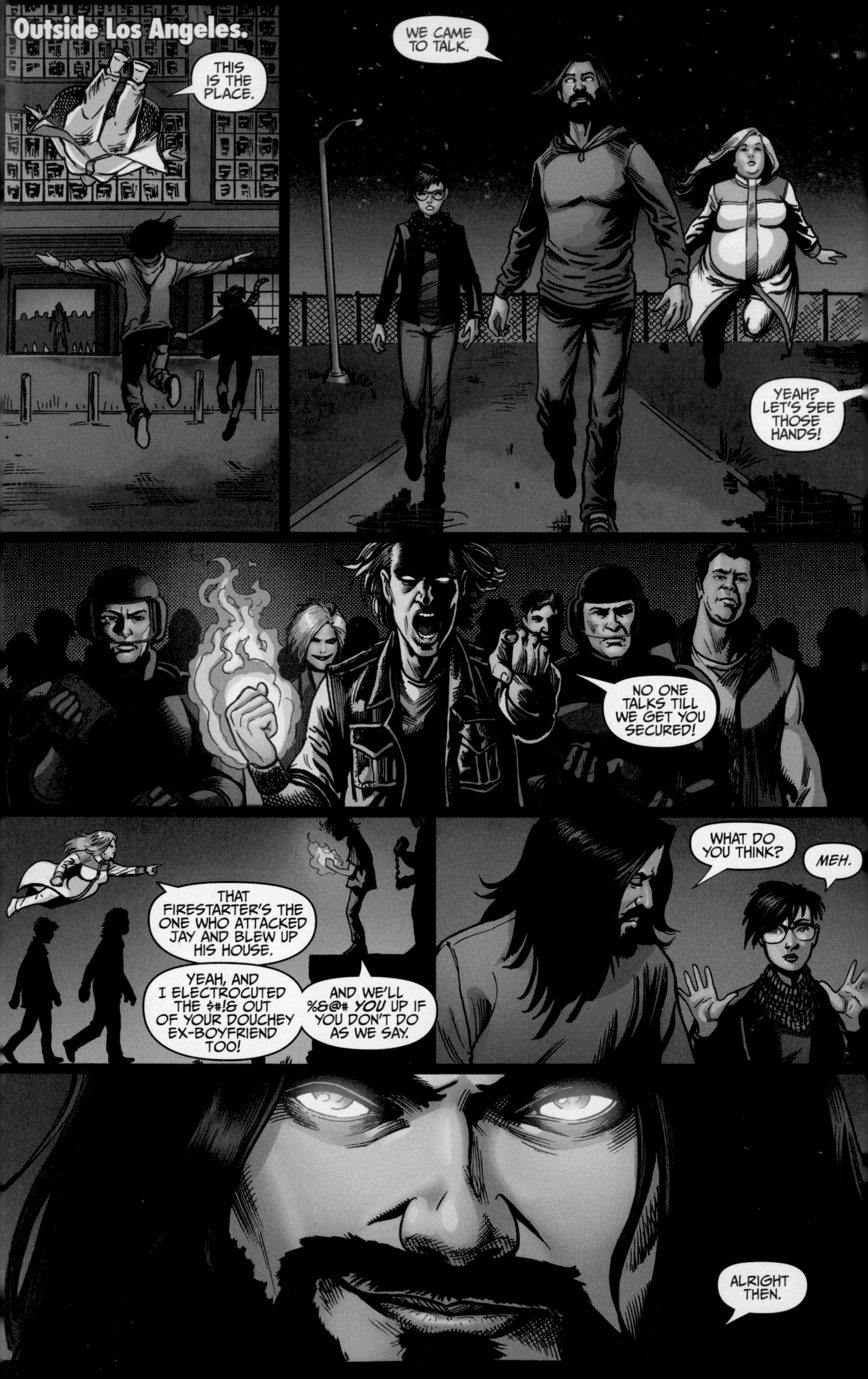

Outside Los Angeles.
THIS IS THE PLACE.
WE CAME TO TALK.
YEAH? LET'S SEE THOSE HANDS!
NO ONE TALKS TILL WE GET YOU SECURED!
THAT FIRESTARTER'S THE ONE WHO ATTACKED JAY AND BLEW UP HIS HOUSE.
YEAH, AND I ELECTROCUTED THE $#!& OUT OF YOUR DOUCHEY EX-BOYFRIEND TOO!
AND WE'LL %&@# YOU UP IF YOU DON'T DO AS WE SAY.
WHAT DO YOU THINK?
MEH.
ALRIGHT THEN.

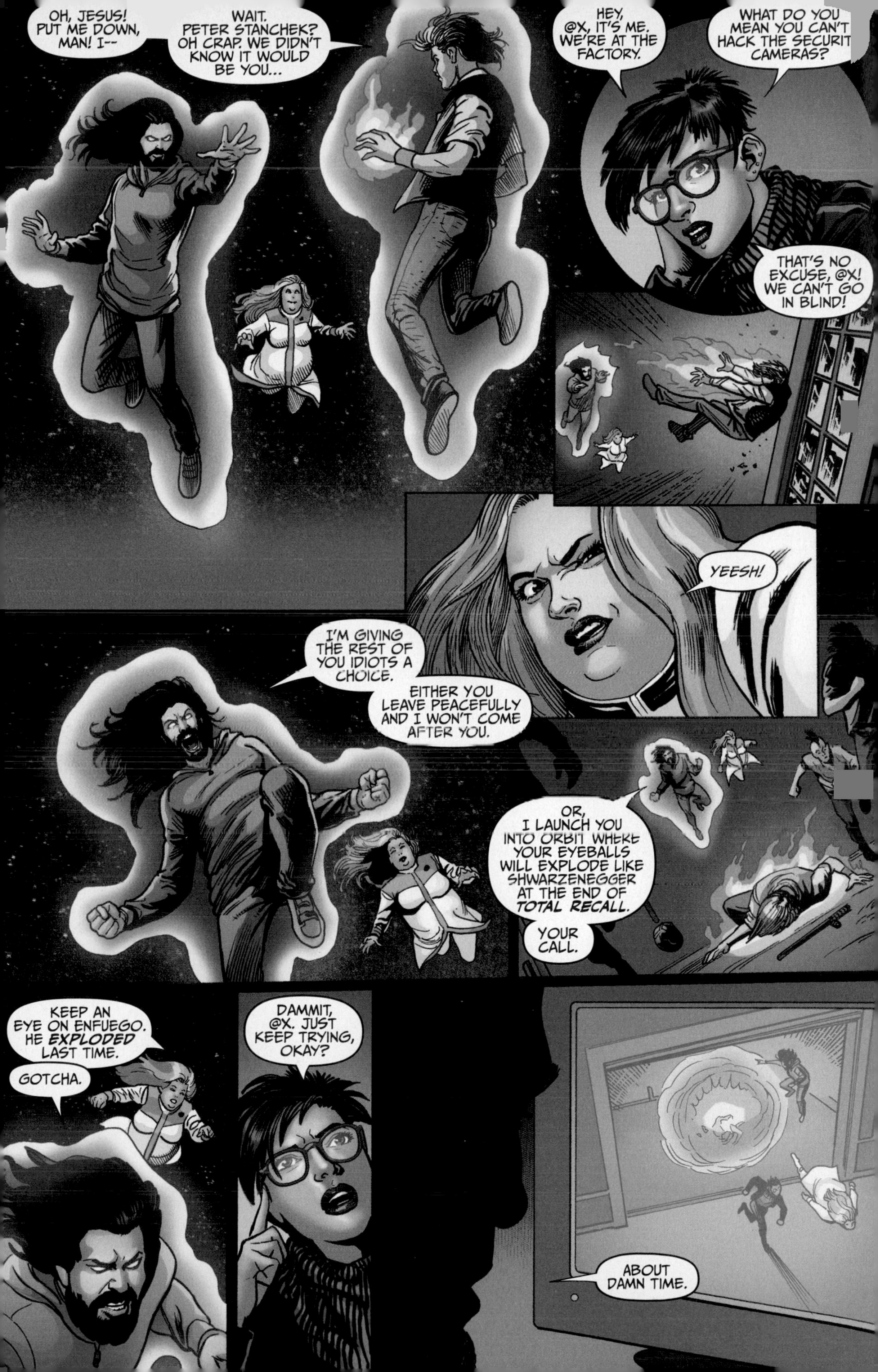

OH, JESUS! PUT ME DOWN, MAN! I--
WAIT. PETER STANCHEK? OH CRAP. WE DIDN'T KNOW IT WOULD BE YOU...
HEY, @X, IT'S ME. WE'RE AT THE FACTORY.
WHAT DO YOU MEAN YOU CAN'T HACK THE SECURIT CAMERAS?
THAT'S NO EXCUSE, @X! WE CAN'T GO IN BLIND!
YEESH!
I'M GIVING THE REST OF YOU IDIOTS A CHOICE.
EITHER YOU LEAVE PEACEFULLY AND I WON'T COME AFTER YOU.
OR, I LAUNCH YOU INTO ORBIT WHERE YOUR EYEBALLS WILL EXPLODE LIKE SHWARZENEGGER AT THE END OF TOTAL RECALL.
YOUR CALL.
KEEP AN EYE ON ENFUEGO. HE EXPLODED LAST TIME.
GOTCHA.
DAMMIT, @X. JUST KEEP TRYING, OKAY?
ABOUT DAMN TIME.

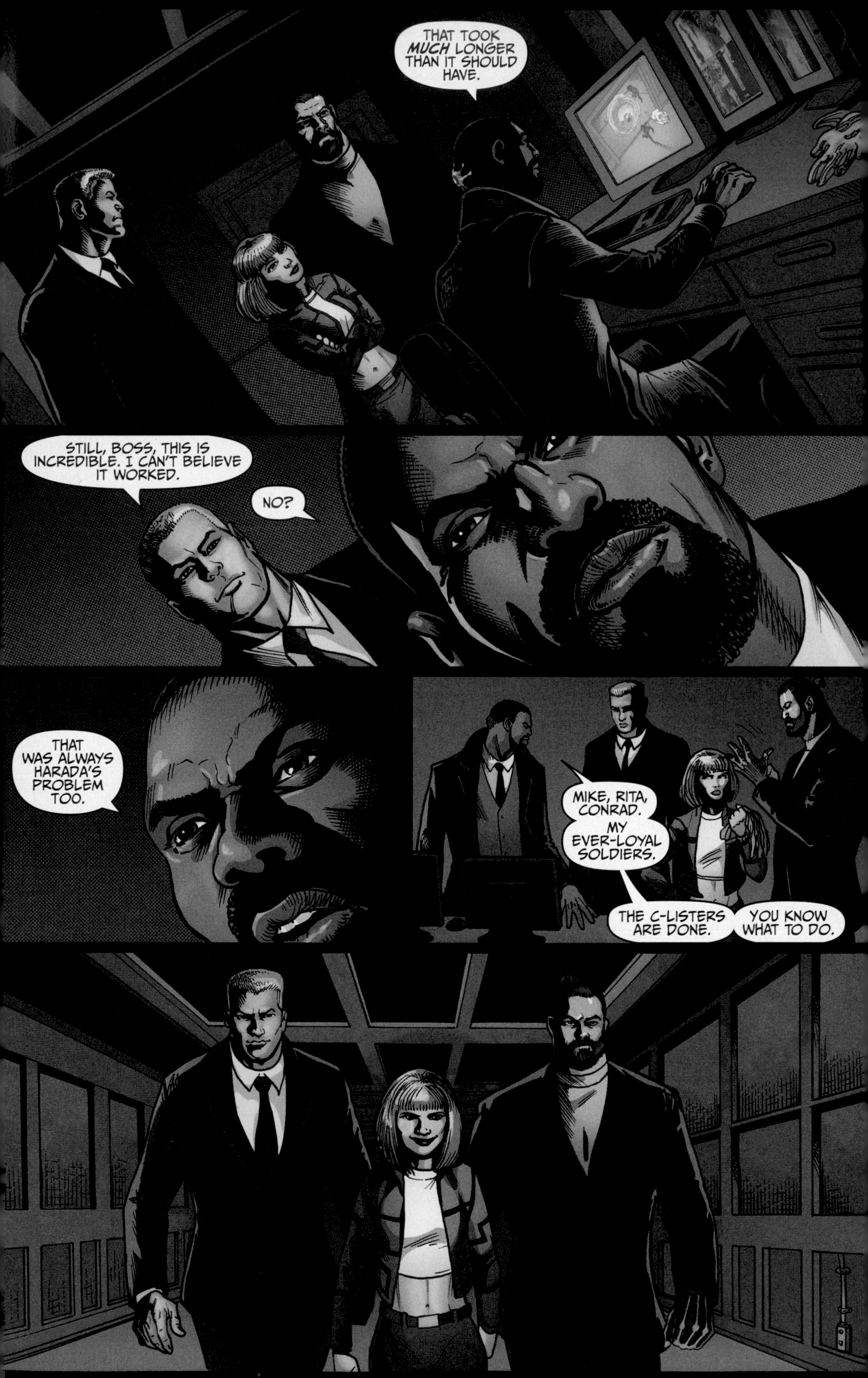
THAT TOOK MUCH LONGER THAN IT SHOULD HAVE.
STILL, BOSS, THIS IS INCREDIBLE. I CAN'T BELIEVE IT WORKED.
NO?
THAT WAS ALWAYS HARADA'S PROBLEM TOO.
MIKE, RITA, CONRAD. MY EVER-LOYAL SOLDIERS.
THE C-LISTERS ARE DONE.
YOU KNOW WHAT TO DO.

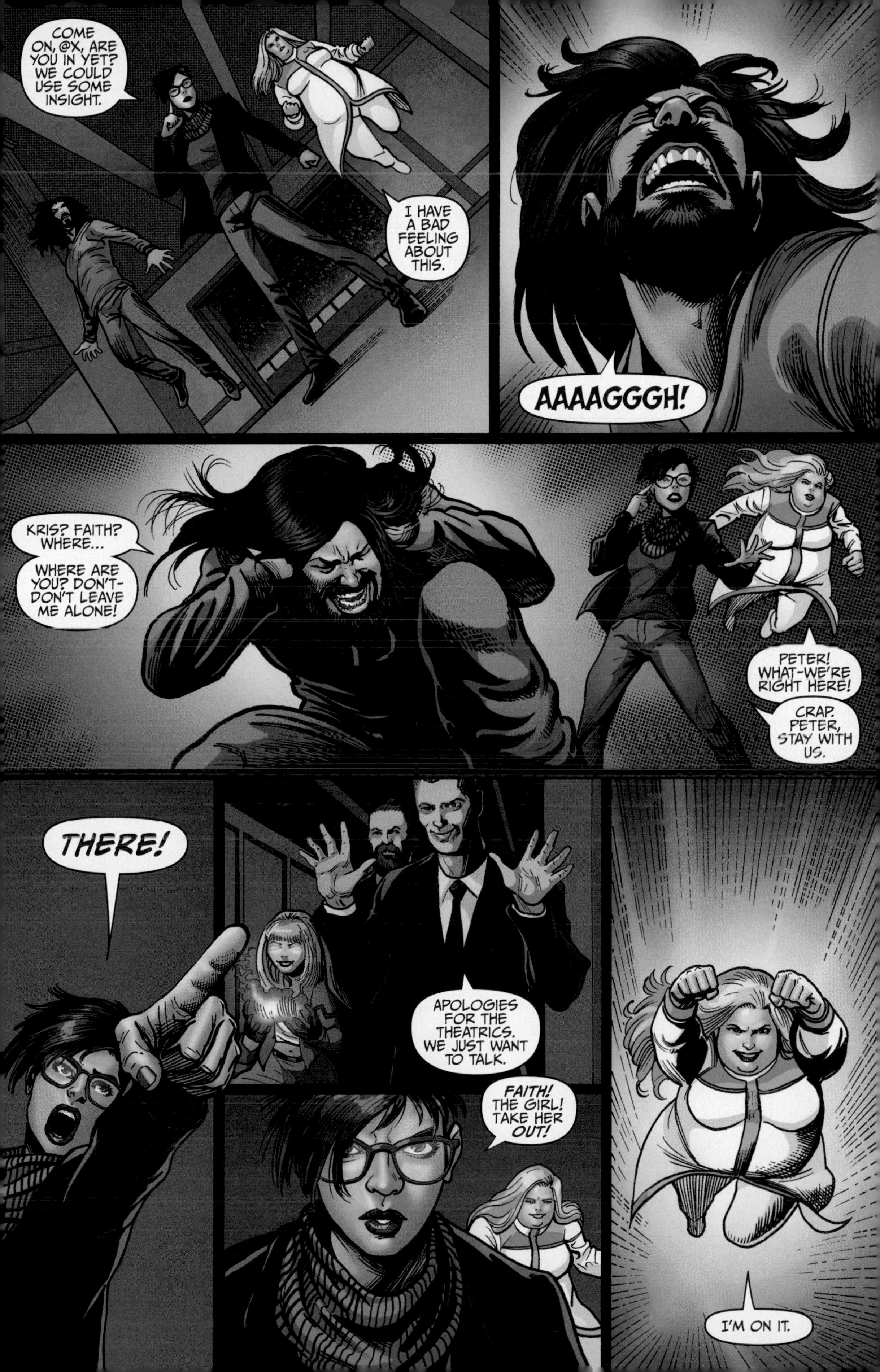

COME ON, @X, ARE YOU IN YET? WE COULD USE SOME INSIGHT.
I HAVE A BAD FEELING ABOUT THIS.
AAAAGGGH!
KRIS? FAITH? WHERE...
WHERE ARE YOU? DON'T- DON'T LEAVE ME ALONE!
PETER! WHAT-WE'RE RIGHT HERE!
CRAP. PETER, STAY WITH US.
THERE!
APOLOGIES FOR THE THEATRICS. WE JUST WANT TO TALK.
FAITH! THE GIRL! TAKE HER *OUT!*
I'M ON IT.

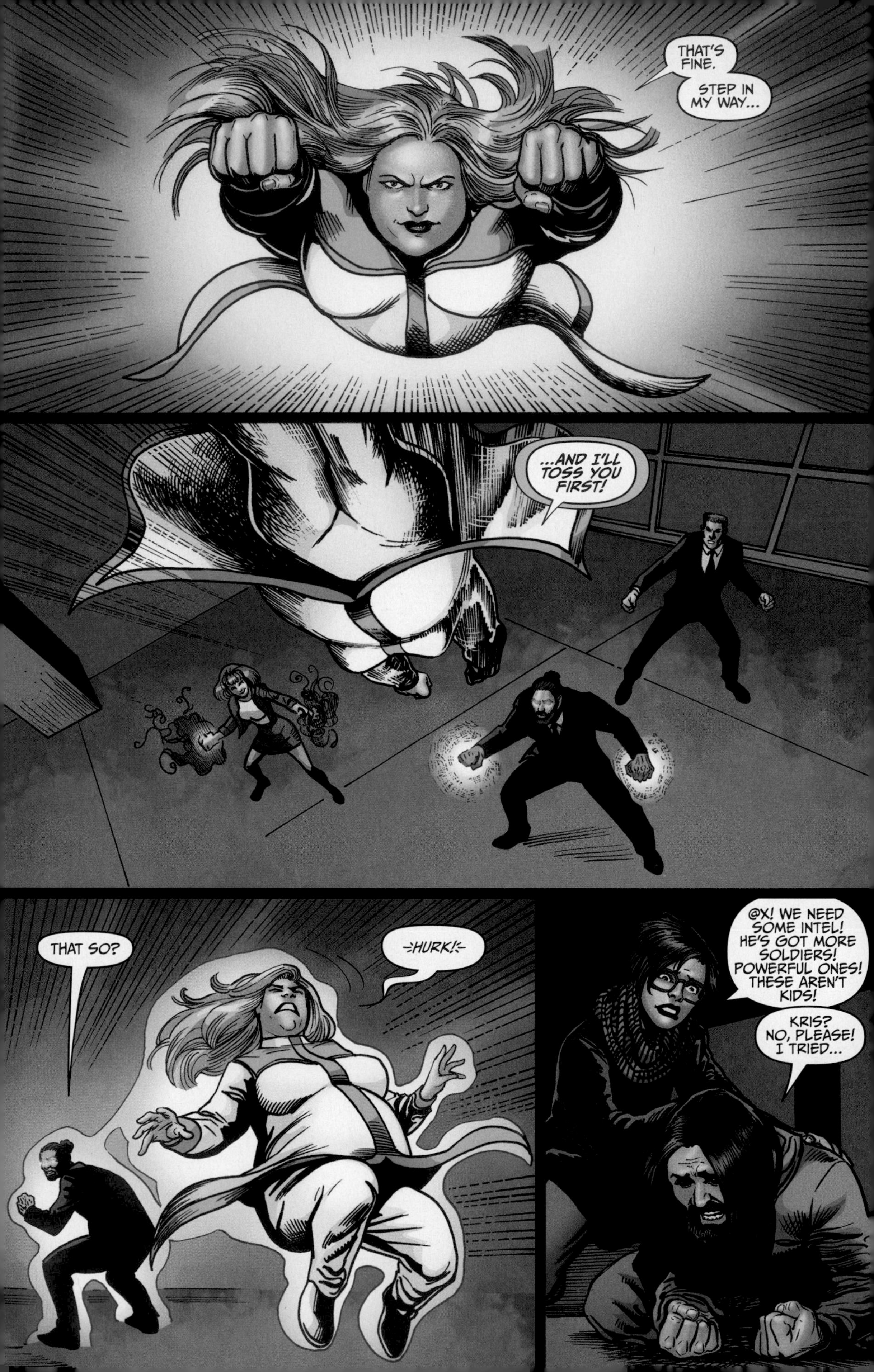
THAT'S FINE.
STEP IN MY WAY...
...AND I'LL TOSS YOU FIRST!
THAT SO?
-HURK!-
@X! WE NEED SOME INTEL! HE'S GOT MORE SOLDIERS! POWERFUL ONES! THESE AREN'T KIDS!
KRIS? NO, PLEASE! I TRIED...

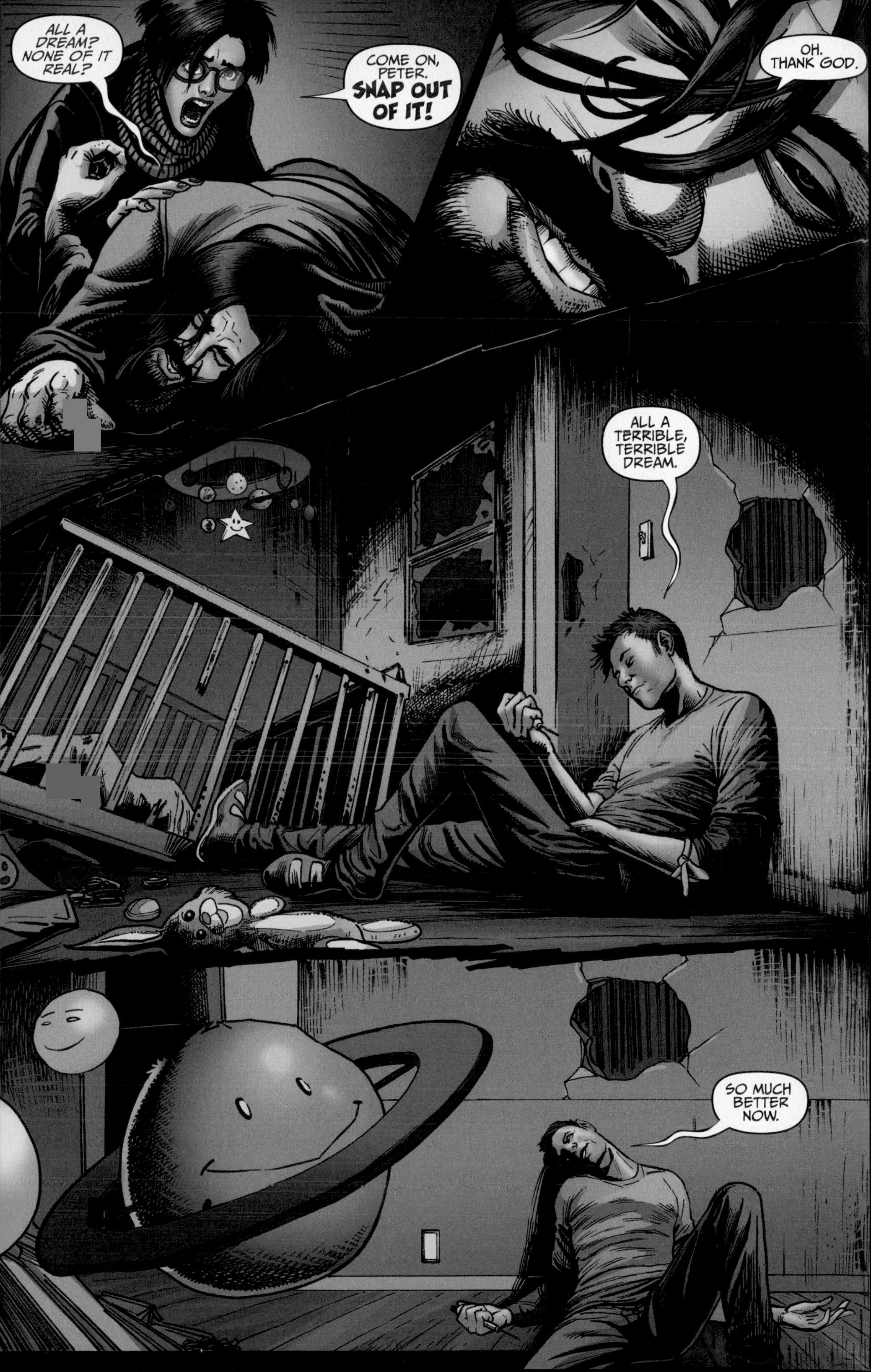
ALL A DREAM? NONE OF IT REAL?
COME ON, PETER. SNAP OUT OF IT!
OH. THANK GOD.
ALL A TERRIBLE, TERRIBLE DREAM.
SO MUCH BETTER NOW.

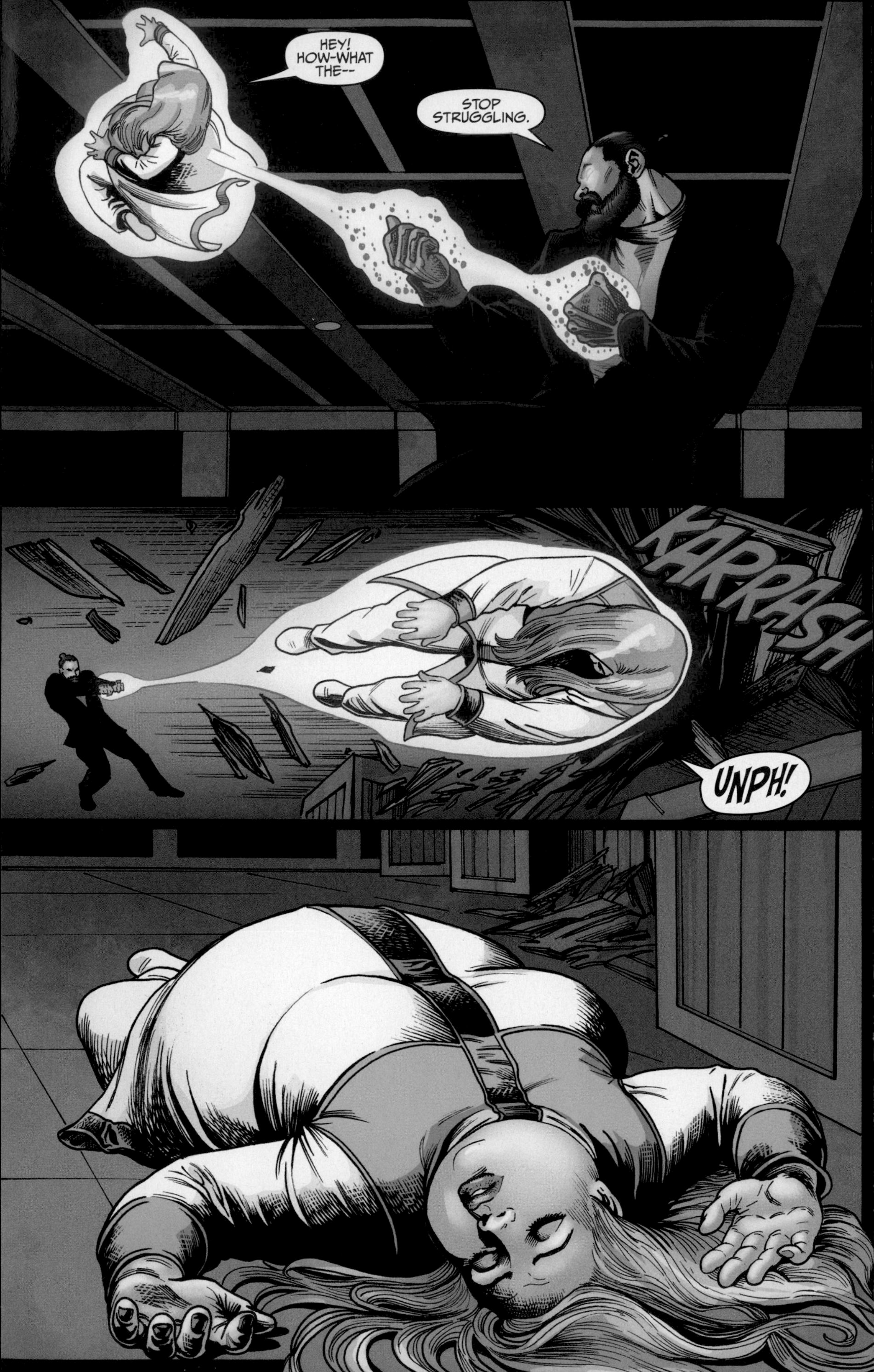
HEY! HOW-WHAT THE--
STOP STRUGGLING.
KARRASH
UNPH!

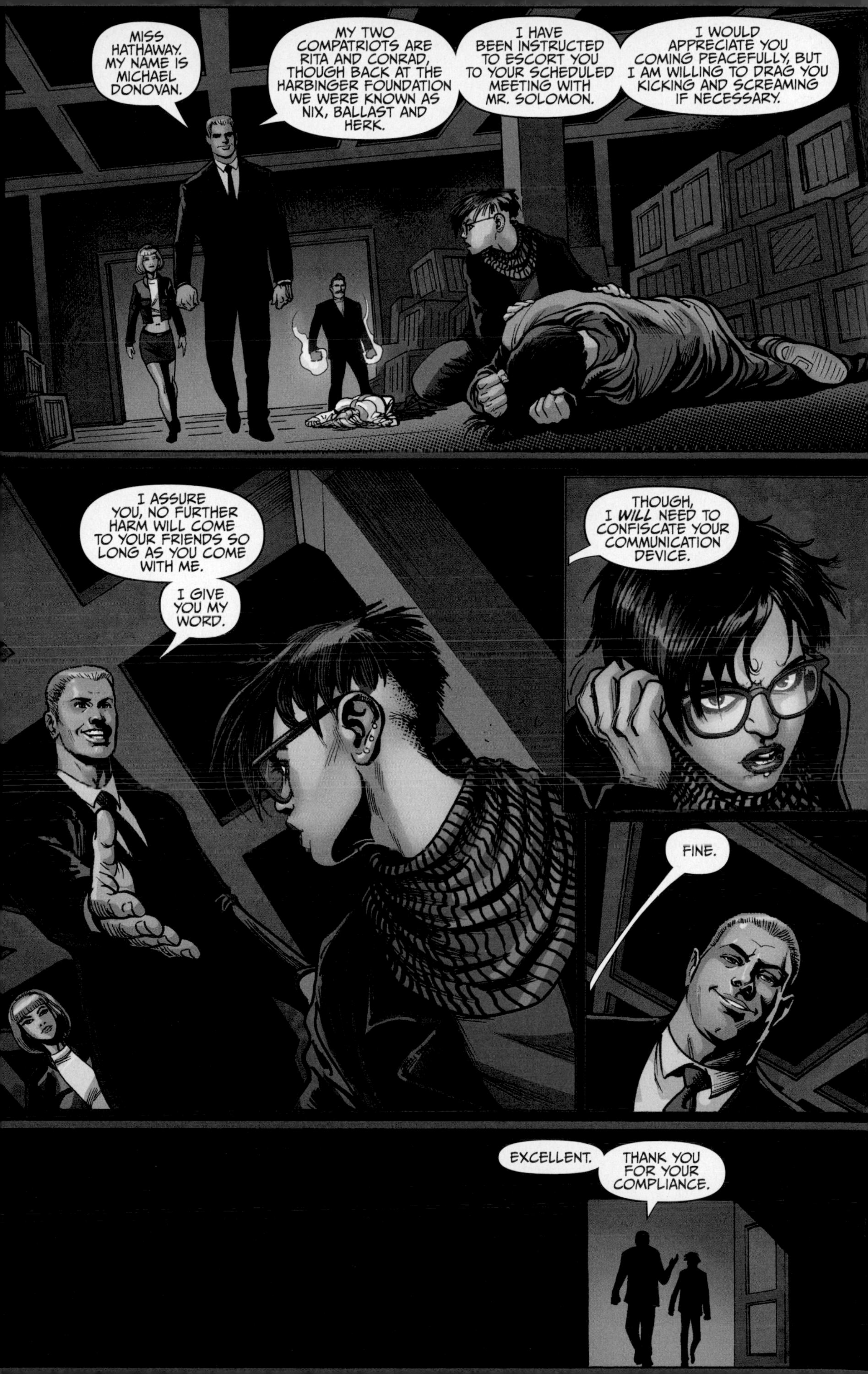
MISS HATHAWAY. MY NAME IS MICHAEL DONOVAN.
MY TWO COMPATRIOTS ARE RITA AND CONRAD, THOUGH BACK AT THE HARBINGER FOUNDATION WE WERE KNOWN AS NIX, BALLAST AND HERK.
I HAVE BEEN INSTRUCTED TO ESCORT YOU TO YOUR SCHEDULED MEETING WITH MR. SOLOMON.
I WOULD APPRECIATE YOU COMING PEACEFULLY, BUT I AM WILLING TO DRAG YOU KICKING AND SCREAMING IF NECESSARY.
I ASSURE YOU, NO FURTHER HARM WILL COME TO YOUR FRIENDS SO LONG AS YOU COME WITH ME.
I GIVE YOU MY WORD.
THOUGH, I *WILL* NEED TO CONFISCATE YOUR COMMUNICATION DEVICE.
FINE.
EXCELLENT.
THANK YOU FOR YOUR COMPLIANCE.

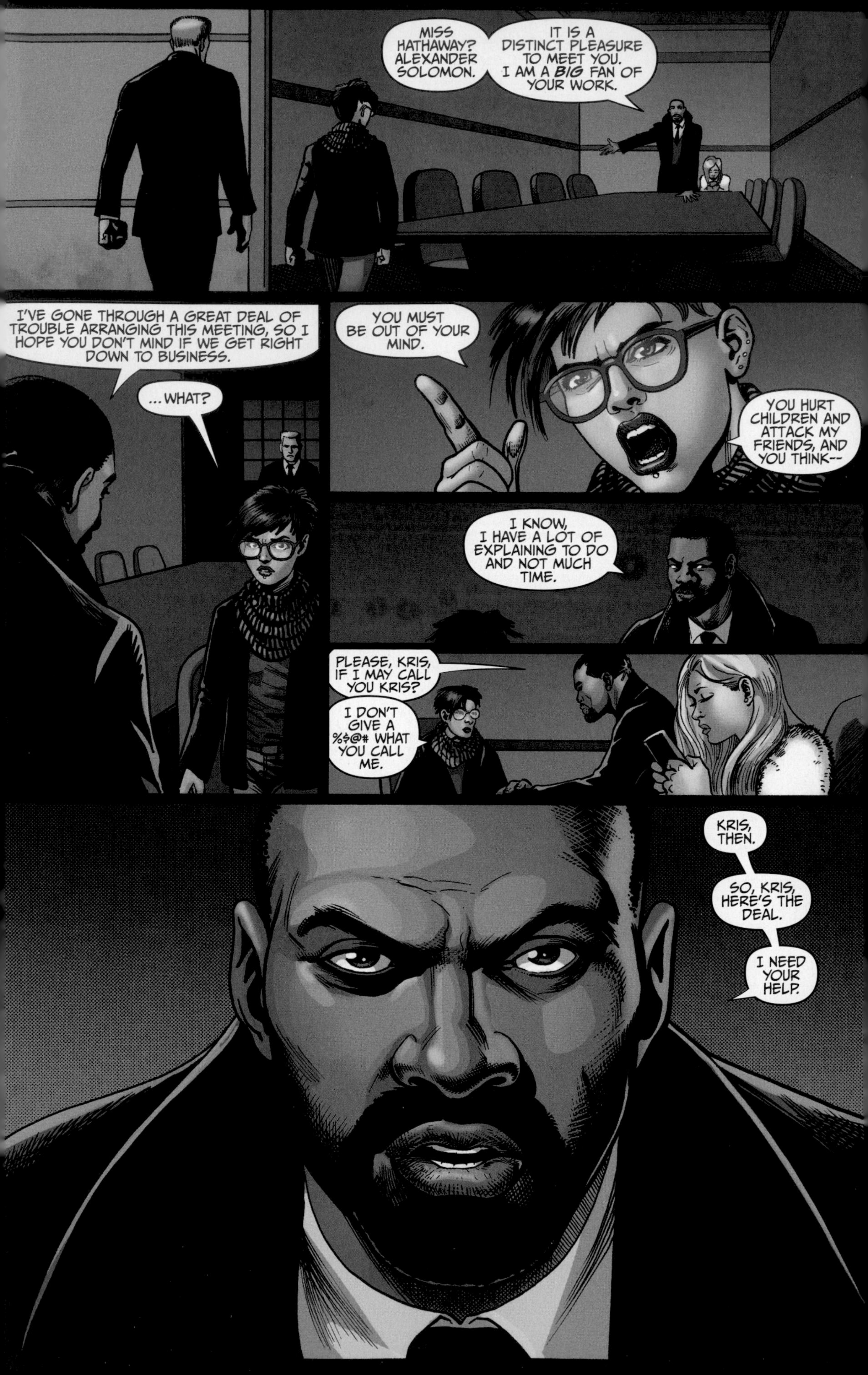
MISS HATHAWAY? ALEXANDER SOLOMON.
IT IS A DISTINCT PLEASURE TO MEET YOU. I AM A BIG FAN OF YOUR WORK.
I'VE GONE THROUGH A GREAT DEAL OF TROUBLE ARRANGING THIS MEETING, SO I HOPE YOU DON'T MIND IF WE GET RIGHT DOWN TO BUSINESS.
...WHAT?
YOU MUST BE OUT OF YOUR MIND.
YOU HURT CHILDREN AND ATTACK MY FRIENDS, AND YOU THINK--
I KNOW, I HAVE A LOT OF EXPLAINING TO DO AND NOT MUCH TIME.
PLEASE, KRIS, IF I MAY CALL YOU KRIS?
I DON'T GIVE A %$@# WHAT YOU CALL ME.
KRIS, THEN.
SO, KRIS, HERE'S THE DEAL.
I NEED YOUR HELP.

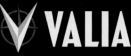

VALIANT | RAFER ROBERTS | DARICK ROBERTSON | JUAN JOSÉ RYP
RICHARD CLARK | BRIAN REBER

#4

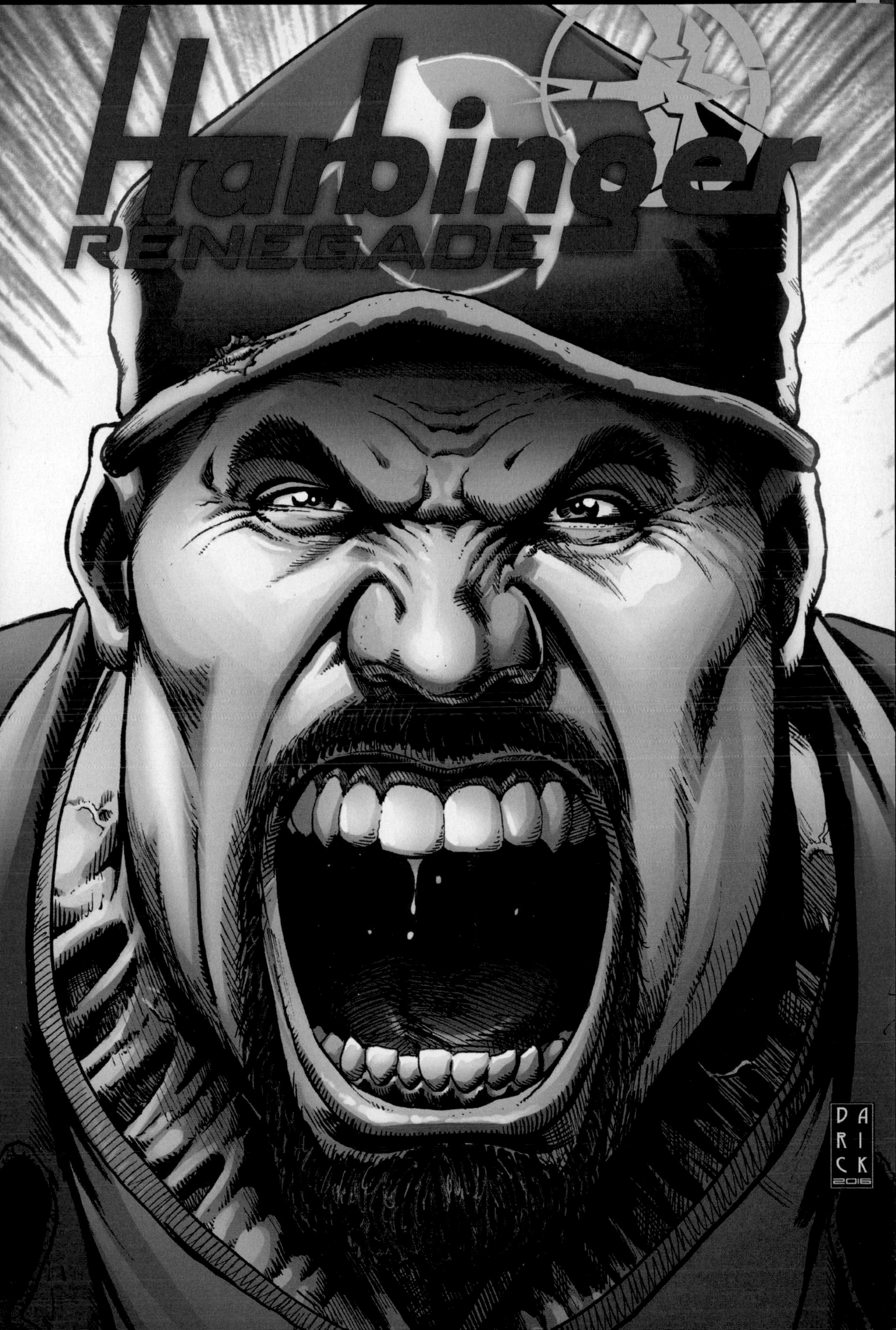
Harbinger
RENEGADE
DARICK
2016

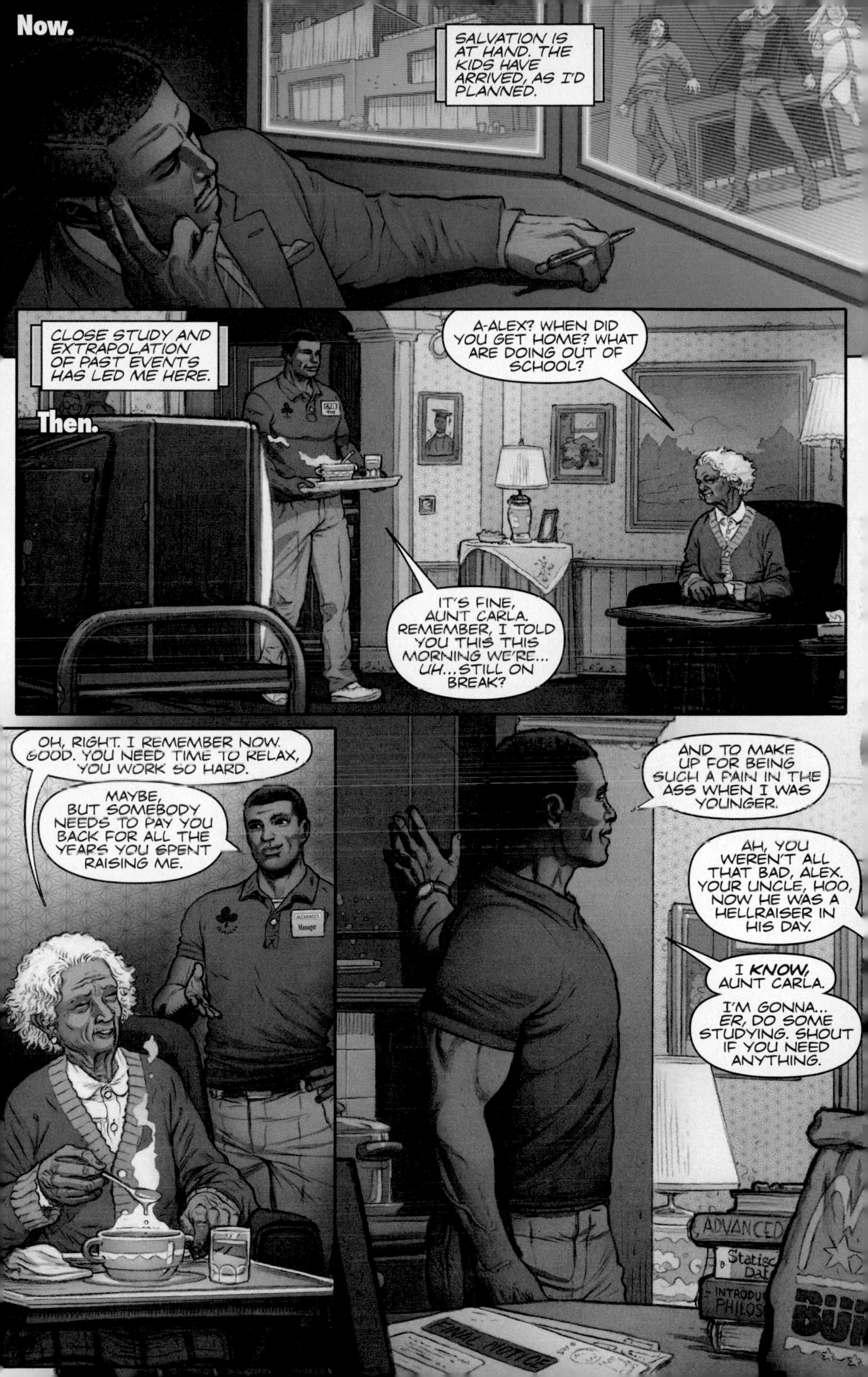
Now.
SALVATION IS AT HAND. THE KIDS HAVE ARRIVED, AS I'D PLANNED.
CLOSE STUDY AND EXTRAPOLATION OF PAST EVENTS HAS LED ME HERE.
Then.
A-ALEX? WHEN DID YOU GET HOME? WHAT ARE DOING OUT OF SCHOOL?
IT'S FINE, AUNT CARLA. REMEMBER, I TOLD YOU THIS THIS MORNING WE'RE... UH...STILL ON BREAK?
OH, RIGHT. I REMEMBER NOW. GOOD. YOU NEED TIME TO RELAX, YOU WORK SO HARD.
MAYBE, BUT SOMEBODY NEEDS TO PAY YOU BACK FOR ALL THE YEARS YOU SPENT RAISING ME.
ALEXANDER
Manager
AND TO MAKE UP FOR BEING SUCH A PAIN IN THE ASS WHEN I WAS YOUNGER.
AH, YOU WEREN'T ALL THAT BAD, ALEX. YOUR UNCLE, HOO, NOW HE WAS A HELLRAISER IN HIS DAY.
I *KNOW,* AUNT CARLA.
I'M GONNA... ER, DO SOME STUDYING. SHOUT IF YOU NEED ANYTHING.
ADVANCED
FINAL NOTICE

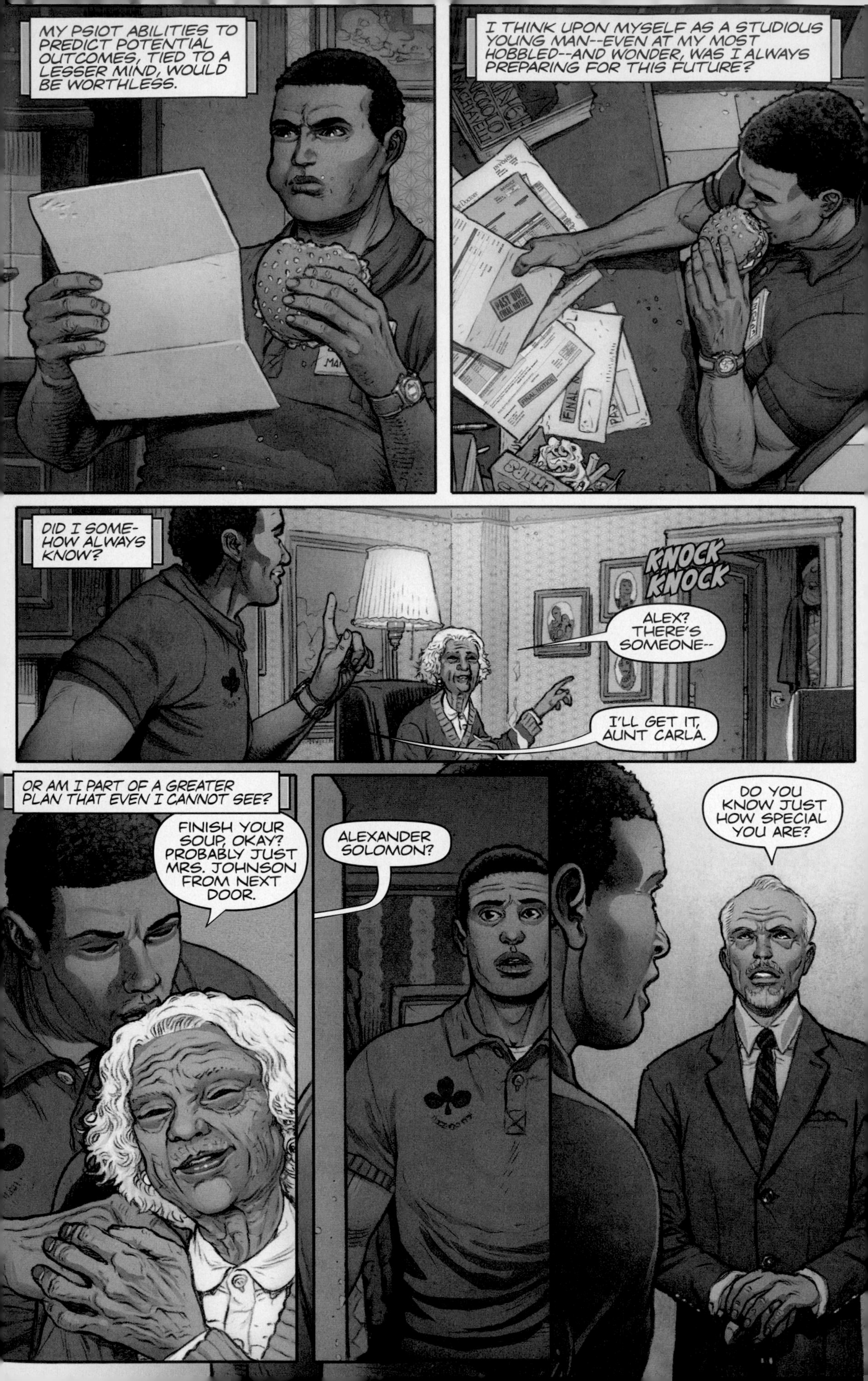
MY PSIOT ABILITIES TO PREDICT POTENTIAL OUTCOMES, TIED TO A LESSER MIND, WOULD BE WORTHLESS.
I THINK UPON MYSELF AS A STUDIOUS YOUNG MAN--EVEN AT MY MOST HOBBLED--AND WONDER, WAS I ALWAYS PREPARING FOR THIS FUTURE?
PAST DUE FINAL NOTICE
FINAL NOTICE
DID I SOMEHOW ALWAYS KNOW?
KNOCK KNOCK
ALEX? THERE'S SOMEONE--
I'LL GET IT, AUNT CARLA.
OR AM I PART OF A GREATER PLAN THAT EVEN I CANNOT SEE?
FINISH YOUR SOUP, OKAY? PROBABLY JUST MRS. JOHNSON FROM NEXT DOOR.
ALEXANDER SOLOMON?
DO YOU KNOW JUST HOW SPECIAL YOU ARE?

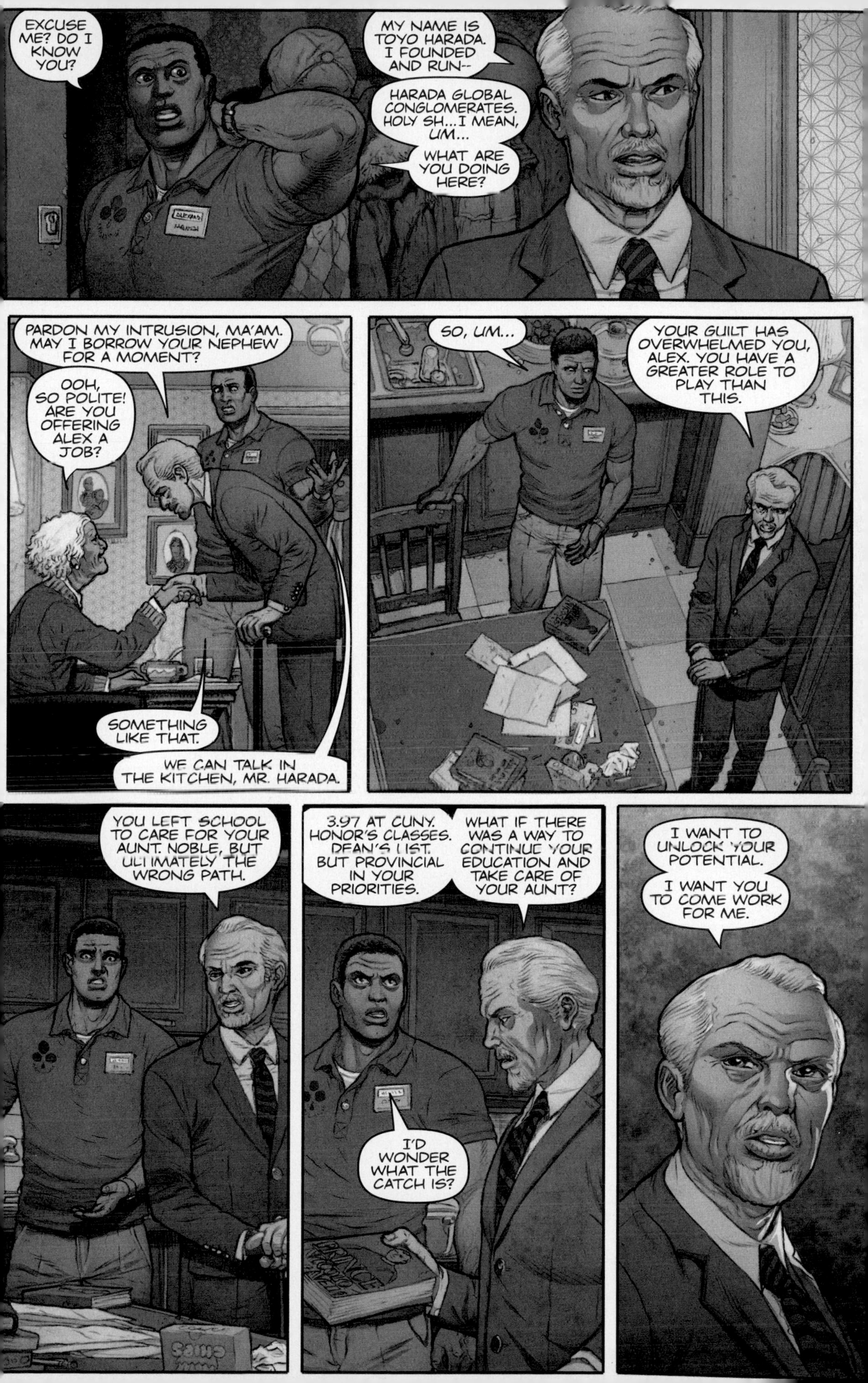
EXCUSE ME? DO I KNOW YOU?
MY NAME IS TOYO HARADA. I FOUNDED AND RUN--
HARADA GLOBAL CONGLOMERATES. HOLY SH...I MEAN, UM...
WHAT ARE YOU DOING HERE?
PARDON MY INTRUSION, MA'AM. MAY I BORROW YOUR NEPHEW FOR A MOMENT?
OOH, SO POLITE! ARE YOU OFFERING ALEX A JOB?
SOMETHING LIKE THAT.
WE CAN TALK IN THE KITCHEN, MR. HARADA.
SO, UM...
YOUR GUILT HAS OVERWHELMED YOU, ALEX. YOU HAVE A GREATER ROLE TO PLAY THAN THIS.
YOU LEFT SCHOOL TO CARE FOR YOUR AUNT. NOBLE, BUT ULTIMATELY THE WRONG PATH.
3.97 AT CUNY. HONOR'S CLASSES. DEAN'S LIST. BUT PROVINCIAL IN YOUR PRIORITIES.
WHAT IF THERE WAS A WAY TO CONTINUE YOUR EDUCATION AND TAKE CARE OF YOUR AUNT?
I'D WONDER WHAT THE CATCH IS?
I WANT TO UNLOCK YOUR POTENTIAL.
I WANT YOU TO COME WORK FOR ME.

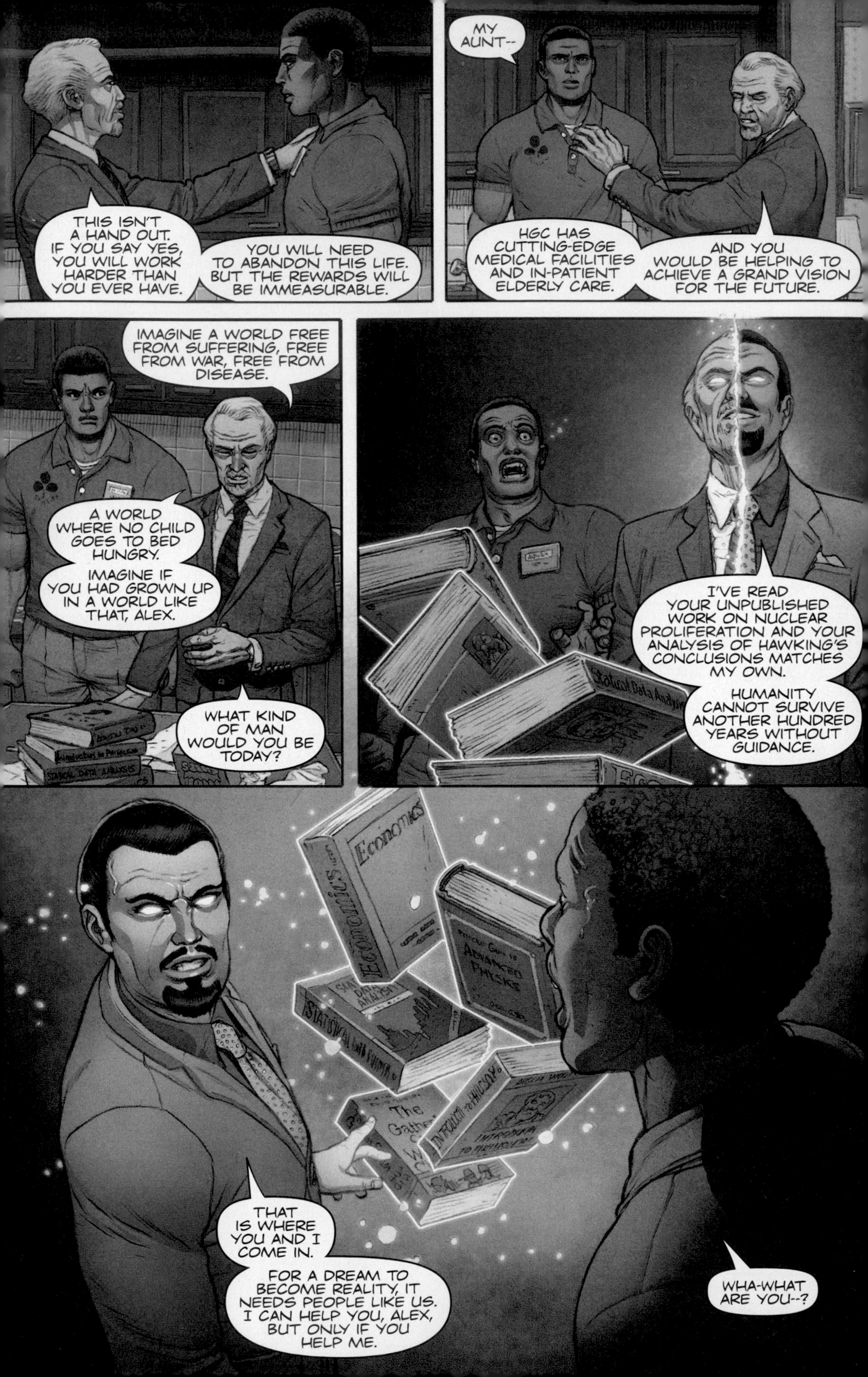
THIS ISN'T A HAND OUT. IF YOU SAY YES, YOU WILL WORK HARDER THAN YOU EVER HAVE.
YOU WILL NEED TO ABANDON THIS LIFE. BUT THE REWARDS WILL BE IMMEASURABLE.
MY AUNT--
HGC HAS CUTTING-EDGE MEDICAL FACILITIES AND IN-PATIENT ELDERLY CARE.
AND YOU WOULD BE HELPING TO ACHIEVE A GRAND VISION FOR THE FUTURE.
IMAGINE A WORLD FREE FROM SUFFERING, FREE FROM WAR, FREE FROM DISEASE.
A WORLD WHERE NO CHILD GOES TO BED HUNGRY.
IMAGINE IF YOU HAD GROWN UP IN A WORLD LIKE THAT, ALEX.
WHAT KIND OF MAN WOULD YOU BE TODAY?
I'VE READ YOUR UNPUBLISHED WORK ON NUCLEAR PROLIFERATION AND YOUR ANALYSIS OF HAWKING'S CONCLUSIONS MATCHES MY OWN.
HUMANITY CANNOT SURVIVE ANOTHER HUNDRED YEARS WITHOUT GUIDANCE.
THAT IS WHERE YOU AND I COME IN.
FOR A DREAM TO BECOME REALITY, IT NEEDS PEOPLE LIKE US. I CAN HELP YOU, ALEX, BUT ONLY IF YOU HELP ME.
WHA-WHAT ARE YOU--?

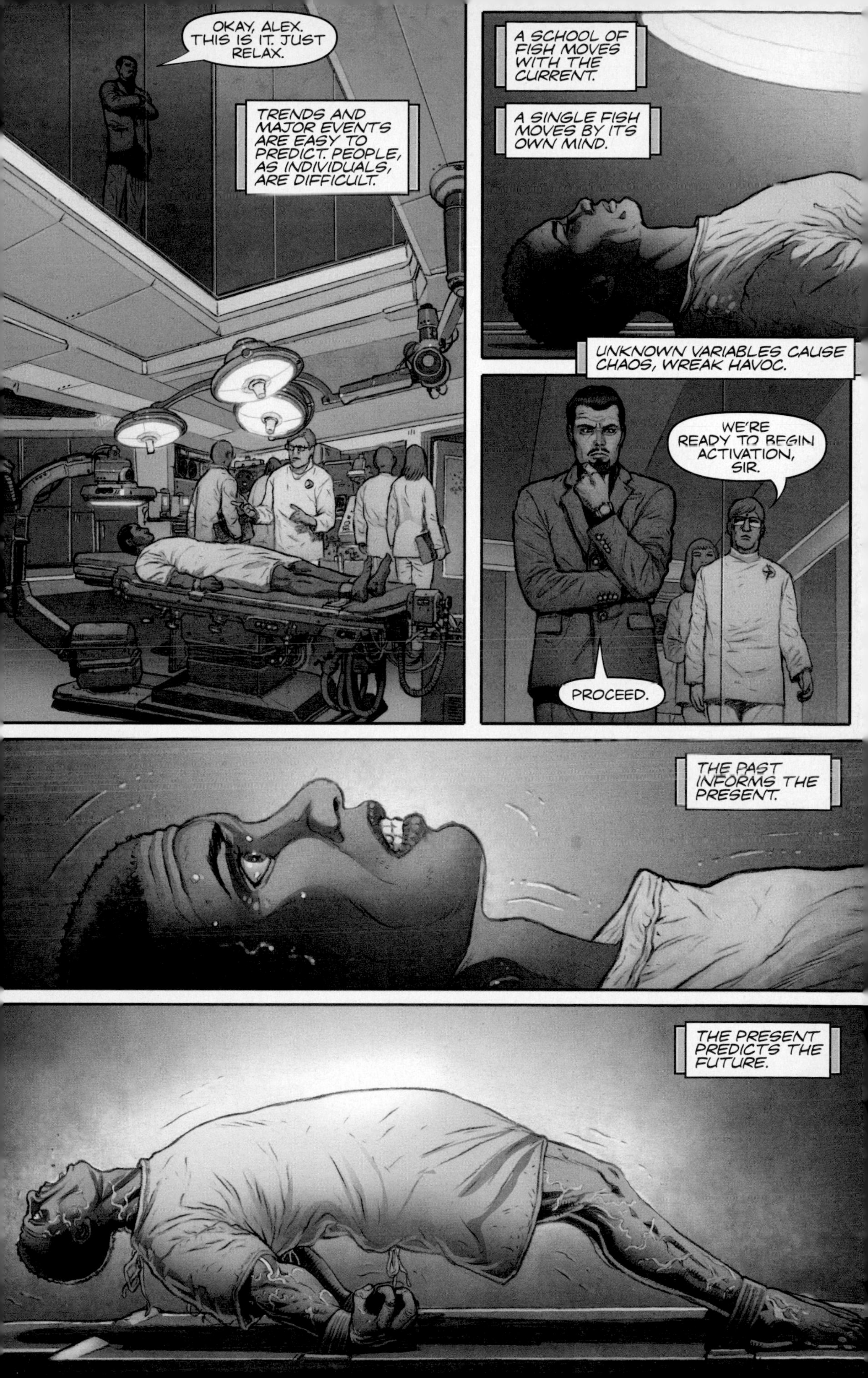
OKAY, ALEX. THIS IS IT. JUST RELAX.
TRENDS AND MAJOR EVENTS ARE EASY TO PREDICT. PEOPLE, AS INDIVIDUALS, ARE DIFFICULT.
A SCHOOL OF FISH MOVES WITH THE CURRENT.
A SINGLE FISH MOVES BY ITS OWN MIND.
UNKNOWN VARIABLES CAUSE CHAOS, WREAK HAVOC.
WE'RE READY TO BEGIN ACTIVATION, SIR.
PROCEED.
THE PAST INFORMS THE PRESENT.
THE PRESENT PREDICTS THE FUTURE.

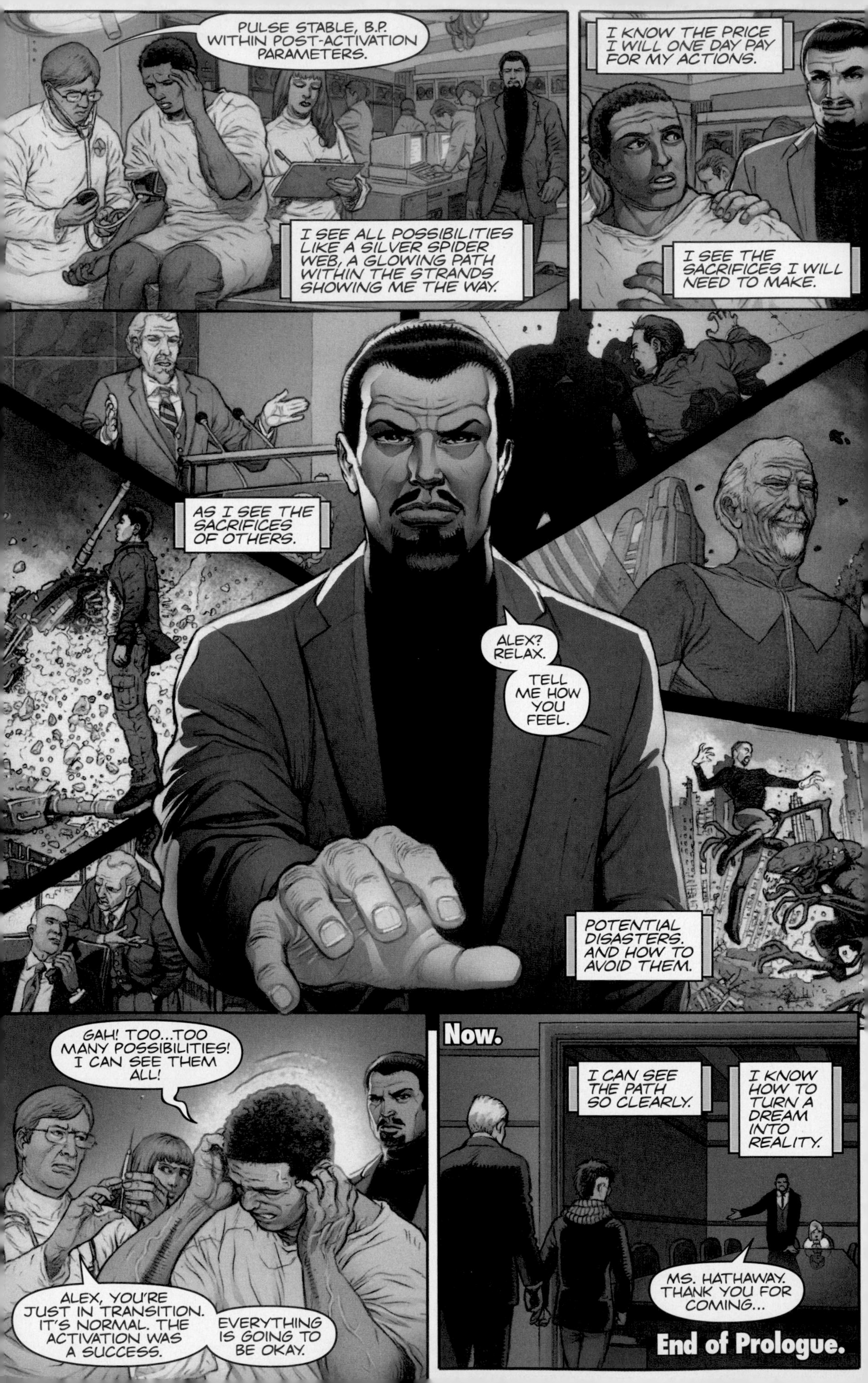
PULSE STABLE, B.P. WITHIN POST-ACTIVATION PARAMETERS.
I SEE ALL POSSIBILITIES LIKE A SILVER SPIDER WEB, A GLOWING PATH WITHIN THE STRANDS SHOWING ME THE WAY.
I KNOW THE PRICE I WILL ONE DAY PAY FOR MY ACTIONS.
I SEE THE SACRIFICES I WILL NEED TO MAKE.
AS I SEE THE SACRIFICES OF OTHERS.
ALEX? RELAX.
TELL ME HOW YOU FEEL.
POTENTIAL DISASTERS. AND HOW TO AVOID THEM.
GAH! TOO...TOO MANY POSSIBILITIES! I CAN SEE THEM ALL!
ALEX, YOU'RE JUST IN TRANSITION. IT'S NORMAL. THE ACTIVATION WAS A SUCCESS.
EVERYTHING IS GOING TO BE OKAY.
Now.
I CAN SEE THE PATH SO CLEARLY.
I KNOW HOW TO TURN A DREAM INTO REALITY.
MS. HATHAWAY. THANK YOU FOR COMING...
End of Prologue.

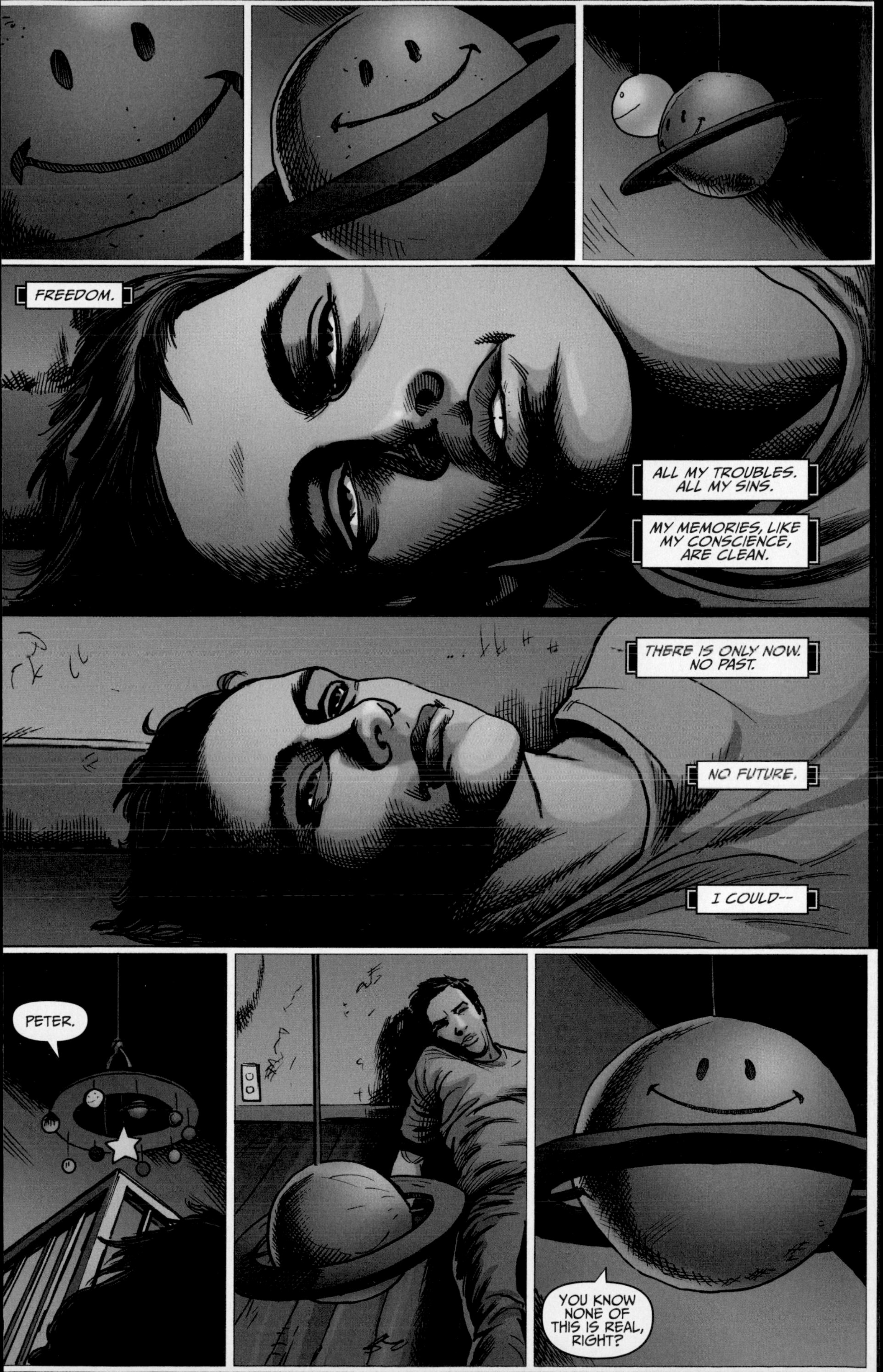
FREEDOM.
ALL MY TROUBLES. ALL MY SINS.
MY MEMORIES, LIKE MY CONSCIENCE, ARE CLEAN.
THERE IS ONLY NOW. NO PAST.
NO FUTURE.
I COULD--
PETER.
YOU KNOW NONE OF THIS IS REAL, RIGHT?

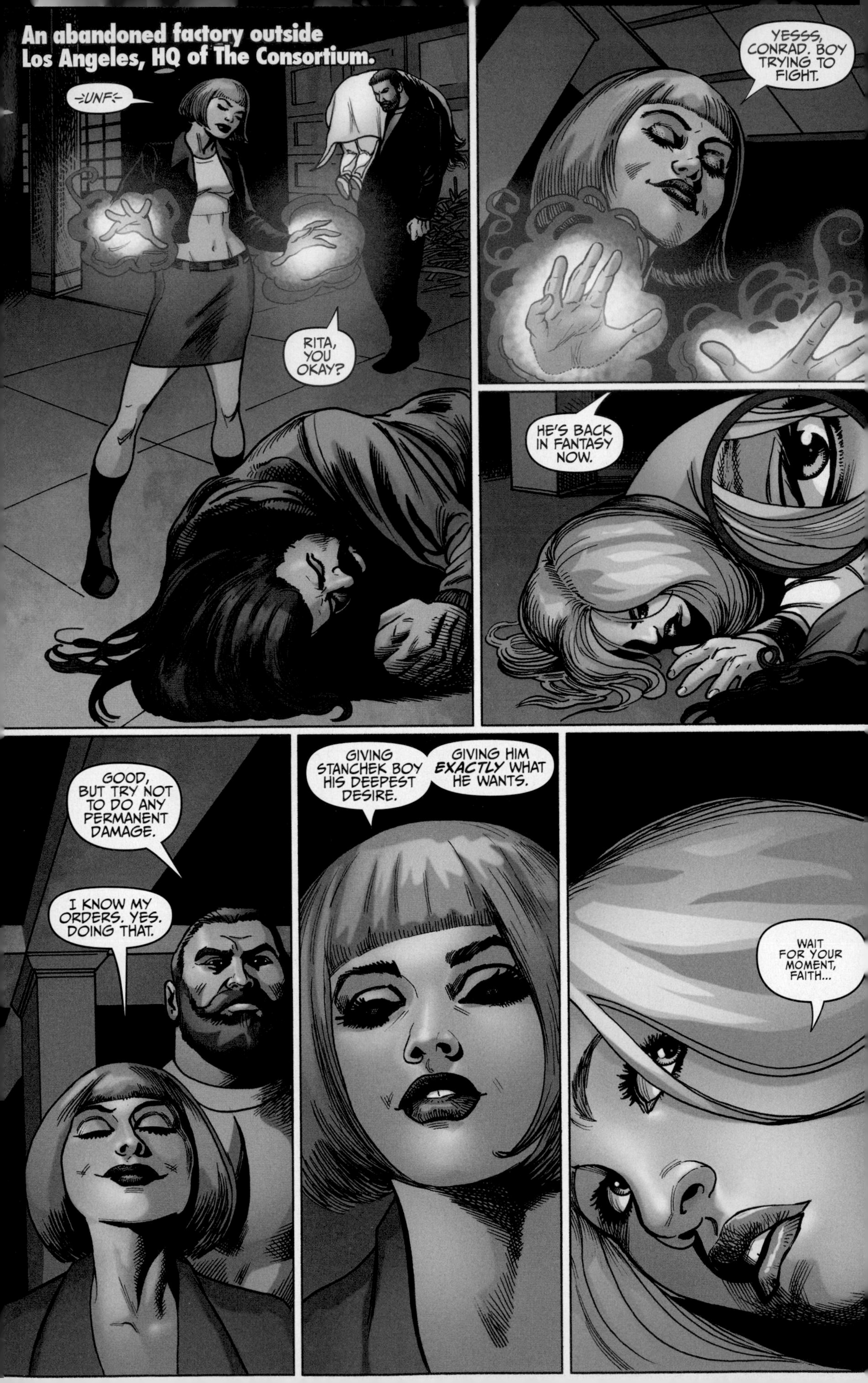
An abandoned factory outside Los Angeles, HQ of The Consortium.
UNF
RITA, YOU OKAY?
YESSS, CONRAD. BOY TRYING TO FIGHT.
HE'S BACK IN FANTASY NOW.
GOOD, BUT TRY NOT TO DO ANY PERMANENT DAMAGE.
I KNOW MY ORDERS. YES. DOING THAT.
GIVING STANCHEK BOY HIS DEEPEST DESIRE.
GIVING HIM EXACTLY WHAT HE WANTS.
WAIT FOR YOUR MOMENT, FAITH...

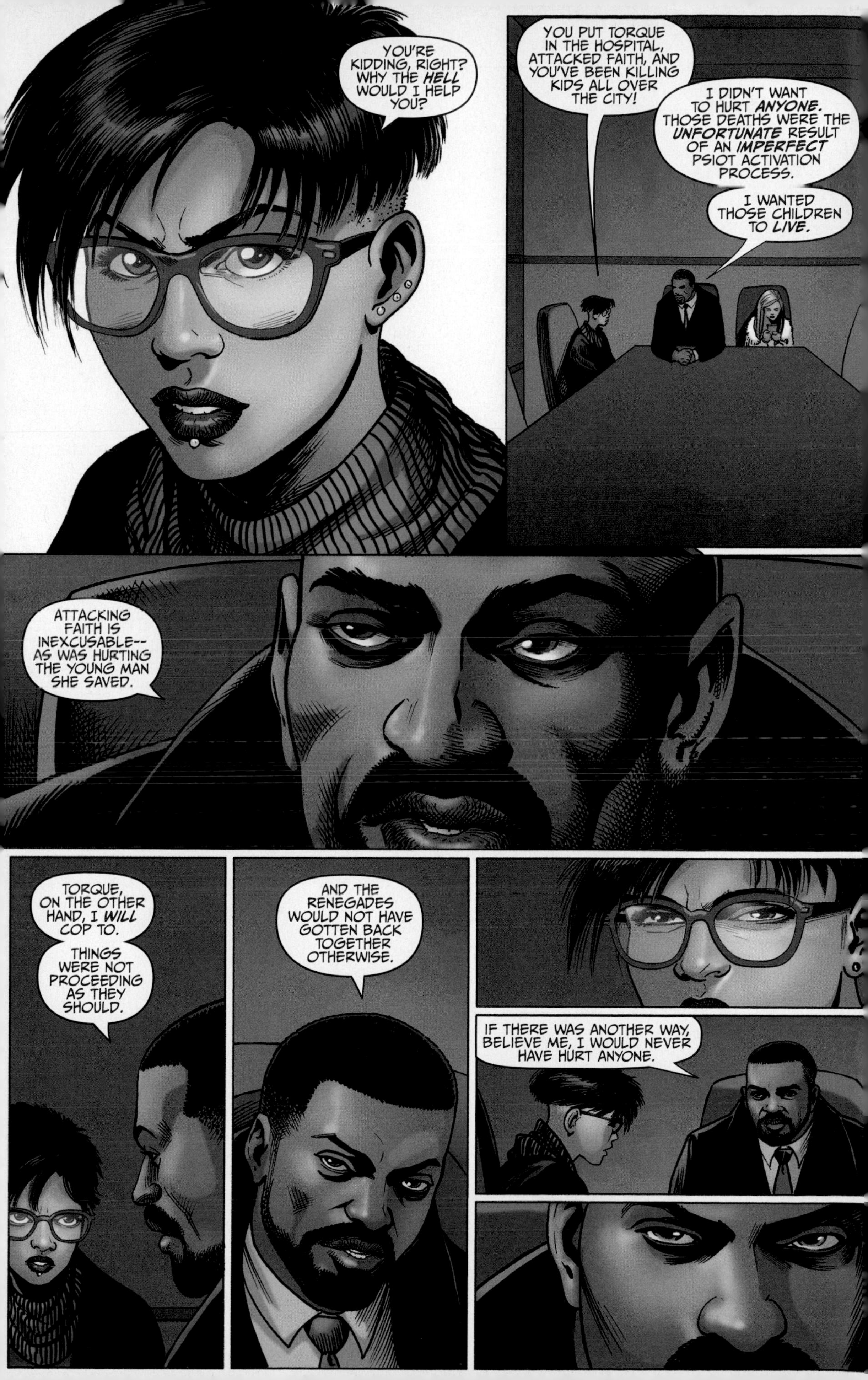

YOU'RE KIDDING, RIGHT? WHY THE HELL WOULD I HELP YOU?
YOU PUT TORQUE IN THE HOSPITAL, ATTACKED FAITH, AND YOU'VE BEEN KILLING KIDS ALL OVER THE CITY!
I DIDN'T WANT TO HURT ANYONE. THOSE DEATHS WERE THE UNFORTUNATE RESULT OF AN IMPERFECT PSIOT ACTIVATION PROCESS.
I WANTED THOSE CHILDREN TO LIVE.
ATTACKING FAITH IS INEXCUSABLE-- AS WAS HURTING THE YOUNG MAN SHE SAVED.
TORQUE, ON THE OTHER HAND, I WILL COP TO.
THINGS WERE NOT PROCEEDING AS THEY SHOULD.
AND THE RENEGADES WOULD NOT HAVE GOTTEN BACK TOGETHER OTHERWISE.
IF THERE WAS ANOTHER WAY, BELIEVE ME, I WOULD NEVER HAVE HURT ANYONE.

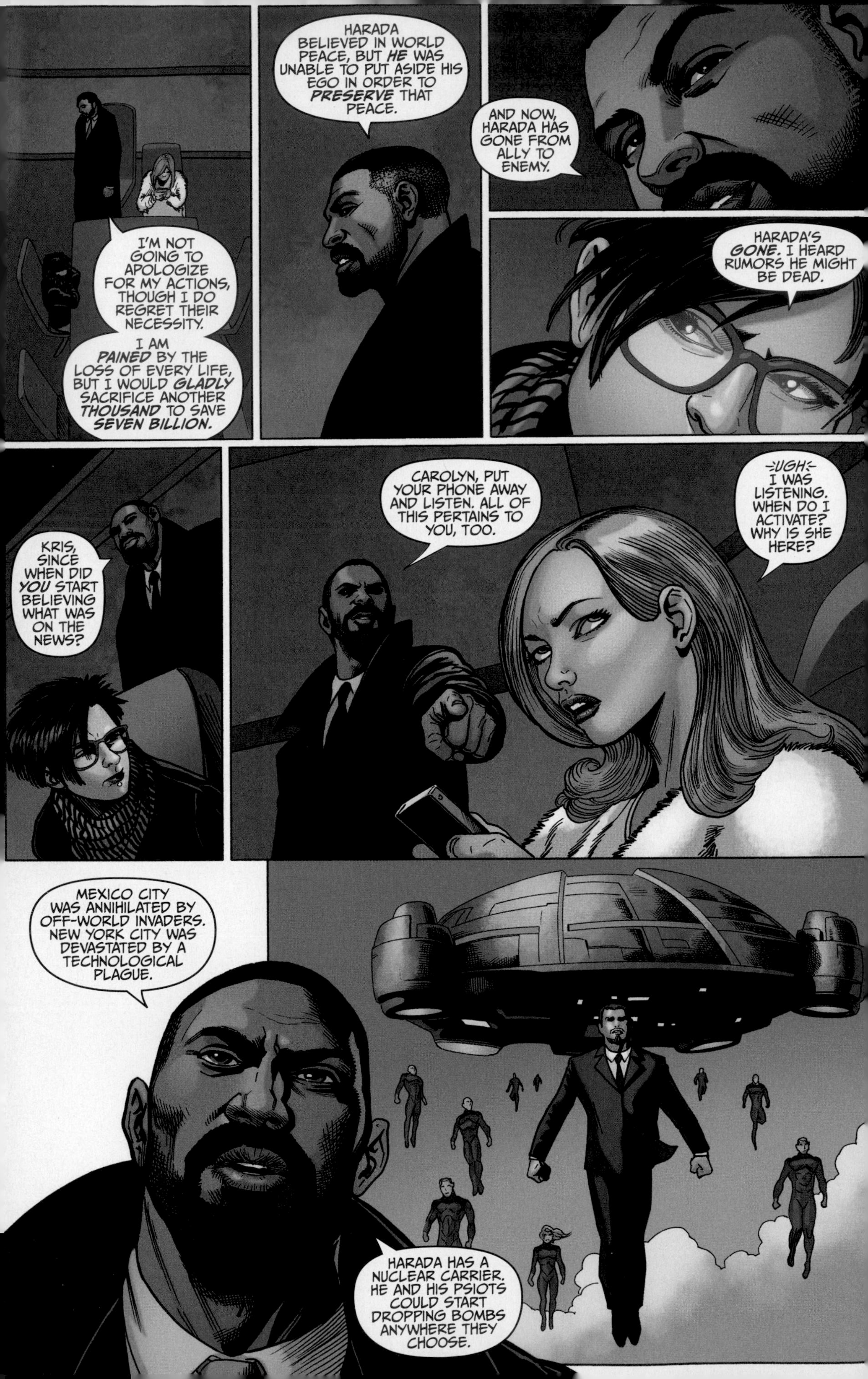
I'M NOT GOING TO APOLOGIZE FOR MY ACTIONS, THOUGH I DO REGRET THEIR NECESSITY.
I AM PAINED BY THE LOSS OF EVERY LIFE, BUT I WOULD GLADLY SACRIFICE ANOTHER THOUSAND TO SAVE SEVEN BILLION.
HARADA BELIEVED IN WORLD PEACE, BUT HE WAS UNABLE TO PUT ASIDE HIS EGO IN ORDER TO PRESERVE THAT PEACE.
AND NOW, HARADA HAS GONE FROM ALLY TO ENEMY.
HARADA'S GONE. I HEARD RUMORS HE MIGHT BE DEAD.
KRIS, SINCE WHEN DID YOU START BELIEVING WHAT WAS ON THE NEWS?
CAROLYN, PUT YOUR PHONE AWAY AND LISTEN. ALL OF THIS PERTAINS TO YOU, TOO.
UGH I WAS LISTENING. WHEN DO I ACTIVATE? WHY IS SHE HERE?
MEXICO CITY WAS ANNIHILATED BY OFF-WORLD INVADERS. NEW YORK CITY WAS DEVASTATED BY A TECHNOLOGICAL PLAGUE.
HARADA HAS A NUCLEAR CARRIER. HE AND HIS PSIOTS COULD START DROPPING BOMBS ANYWHERE THEY CHOOSE.

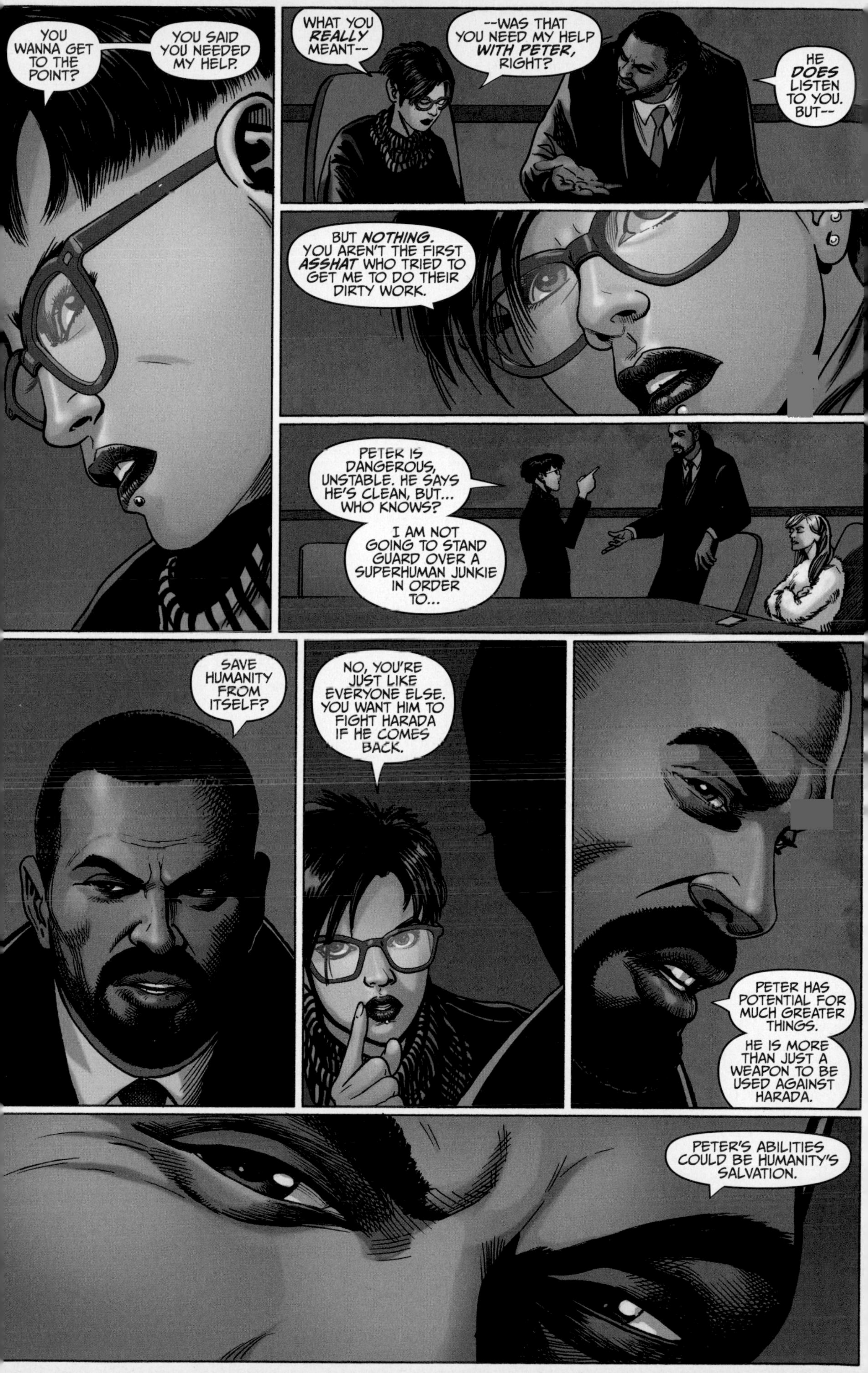

YOU WANNA GET TO THE POINT?
YOU SAID YOU NEEDED MY HELP.
WHAT YOU REALLY MEANT--
--WAS THAT YOU NEED MY HELP WITH PETER, RIGHT?
HE DOES LISTEN TO YOU. BUT--
BUT NOTHING. YOU AREN'T THE FIRST ASSHAT WHO TRIED TO GET ME TO DO THEIR DIRTY WORK.
PETER IS DANGEROUS, UNSTABLE. HE SAYS HE'S CLEAN, BUT... WHO KNOWS?
I AM NOT GOING TO STAND GUARD OVER A SUPERHUMAN JUNKIE IN ORDER TO...
SAVE HUMANITY FROM ITSELF?
NO, YOU'RE JUST LIKE EVERYONE ELSE. YOU WANT HIM TO FIGHT HARADA IF HE COMES BACK.
PETER HAS POTENTIAL FOR MUCH GREATER THINGS.
HE IS MORE THAN JUST A WEAPON TO BE USED AGAINST HARADA.
PETER'S ABILITIES COULD BE HUMANITY'S SALVATION.

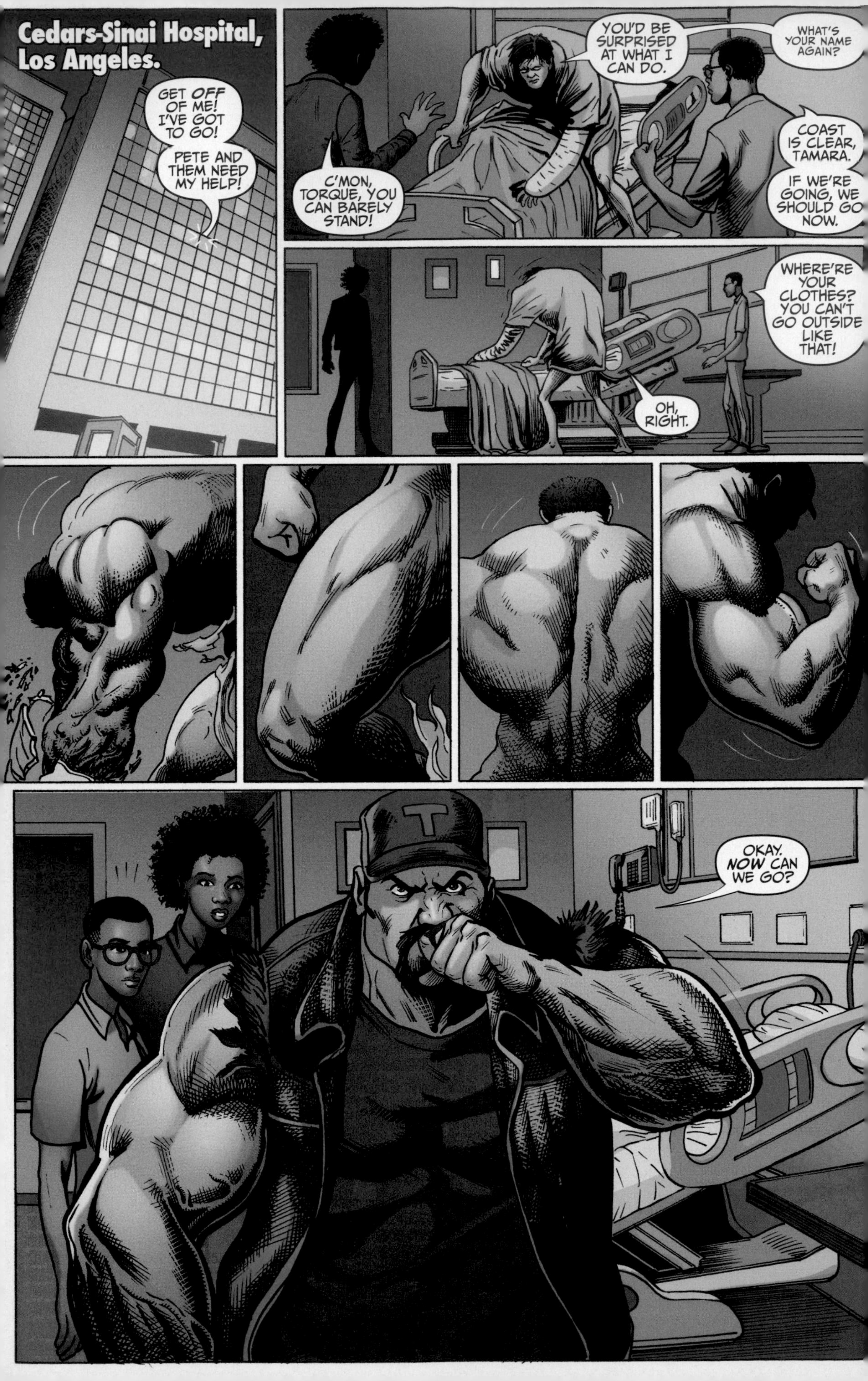
Cedars-Sinai Hospital, Los Angeles.
GET OFF OF ME! I'VE GOT TO GO!
PETE AND THEM NEED MY HELP!
C'MON, TORQUE, YOU CAN BARELY STAND!
YOU'D BE SURPRISED AT WHAT I CAN DO.
WHAT'S YOUR NAME AGAIN?
COAST IS CLEAR, TAMARA.
IF WE'RE GOING, WE SHOULD GO NOW.
WHERE'RE YOUR CLOTHES? YOU CAN'T GO OUTSIDE LIKE THAT!
OH, RIGHT.
OKAY. NOW CAN WE GO?

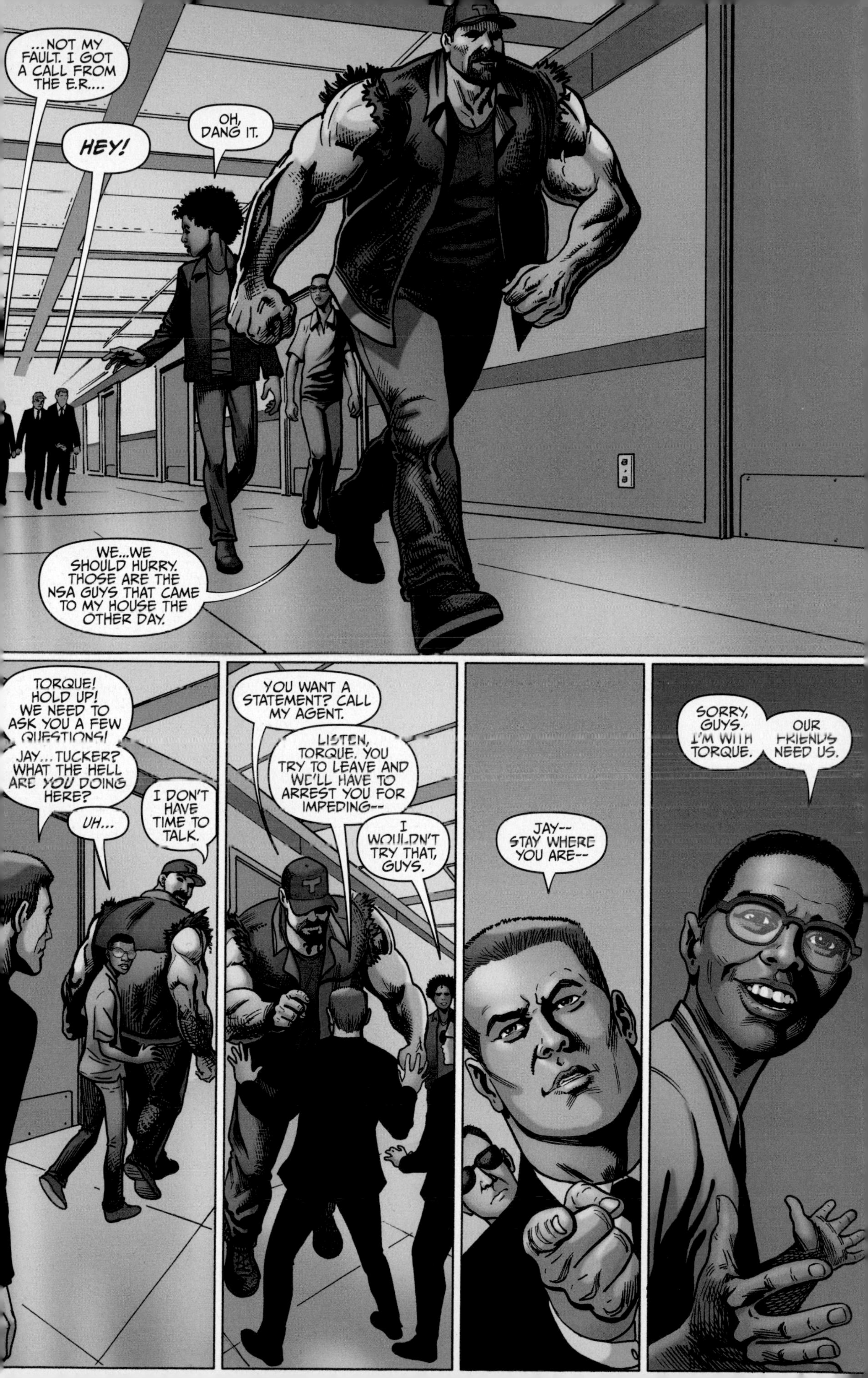
...NOT MY FAULT. I GOT A CALL FROM THE E.R....
HEY!
OH, DANG IT.
WE...WE SHOULD HURRY. THOSE ARE THE NSA GUYS THAT CAME TO MY HOUSE THE OTHER DAY.
TORQUE! HOLD UP! WE NEED TO ASK YOU A FEW QUESTIONS!
JAY...TUCKER? WHAT THE HELL ARE YOU DOING HERE?
UH...
I DON'T HAVE TIME TO TALK.
YOU WANT A STATEMENT? CALL MY AGENT.
LISTEN, TORQUE. YOU TRY TO LEAVE AND WE'LL HAVE TO ARREST YOU FOR IMPEDING--
I WOULDN'T TRY THAT, GUYS.
JAY-- STAY WHERE YOU ARE--
SORRY, GUYS. I'M WITH TORQUE.
OUR FRIENDS NEED US.

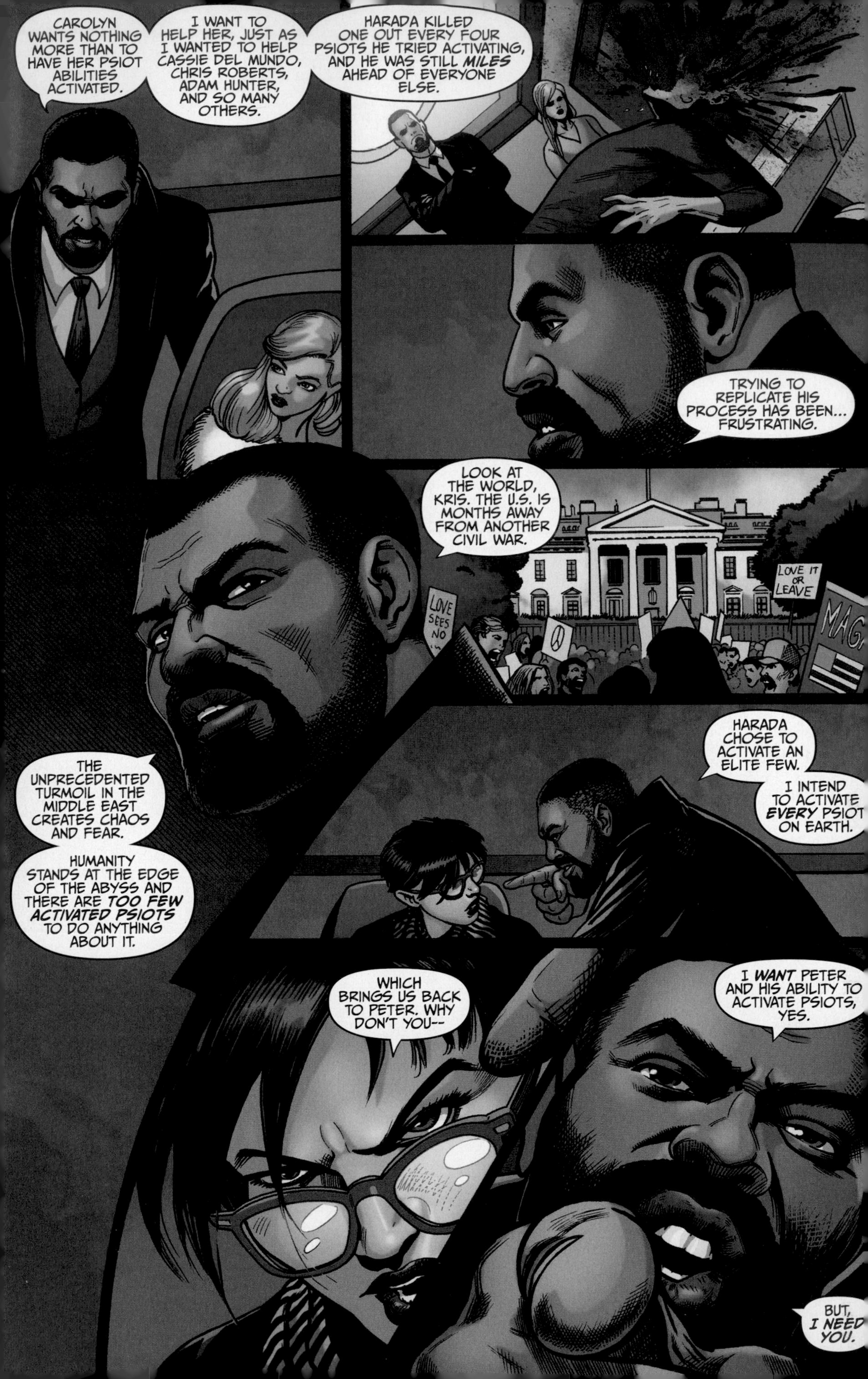
CAROLYN WANTS NOTHING MORE THAN TO HAVE HER PSIOT ABILITIES ACTIVATED.
I WANT TO HELP HER, JUST AS I WANTED TO HELP CASSIE DEL MUNDO, CHRIS ROBERTS, ADAM HUNTER, AND SO MANY OTHERS.
HARADA KILLED ONE OUT EVERY FOUR PSIOTS HE TRIED ACTIVATING, AND HE WAS STILL MILES AHEAD OF EVERYONE ELSE.
TRYING TO REPLICATE HIS PROCESS HAS BEEN... FRUSTRATING.
LOOK AT THE WORLD, KRIS. THE U.S. IS MONTHS AWAY FROM ANOTHER CIVIL WAR.
LOVE SEES NO
LOVE IT OR LEAVE
MAG
THE UNPRECEDENTED TURMOIL IN THE MIDDLE EAST CREATES CHAOS AND FEAR.
HUMANITY STANDS AT THE EDGE OF THE ABYSS AND THERE ARE TOO FEW ACTIVATED PSIOTS TO DO ANYTHING ABOUT IT.
HARADA CHOSE TO ACTIVATE AN ELITE FEW.
I INTEND TO ACTIVATE EVERY PSIOT ON EARTH.
WHICH BRINGS US BACK TO PETER. WHY DON'T YOU--
I WANT PETER AND HIS ABILITY TO ACTIVATE PSIOTS, YES.
BUT, I NEED YOU.

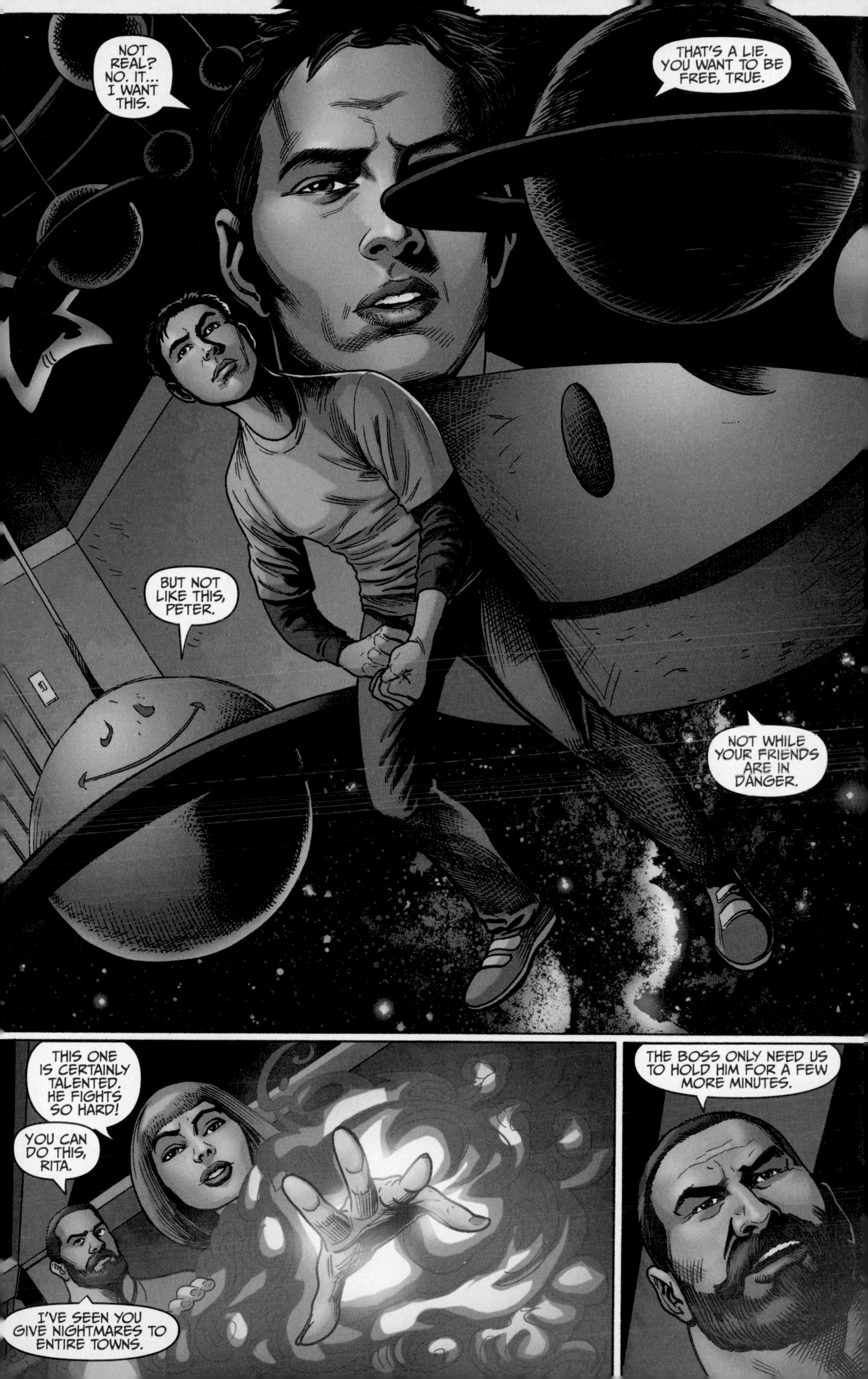
NOT REAL? NO. IT... I WANT THIS.
THAT'S A LIE. YOU WANT TO BE FREE, TRUE.
BUT NOT LIKE THIS, PETER.
NOT WHILE YOUR FRIENDS ARE IN DANGER.
THIS ONE IS CERTAINLY TALENTED. HE FIGHTS SO HARD!
YOU CAN DO THIS, RITA.
I'VE SEEN YOU GIVE NIGHTMARES TO ENTIRE TOWNS.
THE BOSS ONLY NEED US TO HOLD HIM FOR A FEW MORE MINUTES.

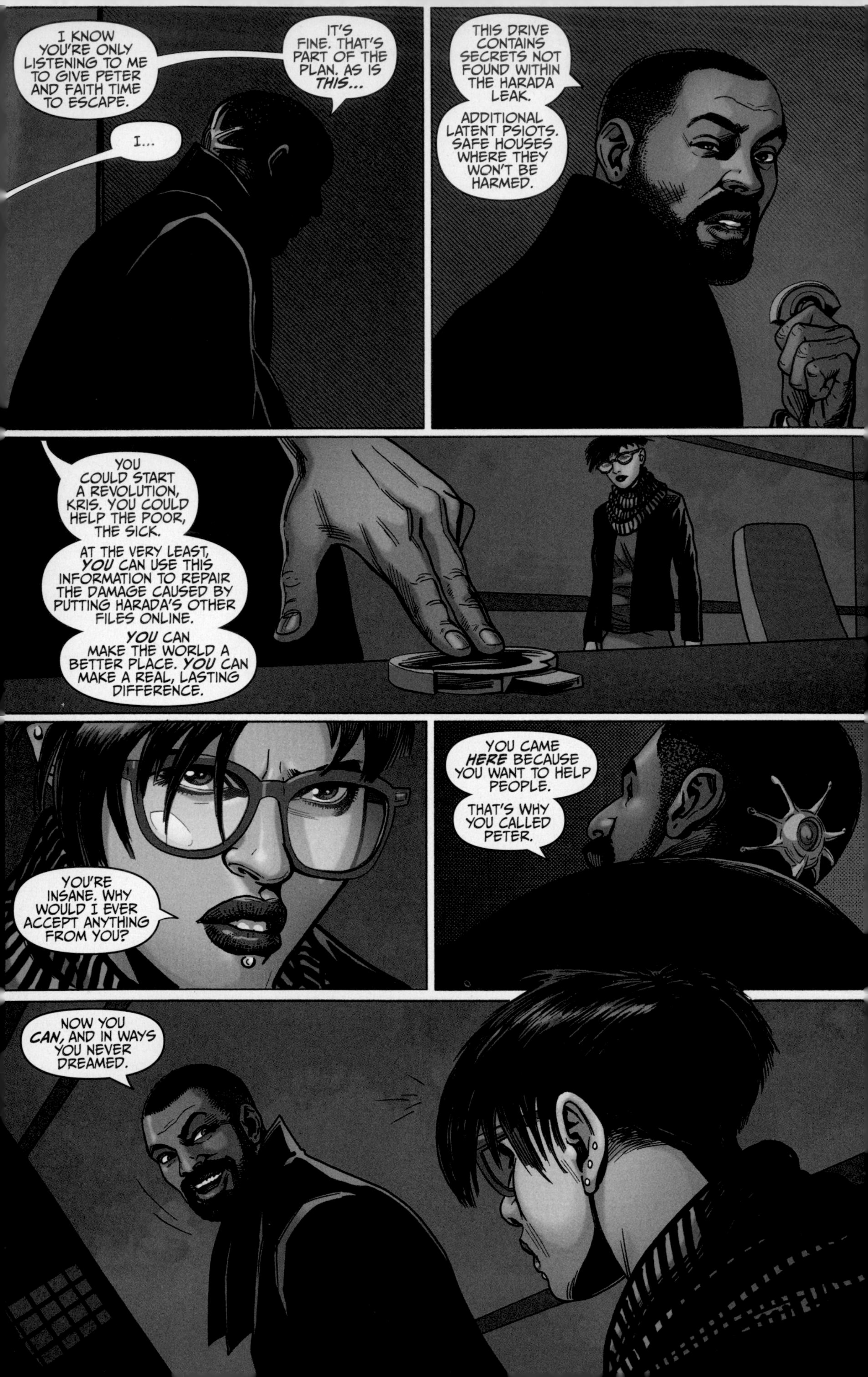

I KNOW YOU'RE ONLY LISTENING TO ME TO GIVE PETER AND FAITH TIME TO ESCAPE.
IT'S FINE. THAT'S PART OF THE PLAN. AS IS *THIS...*
I...
THIS DRIVE CONTAINS SECRETS NOT FOUND WITHIN THE HARADA LEAK.
ADDITIONAL LATENT PSIOTS. SAFE HOUSES WHERE THEY WON'T BE HARMED.
YOU COULD START A REVOLUTION, KRIS. YOU COULD HELP THE POOR, THE SICK.
AT THE VERY LEAST, *YOU* CAN USE THIS INFORMATION TO REPAIR THE DAMAGE CAUSED BY PUTTING HARADA'S OTHER FILES ONLINE.
YOU CAN MAKE THE WORLD A BETTER PLACE. *YOU* CAN MAKE A REAL, LASTING DIFFERENCE.
YOU'RE INSANE. WHY WOULD I EVER ACCEPT ANYTHING FROM YOU?
YOU CAME *HERE* BECAUSE YOU WANT TO HELP PEOPLE.
THAT'S WHY YOU CALLED PETER.
NOW YOU *CAN,* AND IN WAYS YOU NEVER DREAMED.

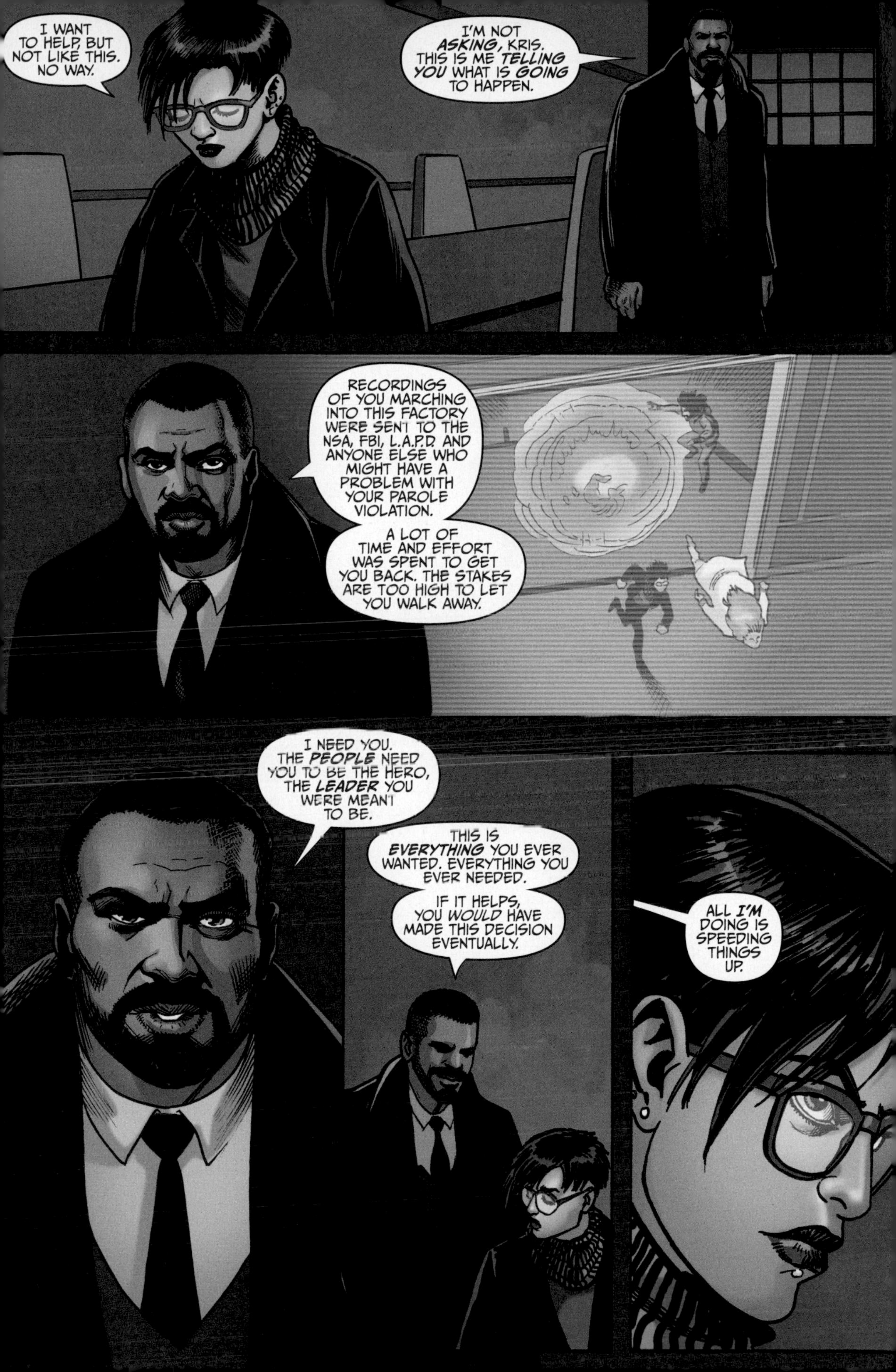
I WANT TO HELP, BUT NOT LIKE THIS. NO WAY.
I'M NOT ASKING, KRIS. THIS IS ME TELLING YOU WHAT IS GOING TO HAPPEN.
RECORDINGS OF YOU MARCHING INTO THIS FACTORY WERE SENT TO THE NSA, FBI, L.A.P.D. AND ANYONE ELSE WHO MIGHT HAVE A PROBLEM WITH YOUR PAROLE VIOLATION.
A LOT OF TIME AND EFFORT WAS SPENT TO GET YOU BACK. THE STAKES ARE TOO HIGH TO LET YOU WALK AWAY.
I NEED YOU. THE PEOPLE NEED YOU TO BE THE HERO, THE LEADER YOU WERE MEANT TO BE.
THIS IS EVERYTHING YOU EVER WANTED. EVERYTHING YOU EVER NEEDED.
IF IT HELPS, YOU WOULD HAVE MADE THIS DECISION EVENTUALLY.
ALL I'M DOING IS SPEEDING THINGS UP.

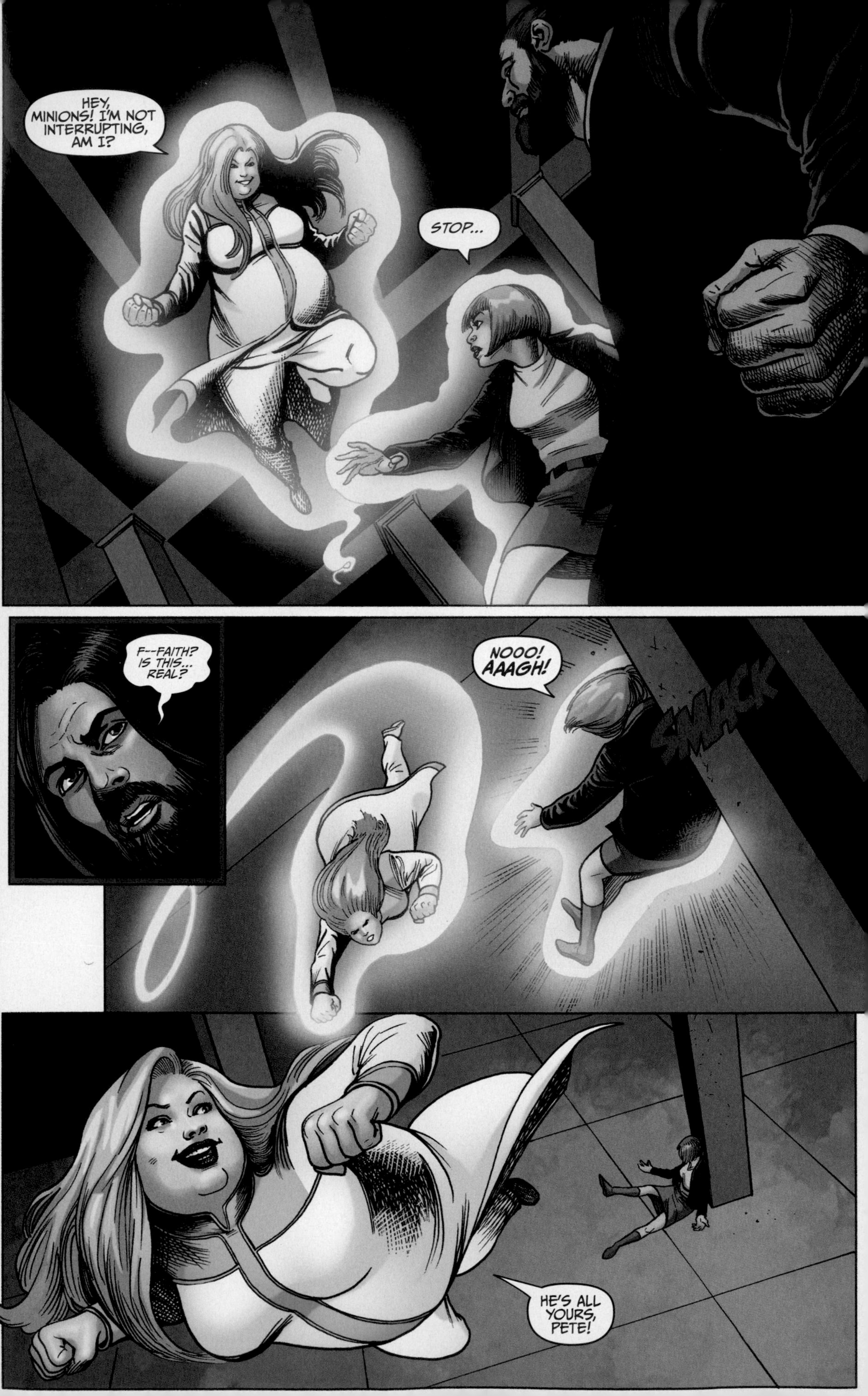
HEY, MINIONS! I'M NOT INTERRUPTING, AM I?
STOP...
F--FAITH? IS THIS... REAL?
NOOO! AAAGH!
SMACK
HE'S ALL YOURS, PETE!

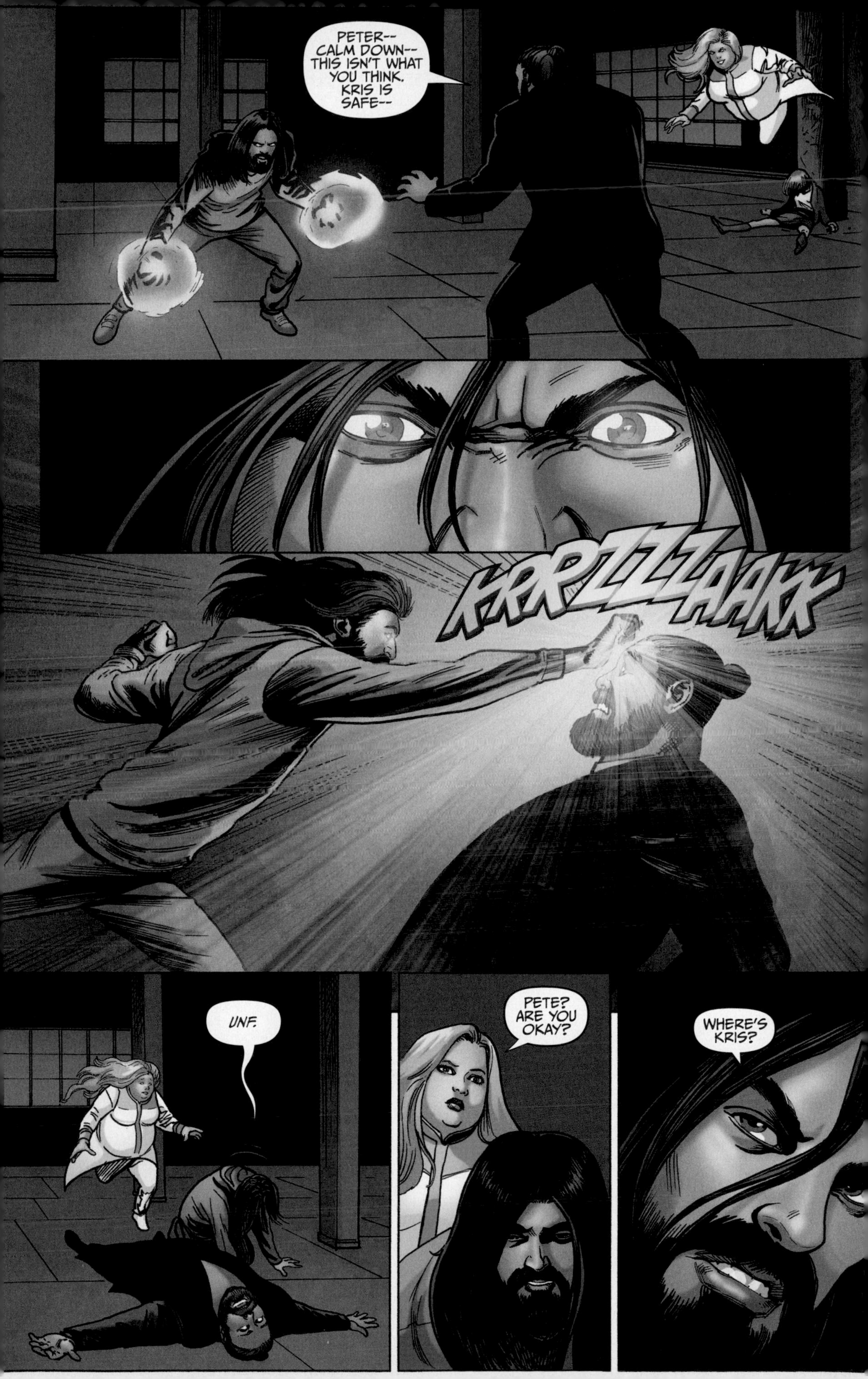
PETER-- CALM DOWN-- THIS ISN'T WHAT YOU THINK. KRIS IS SAFE--
KRRZZZAAKK
UNF.
PETE? ARE YOU OKAY?
WHERE'S KRIS?

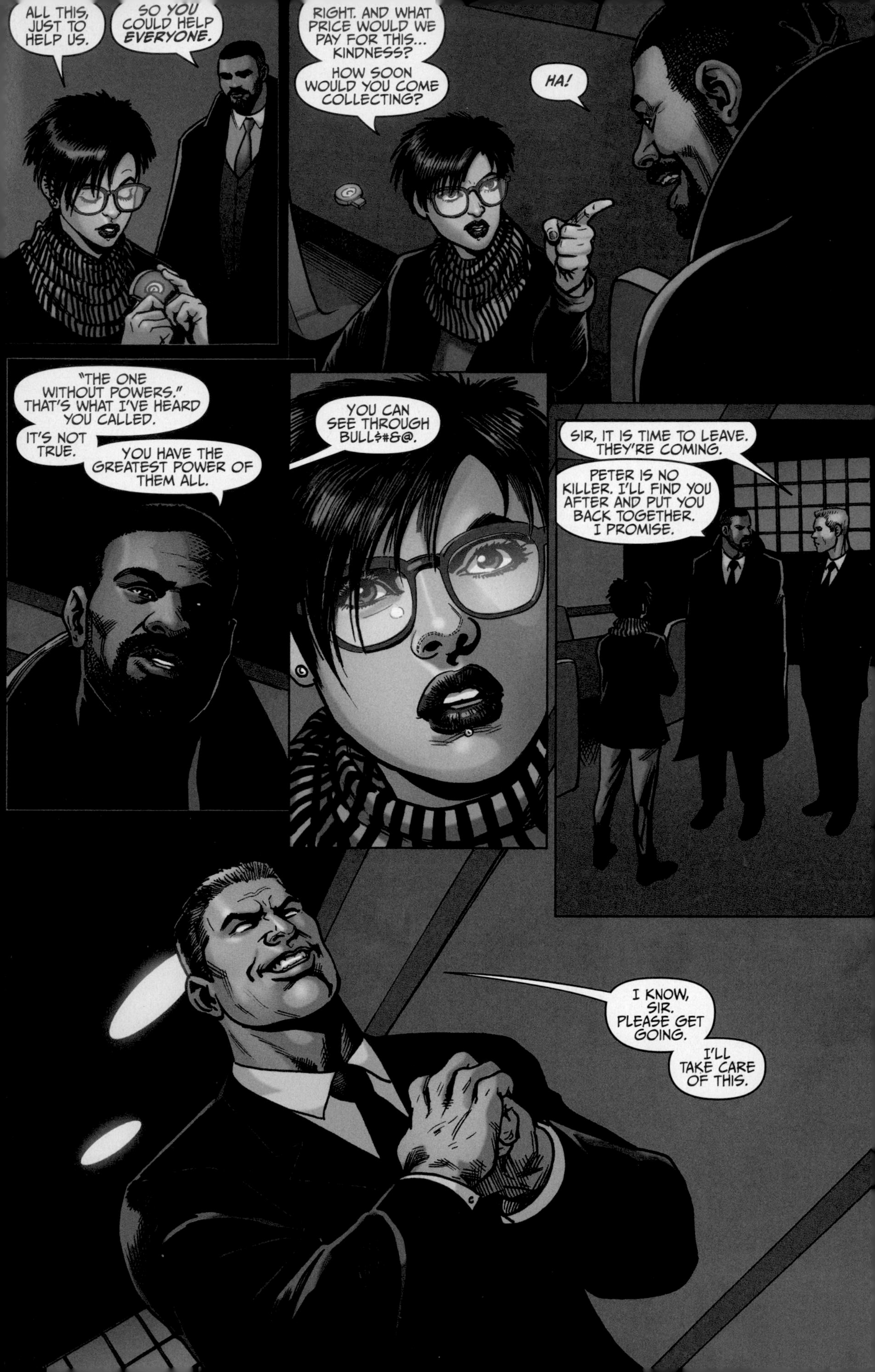
ALL THIS, JUST TO HELP US.
SO YOU COULD HELP *EVERYONE.*
RIGHT. AND WHAT PRICE WOULD WE PAY FOR THIS... KINDNESS?
HOW SOON WOULD YOU COME COLLECTING?
HA!
"THE ONE WITHOUT POWERS." THAT'S WHAT I'VE HEARD YOU CALLED.
IT'S NOT TRUE.
YOU HAVE THE GREATEST POWER OF THEM ALL.
YOU CAN SEE THROUGH BULL$#&@.
SIR, IT IS TIME TO LEAVE. THEY'RE COMING.
PETER IS NO KILLER. I'LL FIND YOU AFTER AND PUT YOU BACK TOGETHER. I PROMISE.
I KNOW, SIR. PLEASE GET GOING.
I'LL TAKE CARE OF THIS.

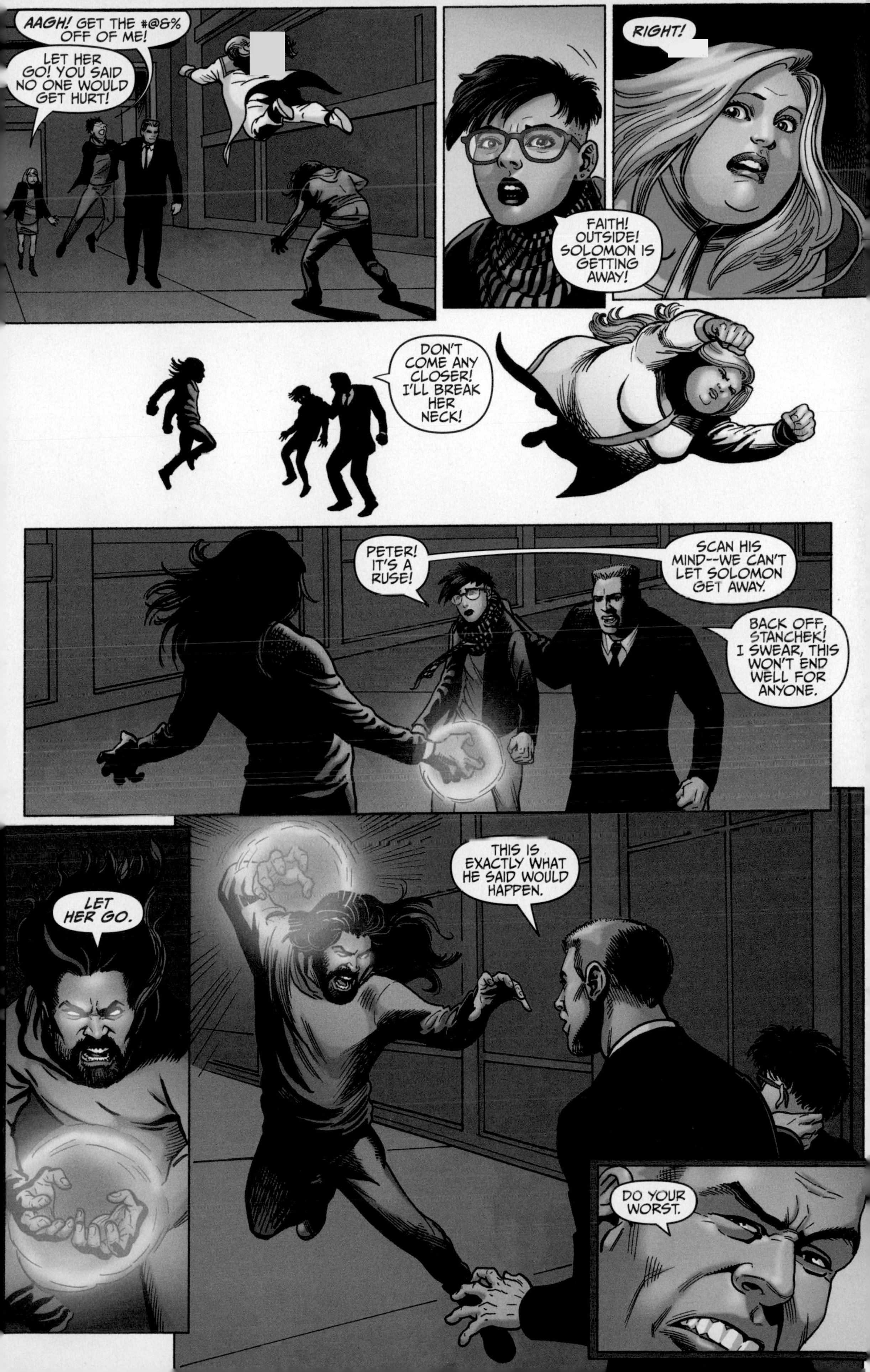
AAGH! GET THE #@&% OFF OF ME!
LET HER GO! YOU SAID NO ONE WOULD GET HURT!
FAITH! OUTSIDE! SOLOMON IS GETTING AWAY!
RIGHT!
DON'T COME ANY CLOSER! I'LL BREAK HER NECK!
PETER! IT'S A RUSE!
SCAN HIS MIND--WE CAN'T LET SOLOMON GET AWAY.
BACK OFF, STANCHEK! I SWEAR, THIS WON'T END WELL FOR ANYONE.
LET HER GO.
THIS IS EXACTLY WHAT HE SAID WOULD HAPPEN.
DO YOUR WORST.

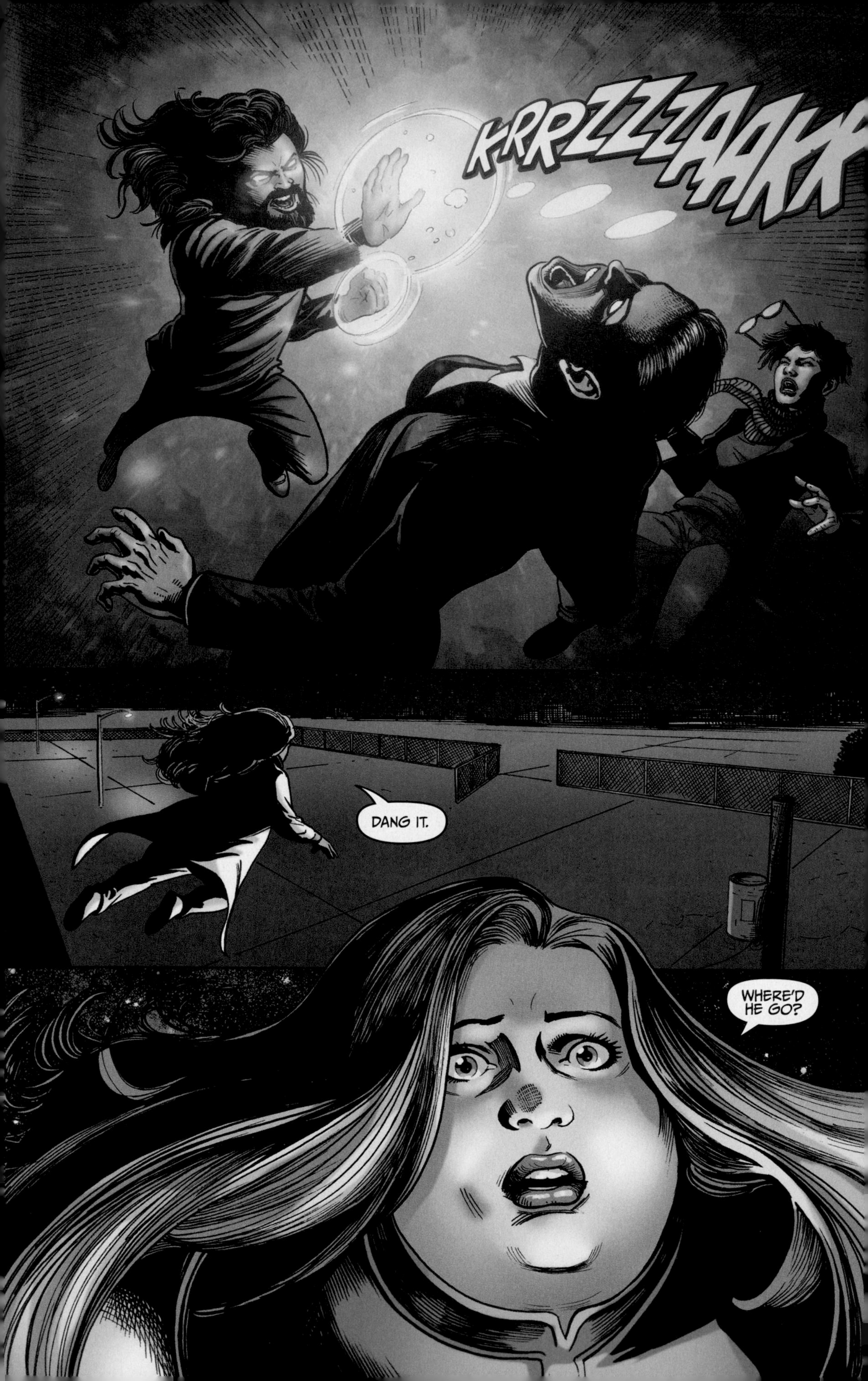

KRRZZZAAKK
DANG IT.
WHERE'D HE GO?

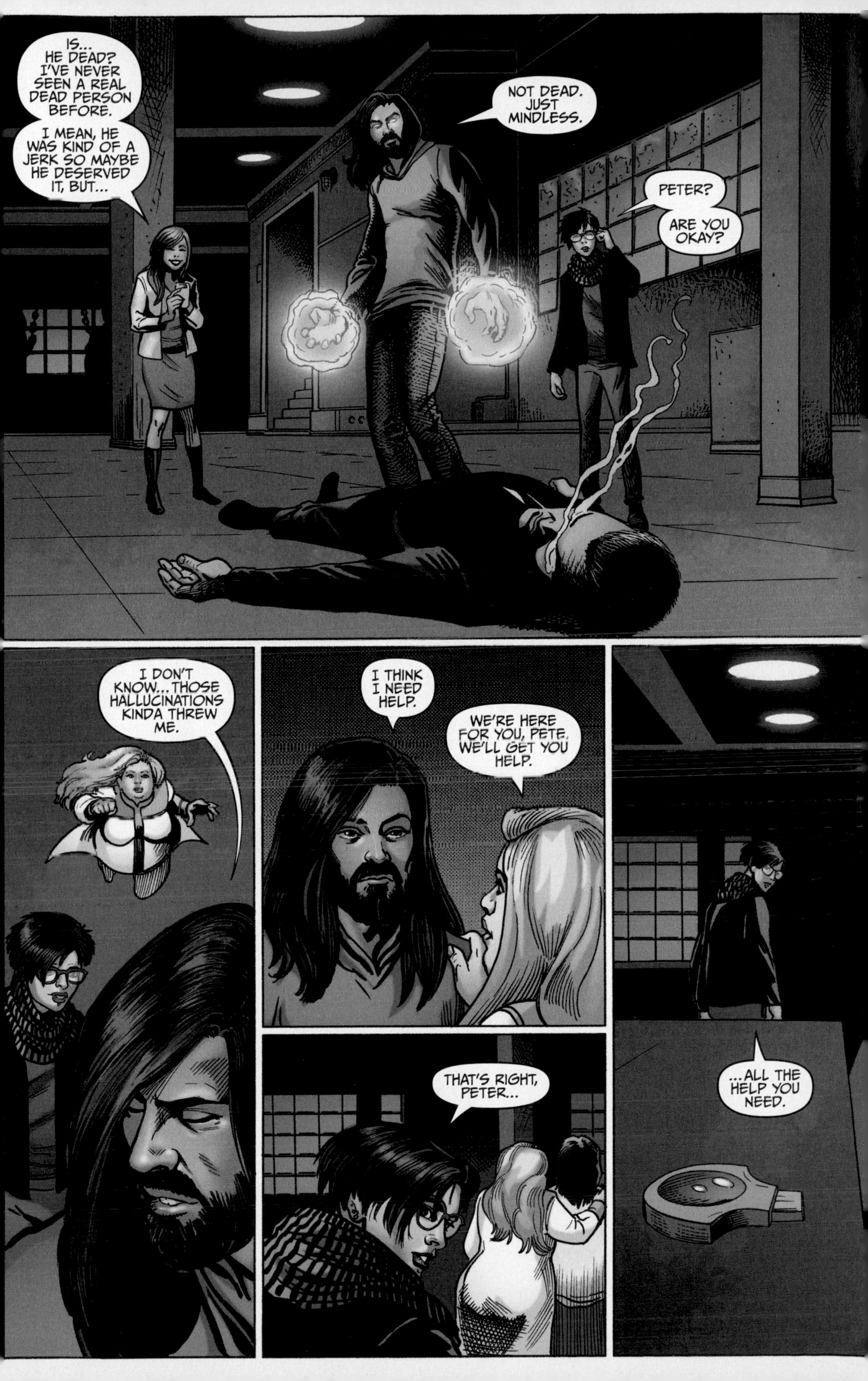
IS... HE DEAD? I'VE NEVER SEEN A REAL DEAD PERSON BEFORE.
I MEAN, HE WAS KIND OF A JERK SO MAYBE HE DESERVED IT, BUT...
NOT DEAD. JUST MINDLESS.
PETER?
ARE YOU OKAY?
I DON'T KNOW... THOSE HALLUCINATIONS KINDA THREW ME.
I THINK I NEED HELP.
WE'RE HERE FOR YOU, PETE. WE'LL GET YOU HELP.
THAT'S RIGHT, PETER...
...ALL THE HELP YOU NEED.

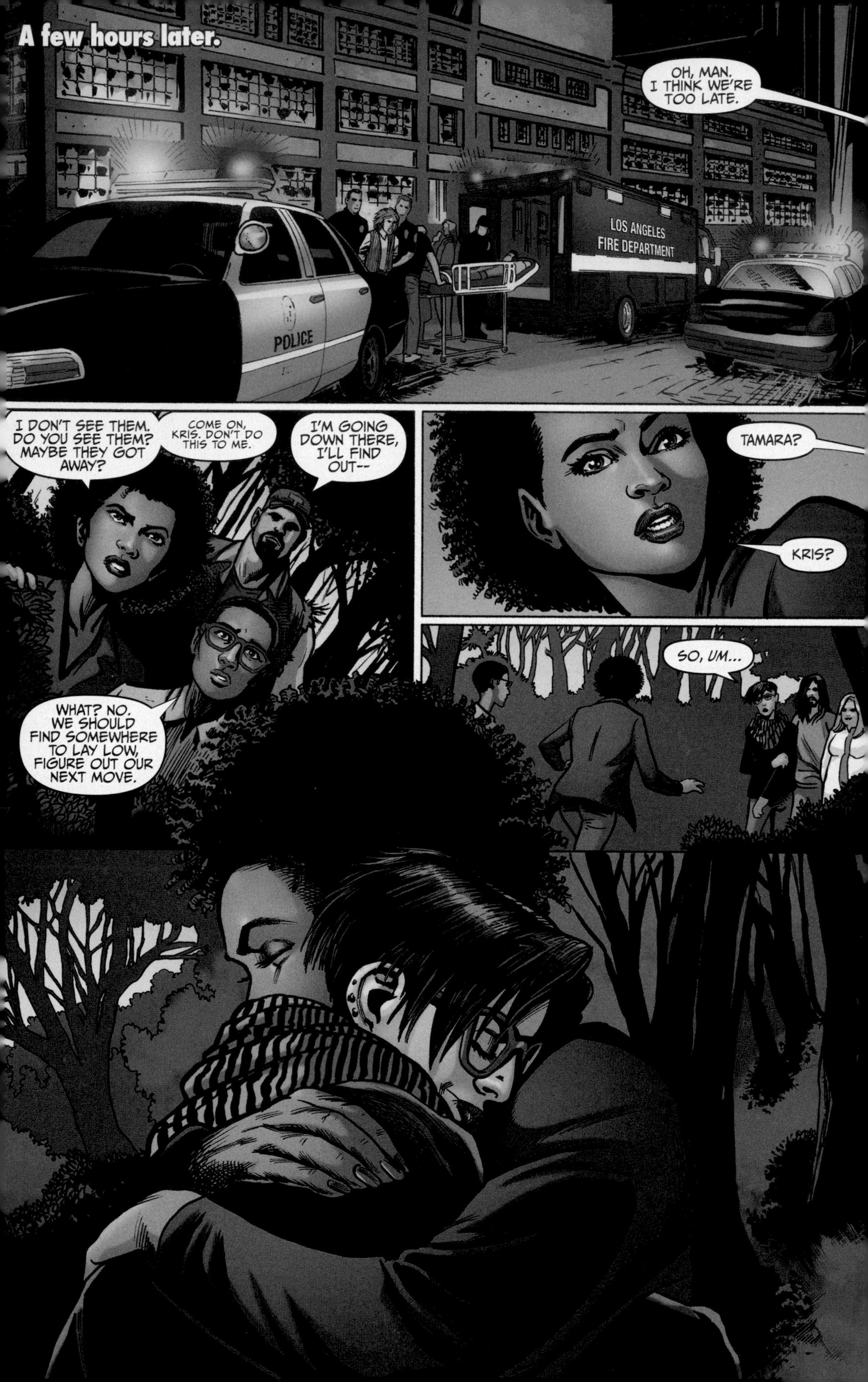
A few hours later.
OH, MAN. I THINK WE'RE TOO LATE.
LOS ANGELES FIRE DEPARTMENT
POLICE
I DON'T SEE THEM. DO YOU SEE THEM? MAYBE THEY GOT AWAY?
COME ON, KRIS. DON'T DO THIS TO ME.
I'M GOING DOWN THERE, I'LL FIND OUT--
WHAT? NO. WE SHOULD FIND SOMEWHERE TO LAY LOW, FIGURE OUT OUR NEXT MOVE.
TAMARA?
KRIS?
SO, UM...

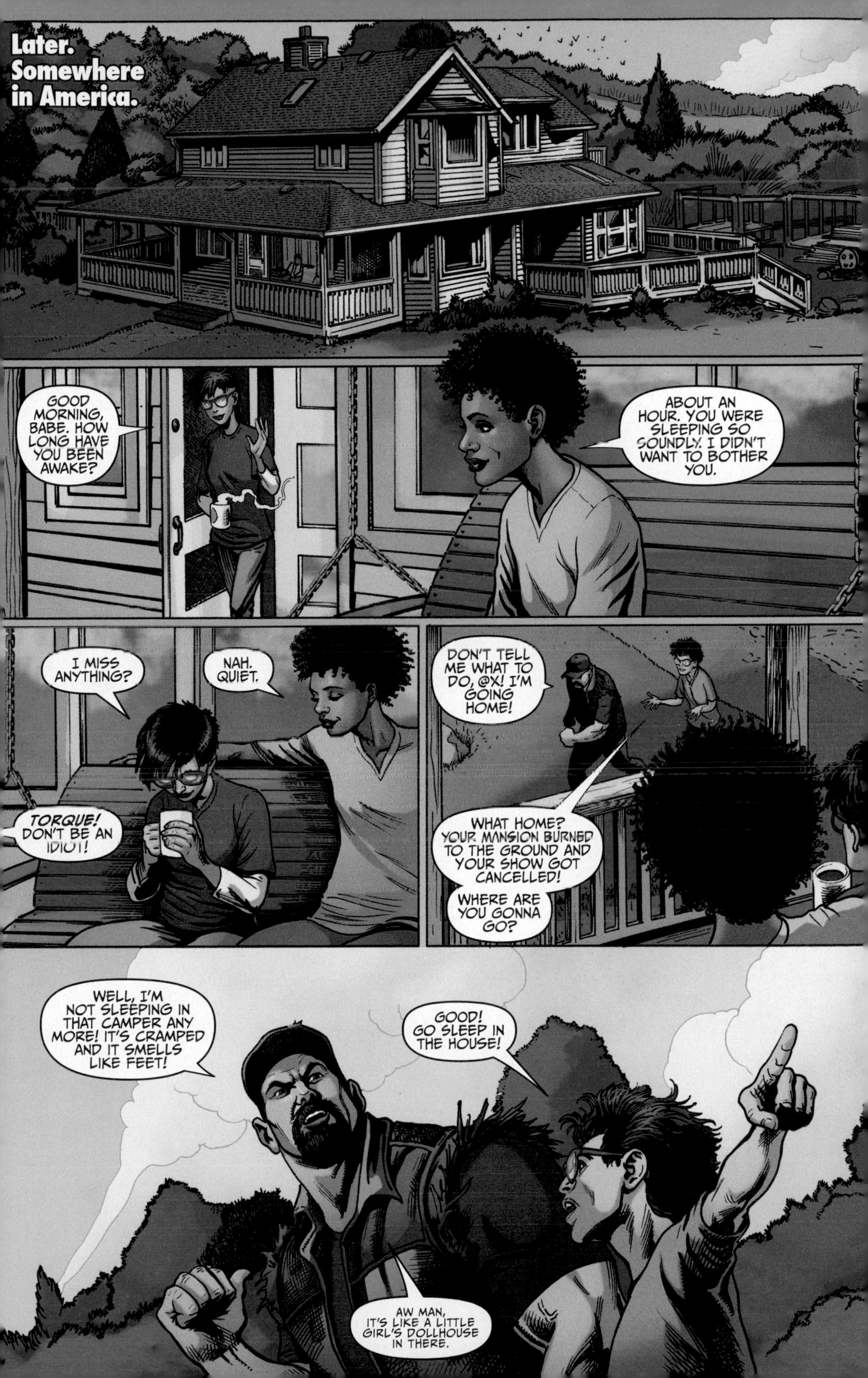
Later. Somewhere in America.
GOOD MORNING, BABE. HOW LONG HAVE YOU BEEN AWAKE?
ABOUT AN HOUR. YOU WERE SLEEPING SO SOUNDLY. I DIDN'T WANT TO BOTHER YOU.
I MISS ANYTHING?
NAH. QUIET.
TORQUE! DON'T BE AN IDIOT!
DON'T TELL ME WHAT TO DO, @X! I'M GOING HOME!
WHAT HOME? YOUR MANSION BURNED TO THE GROUND AND YOUR SHOW GOT CANCELLED!
WHERE ARE YOU GONNA GO?
WELL, I'M NOT SLEEPING IN THAT CAMPER ANY MORE! IT'S CRAMPED AND IT SMELLS LIKE FEET!
GOOD! GO SLEEP IN THE HOUSE!
AW MAN, IT'S LIKE A LITTLE GIRL'S DOLLHOUSE IN THERE.

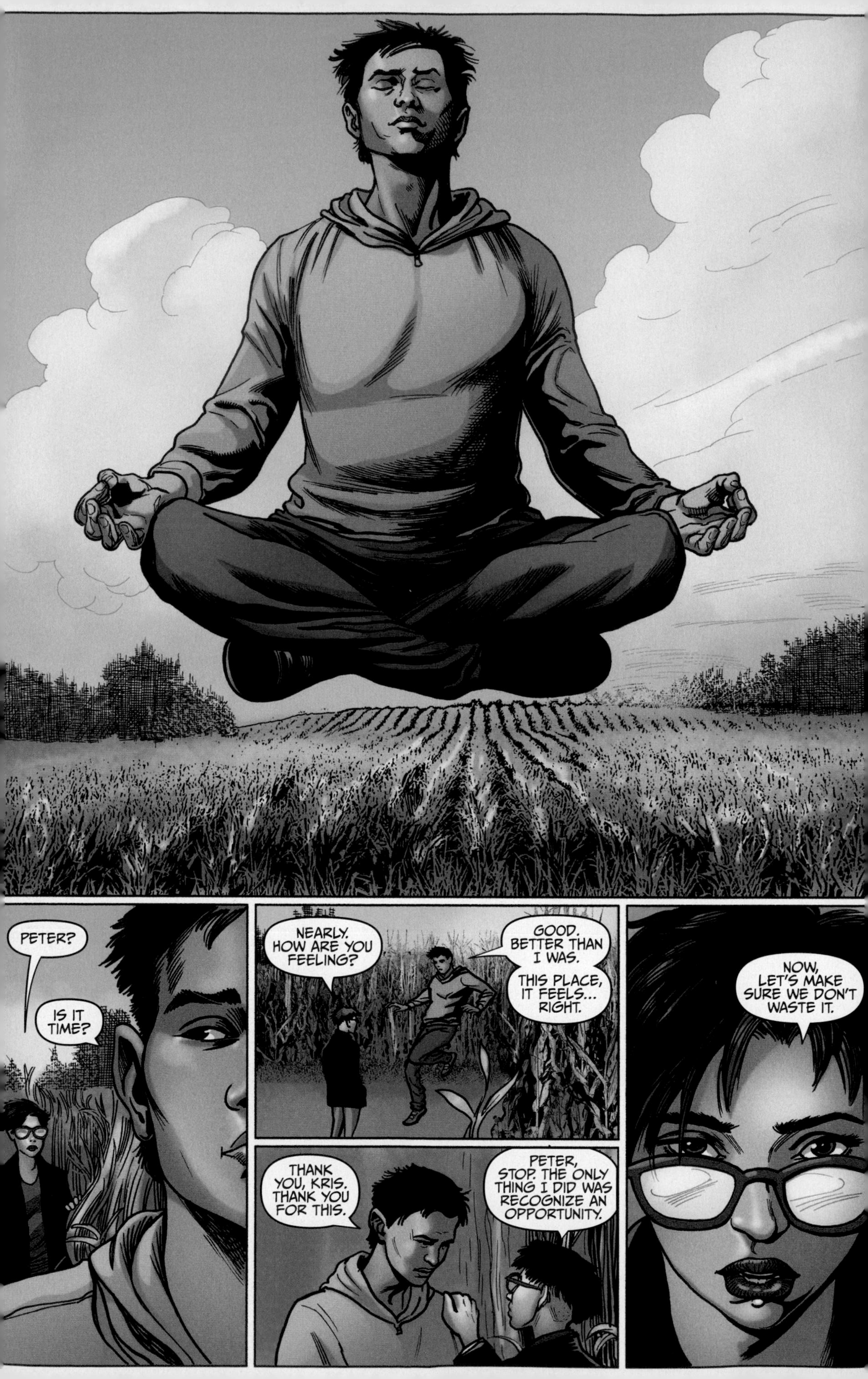

PETER?
IS IT TIME?
NEARLY. HOW ARE YOU FEELING?
GOOD. BETTER THAN I WAS.
THIS PLACE, IT FEELS... RIGHT.
THANK YOU, KRIS. THANK YOU FOR THIS.
PETER, STOP. THE ONLY THING I DID WAS RECOGNIZE AN OPPORTUNITY.
NOW, LET'S MAKE SURE WE DON'T WASTE IT.

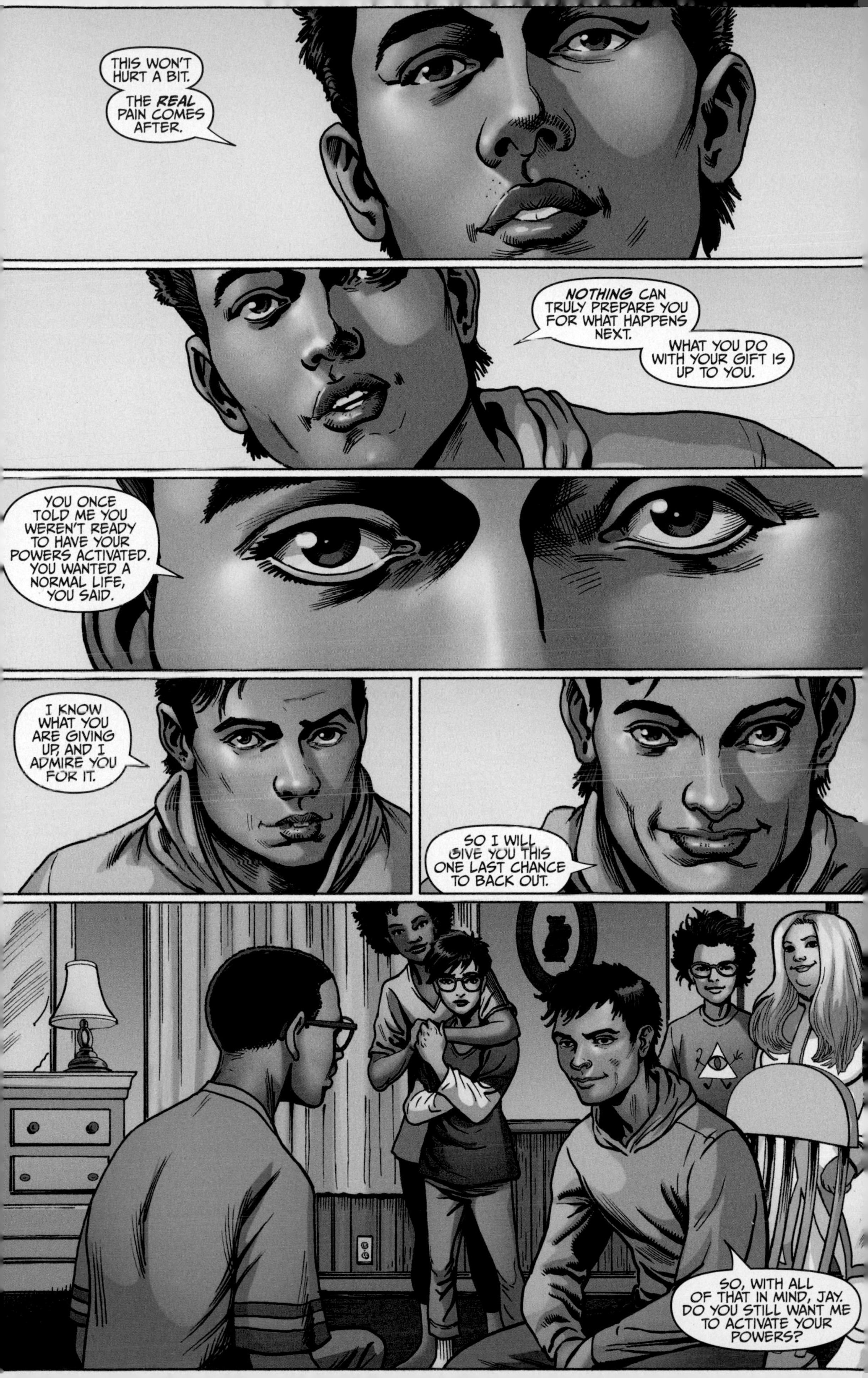
THIS WON'T HURT A BIT.
THE *REAL* PAIN COMES AFTER.
NOTHING CAN TRULY PREPARE YOU FOR WHAT HAPPENS NEXT.
WHAT YOU DO WITH YOUR GIFT IS UP TO YOU.
YOU ONCE TOLD ME YOU WEREN'T READY TO HAVE YOUR POWERS ACTIVATED. YOU WANTED A NORMAL LIFE, YOU SAID.
I KNOW WHAT YOU ARE GIVING UP, AND I ADMIRE YOU FOR IT.
SO I WILL GIVE YOU THIS ONE LAST CHANCE TO BACK OUT.
SO, WITH ALL OF THAT IN MIND, JAY. DO YOU STILL WANT ME TO ACTIVATE YOUR POWERS?

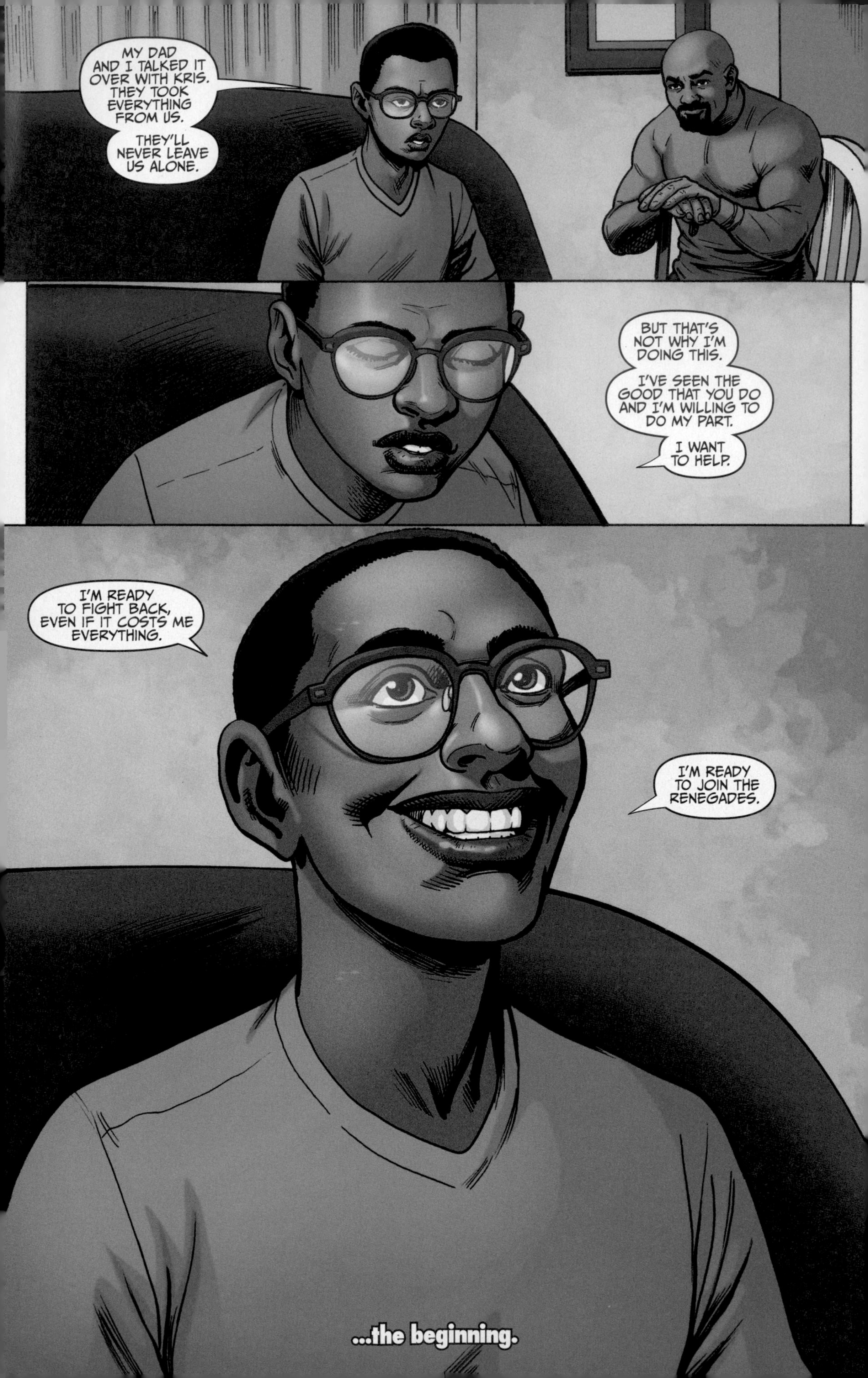
MY DAD AND I TALKED IT OVER WITH KRIS. THEY TOOK EVERYTHING FROM US.
THEY'LL NEVER LEAVE US ALONE.
BUT THAT'S NOT WHY I'M DOING THIS.
I'VE SEEN THE GOOD THAT YOU DO AND I'M WILLING TO DO MY PART.
I WANT TO HELP.
I'M READY TO FIGHT BACK, EVEN IF IT COSTS ME EVERYTHING.
I'M READY TO JOIN THE RENEGADES.
...the beginning.

GALLERY

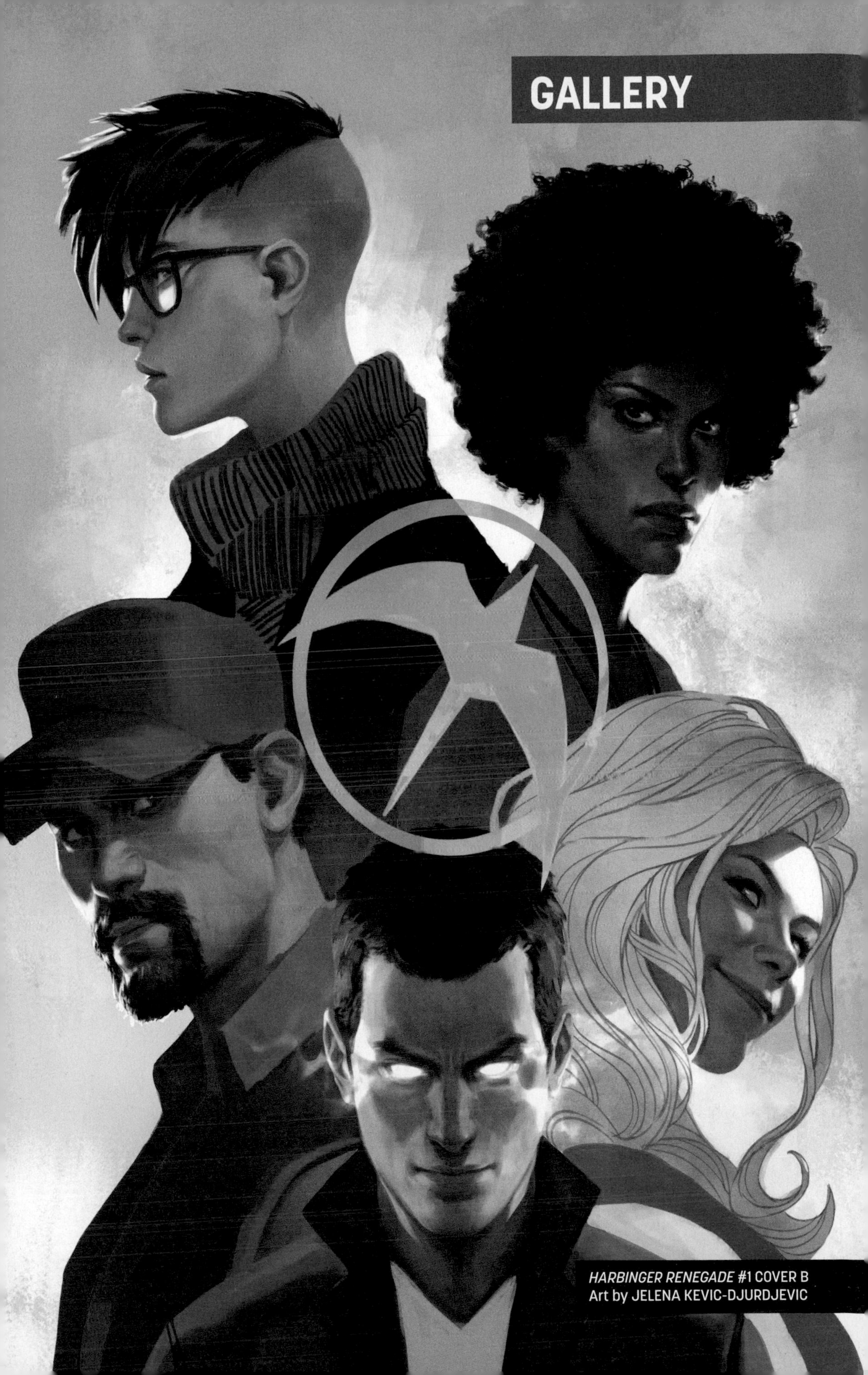

HARBINGER RENEGADE #1 COVER B
Art by JELENA KEVIC-DJURDJEVIC

HARBINGER RENEGADE #1
LOCAL COMIC BOOK DAY 2016 VARIANT COVER
Art by STEPHEN SEGOVIA with MICHAEL SPICER

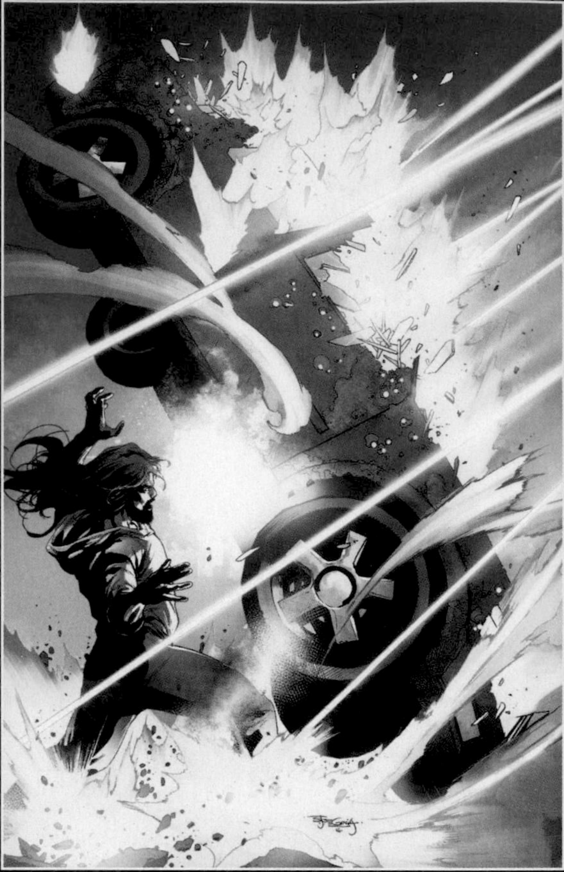

HARBINGER RENEGADE #2 COVER C
Art by MONIKA PALOSZ

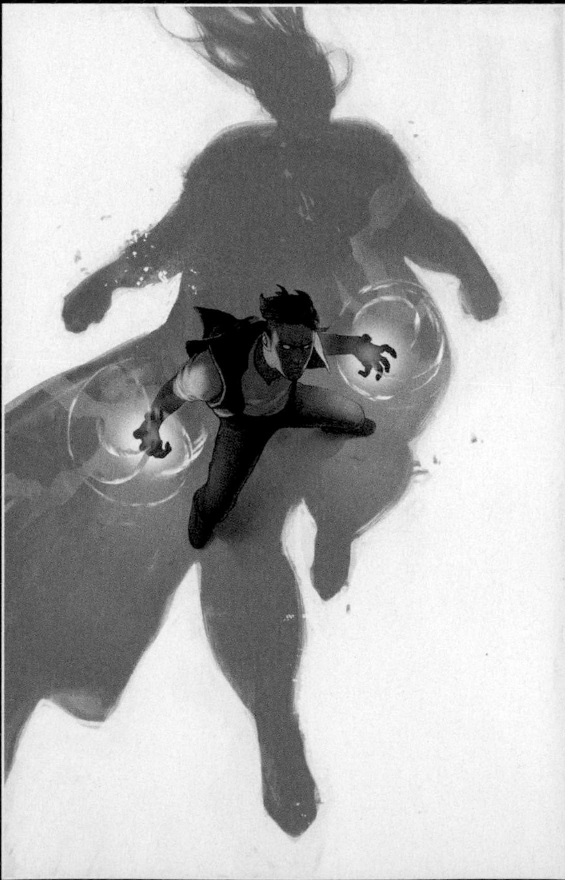

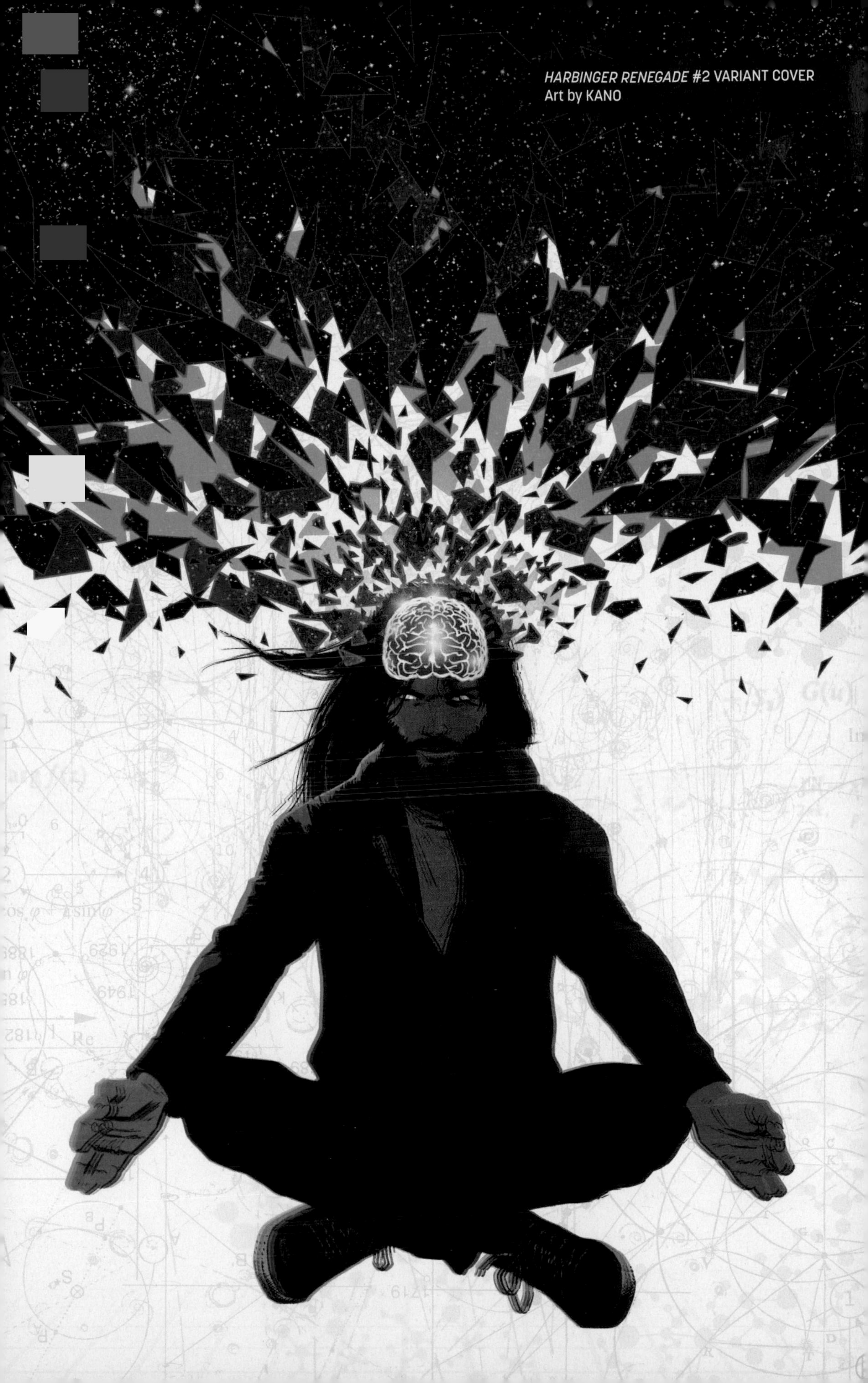

HARBINGER RENEGADE #2 VARIANT COVER
Art by KANO

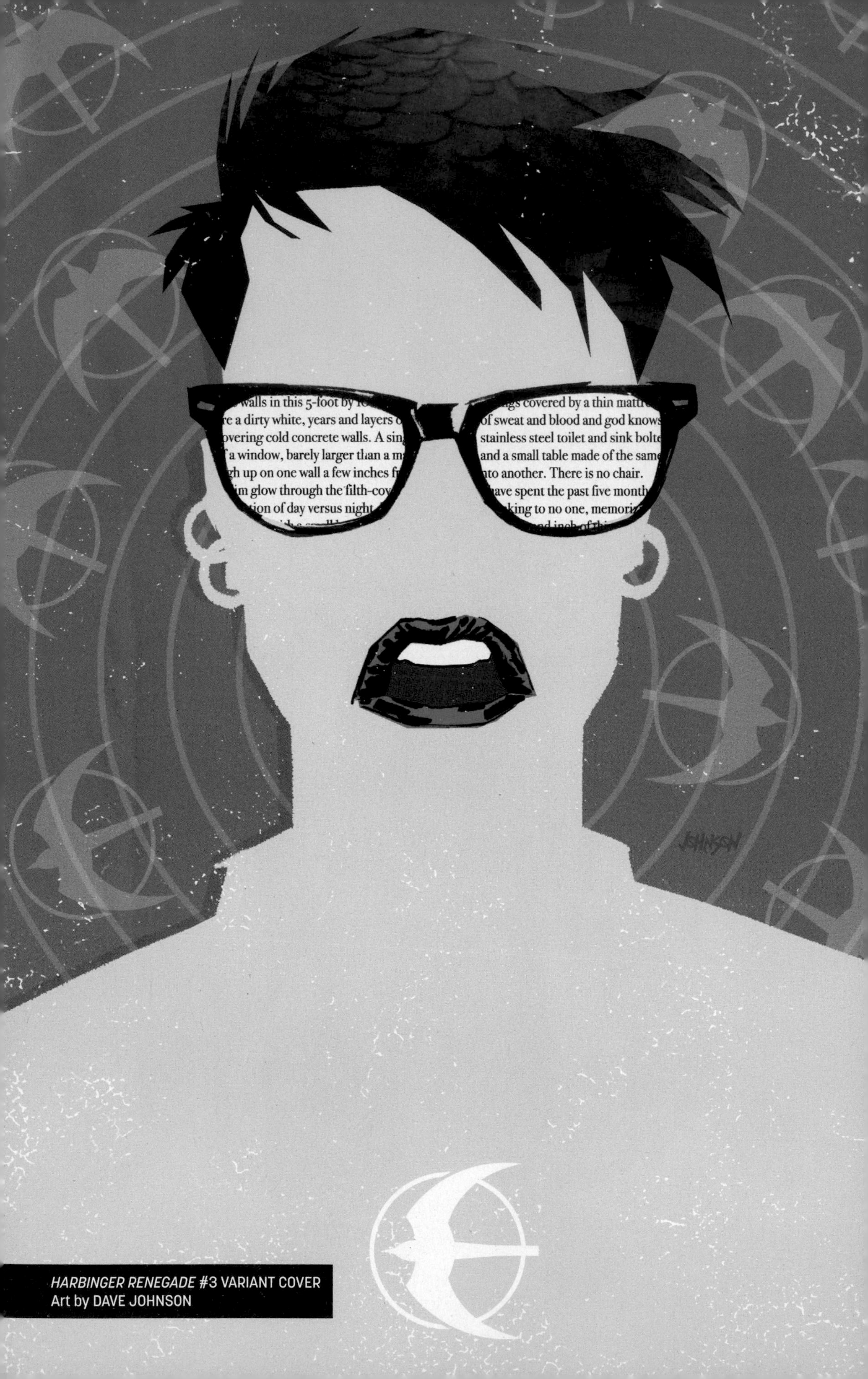
JOHNSON

HARBINGER RENEGADE #3 VARIANT COVER
Art by DAVE JOHNSON

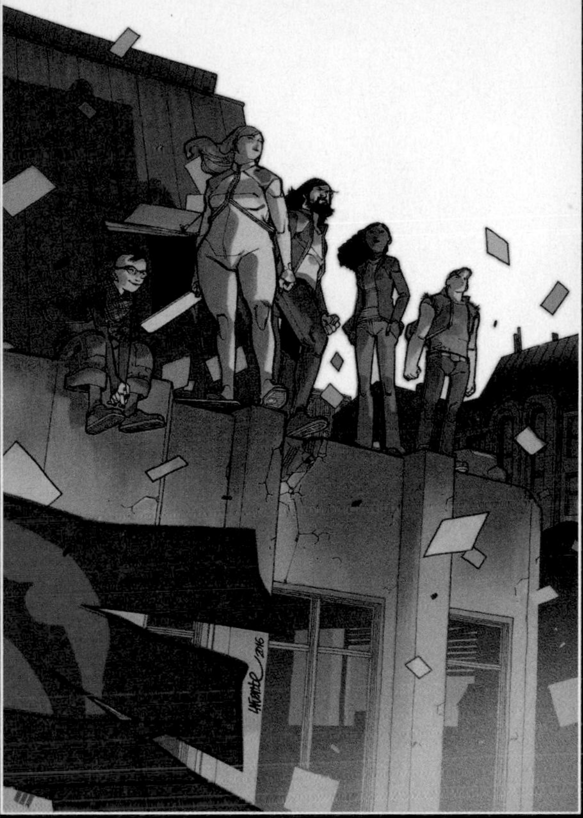

HARBINGER RENEGADE #4 VARIANT COVER
Art by DAVID LAFUENTE

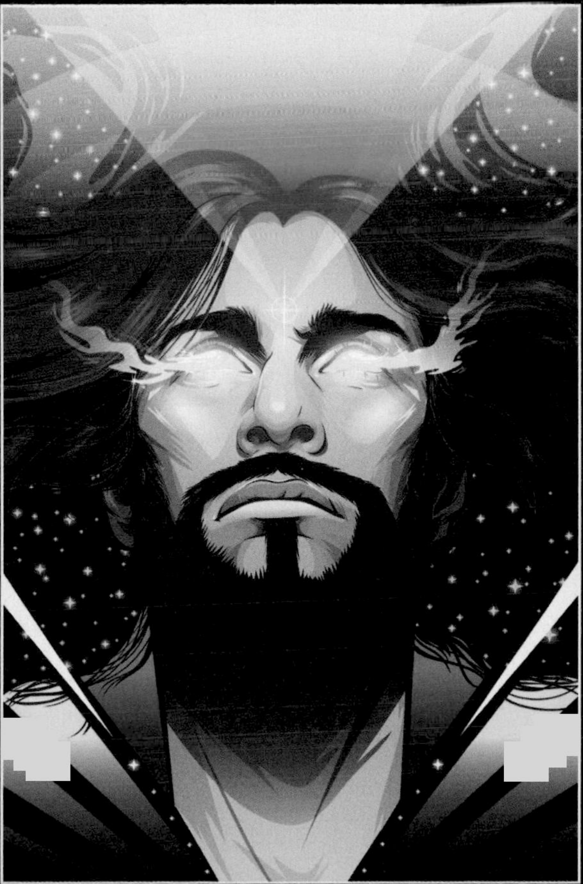

HARBINGER RENEGADE #4 VARIANT COVER
Art by CRYSSY CHEUNG

HARBINGER RENEGADE #1, p. 3
Art by JUAN JOSÉ RYP

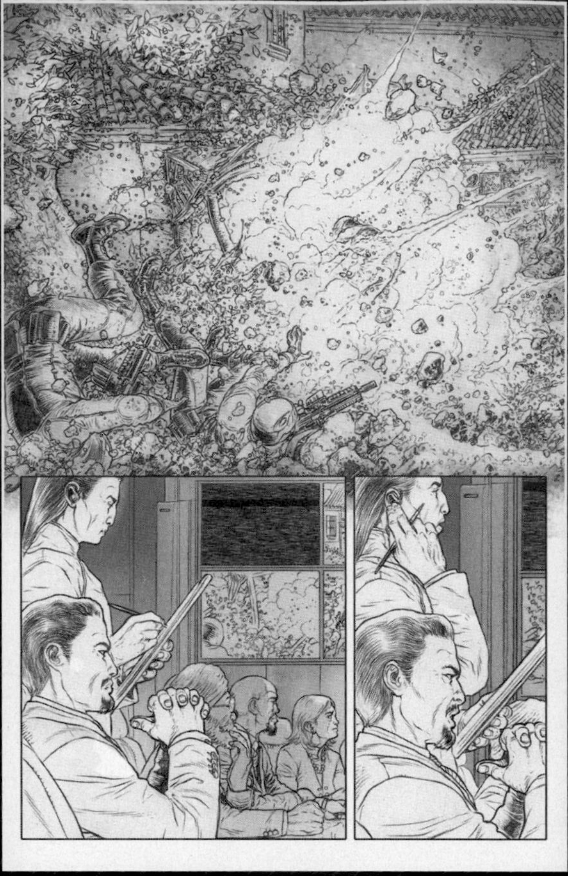

HARBINGER RENEGADE #1, p. 24
Art by DARICK ROBERTSON with RICHARD CLARK

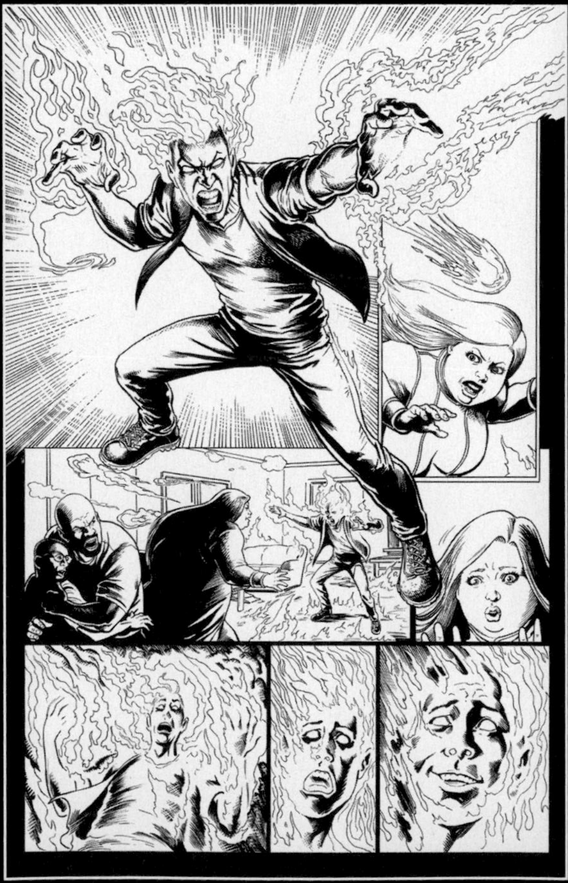

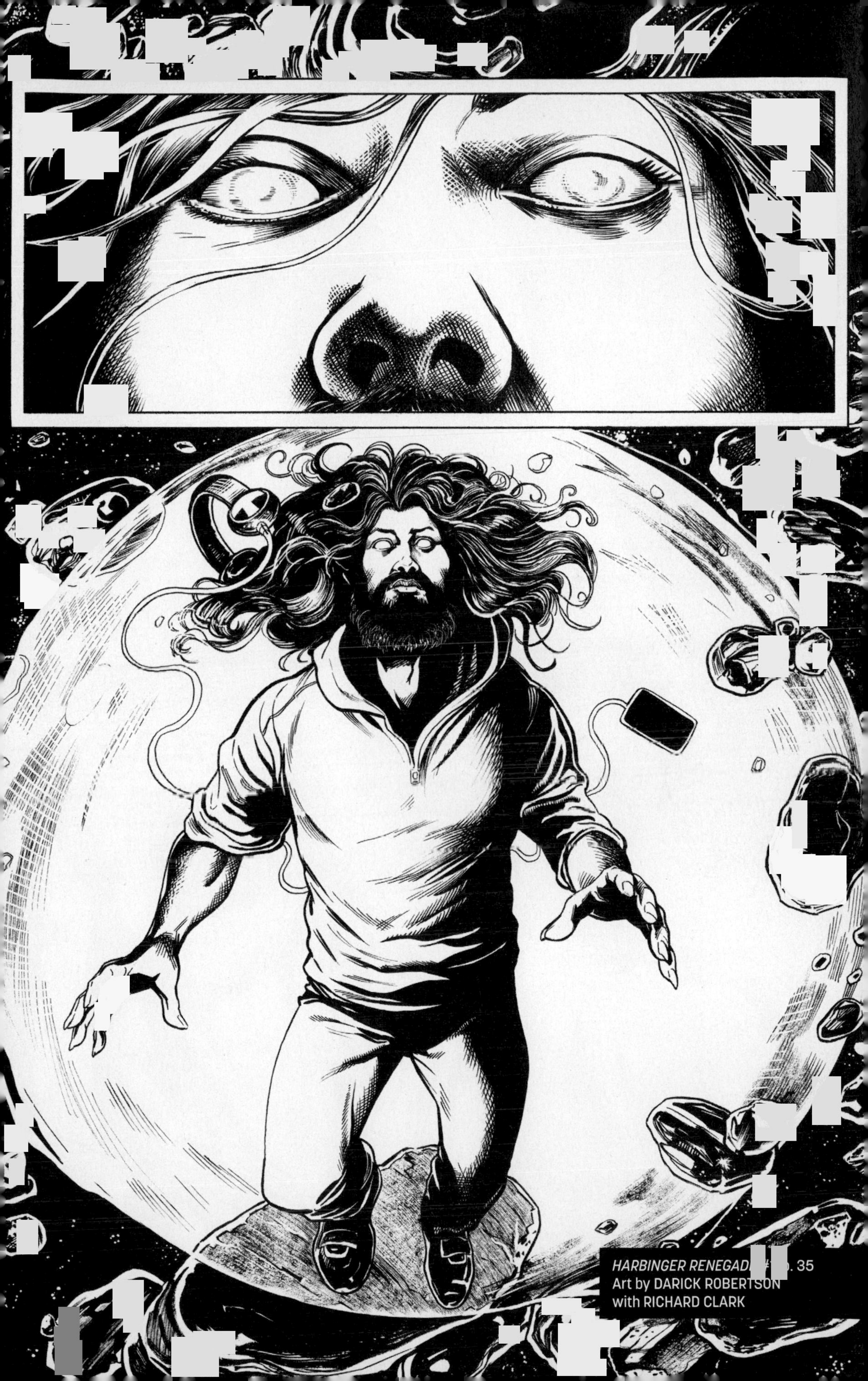

HARBINGER RENEGADE #[illegible]. 35
Art by DARICK ROBERTSON
with RICHARD CLARK

HARBINGER RENEGADE #2, pages 10-11
Art by DARICK ROBERTSON
with RICHARD CLARK

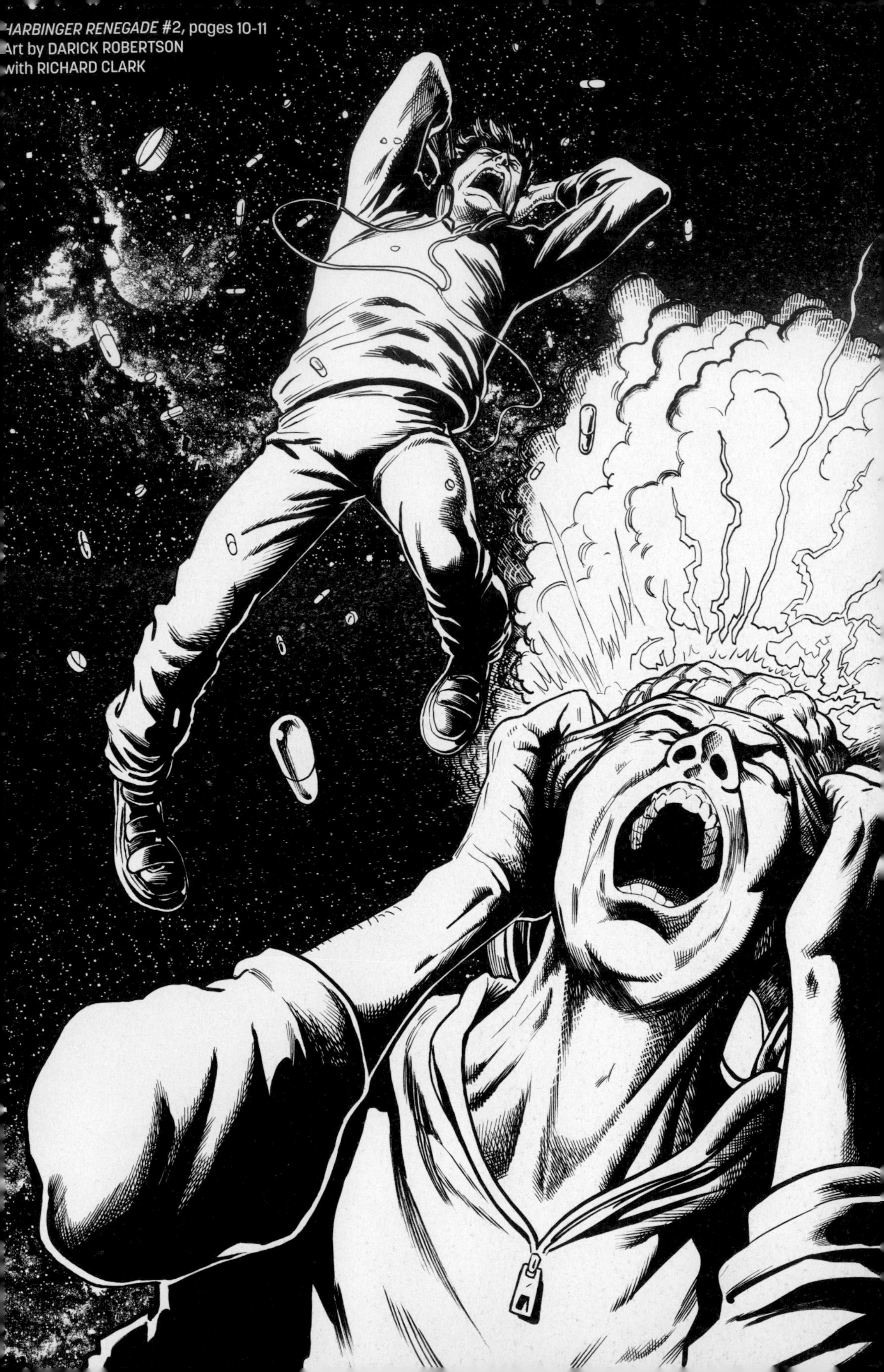

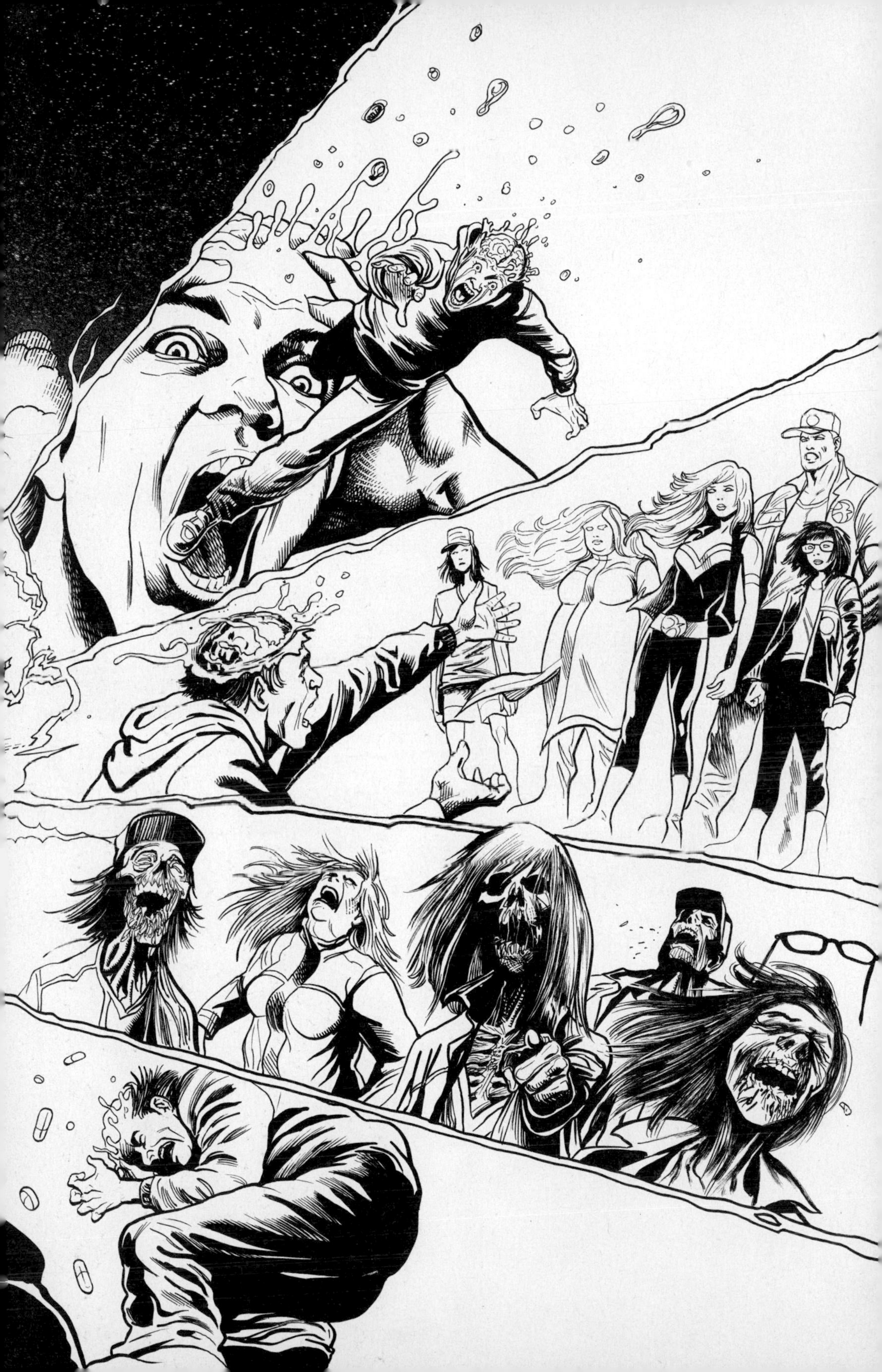

HARBINGER RENEGADE #3, p. 4
Art by JUAN JOSÉ RYP

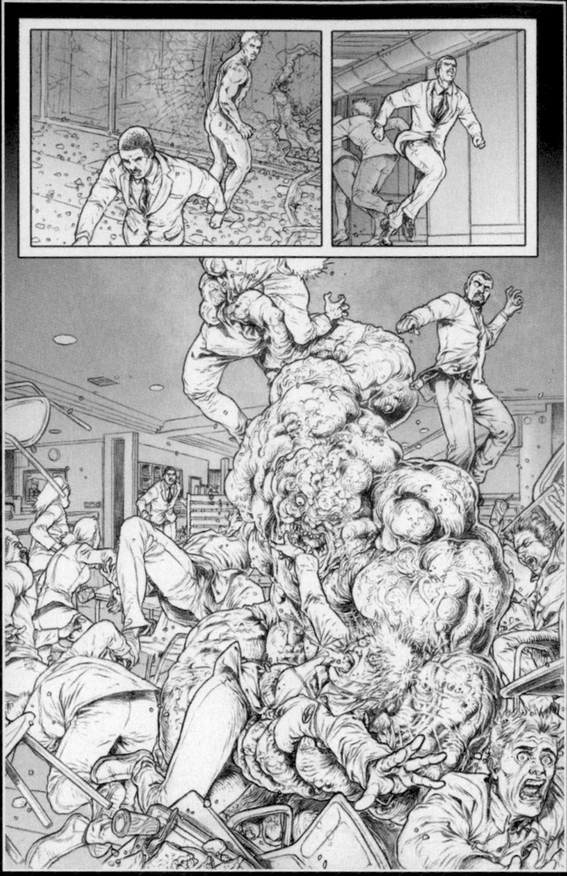

HARBINGER RENEGADE #3, p. 10
Art by DARICK ROBERTSON with RICHARD CLARK

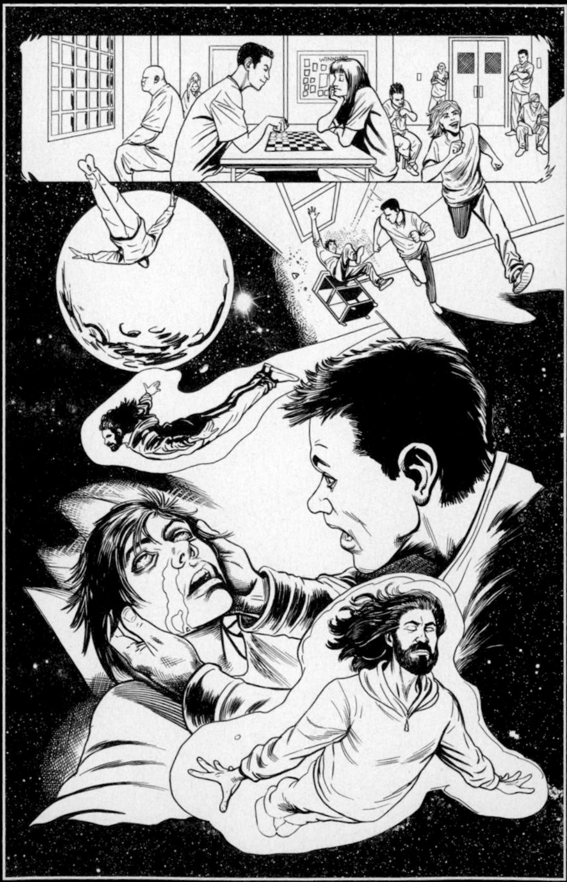

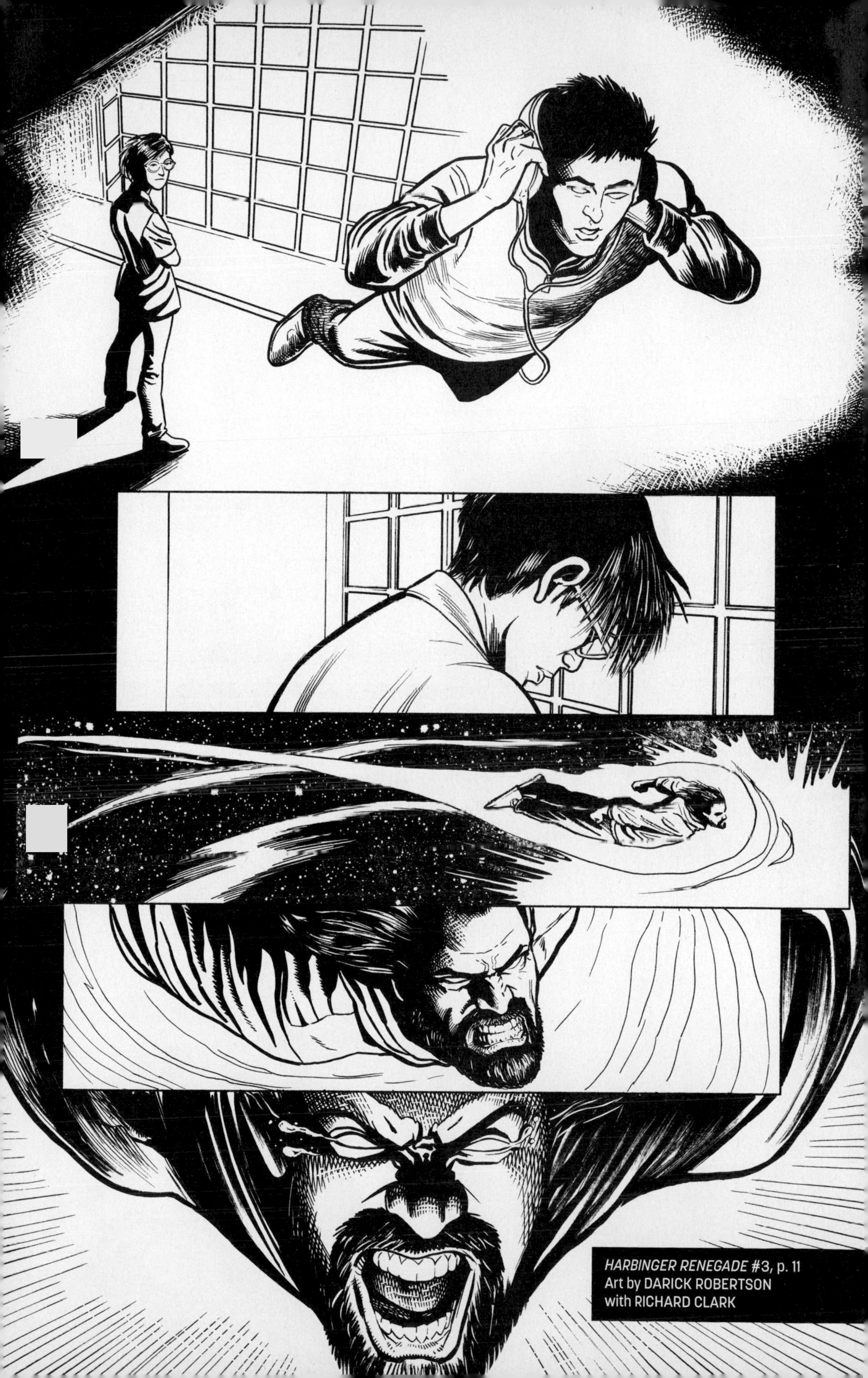
HARBINGER RENEGADE #3, p. 11
Art by DARICK ROBERTSON
with RICHARD CLARK

HARBINGER RENEGADE #4, p. 6
Art by JUAN JOSÉ RYP

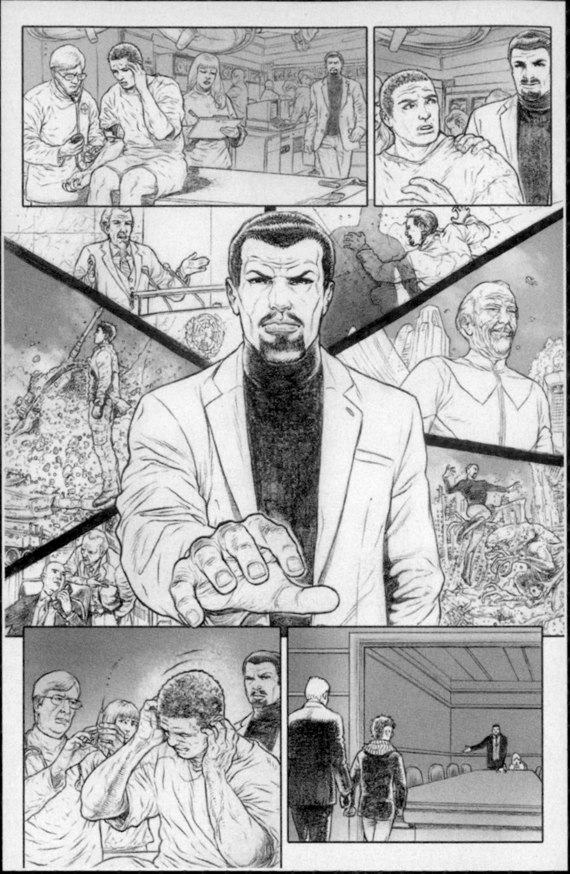

HARBINGER RENEGADE #4, p. 14
Art by DARICK ROBERTSON with RICHARD CLARK

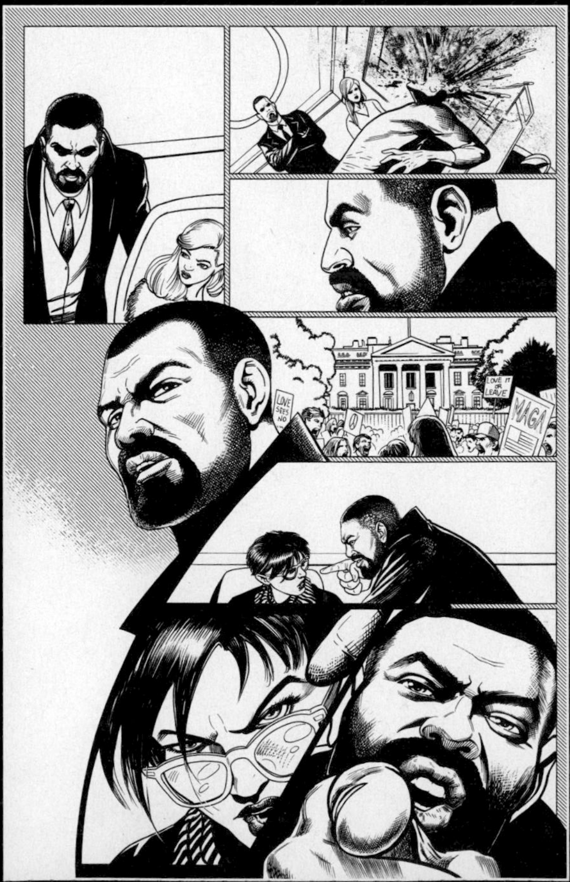
LOVE SEES NO
LOVE IT OR LEAVE
MAGA

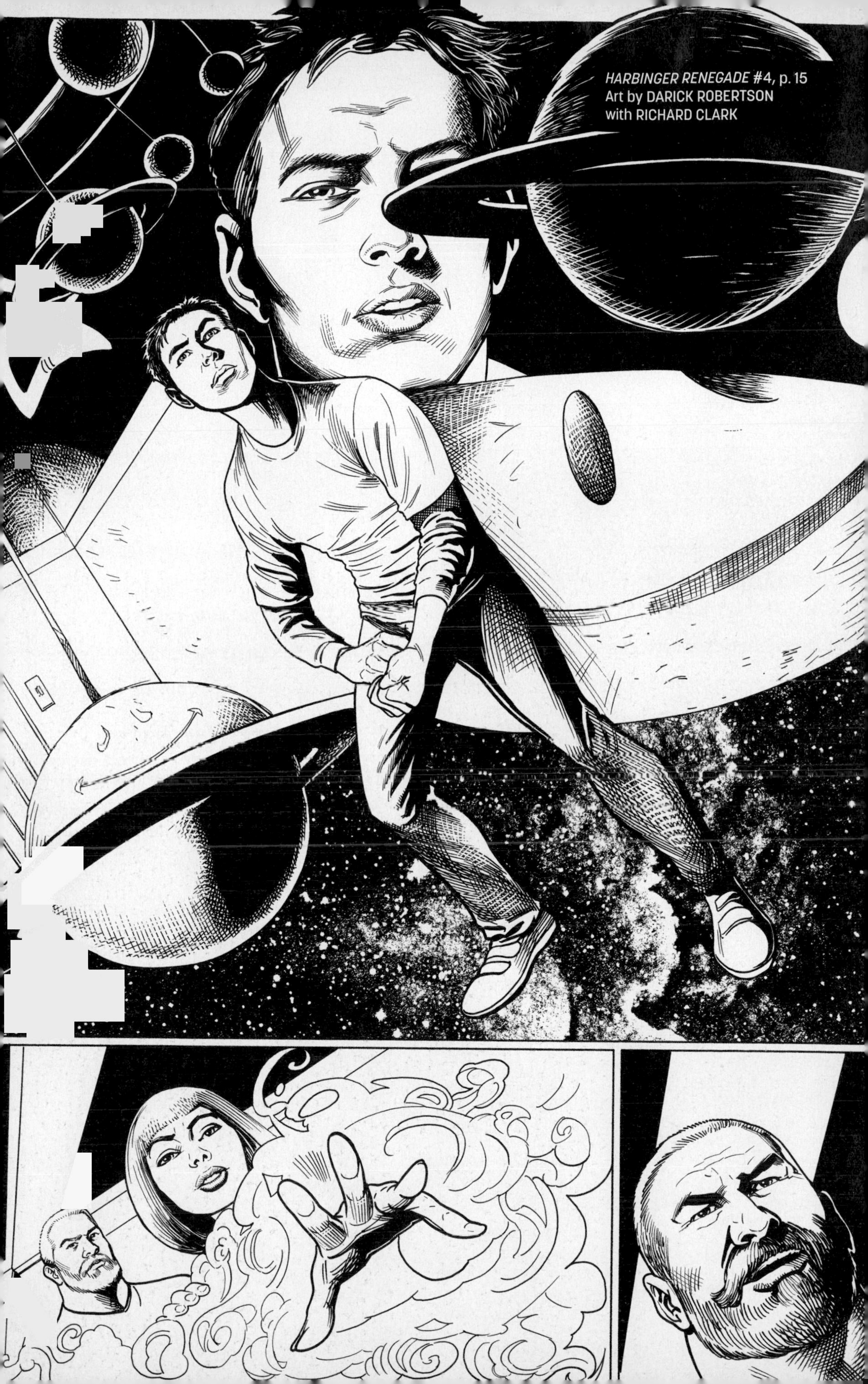

HARBINGER RENEGADE #4, p. 15
Art by DARICK ROBERTSON
with RICHARD CLARK

EXPLORE THE VALIANT UNIVERSE

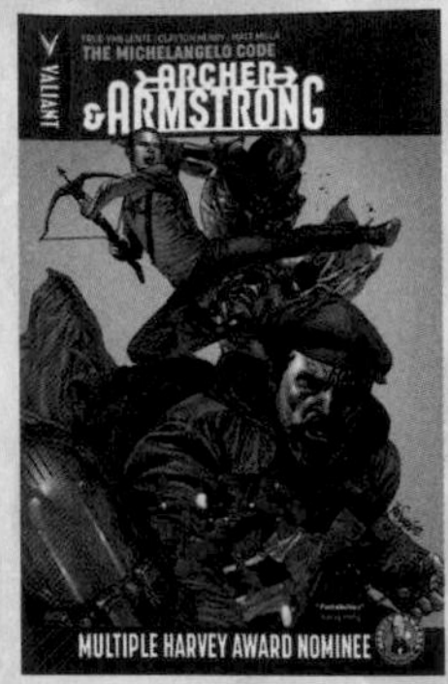
VALIANT
THE MICHELANGELO CODE
ARCHER & ARMSTRONG
MULTIPLE HARVEY AWARD NOMINEE

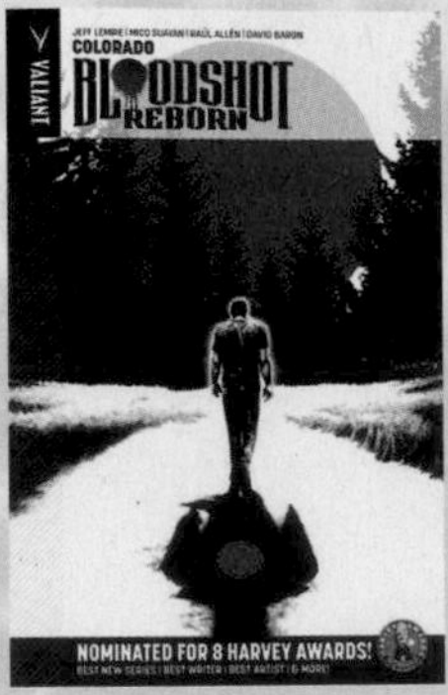
VALIANT
COLORADO
BLOODSHOT REBORN
NOMINATED FOR 8 HARVEY AWARDS!

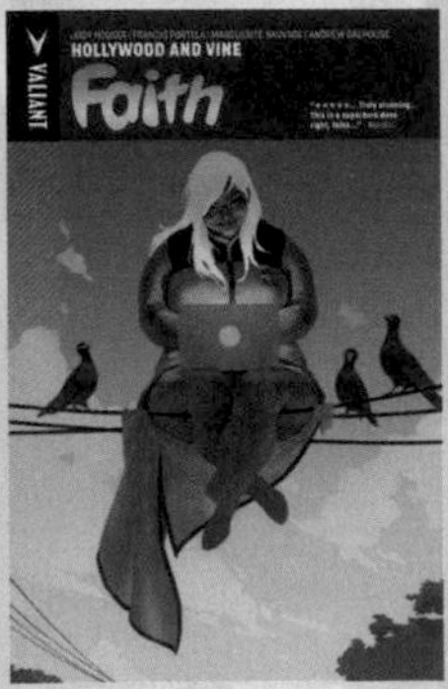
VALIANT
HOLLYWOOD AND VINE
Faith

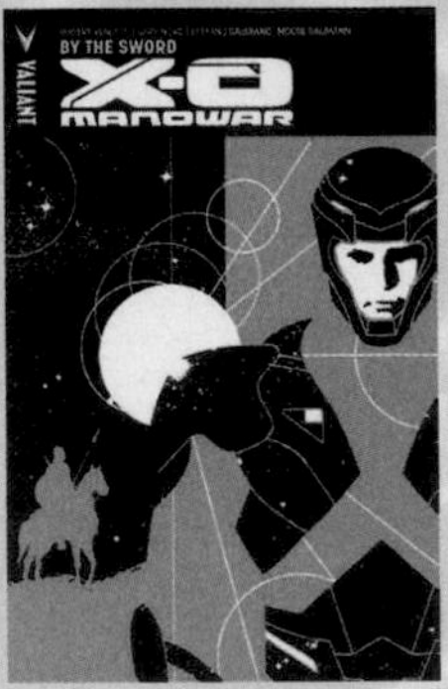
VALIANT
BY THE SWORD
X-O MANOWAR

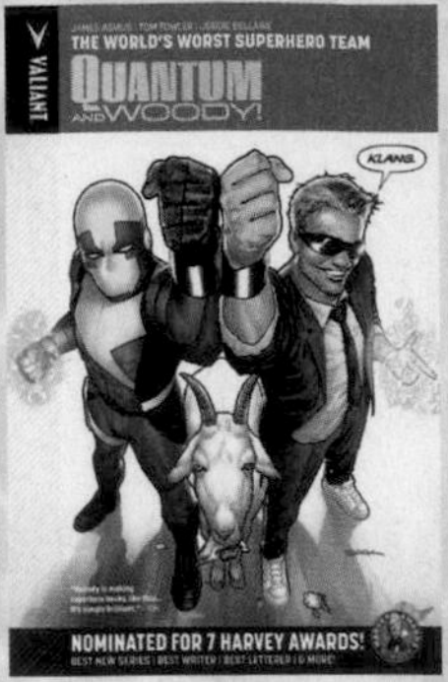
VALIANT
THE WORLD'S WORST SUPERHERO TEAM
QUANTUM AND WOODY!
NOMINATED FOR 7 HARVEY AWARDS!

4001 A.D.

4001 A.D.
ISBN: 9781682151433

4001 A.D.: Beyond New Japan
ISBN: 9781682151464

Rai Vol 4: 4001 A.D.
ISBN: 9781682151471

A&A: THE ADVENTURES OF ARCHER AND ARMSTRONG

Volume 1: In the Bag
ISBN: 9781682151495

Volume 2: Romance and Road Trips
ISBN: 9781682151716

ARCHER & ARMSTRONG

Volume 1: The Michelangelo Code
ISBN: 9780979640988

Volume 2: Wrath of the Eternal Warrior
ISBN: 9781939346049

Volume 3: Far Faraway
ISBN: 9781939346148

Volume 4: Sect Civil War
ISBN: 9781939346254

Volume 5: Mission: Improbable
ISBN: 9781939346353

Volume 6: American Wasteland
ISBN: 9781939346421

Volume 7: The One Percent and Other Tales
ISBN: 9781939346537

ARMOR HUNTERS

Armor Hunters
ISBN: 9781939346452

Armor Hunters: Bloodshot
ISBN: 9781939346469

Armor Hunters: Harbinger
ISBN: 9781939346506

Unity Vol. 3: Armor Hunters
ISBN: 9781939346445

X-O Manowar Vol. 7: Armor Hunters
ISBN: 9781939346476

BLOODSHOT

Volume 1: Setting the World on Fire
ISBN: 9780979640964

Volume 2: The Rise and the Fall
ISBN: 9781939346032

Volume 3: Harbinger Wars
ISBN: 9781939346124

Volume 4: H.A.R.D. Corps
ISBN: 9781939346193

Volume 5: Get Some!
ISBN: 9781939346315

Volume 6: The Glitch and Other Tales
ISBN: 9781939346711

BLOODSHOT REBORN

Volume 1: Colorado
ISBN: 9781939346674

Volume 2: The Hunt
ISBN: 9781939346827

Volume 3: The Analog Man
ISBN: 9781682151334

Volume 4: Bloodshot Island
ISBN: 9781682151952

BOOK OF DEATH

Book of Death
ISBN: 9781939346971

Book of Death: The Fall of the Valiant Universe
ISBN: 9781939346988

BRITANNIA

Volume 1
ISBN: 9781682151853

DEAD DROP

ISBN: 9781939346858

THE DEATH-DEFYING DOCTOR MIRAGE

Volume 1
ISBN: 9781939346490

Volume 2: Second Lives
ISBN: 9781682151297

THE DELINQUENTS

ISBN: 9781939346513

DIVINITY

Volume 1
ISBN: 9781939346766

Volume 2
ISBN: 9781682151518

ETERNAL WARRIOR

Volume 1: Sword of the Wild
ISBN: 9781939346209

Volume 2: Eternal Emperor
ISBN: 9781939346292

Volume 3: Days of Steel
ISBN: 9781939346742

WRATH OF THE ETERNAL WARRIOR

Volume 1: Risen
ISBN: 9781682151235

Volume 2: Labyrinth
ISBN: 9781682151594

Volume 3: Deal With a Devil
ISBN: 9781682151976

FAITH

Faith Vol 1: Hollywood and Vine
ISBN: 9781682151402

Faith Vol 2: California Scheming
ISBN: 9781682151631

GENERATION ZERO

Volume 1: We Are the Future
ISBN: 9781682151754

HARBINGER

Volume 1: Omega Rising
ISBN: 9780979640957

Volume 2: Renegades
ISBN: 9781939346025

Volume 3: Harbinger Wars
ISBN: 9781939346117

Volume 4: Perfect Day
ISBN: 9781939346155

Volume 5: Death of a Renegade
ISBN: 9781939346339

Volume 6: Omegas
ISBN: 9781939346384

EXPLORE THE VALIANT UNIVERSE

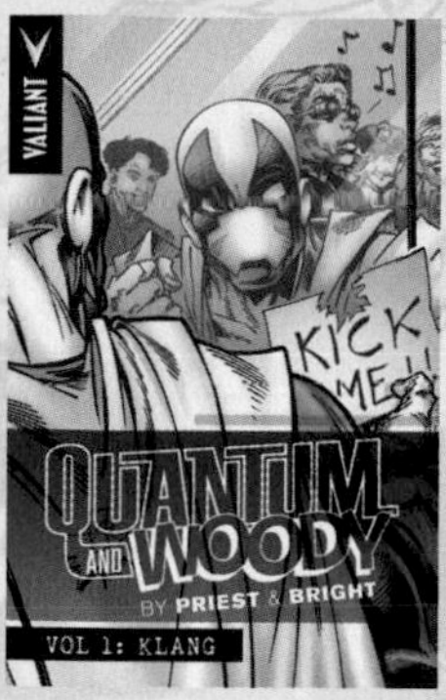
VALIANT
KICK ME!!
QUANTUM AND WOODY
BY PRIEST & BRIGHT
VOL 1: KLANG

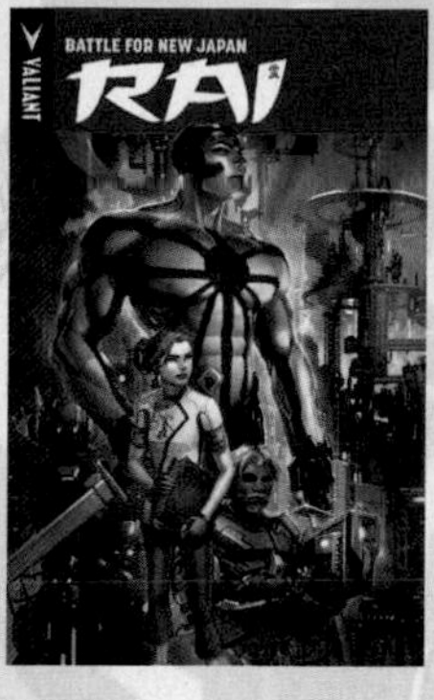
VALIANT
BATTLE FOR NEW JAPAN
RAI

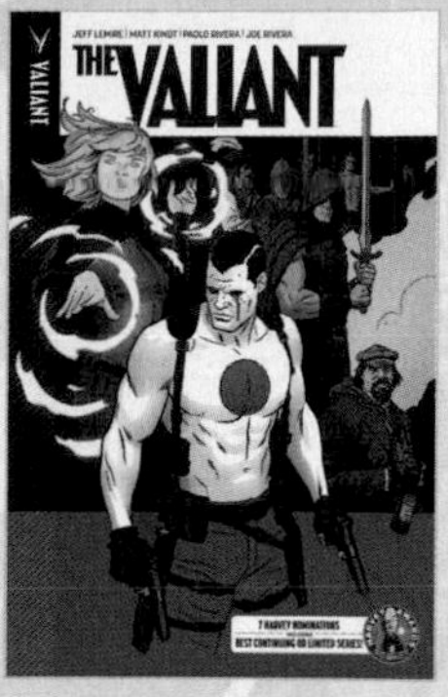
VALIANT
THE VALIANT

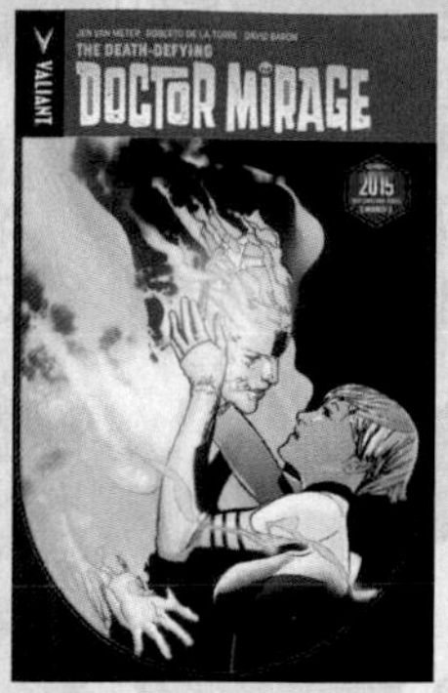
VALIANT
THE DEATH-DEFYING
DOCTOR MIRAGE

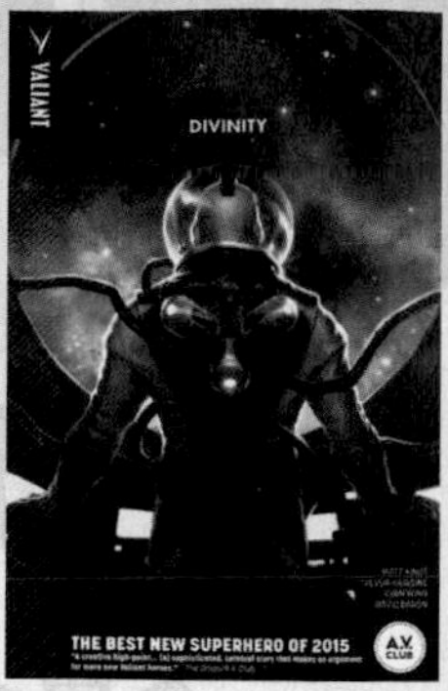
VALIANT
DIVINITY
THE BEST NEW SUPERHERO OF 2015

HARBINGER RENEGADE

Volume 1: The Judgment of Solomon
ISBN: 9781682151693

HARBINGER WARS

Harbinger Wars
ISBN: 9781939346094

Bloodshot Vol. 3: Harbinger Wars
ISBN: 9781939346124

Harbinger Vol. 3: Harbinger Wars
ISBN: 9781939346117

IMPERIUM

Volume 1: Collecting Monsters
ISBN: 9781939346759

Volume 2: Broken Angels
ISBN: 9781939346896

Volume 3: The Vine Imperative
ISBN: 9781682151112

Volume 4: Stormbreak
ISBN: 9781682151372

NINJAK

Volume 1: Weaponeer
ISBN: 9781939346667

Volume 2: The Shadow Wars
ISBN: 9781939346940

Volume 3: Operation: Deadside
ISBN: 9781682151259

Volume 4: The Siege of King's Castle
ISBN: 9781682151617

Volume 5: The Fist & The Steel
ISBN: 9781682151792

QUANTUM AND WOODY

Volume 1: The World's Worst Superhero Team
ISBN: 9781939346186

Volume 2: In Security
ISBN: 9781939346230

Volume 3: Crooked Pasts, Present Tense
ISBN: 9781939346391

Volume 4: Quantum and Woody Must Die!
ISBN: 9781939346629

QUANTUM AND WOODY BY PRIEST & BRIGHT

Volume 1: Klang
ISBN: 9781939346780

Volume 2: Switch
ISBN: 9781939346803

Volume 3: And So...
ISBN: 9781939346865

Volume 4: Q2 - The Return
ISBN: 9781682151099

RAI

Volume 1: Welcome to New Japan
ISBN: 9781939346414

Volume 2: Battle for New Japan
ISBN: 9781939346612

Volume 3: The Orphan
ISBN: 9781939346841

Rai Vol 4: 4001 A.D.
ISBN: 9781682151471

SHADOWMAN

Volume 1: Birth Rites
ISBN: 9781939346001

Volume 2: Darque Reckoning
ISBN: 9781939346056

Volume 3: Deadside Blues
ISBN: 9781939346162

Volume 4: Fear, Blood, And Shadows
ISBN: 9781939346278

Volume 5: End Times
ISBN: 9781939346377

SHADOWMAN BY ENNIS & WOOD

ISBN: 9781682151358

IVAR, TIMEWALKER

Volume 1: Making History
ISBN: 9781939346636

Volume 2: Breaking History
ISBN: 9781939346834

Volume 3: Ending History
ISBN: 9781939346995

UNITY

Volume 1: To Kill a King
ISBN: 9781939346261

Volume 2: Trapped by Webnet
ISBN: 9781939346346

Volume 3: Armor Hunters
ISBN: 9781939346445

Volume 4: The United
ISBN: 9781939346544

Volume 5: Homefront
ISBN: 9781939346797

Volume 6: The War-Monger
ISBN: 9781939346902

Volume 7: Revenge of the Armor Hunters
ISBN: 9781682151136

THE VALIANT

ISBN: 9781939346605

VALIANT ZEROES AND ORIGINS

ISBN: 9781939346582

X-O MANOWAR

Volume 1: By the Sword
ISBN: 9780979640940

Volume 2: Enter Ninjak
ISBN: 9780979640995

Volume 3: Planet Death
ISBN: 9781939346087

Volume 4: Homecoming
ISBN: 9781939346179

Volume 5: At War With Unity
ISBN: 9781939346247

Volume 6: Prelude to Armor Hunters
ISBN: 9781939346407

Volume 7: Armor Hunters
ISBN: 9781939346476

Volume 8: Enter: Armorines
ISBN: 9781939346551

Volume 9: Dead Hand
ISBN: 9781939346650

Volume 10: Exodus
ISBN: 9781939346933

Volume 11: The Kill List
ISBN: 9781682151273

Volume 12: Long Live the King
ISBN: 9781682151655

Volume 13: Succession and Other Tales
ISBN: 9781682151754

EXPLORE THE VALIANT UNIVERSE

VALIANT
HARBINGER
DELUXE EDITION 2

VALIANT
ROBERT VENDITTI | MATT KINDT | JOSHUA DYSART | JOE HARRIS | ROBERT GILL
DOUG BRAITHWAITE | DIEGO BERNARD | TREVOR HAIRSINE | STEPHEN SEGOVIA
ARMOR HUNTERS
DELUXE EDITION

VALIANT
VALIANT MASTERS
JIM SHOOTER | DAVID LAPHAM
CHILDREN OF THE EIGHTH DAY
HARBINGER

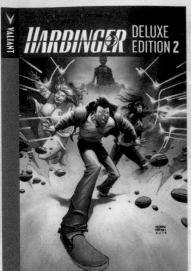

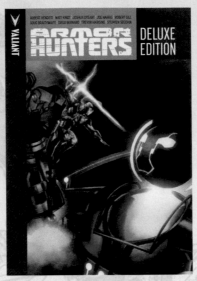

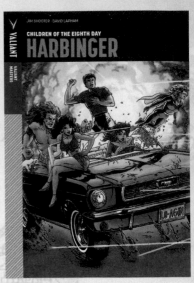

Omnibuses

Archer & Armstrong: The Complete Classic Omnibus
ISBN: 9781939346872
Collecting ARCHER & ARMSTRONG (1992) #0-26, ETERNAL WARRIOR (1992) #25 along with ARCHER & ARMSTRONG: THE FORMATION OF THE SECT.

Quantum and Woody: The Complete Classic Omnibus
ISBN: 9781939346360
Collecting QUANTUM AND WOODY (1997) #0, 1-21 and #32, THE GOAT: H.A.E.D.U.S. #1, and X-O MANOWAR (1996) #16

X-O Manowar Classic Omnibus Vol. 1
ISBN: 9781939346308
Collecting X-O MANOWAR (1992) #0-30, ARMORINES #0, X-O DATABASE #1, as well as material from SECRETS OF THE VALIANT UNIVERSE #1

Deluxe Editions

Archer & Armstrong Deluxe Edition Book 1
ISBN: 9781939346223
Collecting ARCHER & ARMSTRONG #0-13

Archer & Armstrong Deluxe Edition Book 2
ISBN: 9781939346957
Collecting ARCHER & ARMSTRONG #14-25, ARCHER & ARMSTRONG: ARCHER #0 and BLOODSHOT AND H.A.R.D. CORPS #20-21.

Armor Hunters Deluxe Edition
ISBN: 9781939346728
Collecting Armor Hunters #1-4, Armor Hunters: Aftermath #1, Armor Hunters: Bloodshot #1-3, Armor Hunters: Harbinger #1-3, Unity #8-11, and X-O MANOWAR #23-29

Bloodshot Deluxe Edition Book 1
ISBN: 9781939346216
Collecting BLOODSHOT #1-13

Bloodshot Deluxe Edition Book 2
ISBN: 9781939346810
Collecting BLOODSHOT AND H.A.R.D. CORPS #14-23, BLOODSHOT #24-25, BLOODSHOT #0, BLOODSHOT AND H.A.R.D. CORPS: H.A.R.D. CORPS #0, along with ARCHER & ARMSTRONG #18-19

Bloodshot Reborn Deluxe Edition Book 1
ISBN: 978-1-68215-155-6
Collecting BLOODSHOT REBORN #1-13

Book of Death Deluxe Edition
ISBN: 9781682151150
Collecting BOOK OF DEATH #1-4, BOOK OF DEATH: THE FALL OF BLOODSHOT #1, BOOK OF DEATH: THE FALL OF NINJAK #1, BOOK OF DEATH: THE FALL OF HARBINGER #1, and BOOK OF DEATH: THE FALL OF X-O MANOWAR #1.

The Death-Defying Doctor Mirage Deluxe Edition
ISBN: 978-1-68215-153-2
Collecting THE DEATH-DEFYING DR. MIRAGE #1-5 and THE DEATH-DEFYING DR. MIRAGE: SECOND LIVES #1-4

Divinity Deluxe Edition
ISBN: 97819393460993
Collecting DIVNITY #1-4

Faith: Hollywood & Vine Deluxe Edition
ISBN: 978-1-68215-201-0
Collecting FAITH #1-4 and HARBINGER: FAITH #0

Harbinger Deluxe Edition Book 1
ISBN: 9781939346131
Collecting HARBINGER #0-14

Harbinger Deluxe Edition Book 2
ISBN: 9781939346773
Collecting HARBINGER #15-25, HARBINGER: OMEGAS #1-3, and HARBINGER: BLEEDING MONK #0

Harbinger Wars Deluxe Edition
ISBN: 9781939346322
Collecting HARBINGER WARS #1-4, HARBINGER #11-14, and BLOODSHOT #10-13

Ivar, Timewalker Deluxe Edition Book 1
ISBN: 9781682151198
Collecting IVAR, TIMEWALKER #1-12

Ninjak Deluxe Edition Book 1
ISBN: 978-1-68215-157-0
Collecting NINJAK #1-13

Quantum and Woody Deluxe Edition Book 1
ISBN: 9781939346681
Collecting QUANTUM AND WOODY #1-12 and QUANTUM AND WOODY: THE GOAT #0

Q2: The Return of Quantum and Woody Deluxe Edition
ISBN: 9781939346568
Collecting Q2: THE RETURN OF QUANTUM AND WOODY #1-5

Rai Deluxe Edition Book 1
ISBN: 9781682151174
Collecting RAI #1-12, along with material from RAI #1 PLUS EDITION and RAI #5 PLUS EDITION

Shadowman Deluxe Edition Book 1
ISBN: 9781939346438
Collecting SHADOWMAN #0-10

Shadowman Deluxe Edition Book 2
ISBN: 9781682151075
Collecting SHADOWMAN #11-16, SHADOWMAN #13X, SHADOWMAN: END TIMES #1-3 and PUNK MAMBO #0

Unity Deluxe Edition Book 1
ISBN: 9781939346575
Collecting UNITY #0-14

The Valiant Deluxe Edition
ISBN: 97819393460986
Collecting THE VALIANT #1-4

X-O Manowar Deluxe Edition Book 1
ISBN: 9781939346100
Collecting X-O MANOWAR #1-14

X-O Manowar Deluxe Edition Book 2
ISBN: 9781939346520
Collecting X-O MANOWAR #15-22, and UNITY #1-4

X-O Manowar Deluxe Edition Book 3
ISBN: 9781682151310
Collecting X-O MANOWAR #23-29 and ARMOR HUNTERS #1-4.

Valiant Masters

Bloodshot Vol. 1 - Blood of the Machine
ISBN: 9780979640933

H.A.R.D. Corps Vol. 1 - Search and Destroy
ISBN: 9781939346285

Harbinger Vol. 1 - Children of the Eighth Day
ISBN: 9781939346483

Ninjak Vol. 1 - Black Water
ISBN: 9780979640971

Rai Vol. 1 - From Honor to Strength
ISBN: 9781939346070

Shadowman Vol. 1 - Spirits Within
ISBN: 9781939346018

Harbinger RENEGADE | READING ORDER

VALIANT
RAFER ROBERTS | DARICK ROBERTSON | JUAN JOSÉ RYP | RICHARD CLARK
THE JUDGMENT OF SOLOMON
Harbinger
RENEGADE

Harbinger Renegade Vol. 1:
The Judgment of Solomon

VALIANT
MASSACRE
Harbinger
RENEGADE

Harbinger Renegade Vol. 2:
Massacre

Read the origin of the most fearless superteam in comics here in the multiple Harvey Award-nominated series, HARBINGER!

VALIANT
OMEGA RISING
HARBINGER

Harbinger Vol. 1:
Omega Rising

VALIANT
RENEGADES
HARBINGER

Harbinger Vol. 2:
Renegades

VALIANT
HARBINGER WARS
HARBINGER

Harbinger Vol. 3:
Harbinger Wars

VALIANT
PERFECT DAY
HARBINGER

Harbinger Vol. 4:
Perfect Day

VALIANT
DEATH OF A RENEGADE
HARBINGER

Harbinger Vol. 5:
Death of a Renegade

VALIANT
HARBINGER
OMEGAS

Harbinger Vol. 6:
Omegas

Harbinger RENEGADE

VOLUME TWO: MASSACRE

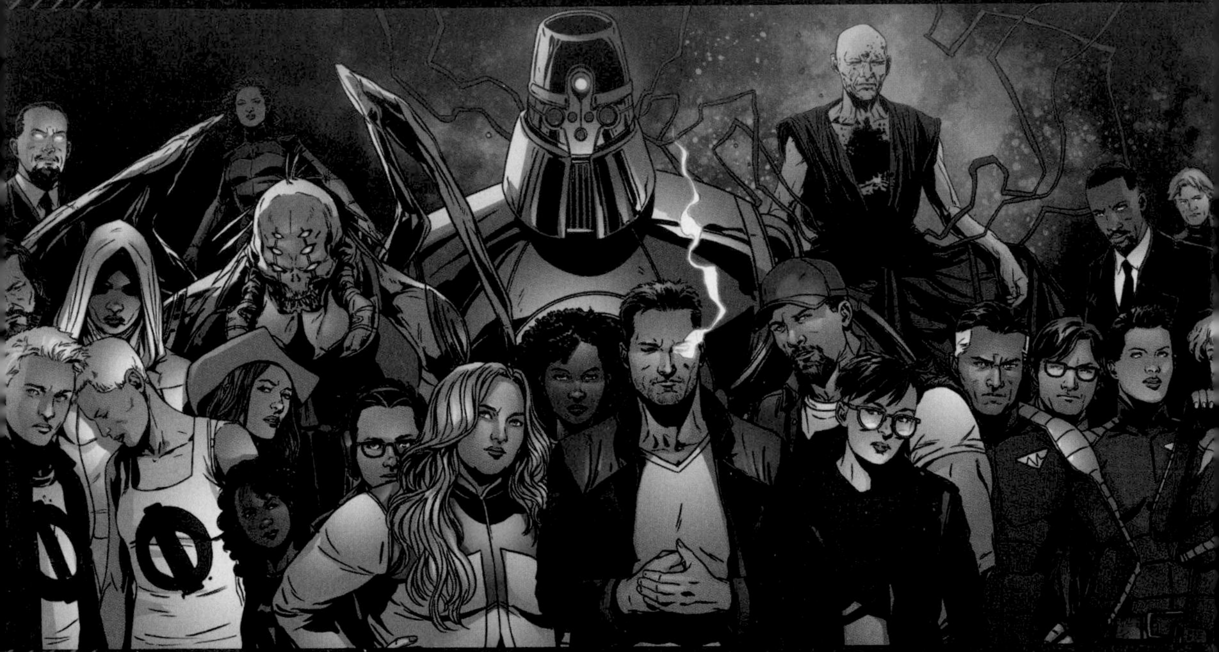

"MASSACRE" BRINGS DEATH TO A MAJOR VALIANT HERO!

Toyo Harada's former protege - Alexander Solomon, a "psiot" with the ability to predict and analyze potential futures - has been waiting for this moment. With the Harbinger Renegades - Peter Stanchek, Faith, Kris Hathaway, and Torque - now reunited as a result of his covert manipulations, his ultimate gambit can now begin. But he's not the only one who has been watching. Major Charlie Palmer has just re-assigned a new division of the militarized psiot hunters codenamed H.A.R.D. Corps to active duty...and they're about to bring a torrent of blood and calamity roaring into the streets of a major American metropolis for an all-out firefight.

The Harbinger Renegades. Livewire. Alexander Solomon. Generation Zero. Toyo Harada. Secret Weapons. Imperium. None of them are safe...and, when the smoke clears, a pivotal Valiant hero will become the first sacrifice of the massive Harbinger War that is to come...

Harvey Award-nominated writer Rafer Roberts (*Plastic Farm*) and superstar artist Darick Robertson (*The Boys*, *Transmetropolitan*) begin THE ROAD TO HARBINGER WARS 2 - right here with a bang that will reverberate throughout the entire Valiant Universe...and claim the life of a major hero!

Collecting HARBINGER RENEGADE #5-8.

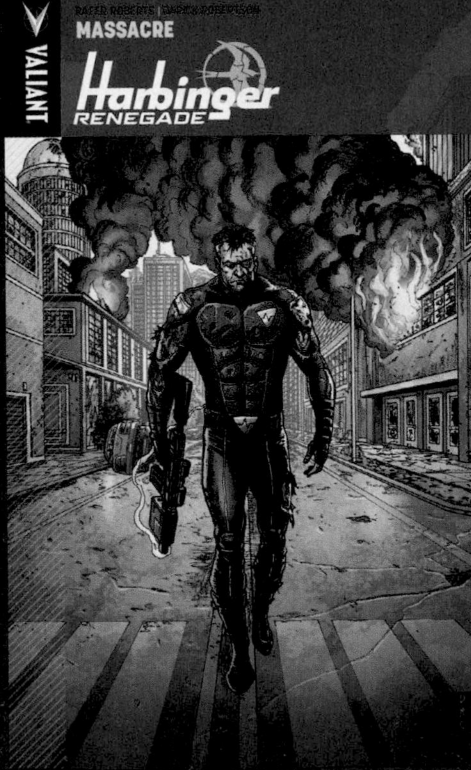
VALIANT
RAFER ROBERTS | DARICK ROBERTSON
MASSACRE
Harbinger
RENEGADE

TRADE PAPERBACK
ISBN: 978-1-68215-223-2